The Geometry of Love

ALSO BY MARGARET VISSER

Much Depends on Dinner
The Rituals of Dinner
The Way We Are

Margaret Visser

THE GEOMETRY
OF LOVE

*space, time, mystery,
and meaning in an ordinary church*

Harper*Flamingo*Canada

The Geometry of Love:
Space, Time, Mystery, and Meaning
in an Ordinary Church
Copyright © 2000 by Margaret Visser.
All rights reserved. No part of this book may be
used or reproduced in any manner whatsoever
without prior written permission except in the case
of brief quotations embodied in reviews. For information address
HarperCollins Publishers Ltd,
55 Avenue Road, Suite 2900,
Toronto, Ontario, Canada M5R 3L2

www.harpercanada.com

HarperCollins books may be purchased for educa-
tional, business, or sales promotional use. For information please write: Special Markets Department,
HarperCollins Canada,
55 Avenue Road, Suite 2900,
Toronto, Ontario, Canada M5R 3L2

First HarperFlamingo ed.
ISBN 0-00-255739-8
First HarperPerennialCanada ed.
ISBN 0-00-639131-1

Canadian Cataloguing in Publication Data

Visser, Margaret, 1940–
The geometry of love : space, time, mystery,
and meaning in an ordinary church

ISBN 0-00-255739-8

1. Church buildings.
2. Church architecture.
3. Church decoration and ornament.
I. Title.

NA4800.V57 2000   726'.5   C00-931208-0

00 01 02 03 04 HC 5 4 3 2 1

Printed and bound in the United States
Set in Aldus

FOR COLIN,
of course

Do you know, I once came across a book which enumerated the uses of common salt and sang its praises in the most extravagant terms, and not only salt but all kinds of everyday commodities. Now isn't it, as I say, an extraordinary thing, Eryximachus, that while all these screeds have been written on such trivial subjects, the god of love has found no man bold enough to sing his praises as they should be sung—is it not, in short, amazing that there should be so little reverence shown to such a god!

Plato, Symposium

Wer den Dichter will verstehen
muss in Dichters Lande gehen.

(Those who poets would unravel
Must to poets' country travel.)
Goethe, Der Westoestlichen Diwan

CONTENTS

ACKNOWLEDGEMENTS

....

I would like to thank the community of Sant'Agnese's church for the welcome they gave my husband Colin and me during two visits to Rome, for taking us in and letting us see and share the breadth and the depth of their commitment to their religion and to each other. The Delia family, Paolo, Paola, Frederica and Stefano, were particularly generous in introducing us to the life of the community. The priests serving the parish, especially Don Giancarlo Guidolin and Don Attilio Haun, gave us indispensable help and support. Among the libraries that have offered their resources to us I must single out the University of Toronto library system, the Columbia University library in New York City, Heythrop College of the University of London, the British Library in London, the British School at Rome, the Deutsches archaeologisches Institut Rom, and the American Academy in Rome. My sister, Dr. Joan Barclay Lloyd, is an expert on the art and archaeology of twelfth-century and early Christian Rome; she has been kind enough to read and correct the book from a scholar's point of view. Any errors that remain are my own. Many friends have read chapters, made suggestions, and offered ideas. I would like especially to thank Emily Visser, Bernard King, Nada Conic, Norma Rowen, Robert Chodos, Louisa Blair, the Petites Soeurs and Petits Frères de l'Agneau O.P. in Rome and Barcelona, Danilo Secchiaroli, Gianfranco Mosconi, and the Rev. Govindu Inna-iah. I am particularly grateful to my unfailingly helpful and supportive editor, Iris Tupholme, to Becky Vogan for her superb copy editing, as well as to my agents Linda McKnight and Zoë Pagnamenta. Emmet Robbins first took us to see Sant'Agnese's many years ago; his suggestion that this church might be the subject for the book was the one we eventually followed. I say "we" because the book is, in fact, a joint venture with my husband, Colin. We set out on this journey of discovery together; we both researched the material, sitting side by side in library after library; and we have discussed every part of it together. It's his book, from many points of view. I dedicate it to him.

PREAMBLE

People who include sightseeing in their travels can scarcely avoid visiting churches. Places of worship—temples, chapels, pagodas, synagogues, cathedrals, and mosques—are often the oldest, and usually the most famous, the strangest, the most beautiful buildings any town has to offer. For these and other reasons, they tend to survive much longer than anything else in the town.

I must have visited hundreds of religious edifices in my life, most of them churches—ugly ones and lovely ones, dusty old neglected ones, plain ones, vulgar ones, and awe-inspiring masterpieces. The famous ones have "guide" books explaining them. These will tell you, typically, how many columns a church has, and also give you their heights and diameters. They will describe for you the façade before which you are standing, and star the objects you are supposed to look at, giving their creators and their dates. All this is potentially useful information, and might serve to focus a resolute visitor's attention. The problem is that guidebooks offer little else.

I remember sitting at the back of a tiny, isolated church some years ago, on top of a hill in Spain. A Japanese tourist was driven up to the front door and led round the building by a guide he must have hired in the town some distance away. The guide told him, in English, the dates of various parts of the building and then proceeded to dilate upon the superb stone vaulting. The tourist did not even raise his head to look at this. He stared aghast—as well he might—at a horrific, life-sized painted carving of a bleeding man nailed to two pieces of wood. When the guide had stopped talking, the man gestured wordlessly towards the statue. The guide nodded, smiled, and told him in which century it had been carved.

Experiences like this one—I have known many—together with my own unanswered questions combined to make me embark on this book. I had once written an account of the meanings, the culture, and the history embodied in a single meal. I set out to do the same thing now with a church: take one particular example and see what I could find out about it. Casting my net as widely as possible in order to explain it to myself, I resolved to look at history and politics, theology, anthropology, art history and technology, iconography, hagiography, and folklore; I would find out about the community of people who used the building. I would discover the meanings of symbols, consider the manner in which this building expresses temporal concepts by means of space, track down if I could both the historical background and the living connotations of each artifact. If there was a statue of a woman in a voluminous pleated garment holding her heart in one hand and a staff in the other, I would find out who she was and what she had done, what her disembodied heart was doing in her hand, why she was wearing those clothes and carrying that staff, and for what reason she came to be represented in that particular church. I would be interested in art, of course, and in the history of beautiful objects (if any) in the church I chose—but I would also want to know what that art was depicting, what it was trying to say.

I had two major problems to resolve before I started the project. First: what church should I choose? I decided early on that it would have to be a Christian church: I simply did not know enough to talk about a mosque or a Buddhist temple. That decision helped me—eventually—to solve in my own mind my second problem: I am myself a Christian. How could I honestly write a non-devotional book about a church without prejudice and above all without appearing to be trying to persuade other people to agree with my own beliefs—with the beliefs expressed, after all, by this church? A friend who is a well-known art historian once told me how, as a student, she had been assured by her colleagues that any scholarly accomplishment in the area of Christian art was out of the question for her because she was a "believer."

It occurred to me then, and I am sure of it now, that it is much more likely to be helpful—not the reverse—to investigate a subject when you know it from the "inside." Such knowledge is not scholarship, of course—but then, neither is being an outsider any guarantee of either accuracy or insight. Surprisingly many people have insisted that in order to understand something you are always better off not participating in it. This attitude has, fortunately, begun to arouse suspicion in recent years, notably among anthropologists: it is no longer thought *de rigueur* to discount what the "natives" are telling you is going on. It has also come to be admitted that no observer, not even a "scholar," has a blank slate for a mind; it is therefore detrimental to truth to claim total objectivity.

In churches, especially Roman Catholic churches, I am a "native," and a lot of what is going on I have known from childhood. Looking for a church to investigate, I chose in the end a Roman Catholic one, small, fairly well known but not too famous: Sant'Agnese fuori le Mura, St. Agnes outside the Walls, of Rome. This is a church I had visited only once before I began researching this book. That occasion was twenty-five years ago. I knew almost nothing about the historical background of the building when I first saw it, but Sant'Agnese's, and little round Santa Costanza's nearby, remained in my memory—small and far and sharply vivid. I recalled grandeur in littleness, gorgeousness of colour (purple, pink, grey, and gold in Sant'Agnese's; terracotta, green, and white in Santa Costanza's), and always there lurked hints of the smell of fresh flowers. I scarcely remembered that in order to enter Sant'Agnese's you had to descend a long staircase—although I did know that somehow the experience of this church went deep.

I felt on that first visit (I was at the time an "unbeliever") that this was a place where you could almost reach out and touch the early Christians of Rome, that this church was uncommonly close to what they would have known and liked. Studying Sant'Agnese's in detail during the past few years has helped me understand just how true that instinctive first response was in a literal, archaeological sense. The church, however, has known many vicissitudes down the centuries, and it is in fact now very modern in its appeal—in its simplicity and clarity of purpose, and even in its modern-and-Baroque "imaging" of early Christian Rome. It is a building that feels as if it has been on a very long journey out of the past, has altered and suffered and gathered accretions, and now it is here with us, still bearing its cargo of memories, and still carrying out the purpose for which it was built.

Little did I guess, when I chose Sant'Agnese's as the church I would write about, how much there was for me to learn! How grateful I am that I did not try (as I once thought I might, to ensure that there was enough subject matter) to take on a large church, a spectacular church, a church with a lot of objects in it! It has taken me years of searching, reading, thinking, and questioning to write this book about a small and simple building and its environment. Not that I feel I have "come to terms" with Sant'Agnese's. It doubtless has a great deal still to teach me. And certainly another author would have written a different account of it.

The book sets out to make this church—and at the same time any other church—more accessible to visitors. It hopes to give readers an inkling of the spiritual, cultural, and historical riches that any church offers. It is for people who are not satisfied with dates and measurements, or with texts that studiously avoid anything that might say what the building is about. When certain beliefs are being expressed, I take them seriously and say what they are, because that is an indispensable part of the explanation. Sant'Agnese's is a building that is intentionally meaningful; it reveals itself most fully to people prepared to respond to its "language."

Each church has its own history, contents, appearance, and atmosphere. But in important respects all churches are alike, and therefore learning to "read" one is to enrich the experience of visiting any of them. It is not necessary to have seen this church in order to get the most out of the book, any more than it is necessary to have eaten a particular meal in order to discover its meaning and history. This church remains merely representative. In fact, its most awe-inspiring aspects may be found in any church, anywhere.

The book takes Sant'Agnese fuori le Mura as its organizing principle. It looks at things more or less in the order in which they present themselves to people moving through the building, beginning with what they see when they walk into it. Chronology does not, therefore, provide the underlying structure of this book; it is the church itself, as it stands today, that shapes the account. Churches are laid out with a certain trajectory of the soul in mind. I have chosen to trust this ancient and intentional order, and to follow it in this book. We know right from the beginning, for example, that the church is dedicated to the martyr Saint Agnes, who is buried here. But it would be untrue to the church's meaning, as well as to the experience of anyone entering the church for the first time, to put Agnes first—either in importance, or in order of presentation. We shall keep catching glimpses of her—a picture, a mosaic, a statue—and her story will slowly unfold for us as we traverse the building. But we come face to face with Agnes only in the last chapter, when we finally reach her tomb, after having walked through the galleries of the catacombs underneath the church to get there. That is where we are supposed to find her: at the end of the journey.

We know, too, that we will find an altar in a Roman Catholic church, and probably statues of saints, and chapels. But it is best, when reading a novel or a poem, or eating a meal, to take things in the order intended: starting at the beginning and moving through the work to the end. A building covers a plot of land; a structure like Sant'Agnese's also has a "plot" in the narrative sense. It is this "plot" that governs the book.

In most respects, this church is like any church—and yet it contains things that are unique to it. A different church would require another book. I shall be examining and considering a wide variety of objects found in this particular building: a pastel drawing of Jesus displaying his heart on his chest, a pair of porphyry columns, a Greco-Roman candlestick, a pew—whatever meets the eye next of a person passing through the building today. Each of these objects has a history, a meaning, and connotations of its own. I shall be explaining, for example, why Agnes in the mosaic has a phoenix embroidered onto her dress; what baptism means to a Christian, and the reason for its symbols, such as the number eight; how the catacombs were dug; what is expressed by a round church as opposed to an oblong one; the technique and history of gold-backed mosaics; and the stories of various saints and martyrs.

Theological background will sometimes be given, but nothing too abstruse: I am not a theologian. I will also from time to time "step back" from some object or place in the church and consider the thought-processes that gave birth to it, positioned it, or made it look the way it does. And I shall occasionally try to express what effect some of the objects in this church have (are *intended* to have) on a person like me, an ordinary, though alas only a very infrequent, worshipper in this particular building.

Although the "plot" of this book is not a sequence in historical time, an underlying chronological movement nonetheless reveals itself: we shall find ourselves moving, on the whole, from the deep past to the present, then back again in time from the present to the past. We shall also constantly bear in mind that a church is deliberately oriented towards consequences, towards the future. The book ends at the church's beginning, with the grave of Agnes, a twelve-year-old girl who was murdered in 305 A.D. She belongs to that extraordinary number, both historical and fictional, of twelve-to-fourteen-year-old girls, the newly nubile, who have acted with force and conviction to catalyze changes in their society: Antigone, Bernadette, Juliet, the Virgin Mary. She is buried, here in this place, underneath the church. Her grave caused the church to be built in the first place, and the church in turn has ensured that her death has never been forgotten. She still demands to be taken into account—and still poses challenging questions, which we shall meet head on. Following the building and its many winding stories is like finding one's way to the centre of a labyrinth. In the end, it is up to each person to make sense of what is encountered there.

1

THE DOOR
SWINGS OPEN:
Threshold

The church stands with its back to the road. It turns away, quietly guarding its secret.

For more than 1,350 years it has stood by the road, and around it once stretched open fields and vineyards. The massive brick walls and towers that encircled the city of Rome were clearly and unforgettably visible, cutting across the landscape to the south.

If you arrive today, say by bus—a two-kilometre ride from Termini Station—you will have to cross the busy road you came on, from the bus stop near a fountain captured in stone. *Acqua Marcia* is inscribed on it, in memory of Rome's first important aqueduct, constructed in 144 B.C. Within the last hundred years or so, the view from here of the city walls has been blocked as the area became first a suburb and then a fairly central district of modern Rome.

Having reached the pavement opposite the bus stop, you look through an iron gate with a walkway leading to a closed door under a porch. To the left of it stands the brick back of the church and its medieval tower—not by any means a spectacular tower, but a strong and graceful one nonetheless. The building not only conceals what it contains, it also marks the spot.

To find an entrance to the building, you can take a small descending side road on your right to a break in the wall on the left; this gateway is invisible from the main street. Or you must walk along the pavement, as I did the first time I came here, and brave a small porch with an arch on columns and a painting over the door, at number 349 via Nomentana; it lets you into a solid medieval monastery building with yellow ochre walls. Once you have crossed into the precinct, you must traverse a courtyard, then walk through the vaulted space that supports another medieval tower, and enter a door on your right. You find yourself at the top of a broad staircase, forty-five steps in all, descending into the church. You realize, with a shock, that the church floor is deep down; the building is much higher inside than it looks from the street. For almost a millennium, until the year 1600, the church was half buried. Only its upper level rose above ground.

The floor level is the same as one of the levels of the catacomb into which the church has been built. These narrow tunnels, with graves cut one above the other into their earthen sides, snake out underneath all of the area hereabouts. There is another much larger catacomb almost adjoining this one; its entrance is just a street block away. The entrance to a smaller, uninvestigated warren has also been discovered. The thundering main road outside, carrying the bus or car you arrived in, passes over a section of the catacombs. There are thousands of graves—in 1924, 5,753 of them had been counted[1]—and several kilometres of tunneling, not all of which has yet been explored.

A single grave among all the rest gives its name to this catacomb and to the church sunk into it: the grave of Agnes, a twelve-year-old girl who was murdered in 305 A.D. She has never been forgotten; the building remembers her.

PERSONAL EPIPHANIES

The word "remember" comes from the same Indo-European root as "mind." And the English word "mind" is both a noun ("what is in the brain") and a verb ("pay attention to," "care"). When one has forgotten, to remember is to call back into the "attention span," to recall. Attention is thought of here as having a span—an extension in space. Forgetting, on the other hand, is like dropping something off a plate, falling off an edge, not "getting" it, but having to do, instead, without it. Remembering is recapturing something that happened in the past; it is an encounter of now with then—a matter of time. Buildings—constructions in space—may last through time as this church has lasted. Such structures can cause us to remember. Their endurance, as well as their taking up space, may counter time and keep memory alive.

This particular church reminds us of Agnes, who was killed by having her throat cut almost 1,700 years ago. But like any church, it recalls a great deal more. One of a church's main purposes is to call to mind, to make people remember. To begin with, a church sets out to cause self-recollection. Every church does its best (some of them are good at this, others less so, but every church is trying) to help each person recall the mystical experience that he or she has known.

Everyone has had some such experience. There are moments in life when—to use the language of a building—the door swings open. The door shuts again, sooner rather than later. But we have seen, even if only through a crack, the light behind it. There has been a moment, for example, when every person realizes that one is oneself, and no one else. This is probably a very early memory, this taking a grip on one's own absolutely unique identity, this irrevocable beginning.

I remember myself, walking along a narrow path in the Zambian bush. The grass was brown and stiff, more than waist-high. I was wearing a green-and-white checked dress with buttons down the front. I was alone. I said aloud, stunned, "Tomorrow I'm going to be five! Tomorrow I'm going to be *five!*" I stopped still with amazement: five-ness was about to be mine! I had already *had* four. The whole world seemed to point to me in that instant. The world and I looked at each other. It was huge and I was me. I was filled with indescribable delight. I took another step, and the vision was gone. But it's still there, even now, even when I am not recalling it.

This was a mystical experience. As such, one of its characteristics was that in it my mind embraced a vast contradiction: both terms of it at once.[2] I was me and the world contained me, but I was not the world. I was a person, but I wasn't "a person"—I was me. A mystical experience is before all else an experience, and beyond logic. It is concrete, and therefore unique. It is bigger than the person who experiences it; it is something one "enters."

People have always, apparently in all cultures, conceptualized the world as participating in, or expressing, or actually being a tension between a series of opposites: big and small, high and low, same and different, hot and cold, one and many, male and female, and so on. Societies of people can have very idiosyncratic ideas about what is opposite to what: a culture can find squirrels "opposite" to water rats, oblongs "opposite" to squares, bronze vessels "the opposite" of clay ones. Anthropologists dedicate themselves to finding out what such classifications could mean; the answers they give us usually show how social arrangements are reflected outward upon the world, and determine human perceptions of how nature is ordered. One result of a mystical experience, therefore, can be a profound demystification.

For no sooner has a culture organized its system of contradictions, than the mystics arise. They steadfastly, and often in the face of great danger, assure their fellow human beings that they are wrong: what appears to be a contradiction in terms is merely a convention, a point of view, a *façon de parler*, no matter how self-evident it may appear. These are people who believe and convince others that they have been lifted out of this world and have seen a greater truth: the opposites are, in fact, one. The Greek philosopher Heraclitus can say, "The way up and the way down are the same." Or: "Step into the same river twice, and its waters will be different."[3]

Such mystic realizations (up and down are one, sameness and difference coincide) have to keep occurring, both for the sake of truth, and for the necessity of realizing that neither our senses nor our thinking faculties have access to, or are capable of encompassing, everything. ("The last proceeding of reason," wrote Pascal, "is to recognize that there is an infinity of things beyond it.")[4] For all the outrage and bafflement with which the pronouncements of the mystics are greeted, we remember their words; in time we learn to appreciate and value them. In our own day, physicists have been talking like mystics for some time: expressing physical reality, for example, as conflating space and time, or declaring that waves and particles (lines and dots) can be perceived to be "the same." The rest of us are only beginning to take in what they are saying.

From the point of view of the person experiencing them, privileged moments—those that allow us to see something not normally offered to our understanding—do not last. Regretfully, necessarily, we cannot remain in such an experience. We move on, into the practical, the sensible, the logical and provable, the mundane. But after one such glimpse of possibility, we henceforth know better. We know what it is to experience two or more incompatible, mutually exclusive categories as constituting in fact one whole. We have seen both sides of the coin, at one and the same time. An impossibility—but it has happened. We may bury this experience, deny it, explain it away—but at any moment something could trigger it, raise it up, recall it. Because it has happened, and cannot unhappen.

One of the consequences of having had a mystical experience is a sense of loss. If only it could have gone on and on, and never had to stop; if only the door would open again! One of the hardest lessons we have to learn in life is that we cannot bring about such an experience, any more than we can make it last. Sex can remind us of it because, like a mystical experience, sex is ecstatic, overwhelming, and delightful; it feels bigger than we are. Drugs can also make us feel as if we're "there" again. So people pursue sex and drugs—experiences they can get, they can have. This other thing, this greater and unforgettable thing, this insight, is not anyone's for the asking. It comes (it always comes, to everyone, at different times and in different ways), and there is no telling what it will be or when or where, let alone how. You can't buy it or demand it or keep it. It is not a chemical reaction, and there is nothing automatic about it.

A mystical experience is something perceived, and it calls forth a response. But you are free to turn away from the vision, to behave as though it never happened; you are free not to respond. (This is something I have had to learn: when I was almost five there was no question of not responding.) The invitation cannot be made to anyone else but you—and not even to you at any moment in your life other than the one in which it is made. I shall never be five again, so no other mystical experience I have will ever again be that one. I shall never again wear that green-and-white checked dress; it is very likely that the path through the brown grass has disappeared. What I have left is the enormous memory, and the fact that it has enlarged all of my experience ever since.

Now a church (or a temple or a synagogue or a mosque—any religious building) knows perfectly well that it cannot induce in anyone a mystical experience. What it does is acknowledge such experience as any of its visitors has had, as explicitly as it can. A church is a recognition, in stone and wood and brick, of spiritual awakenings. It nods, to each individual person. If the building has been created within a cultural and religious tradition, it constitutes a collective memory of spiritual insights, of thousands of mystical moments. A church reminds us of what we have known. And it tells us that the possibility of the door swinging open again remains.

AUDIENCES: CHURCH AND THEATRE

Memory, in a church, is not only individual, but also collective: the building is a meeting house for a group of people who agree with each other in certain important respects. They come together to express solidarity, and they do this by participating in an intensely meaningful performance known as a ritual.[5]

The closest relative of a church is a theatre, where people also come together to witness a scripted performance. There is a stage in a church, and seats for the audience; in both theatre and church, people come in order to live together through a trajectory of the soul. They come to be led by the performance to achieve contact with transcendence, to experience delight or recognition, to understand something they never understood before, to feel relief, to stare in amazement, or to cry. They want something that shakes them up—or gives them peace. Successful drama, like a well-performed ritual, can provoke an experience of transcendence: through feeling, for example, two contradictory emotions at once. Aristotle spoke of *katharsis*—purification— as the aim of tragedy. Catharsis, he said, is achieved by undergoing two opposing movements of the soul—pity (feeling for, and therefore drawing close) and fear (longing to move out of the danger's range)— at the same time.[6]

In a theatre the audience is the receiver of a play, and essential to a play. At an ancient Greek drama the audience was indeed part of the spectacle. The form of the theatre, a huge horseshoe shape, ensured that this was so. The Greek theatres that survive today allow us to imagine what it must have been like, sitting in a vast crowd of fellow citizens with everyone spread out in full view, in broad daylight, fanning out to embrace the round dancing-floor below them. Actors say that an audience can draw out of them their best performances, just through the quality of its attention, its intentness.

A theatre is like a church—not the other way round. "Church" or "temple" is the main category, and "theatre" a division of it. Historically, drama grew out of religious performance (and never entirely left it) in a process wherein the play gradually separated itself from the crowd watching. The distance between watcher and watched is essential to theatrical experience. ("Theatre" comes from Greek *theatron*, a place for viewing.) People come together in a church, however, not to view but to take part. The word "church" comes from Greek *kyriakon*, "house of the Lord"; it is a place of encounter between people and God.

It is perfectly possible to be moved at a spiritual level at the theatre; one can open oneself and be brought to mystical insight, as Aristotle showed us, through attentive watching. (Such experiences, however, can occur anywhere, at any time—indeed, they seem to prefer arriving when we are least expecting them, at times and places we would be least inclined to call "appropriate.") But a performance in a church is permitted to involve people to an extent that the theatre traditionally avoids. People come to participate in it, to join in, and then allow the realization to enter them and work upon them. The whole point of the proceedings is to help them change the orientation of their souls, even though they are also confirming the foundation of their beliefs. They have come to meet, to make the ceremony, and to respond, at a level that may include but goes well beyond the aesthetic. But a church can go on "working" even when there is no performance and no crowd. A person can come into a silent church in order to respond to the building and its meaning. This can produce an experience as profoundly moving as that of attending a performance. The same thing cannot be said of visiting an empty theatre.

MEANING AND RESPONSE

A church like Sant'Agnese fuori le Mura (Saint Agnes outside the Walls) vibrates with intentionality. It is meaningful—absolutely nothing in it is without significance. Even if something is inadvertently included that has no meaning to start with, a meaning for it will be found, inevitably. A church stands in total opposition to the narrowing and flattening of human experience, the deviation into the trivial, that follow from antipathy towards meaning, and especially meaning held in common.[7] Meaning is intentional: this building has been made in order to communicate with the people in it. A church is no place to practise aesthetic distance, to erase content and simply appreciate form. The building is trying to speak; not listening to what it has to say is a form of barbarous inattention, like admiring a musical instrument while caring nothing for music.

The building "refers" to things beyond itself, and it deliberately intends to be a setting where spiritual knowledge receives explicit recognition and focal attention. Sometimes the meanings are highly specific and complex; for the sake of clarity they may even be explained in inscriptions. Other meanings are more general: the nave is "like a ship" (which is what "nave" means), or windows let in light (a symbol of God). But these meanings also engage in intricate play among themselves, arouse further associations, and end up offering some of the most complex meanings of all. And always—silently, intently—the building points at once both to the individual's own inner being and to the things commonly done in the company of other people in the church: the place where "the Word" is read, for example, and the site of baptism, or Christian initiation. The altar table is usually given centre stage, for at the heart of Christianity is a shared meal, together with everything meant by sharing a meal.

Contemplating all these meanings, even when you are alone in a church and there is no performance going on, is intended to help focus your mind and soul. You go into a church to exclude the extraneous, to get away from noise and distractions, to go back into yourself and take a good look at what is there. You go because you want to restore and enrich your relationship with God, by participating in a religious ceremony, by praying, or by just sitting alone in silence. All of the church's "language" exists to help you do this, to get your mind humming and to make you receptive.

It is also supposed to help you keep in good spiritual shape. For one of the central tenets of Christianity is that belief and love and trust and insight, like mystical experience, are given to you. You can't cause a gift such as belief or trust or love—whether felt or received—to be given, although a longing for what is called "grace" will surely be satisfied. Only, when the gift comes, you have to be ready. (Longing for it is part of being ready; Christians say even that to long is already to have received.) It is entirely possible to be so distracted that you don't notice the gift at your doorstep, or to be in such poor shape spiritually that you do not recognize or cannot accept what is being offered. God comes "like a thief in the night." (Notice that in this biblical simile, when God "breaks in" the person is thought of as like a house, a building.)[8] All that a human being can do is be vigilant, notice what is happening, and then respond. A church is there to remind you, to teach you to pay attention, and to awaken the poetry in your soul. It gives you exercise in responding.

TRANSCENDING CONTRADICTIONS

Churches, if we let them, put us back in touch with our mystical experience. At a simple yet eloquent level, they are always bigger than we are, offer more than we can take in. Look forward at the altar, say, and you are missing the crucifix, the rose window, the door behind you. Look at the ceiling and you are leaving out of account the floor, let alone the crypt below it. It is normally impossible to grasp all of a church at once. A church is bigger than I am, but it also represents me. Its plan is the plan of a human soul—and often, indeed, the plan of a human body: head, arms, and torso.

Churches orient us. The word "orientation" means literally "turned towards the east" (*oriens* in Latin means "rising," and so where the sun rises). It is a word derived from church-building: many churches attend to the symbolism of the sun and its movement across the sky, having been built to conform with that cosmic pattern. But "orientation" has now come to mean any direction. A church knows where its centre lies, and what direction it faces; having direction is always part of its meaning. The French word *sens*, which signifies both "meaning" (sense) and "direction," captures the conflation of the two ideas. The direction-ful and meaningful church is an invitation to travel, to stretch our souls and embrace the movement that time imposes upon our lives. Churches express time—but in terms of space.

The use of space to "mean" time and movement is a church's way of preparing the visitor for its final objective, which is to point to infinity or the transcendent, where the oppositions perceived by our human senses are resolved, and all is understood to be one. The Christian religion is itself founded on a vast contradiction; the habit of conflating opposites is indigenous to it. To begin with, Christians believe that Jesus Christ is both God and human. It is an idea outrageous enough to have kept them argumentatively occupied for two thousand years.

Some have thought Jesus was only a man, a very good person; some that he was human until he was baptized by John, at which point he became divine; some that he was never human at all but only appeared to be a man. To preserve the paradox and prevent the exclusion of one of the opposites, the institutional Church kept condemning such ideas—many and ingenious were their formulations—as heresies. (The word "heresy" is from Greek *haireo*, "I choose": heretics are people who choose to believe what they like, regardless of orthodoxy; who bend beliefs to suit themselves. "Orthodoxy," on the other hand, means literally "thinking in a straight line.") But in a sense there is always heresy, simply because Christians cannot—not easily, certainly not constantly, perhaps never—get their minds around the enormity of this central contradiction.

For well over the first thousand years of the Church's history, it was the deity of Christ that was emphasized—not taught as being exclusive, but still used as a lens through which to see things from a "Christian" point of view. Christ was *Pantokrator*, the "All Powerful One," solemn and just, tranquil in his triumph because he had changed the world forever, and very male. Today, that has changed. Christians tend, at least in the West, to think of Jesus in his human aspect, as intensely human as it is possible to be, and as compassionate as the gentlest woman; some can scarcely fit his divinity into the picture. God himself (that is, Christ, as Christians believe) is known to be suffering, even helpless in the face of the evil that humankind has freely chosen to commit. It can be hard these days to feel that God has "the whole world in his hand."

Neither of the two one-sided visions is truly Christian; the Church has always said so. But the Church itself has almost never been able to get it right, except as a formula that it formally upholds. (The "formulas" of the Church are radical and, to those who believe them, inspiring. What the Church as an institution actually does, however, only occasionally rises to the level of its beliefs.) It is absolutely essential to the Christian message to accept that Christ is *both* God *and* human—and that equally, simultaneously, and always. It is indeed impossible to get one's mind around this paradox, yet that, and nothing less, is the crux (a truly Christian word) of everything in Christianity.

A related contradiction is even harder to embrace. God is perceived on one hand as infinite, immense, the creator and sustainer of a universe, the universe whose unimaginable size we are only now beginning to discover; and on the other hand he is believed to be present in every single detail of his creation, to know and hold dear every atom, every speck of dust on every star and planet, to care about every blade of grass, every insect, every human being. To see Christ as both divine and human is to grasp two terms of a contradiction. God's spanning of one and many, huge and minuscule, this instant and always, here and everywhere, omnipotent and vulnerable is even further beyond human imagining—although mystics tell us that in privileged moments they have "seen" this truth. The profoundly Judeo-Christian idea that God is not a theorem or a pattern or a necessity, but a person—an I—takes us even further from common sense. But that is not all: Christians believe that this person ("I am who I am")[9] is the root of love, and eternally loves us. It takes only two words to say the most mind-boggling article of Christian belief there is: God cares.

"I IT AM"

On May 8, 1373, a young woman lay dying, and she experienced God. She later recovered and lived, and wrote down what she had been shown when she met God, in a book called *Revelations of Divine Love*. Julian of Norwich received sixteen revelations in all; after the account of the last one she wrote: "Some of us believe that God is almighty, and may do everything; and that he is all wise, and can do everything; but that he is all love, and will do everything—there we draw back." No matter how horrendous the world's sufferings, no matter how triumphant wickedness looks, God revealed to Julian that "Sin is behovable [that is, necessary or inevitable], but all shall be well, and all shall be well, and all manner of thing shall be well."

God opened the series of revelations to Julian by showing her the universe. "And he showed me . . . a little thing, the size of a hazelnut, on the palm of my hand, round like a ball. I looked at it thoughtfully and wondered, 'What is this?' And the answer came, 'It is all that is made.' I marvelled that it continued to exist and did not suddenly disintegrate; it was so small. And again my mind supplied the answer, 'It exists, both now and for ever, because God loves it.' "

In the twelfth revelation God spoke to Julian in words I shall quote in Julian's original English with its high disdain for consistency in spelling: "I it am, I it am; I it am that is heyest; I it am that thou lovist; I it am that thou lykyst; I it am that thou servist; I it am that thou longyst; I it am that thou desyrist; I it am that thou menyst; I it am that is al; I it am that holy church prechyth and teachyth the; I it am that shewed me here to thee."[10]

"I it am that thou menyst," God said: "I am what you mean."[11]

THE WAY DOWN: INITIATION

There is another way to approach the church of Sant'Agnese. Instead of entering from the via Nomentana, you can take the narrow descending road, via di Sant'Agnese, to the right of the church and enter through the gateway a little way down on your left. You will find yourself in a small piazza. Before you is the façade of the church. By the closing years of the sixteenth century, the building was almost a thousand years old and urgently needed to be restored. The walls were covered in weeds and creepers, wrote Costantino Caetani, who described the work subsequently done; clearing the greenery away meant disturbing the habitations of "serpents and other nasty and poisonous creatures."[12] What is now the front of the church was dug out of the earth—many tons of earth—and we shudder to think of the archaeological damage done. The fabric of the building was then strengthened, the walls cleaned and painted, and the three doors, a big central one and two smaller aisle doors, were created in front at the present ground level.

Today, these doors serve as an alternative entrance or exit. They receive solemn use every year on Palm Sunday, which is "olive branch" Sunday in Rome, where people traditionally carry their own symbol-laden olive instead of palms. The congregation exits from the front of the church and walks in procession, singing, across the little piazza and along a path lined with trees and shrubs to the round church of Santa Costanza nearby. They are recalling Christ's entry into Jerusalem riding on an ass, and his welcome by crowds triumphantly waving branches. It is one of the strategies of religious ritual to make one place "become" temporarily another, for the purposes of re-enactment. Santa Costanza's, as the goal of the procession, "becomes" Jerusalem, and then Calvary, where Jesus was put to death.

But in order to enter the church of Sant'Agnese, it is best to take not the front doors pierced through the façade of the church when it was excavated, but the original entrance, the ancient passage down. This broad, well-lit marble staircase was created during the early seventeenth century. For many centuries before that, however, it had been a dark and slippery descent, with worn, steep, uneven steps. People must have slithered and groped their way down, holding onto each other and steadying themselves against the walls of the tunnel. Many of those who walked or rode out of the Nomentan Gate in the Aurelian Walls of Rome and along the via Nomentana to visit the shrine of Agnes never undertook the tunnel entrance. There is a gallery above the colonnade in the church, often referred to as a *matroneum* or "gallery for women," which provided an alternative to the dark passage.[13]

This upper gallery is at the level of the road, as can be seen from the street outside. There is a gate in the low wall along the street and a walkway leading to a door with a porch over it, near the apse. We saw this walkway and entrance earlier, as we approached the church from the bus stop. The entry from the street directly into the gallery was created in the seventeenth century, and probably replaced a much older one. Originally, there were other entrances into the gallery, both in front and on one or both of the long sides of the church. People would enter the gallery and stand looking down into the church, and they could move around the gallery on three sides of the building. They could not get down from there into the church itself, but they did avoid taking the downward passage in the dark. It may well have been that women usually preferred the gallery to the tunnel.

The passageway itself is considerably older than the present church, which was built in about 630. The lower parts of the left-hand wall of the stairway is of the fabric known as *opus mixtum*, which dates it to the fourth century.[14] It led down, as it still does, to the catacomb and the burial place of Agnes, now resting underneath the church. As a passage into the earth, the tunnel's Christian meanings are superimposed upon the universal symbolism of grottoes and caverns: of the black hole that is a gateway to dreams and visions; of night, sleep, and death; of Mother Earth, who knows all things past, present, and to come, but who speaks indistinctly and in riddles. People who need to see the way ahead may find it by first visiting their fate or destiny, in depth and in darkness. Which, in a sense, is what we do as we descend the steps into Sant'Agnese's.

This, too, is what Aeneas did, at the behest of the Sibyl of Cumae, when he set out, accompanied by his faithful friend Achates, on the last stage of his journey to find and found this city, Rome. Virgil describes the visions Aeneas was granted in the underworld: *sit numine vestro*, the poet prays,

> *pandere res alta terra et caligine mersas.*
> (O Chaos and Phlegethon, oh broad silent tracts of night! Permit me to tell what I have heard; allow me through your aid to unfold secrets buried in the depths and darkness of the earth!)

And then Aeneas and Achates begin the descent, in one of the most famous lines—its unbearably slow rhythm and its beauty are untranslatable—in the entire *Aeneid*:

> *ībānt ōbscūrī sōlā sŭb nōctĕ pĕr ūmbrām.*
> (On they went dimly, beneath the lonely night and through the dark.)[15]

This is the dark, we would say today, of the "unconscious," where the secret of each person's own destiny lies hidden. We must make contact with this darkness; it has a great deal to teach us. It does this in dreams, whose night-enclosed, enigmatic messages we must take care to hear and comprehend. In the seeming "death" of sleep, we come in touch with the roots of life.

It is one of the central paradoxes of Christianity that in order to live, we must first die. It calls us to choose the transcendent, which involves looking away from ourselves and turning outward, towards others and towards God; only then can we know what it is to be fully alive. "Anyone who saves his life will lose it; anyone who loses his life for my sake will save it."[16] One poetic image for this idea is the seed: it must die in the dark, leaving its protective and initially nurturing husk behind, in order to rise and live.[17] Going down into the earth, especially by a dark passage, is a symbol at once of death and rebirth, and of the search for and openness to "unconscious" knowledge. Once such knowledge is comprehended, we must bear it with us out of the place of encounter when we leave. For a church calls us always to exit afterwards, to rejoin the world outside.

In the early thirteenth century the ancient passage down into Sant'Agnese's was given lighting by means of "transenne" (the plural of Italian *transenna*, literally "netting"): pierced stone screens, set into the walls at intervals. Two very small stone screens were found in the top left-hand wall of the passage in 1950; they can still be seen encased in the wall outside. They must have provided very little light. Windows in early Christian churches were often transenne, with the holes separating the stone strips sometimes filled with thin, translucent sheets of selenite or alabaster. The transenne have simple geometrical designs—a common one consists of arching shapes suggestive of waves of water—and wherever these stone screens survive they give dim rippling or starlike lighting effects to church interiors. Such screens, without fillings, were also used for parapets, like the ones now fencing in the gallery in Sant'Agnese's.

At the time when the passage was provided with transenne, there were thirty steps down; they were covered in thirteenth-century cosmatesque (marble mosaic) decorations. At the bottom of the steps were massive bronze doors at the entrance to the church proper. By the late sixteenth century these doors had been stripped of their ornaments and presented a lamentable appearance. But there was plenty of bronze left: in 1587 Pope Sixtus V had the doors taken away and melted down. The bronze went to make the statue of Saint Peter that now stands on top of Trajan's Column, and the statue of Saint Paul, now on the Column of Marcus Aurelius. Today, tall glass doors fill this space; they date from 1884.[18]

In 1590 the entrance passage was given "many windows."[19] Some decades later the thirty steps were removed entirely and the present staircase built. In the process a great many finds were made in the earth under the steps. Out of the soil came ancient Roman marbles, including a number of statues, among them the *Drunk Old Woman* and *Heracles and the Hydra*, now kept in the Capitoline Museum, a *Youthful Augustus* in the Vatican Museums, many burial urns, and a magnificent rock-crystal vase. In addition there were eight out of a set of ten large bas-reliefs in white marble.[20] They depict Greco-Roman myths, and date from the early days of the reign of the Emperor Augustus. These are kept today in Rome's handsome Renaissance Palazzo Spada, in a part of the building now belonging to the Italian government; visitors who want to see them must seek permission. It is well worth making the effort, however, for they are masterpieces of Hellenistic art; it is rare nowadays that works as fine as these should be so little known to the general public. Many of the statues and other works of Roman art found at Sant'Agnese's were taken to Palazzo Verospi (now the Credito Italiano bank) at 374 the Corso, where Shelley once lived. However, they appear to have been dispersed before 1804.[21]

A shrine to Agnes was erected between 352 and 366 A.D., and it stood for three centuries before this church was built. The frontal and sides of its altar were rediscovered when the staircase was repaired in 1884, and they are now on the right-hand wall of the passage down. A bas-relief on one of these slabs shows a young girl praying, her hands lifted in the manner that was then usual for prayer. She probably represents Agnes herself, depicted thus about fifty years after her death. This is one of the most moving objects in the entire church; we shall have occasion to consider it again. Very close by, also now set into the passage wall, is a large, handsomely inscribed marble slab, describing in fourth-century Latin verse the death of Agnes. To this, too, we shall return later.

It is clear from the number and quality of these discoveries that in and around her family's private burial ground, where Agnes' body was laid and later given a stone altar and a small shrine, there were rich pagan Roman tombs and villas, perhaps even a temple or two. The superb columns used in Santa Costanza's (they are second century in date, while the building itself is fourth century),[22] as well as those in the church of Sant'Agnese, are from Roman temples, and perhaps found locally.

By the early seventeenth century uncomfortable dark passages were certainly not in vogue. This was the baroque age, the era of light and of glorying in human creativity and skill. The symbolism of rebirth, of going under water or under earth, and there receiving supernatural vision and new life, still found powerful expression in Church liturgy, but in architecture people preferred to celebrate order, clarity, dignity of bearing, processional pageantry, and an airy grandeur. So Cardinal Alessandro Ottaviano de' Medici and later Cardinal Fabrizio Veralli (the church complex is hung with several armorial shields for each of them) undertook to provide modern Roman Christians with a "new, improved" entrance to the ancient shrine of Saint Agnes, and replaced the medieval staircase with the present one.

The old cosmatesque steps, no matter how uneven, and also the dimness, would have pleased me more. However, I think that the methodical thoroughness of the modern science of archaeology has provided the initiatory passage into Sant'Agnese's with something even better. The experience of descending in scarce light—catching one's breath in wonder as the beautiful church opens out after the turn to the right at the foot of the steps—is still there, although reduced in intensity. But we now also have scraps of marble set into the walls on either side as we go down, whose meaning must enormously enhance any experience of descent into the church. These are fragments inscribed in Greek and Latin, pieces of tombstone from inside the church itself, and from nearby early Christian burials and the catacombs.

Many churches in Rome display their fragments of inscriptions in stone in this manner. Once they have been recorded, these finds are presumably of little importance for archaeologists; being unspectacular, they would merely gather dust in museums. At the places where they were found, however, they constitute a poignant memorial to the people for the enrichment and inspiration of whose lives each church was built. The scraps and segments at Sant'Agnese's are, in fact, sorted and placed in some order upon the walls (they were "systematized" in 1974), but they are fragmentary enough still to look random, scattered, like pieces of a huge jigsaw puzzle awaiting completion, and then decipherment—perhaps in the final coming together of everything, at the end of the world.

Words can be made out: names, many of them Greek, and slices of messages: "To sweetest Epaphroditus" (his name means that he is dedicated to Aphrodite, but he died a Christian); Abilia; Statius; Eufrosine and Decensia who were "buried in peace with the holy martyr." Susanna, whose inscription was set up by her husband, Exuperantius; Honorius, Alexander, Evodia, Phoebe, Terentia Chryse, Abundantius the Acolyte, Inportunus the Subdeacon. The priest (*praesbyter*) Celerinus; a stone for Emiliana (HEMILIANE), "sister of the priest Celerinus," is still in place in the catacomb. Melior Iunior *rediit* "[who has] returned home" to God; Aelia Isidora, Paul, Marcellina, Furius, Euphrosyne, Victor (BIKTΩP), and Assia Felicissima Sucessa, all of whose sibilant names survived.

At the bottom of the passage on the left are slabs set at right angles to the wall. These are opisthographs: slabs with pagan inscriptions that were turned over and reused for Christian graves, such as the one for Valentina. They are set like this today so that both sides of the stones can be read. Upside down and in Greek is the stone of one of the men who dug out the catacomb: Petrus Fossor, Peter the Digger. Thomas "*cum Agni*" got himself buried, perhaps by paying a fee to a digger, close to the grave of Agnes herself; the plaque found might indeed be a contract with a digger rather than his actual funeral stone.

Aelius Heliodorus was only a small child when his earthly life ended. His family engraved PRT on his stone, which means *pax refrigerium tibi*, "peace and delight be to you." By juxtaposing a sign for Christ with the word *deo* (God), Valentinus seems to proclaim—in rejection, it has been suggested, of the Arian heresy—that Jesus was not only human but also God. Publius Aelius Narcissus, buried with Aurelia Phoebilla, brings to mind the family addressed by Saint Paul in his letter to the Christians at Rome: "Greetings to . . . those of the family of Narcissus who are in the Lord's fellowship."[23]

In 1901 during an archaeological dig behind the main altar in the church, a tombstone was unearthed that says (it too is encased now in the passage wall): "Here rests in peace Serena the Abbess (*abbatissa*), who died at the age of 85." The burial date given (in our method of calculation) is May 8, 514 A.D. This date generated great excitement at the time of the find because—given the advanced age of Serena at her death—it meant there was a convent of nuns at Sant'Agnese's as early as the fifth century. This would be the oldest known convent in Rome, and this tombstone remains the earliest known reference to an abbess.[24] Previously, the earliest record of a convent on the site had been three hundred years later, when the *Liber Pontificalis*[25] says that Pope Leo III donated a silver box (*canistrum*) in about 806 to a monastery at Sant'Agnese's. There is scepticism about the meaning of the Serena slab among some scholars nowadays. Perhaps, they say, she was not really an abbess, or at any rate not what we mean by an abbess. Perhaps she did not live at Sant'Agnese's, although she was buried in the church. But there it is: the stone speaks, and it is we who must make sense of it.

There are many more people, many more stones: most often the name is broken off, the message incomplete. The pieces of slab and their inscriptions talk, remember, pray. Many of them are in Greek, the rest in Latin: not our languages, but still we could figure out the meaning of each one, if only we had all of the words. The stones set into the walls stand for thousands more, rifled tombs, broken marbles, lost fragments. As we go down to the church, they whisper to us in a confused murmur of voices. They are, as the Epistle to the Hebrews puts it, "a cloud of witnesses."[26] It is profoundly moving to open oneself to the memory of all these ordinary people who preserved and passed on our traditions to us. Who were they? How did they live? What did they look like? What would I have in common with Melior Junior, or Decensia, or Exuperantia?

A twenty-first-century Christian, after having thought for a moment, can reply: everything that is most important. A modern person would certainly find these predecessors strange, their customs exotic, their attitudes often baffling, their courage at times impossible to imagine. Yet at the deepest level, Christians today believe what they too believed—that with Jesus Christ the world changed forever. Modern Christians want to keep the great insights alive, and wish they could live according to ideals they share directly, profoundly, with these people. Certainly, there have been enormous cultural changes. There are new ideas, new circumstances; the Christian Church has developed and grown. Terrible things have happened, crimes committed often in Christ's name, enormous heroism shown, repression and struggles to regain liberty, decline and renewal. Fidelity and confidence have fluctuated, while vast amounts of knowledge, both factual and spiritual, have been lost and gained during the many centuries since these stones were engraved. And still Christians are one with these dead. They accept the same commitment to love and transcendence of self, belong to the same lineage, can still stand with them, under the same roof.

2

SPACE AND TIME:

Narthex and Ground Plan

The unexpectedness and dimness of the passage down into the church of Sant'Agnese, the time that the descent requires, together with the strong sense the staircase gives of contact with the past, combine to provide an initiation into the church itself, especially for the first-time visitor.

Once you have passed through the glass door at the bottom of the stairs, you discover on your right, here as in any Catholic church, a basin of water called "holy" because it has been formally blessed.[1] This water is for a ritual form of ablution or washing, which signifies purification upon entry, the intention to go in with a pure heart: people dip their fingers into the water and with them make a sign of the cross, from head to chest and from shoulder to shoulder.[2] They do it again when they leave the church, for a church is holy ground—indeed, as we shall see, a church is often cross-shaped ground—and leaving it is as momentous as going in.

What lies before you now is simply a continuation of the passage-way; it turns slightly left and then continues straight on and ends at a door. The door opens into the antechamber of the entrance to the cata-combs. Today, when the passage is lit by electricity, you can see the whole distance, down the steps, through the glass, and as far as the cata-comb door, from the moment you enter at the top of the stairs. There is no groping through the dark; nevertheless, the unexpectedness of finding a long journey still before them, forward and down, makes most first-time visitors pause, then take their time in the descent between the walls that rise on either hand, covered with marble inscrip-tions. There is no sign of any church at the bottom; you are left "in the dark," and must advance and explore before being enlightened.

To your left, after the entrance through the glass partition, is a wall. Doors pierce this wall now, but for many centuries it was blank,[3] and behind it lay solid earth, perforated by warrens full of graves. This area was once very shadowy, lit only by diffused light from beyond the four dark pillars on the right; it is still relatively dim. You naturally turn right, towards the light—and with a rush the space opens out and the generous volume of the church interior rises and widens about you.

Most people arriving for the first time in Sant'Agnese's—and in my case several times thereafter—do not even realize that they have turned ninety degrees to the right to step into the church. They are drawn into the movement, almost unawares. It is like taking the first bite of a delicious meal: the experience is so concentrated and satisfying that the action needed to procure it occurs almost unconsciously, without will or effort. The last step of initiation has been taken, from dim vestibule into the main body of the building. One has scarcely had time to realize that the passage is actually the vestibule of the church.

PARADISE: THE NARTHEX

Such a vestibule is known as a *narthex*, a Greek word meaning "fennel stalk." In the ancient Mediterranean world, a section of a very large fennel stalk was commonly used as a container. For example, Prometheus in Greek mythology stole fire from the gods on Mount Olympus and gave it to humankind, carrying the hot brand down to us enclosed in a *narthex*. A perfume box, too, could be made out of a section of a hollow fennel stalk. The front and transitional portion of a church was known in the Greek Christian world as a narthex, a sacred enclosure. New converts awaiting final initiation into Christianity, the catechumens (literally "those still being instructed"), were sometimes not admitted into the church proper but had to stand in the narthex during church services. Once baptism had been received—a much larger, once-and-for-all-time version of the ritual ablution with holy water at the church entrance—they would formally enter both the building and the institutional Church.

A narthex is ordinarily dim; exterior church doors are usually kept closed or curtained so that the only light in the vestibule comes from the temple beyond it. The preliminary section of many early churches was an enclosed area *outside* the front doors, a courtyard before the temple, often with greenery and flowers and a fountain. It was an area of transition before entry into the building. In Latin the name for it was an atrium (as the courtyard of a Roman house was called), or a *porticus* because it was a pillared enclosure; or it was called a *paradisus*, a garden, but one with biblical connotations. "Paradise" comes from a Persian word meaning a "walled-in enclosure," often a deer park. The word came to denote more vaguely a "pleasure garden." For this reason "paradise" was used to translate the Hebrew word *gan*, or garden, in the Book of Genesis: the place where Adam and Eve lived in delightful innocence before they disobeyed God.[4] The French word for an area in front of a church is *parvis*, from *paradisus*. A narthex inside a church also stands for paradise.

At the culmination of the Christian year, just before midnight on the eve of Easter, an ancient hymn is often sung in the darkness by the light of only the Easter candle. The candle is carried into the church from outside, and symbolizes Christ and the light he brought into the world. The song tells us, among other things, that the mythical sin in Paradise of Adam and Eve, First Man and First Woman—a sin of curiosity, a longing to know and so become "like gods"—turned out to be "a happy fault," *felix culpa*, even though it meant that humankind was thereafter forced to leave Paradise. The fault was happy because it eventually caused God's irruption into human history, the coming of Jesus Christ, "so wonderful a saviour." As Paul put it in his letter to the Romans, with Adam sin "entered the world," but with Christ grace came, "grace abounding": there is far more grace, which is the undeserved mercy of God, than there is sin.[5] The first disobedience was the end of innocence—but still it is seen as standing at the *beginning* of the story of the human race. And similarly, to enter a church we step out of the narthex or "paradise."

Now the next stage of the journey can begin. The "road," the church's central aisle, lies ahead, its length representing the time humanity has before it, the span each person has to live. The church includes within its walls not only the beginning but also the end, the journey's destination. No sooner have we entered than we are presented with a full view of this destination, symbolized by the apse: when the journey is complete and paradise regained, it will be at a higher and eternal level, where the journey will be transfigured and understood.

In the children's game of hopscotch, the origins of which are very old, a pattern of squares is scratched on a bald patch of ground, or drawn in chalk on a city sidewalk. Players, taking turns, throw or kick a stone into the squares in a set order, hopping on one leg to do so; when a pair of squares is reached, landing on both legs is permitted. When a player arrives at the end of the diagram, he or she must turn, then hop back to the beginning and out of the pattern's outline.

Some hopscotch patterns are spiral, with the goal in the middle, like a labyrinth. There the player is said to be "reborn": the next stage of the game is to turn and hop back out. This hopscotch design can be interpreted as a figure of the "journey" of life, as well as a static picture of the soul: of the truth—God—to be found at the heart of every self. Round churches are built in part to evoke such ideas. A different hopscotch pattern resembles the ground-plan of a basilical church with a transverse section or transept. This shape expresses, as we shall see, the spiritual life in time; it also represents a human body, with the double squares (the transept) as the arms, and the far end as the head. The normally rounded hopscotch end-piece is known in many languages as "paradise," or by a word such as "crown" or "glory."

TIME AND SPACE, FATE AND DESTINY

Human beings readily think of time in terms of space. This propensity is built into the English language, and indeed into all languages. Psychologists explain that children learn about space first—up and down, far and near, large and small. Only later do they find out about time, and they do so linguistically, using the spatial concepts they already know. The language itself has already given to spatial words temporal meanings, imitating the order in which a child learns, and perhaps assisting the child by doing so. "Now," for example, is "here" and present to us; it is "the present." What has already happened, what once was present, has moved on and is now absent, as though it has "passed" us. "Present" and "past" are words that give away the unspoken metaphor that we all use to think about time, as a line—a road, a river—in the "course" of which events "take place." A clock face with its moving hands is a spatial area that shows the "amount" of time "gone by," and how much of it is left.

A narrative—a story recounted in time—organizes events into meaningful sequences. When "the plot" in a story is told to us, we demand not just a jumble of facts, but a string or connecting line to join them, disclosing causes, consequences, even form. Often the "line" of connection in stories is pictured as a thread. (The word "line" itself comes from the Latin *linea,* a flaxen thread for making linen.) We speak of "spinning a yarn," and, if we become distracted, of "losing the thread" of the tale or argument. The word "text" is cognate with "textile" because a narrative is thought of as woven, out of threads.

In ancient Greece the propensity to find patterns in events was expressed in a belief in fate, what the Romans called *fatum.* Greek myth spoke of three Moirai ("Sharers Out"), personifications of fate: ancient women who sat spinning the threads or ropes of what is "bound" to happen. (Ancient Roman, Scandinavian, and German mythologies also have groups of three crones who spin and weave the events of the world.) Their names in Greek were Clotho ("Spinner"), Lachesis ("Allotment"), and Atropos ("Not to Be Turned Aside"): we can see from these meanings that one's "spun" fate was exterior to oneself, a "given," yet personal as well as inescapable. The Roman word *fatum* means "a thing said"—it "reports" a sequence of events *before it occurs.* An event that is fated cannot not happen; the plot, *fatum,* or script cannot be changed, as the poet Yeats said, "by an inch or an ounce."[6] It is a length or a weight, a pattern, a line, a thread, a thing, completely existent before it works itself out in time.

It is easy to dismiss such myths as "merely" stories, but they carry a truth we all recognize or they would not fascinate us as they do. Human beings are never in total control of their lives or of everything that happens to them. They often feel forced and dragged into situations and courses of action against their will. It is then that they know what the ancients called fate: unfreedom. Such experience is the context—again the "textile" metaphor—of all moral judgement and spiritual understanding. Every religion states the problem of freedom, and offers its own insights into its meaning.

What Christianity proposes instead of fate is destiny. And, it adds, this destiny is life with God, a personal God, who cares about what happens to human beings. The difference between the two conceptions is important. Whereas fate is allotted or "said" in the beginning, destiny (from which we get the word "destination") is the end, the aim. We are free to walk towards the goal or away from it, just as we are free to walk past a church rather than enter it. Nobody, not even the ancient Olympian gods, could gainsay fate; the Pattern was older than they were. But the Judeo-Christian God is a person,[7] who created all there is out of gratuitous love, who takes a hand in human lives, and who gives meaning to their experience. In the Christian under-standing of the journey towards destiny, it is also possible to get lost on the way, and to be found or saved as well.

The Cross, the human body, and destiny are three of the ideas that have informed the traditional design of many churches for centuries. A church is often cross-shaped—that is, in the form of a human body, with the arms constituted by the transept, the head by the apse, and the heart by the altar. A strong directionality is commonly expressed: a door, then a narthex, and then the long main body of the church or nave, heading directly to the altar and the rounded apse wall beyond it. The people in the church are on a journey, the "journey of life," towards their destiny, which is God. Time—the life of the group, the lifetime of each individual person—is expressed as space. Moving up the nave and aisles is moving towards our end: our aim ("end" as purpose) and also our body's death. Movement and immobility, the temporal and the eternal, time and space: all these oppositions are expressed in a church's geometry.

SACRED SPACE

When people decide to create a sacred space (such space may remain flat, as in many of the Indian or Tibetan mandalas, or eventually have a building or even a whole city constructed upon it), they tend to make the beginnings solemn and instinct with meaning. An ancient Roman temple occupied an oblong area, drawn in a ritual manner by a priest who specialized in prophetically interpreting signs, and who was known as an augur; the building had to be "inaugurated." A *templum* was most literally a piece of earth or a section of the sky, delineated by an augur. When a temple was built, it needed a ritually outlined space, a *templum*.

The word *templum* itself is cognate with Greek *temnein*, to cut: the special area is "cut off" by a boundary from the space around it. Greeks called a sacred "cut off" area *temenos*. In ancient Rome many official state functions—meetings of senators, for example—could take place only once the space for them had been ritually outlined. Inside a *temenos* the augur would draw two lines crossing at right angles. Roman camps, and most Roman cities, made these intersecting lines the two main roads, creating the central and most important crossroad. Around the city or camp or temple was a wall, the sacred boundary.

"Sacred," from Latin *sacer*, meant essentially something that should be respected, and not tampered with or "desecrated." Separateness is an essential element of the notion of the sacred; a sacred area should not be "polluted," that is, mixed up with what has no business invading it. The boundary must not be broken. Cleanliness is the ideal, and purity; sacredness has to do with categories, and keeping them clear. Defilement of the sacred produces in people who respect it a reaction of shuddering and disgust. To give an everyday example, a dinner table is a "sacred" area in a house, especially if it has food on it. So someone's dirty socks (or anything else considered "revolting" by prospective diners) lying on that table, especially once it has been "set" or laid out and thereby ritually set apart for its function, is a form of defilement.

The idea of a bounded area—where what is inside is more special, more focused, and more concentrated than what is outside, and therefore demands purity from people who enter it—is very strong in the related Latin word *sanctus*, holy. The most powerful area in a building may be called the inner sanctum, where only the most important, the most "qualified" people ever penetrate. The strange English word "sanction," which means both "allow" and "forbid," derives its opposite meanings from what is *sanctus*. Something no one dares touch or alter is "sacrosanct"—which doubles the meaning by adding "sacred" to *sanctus*. A holy building, or an especially holy part of one, is known as a "sanctuary." A place that is sacred can act as a refuge for anybody who takes shelter inside it; such protection, which relies upon the "untouchable" nature of the sacred, is also called "sanctuary."

In ancient Greece and Rome a temple was a house for a god; it often stood on a hill, was raised on a podium, and was approached by steps. Around it was a precinct (literally "something with a belt—a cinch—tightly surrounding it"), a space where worshippers could gather; it was not for those who did not intend or who were not allowed to take part in the sacrifices and the feast that followed. The temple proper was not where people congregated. The god's statue stood alone in the temple, in a windowless walled enclosure with a large door in front. Columns stood around the outside of this room, which was called the *cella*. The altar's place was in the precinct, not in the temple; when sacrifice was performed, the door to the god's enclosure was opened so that the deity could watch what was going on.

The sacrifice took place *pro fano*, in front of the *fanum* or "fane," the temple. (*Fanum* is from the Greek root *phan-*, meaning "show," as in "epiphany"; this was a place where the god revealed himself or herself.) What was outside the temple, *pro fano*, also could mean what was not holy, that is, merely—or sometimes appallingly—profane. The distinction between an outlined space and the undifferentiated space beyond it is invariably important.

Christianity was born at the height of the Roman Empire; and when Christians eventually came to build their own churches, they built some of the first of them in Rome. So churches were heavily dependent, architecturally speaking, upon Roman technological and artistic know-how. Christian thinking grew within the matrix of ancient Classical culture. But Christianity was born out of Jewish, not Greek or Roman, religion. The Jews also had a temple, a single building in Jerusalem that focused the nation and provided its ritual centre. Within the "holy of holies," its sacred inner sanctum, this temple held for centuries the written Decalogue or Ten Commandments, fruit of the encounter of Moses with God. The Jewish temple remembered and kept alive that revolutionary contact with the divine. Every Christian church remembers this temple, and often contains features that specifically echo its structure.

SACRED NARRATIVE

But Christians, like Jews, are people of the Word, of memory and narrative; they are the children of time. The physical object that is sacred in Judaism (and therefore in Christianity) is first and foremost the Book, the Bible. There were certainly vast numbers of stories and myths in Greco-Roman religion, but there was nothing like the Bible, a book that is more sacred than any building.

The Bible is not a history book. It has history in it, certainly, but it contains all sorts of other literary genres too: poetry, myths, stories, prophecies, canons of law, commentaries, ethical pleading. The word "Bible" is, in fact, a plural noun (Greek *ta biblia*, "the books"), and that is what the Bible is—many books, many historical periods, many points of view. But behind all of them is a tradition, a continuity, one river through which many waters flow. The purpose of the Bible is to reveal the true nature of God; in doing so, it also shows the ways in which people have missed the truth, or misunderstood it.

The Gospels open the Christian part of the Bible, the "New Testament." A "testament" is writing that bears witness to what has happened. The English word "gospel" is a contraction of "good" and "spell," and means "good news"; the writer of a Gospel is called an "evangelist," from the Greek for an "announcer (*angel*) of what is good (*eu*)." The Gospels, all of which were written in Greek, tell the life of Jesus—but in a manner that little resembles what modern people would expect in a biography. There is no description of what Jesus looked like, for example, nothing about what he did for most of his life, let alone anything about what he "must have" felt. There are no footnotes and no documents adduced, although the writings of the Old Testament are quoted frequently.

In a Gospel, everything is seen in the light of what the writer believes, and the writer never pretends it is otherwise. But he rarely allows himself to address the reader directly; his belief is expressed in the story he tells. Modern writers of biography and history—once those genres and their rules had become set and differentiated from other kinds of writing—have pretended to be objective and unprejudiced, to have obtained and verified the available facts. A Gospel writer, on the other hand, was a witness, giving "news" that he was not afraid to call "good"; he was saying that a new intensity had begun in the relationship between human beings and God, that God had chosen to draw closer to humanity. *Emmanuel*, meaning in Hebrew "God with us," had come, as it had been foretold.[8]

Postmodern thinking has recently come to distrust the notion of any objective reporting of "the facts." It has become necessary to demolish the idea that a writer could have no assumptions, could have no axe whatever to grind when relating a sequence of events or expounding an argument. The New Testament, like the Old, is openly partisan; the writers believe in a meaning, and they present that meaning with the full and open intention of confronting their readers with it. They even challenge the reader to change his or her life and point of view as a result of the confrontation. So unconcerned is the Bible (both Old and New Testaments) about "the facts" that it often presents, without attempting to reconcile them, two or more versions of the same events, told by two or more people, with different perspectives on those facts. What is most interesting, in the Bible, is what "the facts" mean to the reader or listener.

The New Testament offers no fewer than four versions of the life of Christ, each written with a different emphasis and for a different audience. There are enough discrepancies among the four to provide lifetimes of scholarly debate about what the "actual facts" might have been, although in most respects the accounts do agree among themselves. The Gospels, being four, should never let us imagine that there are no assumptions involved, no differences arising out of emphases and points of view. The Gospels, being four, ought to pull the rug out from under any literalist stance well in advance.

The Gospels were written when the Church had already come into being. Indeed, they were written by the Church, from its understanding of events at that time. The intention was to record the message, so that people could hear it and respond to it, each person in his or her own way. Like the Old Testament, the Gospels set out to reveal the true nature of God. They were written out of a sense that people living then had a solemn duty to ensure that these world-shattering events were not forgotten; the story must be handed on.

THE EPIC OF LIBERATION

In the beginning, then, is an epic, told in the many books of the Bible, the world's fullest account of the history of a people from their ancient origins. Running like a great river of memory through the Jewish scriptures is the story of the Exodus, where Moses leads his people out of oppression to liberty.

In the course of this journey, after many adventures, Moses went up to the top of Mount Sinai, and there he met God. He was given a Covenant, or binding promise, that God would grant divine favour to the Israelites provided they obeyed the Covenant Commandments. The Commandments and the Judgements delivered by God to Moses were preserved in the Ark and tent of the Covenant: an acacia-wood box and a portable tent shrine, carried by the people when they journeyed through the desert and into Canaan. Yahweh (God) himself designed it, giving Moses careful measurements and prescriptions for its structure.[9] This tent, carefully recalled by both the temple of Jerusalem and the modern Jewish synagogue, is also the archetype underlying everything in a Christian church. The journey to liberation is still the theme, the story of the Jewish Exodus the founding pattern.

Over the Ark was set a gold plate with depictions of cherubim— celestial beings of mixed human and animal forms—with wings touching, guarding the box and its gold cover, the site of aspersions of blood from animal sacrifices. Its name was *kapporet*, from the Hebrew verb *kipper* meaning "wiping away" (of blood) and hence "propitiatory," "atoning": the blood of the sacrifice on the Day of Atonement or Yom Kippur atoned, in two separate acts, for the sins of priests and people. The ultimate purpose of this ritual was to remember and celebrate the direct encounter with God, of which the Law, and the requirement of uprightness and sinlessness, was the fruit. There was also in the original tent for the Ark, at God's request, a gold seven-branched candlestick, the *menorah*.

The people, however, had apostasized even before Moses came down from his forty days on the mountain with God: they disobeyed the first and fundamental Commandment by worshipping not God, but an idol, the golden calf. Moses had the tent and Ark made, but God's presence was not among the people even then, because they had not remained faithful to the divine revelation; Moses made this absolutely clear by leaving the Ark and tent outside the Jewish camp.[10] Then Moses begged God to forgive and reconsider. God heeded his pleas and gave the people the Covenant all over again, although this time Moses had to write everything out himself; the original prescriptions had been written by God, but Moses had smashed the tablets in rage when he found his people worshipping the golden calf. And then God came once more to live with his chosen people. The story makes the point, central to Judaism and to Christianity, that only God, the one transcendent God, is holy. Nothing else whatsoever is to be adored.

The Ark moved on, bearing the laws and the promises inside it. By the time of the Judges (roughly 1200–1050 B.C.), the Ark was being kept at Shiloh, about twelve miles south of Nablus, in a building called the "house" or "palace" of Yahweh.[11] In about 1030 B.C. it was captured by the Philistines.[12] But the Philistines suffered nothing but trouble until they returned the Ark to Israel. Even then there was no peace until the Ark was brought to where God wanted it, in Jerusalem, which by then was known as the city of David, for King David had made it his capital. The city of Jerusalem was to be the "type" of final and universal salvation, not only for Israel but for all peoples.[13] (The Bible uses "types"—objects and events—that are like riddles to be solved: the answer to the riddle becomes clear only later, when what has been foretold in the "type" comes to pass. What Christians call the Old Testament contains many "types" or adumbrations of what happens in the New Testament.)[14]

King Solomon, son of David, finally built a permanent home for the Ark.[15] When the great temple was finished—it was an immense project requiring the utmost skill and the most precious of materials—Solomon had the Ark placed in the holy of holies, the temple's inner sanctum.[16] The building had taken seven years to complete, sometime during Solomon's reign, between 965 and 928 B.C.

THE JERUSALEM TEMPLE AND THE SYNAGOGUES

The Temple of Solomon in Jerusalem stood on a platform on a hill, in an area probably about fifty yards north of the present Dome of the

Rock. Two free-standing bronze pillars rose at the top of the steps in front of the entrance, forming part of what was known as the *ulam*, a vestibule, porch, or narthex fifteen feet deep. From there the priests, and the priests alone, could enter an oblong space, the *hekal*, which is calculated to have been sixty feet long and thirty feet wide. The shape of this temple—similar as it is to the form of many a church today, including Sant'Agnese's—had very ancient Middle Eastern roots. A hint of its antiquity can be glimpsed in the word *hekal*. It derives from Sumerian *È-GAL*, "great house," referring to the house of a god or a king. The great temple culture of the Sumerians, in modern Iraq, lasted from the fifth millennium to the twenty-fifth century B.C. Abraham had set out for Canaan from Ur, the temple city built by the Sumerians, probably during the early second millennium B.C.

At the end of the *hekal* of Solomon's temple, opposite the entrance, was a square room, probably reached by climbing steps. It was a cubic space thirty feet by thirty feet by thirty feet, closed off with olive-wood doors sheathed in gold. This was the holy of holies, the Sancta Sanctorum, the *debir* in Hebrew. In this room—into which no one could enter but the high priest, and he on only one day in the year—stood the Ark containing the Covenant, watched over by two fifteen-foot-high golden cherubim, whose extended wings reached from wall to wall.[17]

The altar for animal sacrifices rose in the courtyard outside the temple proper (*pro fano*). Near it was a huge basin known as the "sea of bronze," resting on the backs of twelve bronze bulls; there were also ten tables supporting bronze basins. The priests used the "sea" for their own ablutions, and the other basins for purifying the sacrificial victims.[18] Sacrificial blood entered the *debir*, or holy of holies, only on Yom Kippur, the Day of Atonement, when it was poured onto the golden *kapporet*, also called God's "throne." When the high priest went into and came out of the holy of holies, crossing the ultimate boundary, he changed his clothes and washed himself from head to foot.

The temple of Jerusalem "stood for" or refracted the entire cosmos: the sea (the "bronze sea" or giant laver in the court outside), the earth (the *hekal* with the altar of perfumes, the golden "tree" or menorah, the "showbread" or fruit of the earth formed into twelve loaves symbolizing the twelve tribes of Israel), and heaven, the dwelling place of God (the *debir*, recalling the meeting of Moses with God on Mount Sinai and containing the Commandments in the Ark). The two bronze pillars that stood in the narthex or *ulam* are of unknown significance. Perhaps they referred to the two mystical trees in Paradise, the Tree of Life and the Tree of the Knowledge of Good and Evil; if so, the *ulam* was symbolic of Paradise, *gan eden*.

The temple stood for nearly four centuries, until the Babylonians under King Nebuchadnezzar invaded Jerusalem in 587 B.C. The temple was burned down, and the Ark of the Covenant disappeared. All the gold and precious metals from the treasury were stolen, as well as the bronze from the two great pillars and the "sea." The survivors of the battle were deported to Babylon.[19]

Yet during the exile Ezekiel prophesied that the time would come when a new temple would rise. He described it in detail.[20] In his vision it was similar, but not identical in measurements, to Solomon's temple. This time, however, the temple was symbolic, an embodiment in the mind of reunion and wholeness, of a return home from exile, of cohesion and order, harmony and balance: everything about this visionary temple was triumphantly symmetrical. Then the vision shows us a marvel. Ezekiel says that he was taken to see the fountain of water that would well up in the temple. It poured out from under the threshold to the east, since the temple faced east. This water became a stream, a river, a flood; it flowed into the Dead Sea and made the salt water fresh, so that it teemed with fish and water creatures. Trees grew in profusion around it, and people fished in the water and lived on the fruit of the trees and used the leaves for healing. The temple of Ezekiel's vision would turn the desert into Paradise, and death into life.

In 538, when the Jews returned from their forty-nine-year exile in Babylon, their Persian rulers permitted them to rebuild the temple. It took twenty-three years of intermittent work to restore it. The Ark was not remade, and the *debir* of the temple was left empty except for a new *kapporet* to receive the blood offering,[21] with its function of ritually focusing God's presence inside the holy of holies. But the hope stirred up by visionaries like Ezekiel was henceforward unforgettable.

The idea of a new temple began to grow. It was also increasingly believed that a saviour would come to Israel.[22]

During the reign of King Herod I, the Great (73 B.C.–A.D. 4), the temple was rebuilt and refurbished. He doubled the size of the Temple Mount and created a podium thirty-six acres in extent to support a huge complex of buildings in addition to the temple. He recreated the menorah, the single gold candlestick that had graced the original tent in the wilderness, with seven branches holding cups in the form of open almond blossoms and lamps filled with pure olive oil. The veil that hung in front of the *debir* or inner sanctum, also required in the Exodus prescription, was woven again in wool and linen of violet and scarlet and crimson, and worked with cherubim. A second, less magnificent curtain hung at the entrance to the temple from the *ulam* or narthex. The purpose of the two veils was to separate; the curtain hanging before the *debir*, in particular, served to draw the line between "the holy place and the holy of holies."[23]

The temple was surrounded by courtyards that progressively sifted out the impure and prevented them from approaching the central and most sacred area. An external wall around the temple precinct prevented Gentiles (non-Jews) from entering the temple area at all; warnings were set up in Greek and Latin (two of them have been found) forbidding any foreigner to set foot on this ground on pain of death. Jewish women were allowed only in the outermost court of the temple precinct; then—purer—came the court of Israelite men; then came the court of the priests, purer still. Only priests could penetrate the temple proper, the *hekal*. Only the high priest was permitted, and that only once a year, to pass beyond the veil that hung before the holy of holies.

This was the temple precinct that Jesus knew. He would not have been allowed into the temple proper, because he was not a priest. The grandeur of the entire complex, its ancient story, deep significance, and profound roots should be present to anyone who hears that Jesus said he came both to fulfill the Law and to replace the temple—that indeed he *was* the real temple.

The temple in all its splendour was demolished by the Romans in 70 A.D., when they destroyed Jerusalem. On the Arch of Titus in Rome is depicted the scene of the Roman army returning in triumph with their booty, including what is apparently the gold candlestick, the menorah, from the temple. They ruthlessly wiped out the entire complex of buildings and pillaged its riches. But the temple that Ezekiel foretold, the visionary temple, lived on.

There had been only one temple, the one in Jerusalem. But Jews had other shrines, and they also performed religious rituals at home, as they do to this day. In addition, they had meeting houses for prayer, meditation, and instruction. The Greek word for such a building is a synagogue, literally a "coming together." It is still unknown when the first synagogues were conceived and built, but they represented a wholly new idea of communal religious observance. They were flourishing at the time of Jesus, who began his public ministry in one.

The form of the synagogue made reference to the temple. Then as now it was usually rectangular in plan, with a shrine-cupboard containing the rolls of the scriptures set in one wall. It also had a raised platform in the midst (*bema* in Greek) on which sat the elders and officials of the synagogue, and from which much of the service was conducted. The alcove for the scriptures recalls the *debir* at the temple, the place where the Ark containing the Covenant was kept. The *bema* can be thought of as an echo of the *hekal*. A synagogue is for hearing and learning and discussing the Word: the history, traditions, prayers, and commentaries of the Jewish people. With the destruction of Jerusalem in 70 A.D., the Jews had to learn to do without the temple. The practice of sacrifice ceased. The many synagogues took over the role of religious centres.

THE COMING OF CHRISTIANITY

In the earliest days after the death of Jesus, his followers continued to attend the still-standing temple. They also met together wherever a room large enough to contain the group could be found.[24] The Jewish scriptures remained their foundational book, as they still are for Christians today. For larger meetings they had the model of the synagogue, which was intensely familiar to them: almost all of them were Jews, and Jesus himself had been a Jew who was deeply committed to his people's religion.

The word "Christian" was not coined till some decades later—probably by Gentiles, and as a term of opprobrium.[25] The first Christians continued simply to be Jews, or Judaizing Gentiles. However, they differed from their fellows in their belief that the Messiah, or "Anointed One" foretold, had come. He had turned out to be not a triumphant warrior or a master politician, but someone they had personally known, their own friend, a poor man, someone of immense personal power but of no account in the world of public affairs, an innocent man, utterly committed to nonviolence, who had suffered the death of a criminal. Such a Messiah could not have been more unexpected (although, in the Christian interpretation, his character had in fact been foretold in the Jewish scriptures).[26] For Christians, Jesus and none other was the Messiah, *Christos,* "Anointed One" in Greek. Not only that, but they also believed Jesus was no longer dead; he was still with them. In Jesus, they came to be convinced, God himself had become human.

The temple at Jerusalem is very much a part of the narrative concerning Jesus in the four Gospels. But the actual temple, from a Christian point of view, was always destined to pass away. Indeed, at least three of the Gospels were written after the temple had been destroyed (that of Mark may have been the exception). The temple, however, was an embodiment of the story of God's chosen people and a sign or "type" of what was to come; for Christians it was subsumed in Jesus and in the Church. Christians believed that Jesus was what the temple had anticipated; he was the "presence of God" that it promised.

The climactic end of Jesus' life began with his outrage at the people's lack of respect for "his father's house"—the temple. (The rage of Jesus recalls that of Moses when he found his people worshipping the golden calf.) So important was this incident in the memory of his disciples that all of the Gospels record it, and John places it very near the beginning of his account.[27] It took place in the outer esplanade of the temple, the only area where Gentiles were allowed. There Greek and Roman currency was exchanged for Jewish and Tyrian shekels, and animals and birds were sold for sacrifice. Even Jesus' own parents, when they had presented him as an infant at the temple in accordance with the laws of Israel, had changed their money for shekels and bought birds for the mandated sacrifice.[28] But in his rage Jesus pushed over the tables, made a whip of cords, and thrashed the money vendors and the salesmen out of the "den of thieves" they had created. It was shocking behaviour, and clearly arose from his sense of reverence for God's holy place.

But the source of the drama was even more revolutionary than it looks to us at first sight. Certainly, the market must have seemed crass—rather like the sale of tasteless goods outside many a church or shrine today. But there was more: the market itself and its relegation to a profane place outside the temple proper had a solemn purpose, and that purpose was purity. The market ensured, first, that only animals deemed pure would be sacrificed in the temple. Further, Greek and Roman money was considered impure, and its impurity would contaminate the animals it paid for. Pagan money, idolatrous money with the picture of the divinized emperor on it, was therefore not allowed in the temple; it had first to be exchanged for shekels. To attack the market was symbolically to strike at the exclusivity, the relentless purity, of the temple itself.[29]

Immediately after this incident Jesus said to the people who remonstrated with him, "Destroy this temple, and in three days I will raise it up." They were furious, and contemptuous of his folly; the charges at his trial included the blasphemy of this remark. But they had not understood the riddle. By "this temple" Jesus meant himself; he was saying that he had replaced the temple. His kingdom was not to be protected and privileged by means of purity. He himself was not sacrosanct: his body would be agonizingly pierced, and his heart pierced again after his death. He saw to it that everybody could have access to him by means of the endlessly reproduced bread that is his body, "this temple." No one would be excluded, unless people wished to exclude themselves. And he would "raise the temple up" from death, in three days.

When Jesus died on the cross, Matthew relates that "the veil of the temple was torn in two from top to bottom."[30] Henceforth, Christians believed, the holy of holies would lie open for all to approach it; salvation history was beginning a new era.

44

"Christianity" is the name of a continuing endeavour to take up and live the implications of the life and death of Christ, of the belief that in him God has broken into human history. Within the family of institutions that try to remember the insights they receive from him, there are many cultures, many tastes and traditions, many differences of attitude and emphasis. These are expressed especially vividly in the buildings they occupy.

Some Christians prefer to worship God at home and in private, or with other people in something ad hoc—under some trees, say, or in a garage or a shed or a school basement. And indeed, according to the Gospels Jesus instituted the Eucharist in a dining room borrowed from a friend, and foreshadowed this event in the multiplication of loaves and fishes in an open field and in the hills beside a lake.[31] When Christians meet in buildings the architectural possibilities range widely, from the austere to the exuberant. Everything is to be found, from the simplest halls or meeting houses—to modern churches that may be purely functional or make dramatic "statements"—to imposing, fortresslike stone buildings, perhaps accommodating here and there a minimum of artistic heightening—to magnificent and elaborate Gothic cathedrals and their progeny—to luxuriously decorated churches (Sant'Agnese's could be classified as a minor example)—to Baroque edifices revelling in deliberate excess—to garish constructions choked with statuary and clutter, ranking low in the judgement of people of "good taste."

But why have churches at all? The very idea of having such a thing as a church building must be questioned, given Christianity's founding story. For a Christian, not to ask this question, or even to feel comfortable about his or her answer, is to deny something that lies at the heart of Christianity. God, or the truth, is not confined to the Church, let alone by church buildings. Every Christian should remain deeply suspicious of churches—both as buildings and as institutions; it is part of following Christ.

The paradox is there from the beginning. For example, when Jesus hounded the money-changers out of the temple, he wanted people to respect God's house—even as he proposed to replace it. Churches can be confining and deadening—and churches may liberate and enliven. Buildings are unnecessary—but needed. Churches remain—but they remain in order to keep alive a message that is all about movement; about hope and change. In short, a Christian church seems to be—and quite consciously is—a contradiction in terms.

3

TRAJECTORY:

Nave

From one point of view, the mystical, Christianity is a series of oppositions transcended. From another, the ethical and psychological, Christianity turns the value system of what Jesus called "this world" on its head. By "this world" Jesus meant the world as it is at present organized, insofar as it stands in deliberate opposition to God's will. The ideal that Jesus revealed is "the kingdom of God," in which power, selfishness, and violence are rejected. In this alternative order, the poor own the kingdom, the merciful receive mercy, the gentle "inherit the earth." And those persecuted for the sake of the truth are, if we could only comprehend the breadth of the perspective offered, fortunate and blessed.[1]

The church of Saint Agnes was built in honour of a young girl who was put to death because of what she believed. She was buried here, in this place, by her family and friends. The people who shared her beliefs visited her grave, and were convinced, not that the cruel brevity of her life was a shame and a waste, but that she had shown a bravery and integrity that they all wished they could attain.

Being a young girl, in those days much more than in ours, meant having no power, no prestige—not even any social autonomy, let alone heroic "prowess." And yet Agnes had managed to express the depth of her conviction, and to find the courage to face its consequences at the hands of "this world." To take her for a hero, to visit her grave and honour her, was to express one's own belief, while deliberately choosing the opposite of what was generally thought brilliant and worthy of admiration.

People kept coming. They wanted to stand before the remains of an actual human being who had freely, indisputably, and spectacularly embraced God. Agnes was little—but her courage was magnificent; a person unknown during her life and of no account—yet whose integrity of soul the massive and concentrated power of the Roman state had been unable to crush; a very young girl—but (in the opinion of these people) a great hero. They also believed that she had died, but lived; that she could still help them to see what she had seen, and even to do what she had done; that she could share her gifts if they sufficiently longed to receive them.

They turned their backs, therefore, on the glory of marble and gold, the great monuments and marvels of central Rome, arguably the most magnificent city ever created. Instead, they travelled out into the country to visit a simple burial space in a catacomb.

THE CATACOMBS

In ancient Greece and Rome, death, and in particular dead bodies, were considered utterly revolting; the dead polluted the living. Dead bodies were disposed of outside the city walls. Beside roads leading to and from Rome, sometimes in the gardens of private estates, tombs above ground and hypogea (graves under a family's burial plot: the word means literally "under the earth") were constructed. Many of the dead were cremated; the bodies of those too poor to afford named graves would be thrown into communal lime pits. Roman law forbade any touching, moving, or otherwise tampering with dead bodies. (Respect, in pollution beliefs, is achieved by avoidance and underwritten by disgust.) The loathsomeness of corpses made them the family's business: the family had to bury their dead, and the Roman government was only too happy to leave them to it.

Whatever their religious belief, people were accustomed to visiting these burial places, as people do today, to remember family members and friends, and to care for their graves. (Part of the horror of being dumped when dead into a lime pit was the impossibility of such visits and such remembrance occurring.) There was something festive about visiting a grave to commemorate a relative's death; you walked out of Rome into the country, a distance often of a mile or two, carrying provisions for a meal, and made a day of it. People could sit, enjoying the bucolic surroundings, and picnic at the family's burial site. There was also a sense, more or less explicitly believed in, that when friends and relatives ate together at or above the graves they were somehow including the dead people in the party, cheering them up, warming them with love and remembrance, and even sharing food with them: people made libations of wine and left food for the dead.

In the late second century Romans, and in particular Jews and Christians, began to bury their dead in catacombs.[2] The city of Rome is built on soil shot through with seams of tufa, formed by chemical precipitation from volcanoes that erupted between two and a half and three million years ago. Tufa can take a multitude of forms. Certain tufa seams have the consistency of clay, which hardens on exposure to the air; it was into these that the catacombs were dug.[3] The system was economical because it saved space; all that was legally required was proof of ownership of the surface area, underneath which gallery after gallery could be excavated. Catacombs are found in places other than Rome, including Naples, Syracuse, and Malta. Christians living in places lacking tufa continued to bury their dead in ordinary cemeteries.

Pozzolana, a non-cohesive form of tufa, was invaluable to the Romans because they used it to make an excellent cement. (It is named after the cement quarries near the town of Pozzuoli on the Gulf of Naples.) The Romans dug assiduously for pozzolana. They perforated the earth in several areas around Rome with quarries called *arenariae*, "sand pits." Catacombs tend to be associated with pozzolana warrens; sometimes Christian burials are found inside their wide, irregular tunnels.

The Roman authorities knew perfectly well the Christian predilection for burying their dead in catacombs, which were usually associated with surface cemeteries. Christians were allowed to dig through the tufa as much as they liked, provided they owned and duly registered the land directly above the galleries full of graves. Christians would club together and buy such land, or rich converts would donate it. When galleries covered the whole area under a given surface, a new set of passages was excavated underneath them, or a passageway was deepened. The result is that in many high catacomb galleries, or where there are several levels of passages, the graves on the lowest level were dug last. Tunnels frequently come to an abrupt end underground because it was illegal to dig beyond the surface plot.

Air and light were provided in the galleries by a series of shafts rising to the surface; it was also via these openings that the tufa was extracted from the tunnels. Jerome describes, in about 413 A.D., how he and his friends used to visit the catacombs when he lived in Rome in the 360s. "Often I would enter the crypts, deep dug in the earth," he wrote, "with their walls on either side lined with the bodies of the dead. . . . Here and there the light, not entering through windows but filtering down from above through shafts, relieves the horror of the darkness."[4] The early Christians called the catacomb galleries *cryptae*, which means "hidden places" in Greek. Much later it became common for churches to have chapels underneath them, called crypts. These crypts ultimately derive from the ancient custom of building churches, such as Sant'Agnese's, over the bodies of saints buried in the catacombs.

A Christian corpse was given a simple embalming treatment with spices and scented ointments. Before burial, the body was covered with quicklime and then wrapped in a linen shroud. It was usually placed in one of the burial slots now called *loculi* ("little places"); more lime was sometimes added, and tiles or bricks or a marble slab closed the aperture. In graves that have been opened in modern times, the balm has become a reddish dust that still gives off a pleasant scent when burned; the lime, now hardened, often preserves the imprint of the shroud. Yet for all this care, catacombs must commonly have smelled of decay. Glass perfume flasks are often found in catacomb galleries. Visitors probably used perfumes to overcome the smell; they certainly sprinkled perfume onto the slabs closing the loculi.[5] The custom was also an evocation of life, not unlike that of bringing flowers to the graves of the dead.

A modern myth about early Christians is that they hid in the catacombs during the various persecutions. There was certainly clandestinity in these terrifying periods—Christians met for religious services in private houses, and must have hidden in private houses from time to time. But the catacombs, which the Romans occasionally confiscated to prevent Christians from meeting in their grounds, would not have made feasible hideouts because they were too well known. In any case people could not have survived for long down among the dead.

In the earliest catacombs all Christians received the same burial;

later some were given larger and more decorative tombs inside *cubic-ula* (square rooms containing all the graves of a particular family and its dependants), but the impression remains of an egalitarian togetherness. The community took responsibility for the burial of even its poorest members; it was one of the advantages of being a Christian, especially among the poor. Very often a grave had only the person's name written on it, but after about 250 A.D. more information began to be supplied. At more and more of the graves, especially those dug after Christianity was officially sanctioned in 312 A.D., the walls are plastered and then decorated with simple painted pictures, of enormous historical and iconographical interest. Occasionally, the family pressed a small object into the tufa wall outside the grave: a finger ring, a bone doll for a child, a sign showing what a man had done for a living.

There are about sixty catacombs, of varying sizes, around Rome; Sant'Agnese's is a fairly small one. A large catacomb, such as that of Priscilla or of Domitilla, has from six to eight miles of explored galleries, every one of which has several layers of loculi. The Roman catacombs have been rifled many times over the centuries, and most graves are now empty. They nevertheless provide unparalleled evidence about the lives of ordinary people, including the very poor, during the more than three centuries the catacombs were in use, from the late second century to the sixth century A.D.

Christians, like their pagan contemporaries, visited their dead.[6] However, Christians tended to gather in groups to do so, at the cemeteries and catacombs outside the city walls, in the secluded, "impure" places where the Roman state was not inclined to interfere, and where it was an ancient right of the family to bury and mourn their own. There was a tradition in Rome of burial societies, whose members paid dues and met regularly to deal with cemetery business. Many of these private clubs served social purposes other than merely facilitating burials; they were for making and meeting friends, and usually offered premises for holding dinner parties as well. It is likely that, in the early years, Christians often met together in the context, and sometimes under the pretext, of belonging to such clubs.

Christians were drawn together at the graveside not only to celebrate their own families but also, as a larger Christian community, to celebrate their heroes, the persecuted dead. The body of a person killed during one of the recurrent periods of persecution, for disobedience to the state because of his or her religious beliefs, was often handed over to the family for burial, like any other dead body. To Christians, people killed in these circumstances were martyrs, literally "witnesses" to their beliefs. The Greek and late Latin word *martus* ("martyr") derives from the same root (*mar-* and *mer-*) as *memor*, memory, a "keeping in mind." Early Christians remembered the graves where martyrs were buried, and built shrines or martyria to mark out and honour a burial place that the community invested with particular significance.

CONSTANTINE'S BUILDINGS IN ROME

When the new emperor, Constantine, decided after his victory over Maxentius in 312 that he would legitimize Christianity, he not only restored to the Church its confiscated property, but also began an ambitious program of church building. He donated the area and buildings known as the Laterani, which was part of his wife's dowry,[7] to the bishop of Rome for an official residence and administrative centre, and next door to it he built the Basilica of the Saviour, just within the city walls. The baptistery of the basilica, separate from the main building, was dedicated to John the Baptist. By the twelfth century its name had become attached to the church, which is why the Lateran is known today as St. John Lateran. A hall in a palace occupied by Constantine's mother Helena, also just within the walls, was converted into the church of Santa Croce in Gerusalemme. It was so called because Helena brought from Jerusalem to Rome a piece of what was believed to be the cross on which Jesus had died, and placed it in the church, to which it gave a status similar to that of a martyrium.

The other churches built under the auspices of Constantine, both in Rome and in Palestine, were conceived of not as regular meeting places for Christian communities but as martyria or memorials of sacred events. By the early fourth century many people in Rome, perhaps as much as a third of the population, were Christians, and they already had many places in the city in which to meet for regular prayer.[8] These centres also housed offices and living space for the clergy, and depots of clothing and food for the poor. Some of them were private houses donated to the community and named after the original owner: titulus Clementis, titulus Caeciliae, and so on. (Strictly speaking, a titulus was a marble plaque set into the wall of a house with the name of the owner carved on it, establishing his or her title to the property.) There were twenty-five such tituli by the end of the fourth century, many of which still survive in modern Rome. Even before 312, a few large halls had been built specifically to serve as Christian meeting places or churches. The remains of one such pre-Constantinian hall lie alongside the present church of San Crisogono in Trastevere. Martyria, on the other hand, were of necessity built in the cemeteries, and therefore outside the walls of Rome.[9] They were too far away for daily or even weekly church-going. People went out there occasionally, as a kind of pilgrimage, to visit their dead and to pray at the burial place of a saint.

The great basilica of St. Peter rose across the Tiber River, on top of a cemetery on the slopes of the Vatican hill beside Nero's circus, where Christians remembered that the Apostle Peter had been put to death and next to which they said he had been buried.[10] The ground was levelled at enormous cost and effort so that the church should stand directly over the nondescript grave that the Christians believed was Peter's. The site of the Lateran had no connection with a martyr. It was chosen for purely practical and administrative purposes, and because it was available. The buildings on it always remained primarily official. In contrast, it was the idea of who Peter was, what his death meant, and the actual place of his burial that really appealed to Christians.

As Rome's power and population declined, the Lateran, although it was within the city walls, gradually became marooned in uninhabited land, and the popes[11] found themselves having to travel tiresome journeys to and from the actual life of the city. Slowly, during the course of many centuries, the area around St. Peter's was incorporated into Rome. In the fifteenth century, the popes finally capitulated and moved definitively to St. Peter's.[12] The Lateran remains the cathedral of the pope in his role as bishop of Rome, but its fame continues to be overshadowed by that of the martyrium of Peter.

All Constantine's foundations at Rome were made in the twelve years between his victory at the Milvian Bridge in 312 and his departure for Byzantium, where he founded "the new Rome," Constantinople, now Istanbul. The Constantinian foundation at the catacombs of Sant'Agnese was made, in fact, soon after the emperor left Rome. Sant'Agnese's, like St. Peter's and St. Paul's, is one of the martyria that stood in the cemeteries, and therefore in a ring around but outside the walls of Rome. Eleven out of the original thirty-eight martyria still remain.[13] As Sant'Agnese's is a fairly stiff walk from the present gate in the Aurelian Walls, the Porta Pia, visiting the catacomb must have been a special event rather than a daily occurrence. On the anniversary of her death each year, on January 21, Christians gathered there in increasing numbers.[14]

The small loculus in which Agnes had been laid was probably first isolated inside the catacomb, and then enclosed in an arched shrine with an inscribed eulogy affixed to it. Later a small oblong church, almost buried in the hillside, was built over the grave in order to accommodate visitors. In about 630 A.D. the present church replaced the earlier building. It was no longer than its predecessor, though made broader by the addition of aisles. The resulting building, without the chapels that were added later, measures roughly 78 feet by 42 feet; the apse is a further 8 feet deep. There was no doubt, in the minds of either the founder of the church or its architect, what the ground plan and the general disposition of the church should be: it has, naturally, the shape of a basilica.

BASILICAS

A basilica is a pre-eminently Roman type of building, the kind Constantine and his advisors chose to erect when he first set about throwing up huge edifices, at the Lateran and over or beside martyrs' shrines, for the Christian community. The Christian version of the basilica commonly used in Rome had a half dome, rising from a half cylinder, at one end. It was the ancient Romans who developed and most confidently expounded the architectural technology of the arch, the vault, and the dome.[15] Ancient Greek temples, for example, for all their beauty and sophistication, employed neither domes nor arches. Roman temples, unlike basilicas, were archaizing structures that avoided domes and arches, although cylindrical temples existed in Rome as in Greece, and were invested with special connotations. Also typical of the first Christian basilicas in Rome was their construction out of brick, the traditional Roman medium for most public buildings; Greek and Roman temples tended to be made of marble.

The word "basilica" means "royal" in Greek, but ironically enough, as an architectural term it is known to us first in the context of Republican Rome in the early second century B.C. The Basilica Porcia was built on the south side of the Roman Forum by Cato in 184 B.C., and named after himself (Marcus Porcius Cato, the Censor). Five years later the Basilica Aemilia was erected close by (the remains of its first-century A.D. restoration are still visible in the Forum today); subsequently, the Romans built basilicas all over their empire. These buildings played a role similar to that of stoas—edifices with colonnaded porticoes that edged Greek and Hellenistic agoras, providing shade but also open air. The agora was the Greek equivalent of the Roman forum or central city square. Basilicas, like stoas, were large and multi-purpose public buildings. But unlike stoas, they were wholly enclosed: if there were rows of columns, they stood not outside but inside the basilica's walls.

Basilicas were used as markets and tribunals, as meeting halls for the military, or for holding fiestas. They were also components of the gigantic public Roman baths. Their main feature was that they were large enough to accommodate a lot of people. The principle remained the same when basilicas became churches: Constantine's Lateran basilica, which was larger than those in the Forum, provided space for a congregation of three thousand. A basilica, moreover, could be quickly constructed: it was oblong, made of bricks, and had a timber roof covered with tiles rather than a vault. For extra breadth, Christian basilicas were provided with side aisles. These were separated by rows of columns from the central part, the nave; the aisles could be closed off from the nave at will with curtains. In order to let light into the longitudinal nave, it was given walls higher than those of the aisles, and these higher parts of the walls were pierced with windows to form a "clear storey," or clerestory, above the columns.

The hugeness of the early Christian basilicas not only allowed them to accommodate large crowds, but also encouraged processions inside them in the course of the liturgies. Almost from the beginning, the aisles in certain very large Christian basilicas were made to join up at the apse end, thus forming a U-shaped route leading up one aisle, around the apse, and back down the other aisle—and then across the narthex and up again if desired. The apse bend in such an arrangement is called an *ambulatory*, a "place for walking."

The long walls of a basilica were straight and plain. There were no chapels let into the sides; those in Sant'Agnese's today were added in the seventeenth and nineteenth centuries. The one complexity in the building's periphery was the apse, usually a semidome. ("Apse" is from the Greek *haptein*, "to grab": each end of a curved apse "holds on" to the ends of the straight sides of the rectangular building.) In ancient Roman multi-purpose halls the apse could be at one short end, at both short ends, or in the middle of one of the long sides, in which case the entrance was in the side opposite. An apse arched over a raised platform; it marked out as special whatever took place there. When a basilica was used as an administrative building, the magistrates would sit in this space, as would the emperor, if present. The emperor sat in the apse of the basilical audience chamber of his palace; and it was in the apse, too, that a statue of the emperor was commonly placed.

A Christian basilica was always longitudinally ordered; the flexibility of pagan Roman buildings on this point was forgone. From among the varieties of basilica that the Romans had created, Christians chose the oldest version of all, with narthex, then nave, then the apse opposite the entrance, just as the Jerusalem temple had progressed from *ulam* to *hekal*, with the *debir* as the climax. In or before the apse of a basilica Christians placed the altar. In a church like Sant'Agnese's, the altar is sheltered under a ciborium or canopy.

JOURNEYS OF THE SOUL

The floor of the central aisle at Sant'Agnese's is a plain path of pale grey veined marble, pushing aside to left and right the overall floor pattern in light and dark grey. The purpose is to emphasize the route straight forward. This floor is quite modern. It was made from marble left over from the repaving of the basilica of San Paolo fuori le Mura when that basilica was reconstructed in 1854, after its destruction in large part by fire. It is certain, however, that earlier floors, including the magnificent medieval mosaic pavement the church once possessed, would have made the same statement.[16] The medieval floor doubtless included, as do other surviving floors of the same period, porphyry circles surrounded by decorative mosaic patterns and set in a row up the centre. The clergy would have used these designs to mark out places and distances as they performed elaborate processional liturgies—rather as a stage is marked to show actors where to stand.[17]

On either side of the central aisle are the pews, which are benches with kneelers, and the chairs. ("Pew" originally meant a raised and enclosed wooden stall for a preacher. It is from *pes*, "foot," and is related to "podium," the word for a "stand." In English Protestant usage the word came to mean a private, sometimes raised bench enclosed with doors; and then an ordinary open bench for members of the congregation.) This seating and kneeling arrangement was certainly not what the church was designed for: originally at Sant' Agnese's people stood during church ceremonies.

The central aisle or "road" forward in any church is a symbol of the length of a life: the life of all creation, of all humanity, of the Church as a community, of each individual person. The "journey of life" symbolized in the floor of a church nave is accompanied by many other significant journeys in Jewish and Christian memory. There is the journey of Abraham, trusting that he would find the Promised Land; and the Exodus journey of the Jews (the Greek word *exodos* means a "way out"), a wandering for forty years in the desert as they struggled to achieve a liberation from oppression.[18]

Exodus is a central theme in the Christian imagination, as it is in Judaism; the great biblical liberation stories are narrated at the yearly vigil of the Resurrection, Easter eve. Christ's breaking out of the tomb is for Christians the climactic event in the series. The penultimate journey towards the Resurrection was Christ's journey to his crucifixion, his being forced to carry the instrument of his own torture and death out of the walls of Jerusalem to the hill called the Skull, *Golgotha* in Hebrew, *Calvary* in Latin. This journey is commemorated in every Catholic church by the Stations of the Cross.

In Sant'Agnese's, the Stations of the Cross are very simple and sober, modelled in plaster stained to look like wood and hung on the walls along the aisles, so that people can walk the journey past them, pausing at each one.[19] The Stations are fourteen episodes from the crucifixion of Jesus, from his condemnation to his burial and including his road to Calvary. From early times Christian pilgrims to Jerusalem would walk through the city, where they were shown places said to have been exactly where each event took place. Some of these episodes are quite unscriptural and almost certainly imagined by people who felt they "must have," "should have" occurred. The "places" where these events "happened" were then supplied also, in Jerusalem.

For example, a woman named Veronica is said to have wiped the face of Jesus, covered with blood and dirt and sweat; the imprint of his face, a "portrait," remained on the veil. The story expresses the longing of Christians for a picture of Jesus, so they could know what he looked like. Veronica stands for the pity and regret Christians feel about the death of Jesus, their wish that it had not happened, that it could have been avoided. Veronica probably never existed, but her story expresses things many people care about, and so they agree to tell it: in this sense Veronica enacts a Christian myth, much as Oedipus enacts a Greek one. Her deed, which is one of the Stations of the Cross, has become more "real" than most documented events in history: the figure of Veronica has been a catalyst for personal response to the revelation of God's love in countless people.

Beginning in the fourteenth century, members of the Order of Saint Francis of Assisi, living in Jerusalem and entrusted with the care of the holy places, "systematized" the Stations of the Cross, gradually giving them a canonical number and order. Not everybody could visit the Holy Land, of course. But this has never been a major problem for Christians. A way was provided for people to visit the Holy Land and to follow the journey of Jesus to Calvary "in spirit," without actually going there.

"Stations of the Cross" were made and placed in every church: a picture of each event, with spaces left between them.[20] The spaces are important: they allow people to "walk the distance," making their own "journey" of spiritual accompaniment, responding inwardly, in their own way. At each picture the devotee stands still (is "stationary") and contemplates the picture and its meaning for him or her. During a service the clergy may make the journey while the people simply stand in their pews, turning to face each Station.

Following the Stations of the Cross is only one of many journeys that take place in Sant'Agnese's. The priests and their ministers enter the building in procession to begin services. They walk in procession with candles to the podium when it is time to read aloud passages from the Bible, and to give commentaries on their meaning. People walk up the central aisle to the altar to present offerings during Mass, and then again to receive Communion. They approach and embrace the Cross on Good Friday, the day of Christ's death. They walk up the aisles to see the elaborate crib created every Christmas by members of the congregation, and in this they are imitating the journey of the shepherds, the journey of the Wise Men following the Star, and indeed the journey of Mary and Joseph searching for a place where Jesus could be born. During Advent (the four weeks preceding Christmas) the present congregation of Sant'Agnese's leaves the church to walk in procession through the neighbourhood, following an exuberantly cometlike star mounted on a slowly moving car, in memory of the Wise Men.

And the church itself represents a journey. There are three main symbols here. The first is Exodus, signifying the journey of all humanity towards liberation. Taking its cue from the Jewish Bible, a church thinks of itself as a tent carried by the people, as the Jews carried the Ark of the Covenant on their quest for the Promised Land; the church is searching for and journeying towards the kingdom of Christ, and the "heavenly Jerusalem" at the end of the world. Secondly, a church must reflect the fact that Christianity is a religion of both sudden revelations or conversions, and ongoing transformation—both in history and in every individual soul. The space traversed from entrance to altar and apse expresses change, both dramatic (all at once) and gradual (requiring the course of a lifespan). Finally, the church as "journey" recalls the words of Jesus: "I am the way, the truth, and the life. . . ."[21] And so the building erases itself before what it represents, namely Christ himself, who now "is" the temple and the path we are to follow. These bricks, marbles, and mosaics were set up in full consciousness that all they can do is point to what they mean.

LABYRINTH

The spatial metaphor of a journey is essentially one-dimensional: life as a line. But to join two ends of a line on a flat surface is to achieve another dimension: an area. A labyrinth is a confusing warren, where the object is to arrive, eventually, at the other end of the path, its goal. This is usually in the middle of the design; the traveller then has to find the way out again. The route cunningly turns and twists, and so fills out a two-dimensional space.

There are two kinds of labyrinth. In one, there is a correct route and there are many dead ends: every choice of direction is consequence-laden, and it is easy to travel a long way in error. (The word "error" in Latin means a wandering—*erro*, "I wander"—away from the correct route.) The other kind of labyrinth is unicursal: there is only one way, and it surely arrives at the goal, although the route often seems to be wrong and the traveller appears to be walking in a direction that will never reach its destination.

Both kinds of labyrinth are used metaphorically in Christian think-ing. The first is often found in narrative, in stories like that of the Quest for the Holy Grail. It is also embodied in mazes, which are a form of physical riddle and a test of prowess. (The word "maze" is related to "amazement.") This type recalls the origin of the word "labyrinth" in Greek myth, where Theseus might never have emerged from the Cretan Labyrinth had he not been supplied with a coil of thread (the name for which is a "clew," the origin of the word "clue") to follow back to the entrance. You cannot see over the walls of a maze if you are walking in it: the experience recalls the frustrating puzzles of human existence. Cleverness and luck are what you need in order to succeed; but these gifts are, in fact, the outward expressions of profound psychic knowledge and readiness, of openness to the possi-bility of epiphany.

The second type exists in space, but it is spread out for us to see it whole. In certain medieval churches—in Amiens cathedral or in Chartres—it is still possible today to walk the labyrinth, a mini procession or pilgrimage laid out for that purpose in the floor. These labyrinths are always unicursal. All you need to do is choose to start—to enter the labyrinth and then to persevere to the end, no matter how far the twisting road seems to be taking you from your goal. The road symbolizes a human life with all its difficulties and failures, and the common feeling of being lost; the message is that mental agility is not the most important gift for the spiritual life. But the road here is also Christ, "the way, the truth, and the life." He is the thread—both meaning and guide—and also the goal. The Judeo-Christian God is "the Alpha and the Omega," the beginning and the end, imaged by the first and last letters of the Greek alphabet—and, it is implied, including the whole series of letters in between.[22] At the centre of a church labyrinth is Christ, eternal bliss, the soul's core.

Whereas a labyrinth's "end" is its centre, a basilical church's "road" moves straight ahead, from Alpha (Jesus also said, "I am the door"[23]) to Omega, the apse and God. In a unicursal labyrinth the goal is visible from the start, just as one can see the apse, or Omega, as soon as one enters a church; but still the distance needs to be covered. Another of the great Christian opposites, articulated in many ways in Christian art, is "already" versus "not yet." Both are true, at one and the same time, paradoxical as the claim most certainly is. Christians believe that salvation is already here, because Christ has come; the truth has been revealed. However, there is a long way to go yet: paradise regained and the end of the world are still to come. The kingdom is to be struggled for; it is both present among us, and not yet. The journey is ongoing.

SAILING

From earliest days Christians have symbolized the organizational Church as a ship. In the ancient Mediterranean world, where roads were few and mountainous regions common, travel was often achieved more swiftly by sea than overland, so a ship was an obvious symbol of movement. People in a boat relied utterly upon it for safety as they steered it towards harbour, the "safe haven" of arrival at their destination. A ship stood for protection from the sea—but also for venturing into the unknown.

The image is a composite one, drawn from Greek, Roman, and Jewish metaphors for life's perilous journey, and also from the Gospel narrative. In the Jewish myth, Noah's ark saved both nature and humanity from the flood that threatened to destroy life on earth:[24] a common symbol for the Church, and also for a church, is the ark, with its hugely diverse mixture of creatures on board, afloat amid the murderous tumult of "this world." Apart from Noah's ark, Old Testament marine metaphors are few, for Israel was not a sea-going people.

Shipping symbolism is, however, to be found everywhere in the literary tradition of the Greeks, reflecting the importance to them of sailing, both in commerce and in war. Always the sea is presented as changeable and dangerous, the Mediterranean being peculiarly prone to storms: the sea is a major metaphor in Greek literature for fate and necessity, or circumstances otherwise beyond human control. Greeks also elaborated the metaphor of the "ship of state," protecting the citizens within its hold.

The Gospels, for their part, record that the twelve men Jesus chose to begin spreading his message across the world were most of them fishermen. They worked the Sea of Galilee—a body of water liable to sudden storms. Saint Paul on his journeys around the Mediterranean, as we learn from his letters and the Acts of the Apostles, suffered shipwreck repeatedly. Fishing, boats, storms, and water are therefore common themes in the New Testament.

Christians were struck by the resemblance of a ship's mast and its crossbar, known as a "cross-tree," to the primary Christian symbol, the Cross. Like a ship, the Church carried people of many different origins; Christ was the pilot; the Roman double rudder was "the two Testaments." Sails and rigging were "stretched out" like love for others or like Christ himself embracing the Church. The rigging was a cosmic ladder, a "way up" towards God. Human technology—the craft of ship builders, sailing by the stars, understanding the winds, the plotting of routes—enables the ship to arrive where it wants to go, just as the Church is led by God's Word, by grace and response, by wisdom, and by fixing its sights on its goal.[25] The point of the ship metaphor, however, is above all movement forward, towards the world's destiny, and also towards both end and fulfillment for the individual. On some of the burial tablets fixed to the walls of the passage down into Sant' Agnese's church, a simple anchor is incised, a typically Christian symbol signifying salvation, the end of the "sea voyage" of life, and eternal rest with God.

A church building, too, is thought of as a ship, sailing onward, bearing the congregation inside it. In an "orientated" church—one built so that the congregation faces east—the "ship" sails east, towards the dawning of eternal bliss; if turned westward it is directed towards the world's end, "the setting of the sun." (Sant'Agnese's church "sails" roughly eastward.) The word "nave" means "ship," *navis* in Latin. Aisles are literally "wings," Latin *alae*: the rising and dipping banks of oars on either side of a ship always reminded the ancients of wings, making the boat "fly" forward. The fact that the wooden beams of church roofs were often left exposed must also have encouraged people to think of travel in the hold of a ship. The symbolism turns on a series of imaginative linkages: from group to building, to ship, to movement. Thus the building is turned into a metaphor for a journey; stationary space signifies moving time.

MOVING ON

People today have largely abandoned static models of reality for a distinctively dynamic view of the way things are. Plato's eternal Ideas have been placed on the shelf, while the Greek philosophers who claimed that "all is movement and change" are more than ever in vogue among philosophers and theologians as well as ordinary people. Today mobility—both physical and social—tends to trump ideals such as rootedness or commitment. The Church, too, chooses now to stress its "pilgrim" aspect over its stability. (Its stake in the "perennial" or static model remains, of course, as the other term in this pair of opposites.)

Christians today tend to see themselves as foreigners, though living very much in the midst of "this world," struggling on, risking everything, but believing in a destiny; people on a journey that is full of pain and danger, but deliberately undertaken because of the end in view. They also believe that the kingdom is not only "still to come," but is already here. Their hope, despite the cosmic scale of the project, rests upon faith that "absolutely nothing can separate us from the love of God."[26] The word "pilgrim" is from Latin *peregrinus*, "travelling away from home." Modern people look for the expression, in a church, of this view of Christian commitment.

In the church of Sant'Agnese itself, everything about the journey metaphor is, of course, spatial. The passage downward is initiation, finding the way to where there is a new beginning. The threshold at the door of any church represents the interruption of the course of history that was Christ's coming and the Church's founding, and also the place of beginning for each person entering. The narthex or "paradise" is still there when one has stepped into the church and onto its central "road." The distance covered endures even as the travellers press onwards, just as a road or a route on a map exists both before and after the trip. The "end"—the apse—is in view from the beginning. The church contains both the road and the movement upon it. In a Christian temple, the past is never to be forgotten or disowned or discounted: it is part of each person, as it is part of the Church, and also part of what this building expresses. In a church the future is always open, while the past is never shut off.

THE ACCOMPANIMENT OF COLUMNS

The columns on either side of the nave in a basilica enhance the sense of a road ahead. They allow the eye to measure the length of the nave by their regular spacing, and as they appear to decrease in height and press together at the end of the sightlines, they visually underline both the stability of the building's structure and its dynamism.

Columns are for support; they are bearers of weight. The earliest temples, in ancient Greece, for example, are known to have had wooden columns. And all columns continue to remember trees, to the point where an ancient Egyptian or a classical Greek or Roman column unfolds into a severely controlled arrangement of leaves and tendrils at the top. A nave resembles a "tree"-lined avenue.

The shaft of a pillar can be so vast as to dwarf a human being, but always we remain aware that human technology made it: a column is a deeply enculturated object. Yet—and perhaps in part for that very reason—we tend to humanize a column, to think of it as like a person.

Verticality in itself is for us a primary human characteristic: we are proud of our "erectitude," our two long legs and what we call our "spinal column." A string of pillars seems to stride through space. The floor on which a colonnade stands is called a stylobate. *Stylos* is Greek for "pillar" and *bates* is "one who treads": the columns "walk" the stylobate.

A column ideally feels like a living thing, taut with energy. For this reason, the beauty of a column often includes *entasis*, "swelling" or "exertion" in Greek: the outline of its shaft will curve outwards very slightly in the middle, and gather itself more tightly at the top. A straight-up-and-down column forgoes this tension and movement, and nearly always ends up looking mechanical and lifeless. The leafy or otherwise elaborated and figured top is called a capital, meaning that it is also like a head (Latin *caput*).

Sometimes architects and sculptors join forces and turn columns into statues, stone people charged with carrying the weight of the building for ever. Caryatids, they are called, after the female virgins who danced for Artemis at her great temple at Caryae in Laconia.[27] The ancient Greeks called pillars carved in the shape of male statues *atlantides*, after Atlas, who once carried the world on his back. ("Atlas" means "very enduring" in Greek.) Christians very early spoke of the Apostles as columns: James, Peter, and John are "pillars" in Jerusalem for Paul;[28] Paul himself (the Apostle to the Gentiles) and Peter are called "pillars of the Church" in the Letter of Clement (ca. 96 A.D.).[29] The columns of a church basilica represent the founders, but they also represent "supporters," everyone who belongs to the Church.[30]

In the Greco-Roman world, columns had become an essential component of architectural beauty. The Roman basilica, plain as it was on the outside, loved grandeur within, and beautiful columns provided undeniable splendour. The early Christian basilicas could be built quickly and relatively cheaply of brick; and columns were easy to find. Rome by 313 A.D. was a forest of columns: Romans had been collecting stone and cutting columns for centuries. Much of the work was done at quarries all around the Mediterranean, before the shafts were shipped for polishing and finishing at Rome. Columns had also been stolen from all over the empire, as when Sulla had the columns of the

Athenian Olympieion brought to Rome in 86 B.C. to embellish the Capitol.[31] Christians, under Constantine, began a career of taking columns from pagan buildings to adorn their churches.

In the ancient world one of the essential characteristics of a magnificent building had been the similarity of the columns adorning it. They were made as a set for this particular temple or stoa or portico and no other: that was part of their strictness, part of their extravagance. (In his *"Cantique des colonnes,"*[32] the French poet Paul Valéry calls the columns of a Greek temple *"pieusement pareilles,"* ("dutifully identical.") He also describes them as "incorruptible sisters"— *colonnes* are feminine—and "servants without knees.")

Christians in late antiquity, perhaps unable to afford the luxury of a full complement of specially made columns, would content themselves with looting pillars here and there from pagan monuments: early churches often have columns and capitals of various designs, even of differing sizes, reflecting the variety of their origins. And Christians did not mind this: they quickly began to see in the hodgepodge of lifted goods a symbol of diversity among the people who became Christians. The inclusion of absolutely every kind, class, and race of person, from anywhere, has always been a distinctive mark of Christianity.

In a similar investment of a material necessity with a satisfying new significance, a Christian basilica could be thought of as having turned a classical temple inside out, much as Christianity in important respects stood classical culture on its head. The columns around the outside of a pagan temple (as opposed to a basilica) have migrated indoors to make a Christian temple, as has the altar, which is now no longer for bloody sacrifice.[33] And the traditional Roman basilica, plain without but extravagantly marbled within, could express for Christians the revolutionary ideal of a human being who has chosen an unassuming exterior but spiritual riches "in the heart."

Columns were to have a very long history in Christian architecture. By the Gothic period, in the great cathedrals of France and other countries to the north, columns were to become bundles of narrow reeds of stone, springing high and then fanning out into the tall vaults they carry. In Rome, however, churches have always been made in a spirit of balance and repose; the lucid harmonies of Greco-

Roman architecture remained what people living in Rome felt to be "right." The solemn, grounded feeling produced by a broad, solid Roman church is totally different from the soaring aspiration of Gothic. (Rome possesses, indeed, only one Gothic church, Santa Maria sopra Minerva, near the Pantheon.)

Roman church columns carry either entablatures—straight stone beams, adding a powerful horizontal element to the verticality of columns—or, as at Sant'Agnese's, a series of round arches. Arches are literally as well as symbolically dynamic forms: they carry stress, channelling the downward thrust of the upper parts of structures into the earth via walls, pillars, and columns. They appear to leap and fall, like water or moving objects; arches surmounting columns produce a graceful lightness, turning a stride into a decorative dance.

Sant'Agnese's has rows of columns bearing arches on two levels around three sides of the building. In addition to these are four built pillars that also help to carry arches: two cruciform ones at the narthex end and two rectangular ones beside the apse. From the gallery (originally at street level) people could look down into the deep interior of the church. The gallery columns are both thinner and shorter than those that support them from below.

For the visitor standing in the nave, the floor level of the gallery underlines the horizontality that is essential to the tradition of Roman buildings. At the same time the gallery itself harbours space. The smaller columns above invite comparison with the heavier lower ones, and look higher because they are smaller. And the nave's walls higher still are pierced with windows, a bright arched space for every dark arched space in the gallery. The windows are smaller than the gallery's arched spaces, though similar in shape: again, this makes them look higher than they are.[34] Everything has been done to make the little church, buried underground for half its height, feel nevertheless airy, graceful, varied, and light inside.

The nave is much wider than the aisles,[35] but, thanks in part to the columns, it maintains its role as "avenue" leading to the altar and the apse behind it. The nave is only twice as long as it is wide, however, and the altar area takes up much more of the space in front of the apse than is evident at first sight: out of eight intercolumnar spaces created by the seven columns and the pillar on each side, the altar and its steps occupy three. This makes the space for the congregation broader in relation to its length than is usual in this kind of church. Sant' Agnese's, then, is short for a basilica and very high for its length. There is no transept; the church is "monoaxial," all moving forward.

On top of each column capital in the gallery is a pulvin (from *pulvinus*, "cushion" in Latin): a block placed between the capital and the arch. The pulvins for the gallery's columns, the galleries themselves, and also the proportions of the church in general point to Eastern, which is to say Byzantine, influence. When we look at the apse mosaic, the Byzantine background of the building is even clearer. And if you measure Sant'Agnese's in Roman feet, you get fractions; if you measure it in Byzantine feet, the measurements are in round numbers except for one half-foot result.[36] Sant'Agnese's is a basilica, all right, but a basilica wedded to Byzantine taste. It is likely that the architect was Byzantine, although the workmanship in the building is believed to have been Roman.[37] We know that Byzantine artists fled in large numbers to Rome during the period 726–843 A.D., when the Eastern Church embraced Iconoclasm and banned all images. But Sant'Agnese's, built a hundred years beforehand, shows us that there were highly appreciated Byzantine artists working in Rome before the diaspora caused by Iconoclasm began.

The church in Rome that most closely resembles Sant'Agnese's is the earlier of the two joined churches that now form San Lorenzo fuori le Mura.[38] This basilica was erected forty-odd years before Sant'Agnese's, over the grave of the martyred deacon Lawrence. It, too, was built into a catacomb outside the walls, with galleries to provide access at street level.[39] It has similar proportions, and a similar Byzantine cast. San Lorenzo's is a more "masculine" building, however, with its straight entablatures rather than arches, and its more massive pillars. Both churches display an apparently deliberate variety among their columns.

CONNOISSEURSHIP AND CAPITALS

Sant'Agnese's has sixteen large columns at the lower level, sixteen little ones in the gallery, and four to hold up the ciborium (the dome over the altar). The six large columns that flank the altar, three on either side, are all exceptional. There are four of precious pink portasanta marble from the Greek island of Chios, the subtle colour of which, as we shall see, gives the tone for the colour harmony of the entire church. There are two columns of grey-white pavonazzetto marble standing on either side of the altar steps. (*Pavonazzetto* means "bluish," and the marble came from Phrygia in Asia Minor, modern Turkey.) They are famous examples of virtuosity in columnar carving. Grooves run straight up the length of each column, each groove or flute containing another, which contains another, and so on. Each column has 140 flutes: twenty broad flutes and another six within each of these. All of them join up with their opposite numbers inside each broad flute in elegant curves at the top and bottom of the column. There is nothing bombastic about this exquisitely difficult, totally achieved workmanship; the overall impression is of quiet grace.

In the past the love of columns could become an obsession, one that can gradually grow even in a modern visitor to a church like this one. Originally spoils from pagan buildings, columns could also migrate from church to church in the various heats of rivalry. As late as the seventeenth century column envy nearly cost Sant'Agnese's four of her best pillars: two of the pink portasantas and the two fluted pavonazzetto columns almost went to embellish the new funerary chapel for the Aldobrandini family in Santa Maria sopra Minerva. Only the vigilance of the abbot of Sant'Agnese's monastery (the future Pope Leo XI), and his diligence in very quickly finding substitute columns on the antiquarian market, saved these glories of the church from leaving for somewhere else. Pope Clement VIII, himself a member of the Aldobrandini family and in whose name the transfer was to be carried out, accepted both the column replacements and the veiled reproach, and rewarded the abbot with a sapphire ring.[40]

Column connoisseurship involves appreciation for the provenance and quality of the materials and their colouring. But a great deal more enters into it: the way irregularities of size are overcome in a church full of columns taken from different buildings; form and carving skill in the column bases; the subtle entasis of the shafts, which might also have sophisticated surface fluting; and, very particularly, the capitals.

The builders of Sant'Agnese's carefully picked the columns they pilfered from classical buildings; they then meticulously planned just where they should go in the church. For example, in the gallery the shafts of the columns around the entrance have spiralling grooves on their surfaces, while the columns near the altar are fluted. The others are alternately plain and fluted.

It mattered intensely where a column with a particular capital was put. Apart from the Tuscan order, ancient Rome had inherited from the canonical orders of Greece three types of columns, each with a distinctive capital. Capitals were Doric, Ionic, Corinthian, and—the Roman contribution—Composite.[41] Each had its own status. Romans used Composite capitals to express their own glory—on triumphal arches, for example, such as the Arch of Titus, which celebrated the crushing of Jerusalem (70 A.D.). On the Colosseum (72 A.D.) columns and capitals of the Doric order adorn the first and lowest level of the building, Ionic the second, and Corinthian the third. Composite was reserved for the emperor's entrance and for the building's interior, where the Roman populace and its rulers would sit and watch the gory games. The sequence here of Doric–Ionic–Corinthian–Composite exemplifies the status of the orders, from lowest to highest, with Composite highest of all.[42]

The status of the orders is preserved at Sant'Agnese's. At the entrance into the nave from the narthex stand two dark granite columns with Composite capitals. They clearly announce that stepping from the street into the house of God is a momentous act: you are leaving the world outside to enter a place that represents your own inner being, your deepest desire and transcendental destiny. After the entrance and along the nave the columns are of a lighter colour and have Corinthian ("lower" than Composite) capitals. The finest columns stand around the altar: fluted ones with Corinthian capitals and pink ones crowned with Composite. (These capitals look unfinished. They may have been made as late as the seventh century, perhaps when the church was built. But their Composite order is unmistakable.)

In the gallery the little columns over the narthex have Ionic capitals. The capitals of the other small columns alternate Composite,

Corinthian, Composite, Corinthian, the length of the nave; four of them date from the fifteenth century.[43] The spaces between the upper columns were closed off with panels of marble, forming parapets, a necessary protective barrier when people came into the church at gallery level and stood there, craning towards the altar. These panels disappeared in 1600, to be replaced first by balustrades echoing those still standing in front of the altar, and then, in 1855, with the plain transenne, pierced by circular and cross-shaped holes, that are still in place.

Today, the gallery is never used, except for the part over the narthex, which contains the organ.[44] The old entrances from the street are closed. Once a year during the saint's week in January, the church's custodians—who, like the organist, can enter the gallery from a spiral staircase leading from the right-hand aisle or from the adjoining canonry—drape over the parapets a series of handsome red hangings kept for that purpose alone. The hangings are red because Agnes spilled her blood as a martyr. It is common practice in Mediterranean countries for people living in the houses and apartments that line the route of a parade to decorate their balconies by hanging rugs or bright drapery over them. The hangings at Sant'Agnese's treat the nave, appropriately, as a street during a fiesta.

CARVING, COFFERING, AND COLOUR

Above the nave of the church stretches the carved wooden ceiling, like a lid on a rectangular box. It was added in the seventeenth century and hides from our view the simple wooden beams and tiles that roofed the church on their own for a thousand years previously. (The central horizontal beam of the roofing structure must have stressed again the movement forward that is represented by the central path of the nave's floor.) The present ceiling, coloured predominantly in pink, plum, blue, ochre, and gold, is coffered. Curling fronds, white and gold on plum and blue, decorate the sunken panels.

Three carved figures of women look down on the congregation from large cross-shaped spaces set the length of the nave. In the centre is Agnes with her lamb and her martyr's palm. Nearest the door is Constantina, daughter of Constantine, with an empress's crown tall on her head, carrying a budding plant with three branches, probably referring to the Trinity. Nearest the apse is Saint Cecilia, virgin martyr and patron saint of music, with her attribute, a set of organ pipes. St. Cecilia's church in Trastevere was the favourite place of worship of Cardinal Paolo Emilio Sfondrati, under whom repairs to Sant'Agnese's were completed. He inaugurated the ceiling in 1606.[45] On September 20, 1870, when armies advanced on Rome along the via Nomentana, a cannonball fell onto the basilica, smashed a hole in the roof, and damaged the ceiling; repairs were made a year later.

The colours in the big portasanta marble columns that stand round the altar—a deep pink with grey inclusions—provide the church with the keynote for its colour scheme. The background colour throughout is pale and darker grey for the marble floors and apse walls, the painted side walls, most columns, and all capitals. The pink is picked up by the eight pink marble sections of the dome over the altar, with its grey and white cornices, ribs, finials, and capitals. It deepens into porphyry in the gorgeous small columns holding up the dome, the echoing porphyry verticals of the pilasters in the apse, and the porphyry horizontal band above them; and it metamorphoses into purples in the robes of the figures in the mosaic above. Gold gleams from the mosaic background and from the ceiling; ochre and pink (an exact match for the pink of the columns) are the main colours of the ceiling, together with plum and blue for the sunken coffers. (Coffering, the imposition of geometrical design upon ceilings representing the heavens, "means" the cosmic order of the skies). Light and dark blues are the colours of the starry circular heavens in the mosaic, out of which the Hand of God reaches with the crown of martyrdom for the saint.

During the annual week of festivities in honour of Saint Agnes, red and plum velvet hangings with gold embroidery clothe the apse; there are red hangings at the parapets of the gallery and also at the door to the canonry from the street. Passersby note the hangings and know that the church of Sant'Agnese is celebrating its feast. The clergy wear seventeenth-century red and gold vestments on the saint's special day, January 21. Pink and purple flowers (orchids on the occasions I have been there) deck the altar. The overall effect is delicate, solemn, and intensely female.

4

ALPHA AND OMEGA:
Altar

The church of Sant'Agnese is designed so that the entering visitor will see the rounded apse as the end of the journey that starts at the door. But the building can just as well be understood as beginning with the apse and growing out of it: the structure, from this point of view, emanates from a vertical line in the middle of the wall behind the altar. The arms of the curved embrace issuing from that invisible line extend as far as the façade. The church as a spatial entity represents the mystery that one day we shall discover that the beginning and the end of time, Alpha and Omega, are one.

The apse, a quarter-sphere rising above a half-cylinder, imposes on the end of the nave and gallery a transitional section in the shape of a great arch, as high as nave and gallery combined and as wide as the entire nave. The human eye naturally reaches for the highest point of this enormous archway, and this teaches at once the height of nave plus gallery. Higher yet are the windows round three sides of the building; on the fourth wall, above the blue arch, is a fresco depicting the execution of Agnes.[1] A little girl in white kneels on the ground between two burly men; one of them seizes her hair while the other grasps his bared sword. To the left, on a high throne, sits the Roman prosecutor; there are other people at the scene, watching. An angel flutters in the sky above, holding ready the martyr's crown and palm.

Written on the arch and facing into the church is a quotation from the hymn to Agnes by the Spanish-born Roman poet Prudentius (ca. 400–405 A.D.):

O virgo felix, o nova gloria,
caelestis arcis nobilis incola.[2]
(Oh happy virgin, oh glory unknown before,
noble dweller in the height of heaven.)

And immediately below the inscription from the viewer's perspective, in the apse itself, we see Agnes in a blaze of seventh-century gold mosaic,[3] flanked by two clerics—both of them popes, and both subsidiary to her.

Within the curve of the apse and below the great arch, sheltering the altar, stands the ciborium. This is a pink marble dome made of eight curving sections, lifted on four small porphyry columns that rise from pedestals the height of the altar. At the four corners over the columns are finials made of flourishes of acanthus leaves. The space between altar and dome is a perfect cube, with the columns at the four corners. On the square marble slab supported by the columns under the dome is carved a dove with outspread wings, hovering over the altar. On the altar is the tabernacle, which in this case is in the form of another domed edifice, itself resembling a diminutive church. It is an intricately carved and inlaid modern work in marble and gold.[4] Inside it is the still point around which the entire church revolves: the consecrated bread of the Eucharist, contained in its cup.

The church can be read in yet another way, as a series of containers enfolded one within the next, with the heart and seed of the whole held in the cup enclosed in the tiny domed tabernacle on the altar. The altar, a table for the celebration of the Eucharist, supports the tabernacle. Over it is the domed ciborium, or canopy. The word "ciborium" is derived from *kiborion*, the Greek name for the seed container of the Egyptian water lily: these shells used to be cut in half to form bowls. The cup inside the tabernacle on the altar is also called, if it has a lid, a *ciborium*; it is known as a *chalice* if it is open like the calyx of a flower.[5] Above the dome, covering the tabernacle with the cup inside it, stretches the apse, itself a cupped hollow, with the figure of Agnes floating upon a background of celestial gold. The apse is a figure of the heavens and of eternity, which Agnes, according to Prudentius in his inscription on the arch, now inhabits. In this manner the church becomes a symbol of the vast cosmos, shell contained within shell, as the ancient Greeks, and after them the Romans, and then the scholars of the Middle Ages, envisioned it. The Eucharist is the focal point, the life and heart of the whole. It is the point of encounter between God and humanity in Christ. And it is available to everyone.

In the Eucharist, God—infinite vastness—enters into the person who eats this bread and drinks this cup. It is as food and drink—the object for human beings of endlessly renewed desire, necessary, simple, ordinary, to be broken and shared, of external matter that becomes internal, and which then turns into the very substance of the eater—that the Christian God of love sacramentally gives himself to human beings. In spatial and temporal terms, always and everywhere become, in the Eucharist, one with here and now.

THE SANCTUARY

Rome is a city of domes. Their calm, round forms rest like bubbles across the city's skyline, softening its raggedness and providing foci for the urban landscape. The oldest great dome is that of the Pantheon, which has stood for nearly 1,900 years: a Roman temple, converted into a Christian church.[6] Other church domes, all of the following ones Renaissance and Baroque, include those of St. Peter, Sant'Andrea della Valle, San Carlo ai Catinari, Santa Maria di Loreto and Santissimo Nome de Maria, the twins Santa Maria dei Miracoli and Santa Maria in Montesanto, the Gesú, San Carlo al Corso, San Giovanni dei Fiorentini, and the dome of Saint Agnes' other church, the downtown Sant' Agnese in Agone. These later large domes—they have dozens of baby sisters—exhibit triumphant technological mastery in the service of generous, familiar, comforting, essentially female form. All of them, beginning with the dome of the Pantheon itself, are drenched in the symbolism of the heavens and totality, of the round cosmos. *Kosmos* in Greek means not only "world" but also "order and decency" and "decorative comeliness." (From *kosmos* we get the word "cosmetics.")

When little Sant'Agnese fuori le Mura was taken in hand, repaired, and refurbished in the first years of the seventeenth century, it was felt that the church deserved a dome. Michelangelo's dome over St. Peter's had been finished, after the master's death, by Giacomo Della

Porta in 1590.[7] It seemed self-evident just after 1600 that Saint Agnes and her foster-sister Saint Emerentiana (for there are, as we shall see, two martyrs buried under the altar at Sant'Agnese's) would prefer to have a dome over the altar.

The medieval chancel arrangements were impatiently swept away: the *ambones*, which were two raised tribunes or platforms to the left and the right, from which the scriptures were read out (the word is from the Greek *anabainein*, "to go up"); the choir screens; and the medieval ciborium. (The gilded bronze ciborium offered by Pope Honorius in about 630[8] had almost certainly been stolen during one of various armed raids upon Rome over the centuries; it had long since been replaced by a medieval marble structure.) The altar was broken open to verify the presence inside it of the bones of the two young martyrs. A new altar had therefore to be made; it was created out of coloured marbles inlaid in handsome geometrical patterns. All that was saved was the huge porphyry slab, 1.95 metres by 1.12, that had formed the tabletop proper, the *mensa*. This had probably been part of the original seventh-century altar, and it is still in use today.

What was broken and discarded was ninth-century slabs and thirteenth-century cosmatesque work (mosaics in marble, named after a family of Roman marble cutters and designers called the Cosmati). The thirteenth-century marble structures had been of white and grey marble inlaid with red and green porphyry, and decorated with fine red and gold mosaic borders. (The entire floor of the church, together with the steps leading down to the building, were also in cosmatesque floor mosaics.) Some idea of the magnificence of the sculpted and mosaic-inlaid chancel complex can be gathered from pieces recovered when restorations were undertaken in the canonry[9] next door in the early twentieth century. For three hundred years these fragments had lain face down, forming part of the kitchen floor. Some of them are now displayed in the passage leading to the church, on the lower left-hand wall. The least damaged piece was repaired and reused as the beautiful eight-panelled front of what is today the altar of the Saviour, in the second chapel on the right.[10]

In 1621 the new main altar was in place over a new silver casket containing the saints' bones, and the new domed ciborium rose over them both; the complex was inaugurated by Pope Paul V. The marble for the dome had been chosen to match in colour the four magnificent pink and grey portasanta columns, two on either side of it. The four small supporting columns of porphyry are almost certainly of ancient Roman origin; they may well have been reused in the medieval altar complex, and saved from it.

The two front columns of the four are considered by column-lovers to be among the finest specimens of tooled porphyry in existence. Their gleaming dark red-purple surfaces are stippled with tiny white beads of quartz crystals, which lend an extraordinary vibrancy and depth to their colouring. This most precious kind of porphyry is known as *lattinato* ("milk-flecked") because its minute inclusions are white; the fine rear columns of the ciborium, which are also slightly narrower than the front ones, have speckles that are merely pinkish.

Behind the ciborium, the lower part of the curved apse is covered with nine sheets of streaky grey pavonazzetto marble—rare because of their height—divided by strips of porphyry. The tall pavonazzetto panels create unbroken vertical streaks, dark bluish grey on light grey, that are echoed by the porphyry strips. A broad horizontal band of porphyry with a narrow carved cornice marks the height of the columns in the nave.[11] The ten perpendicular porphyry strips both echo the columns and emphasize the embracing gesture of the apse.

Sant'Agnese's is one of 123 ancient churches in Rome that become the *tituli* or "titles" of cardinals when they take up their offices. It is the churches, not the cardinals, that are titles.[12] A cardinal, who usually lives abroad, is expected to take a special interest in his titular church, and to visit it and say Mass in it when he is staying in the city. The present titular cardinal of Sant'Agnese's lives in Rome; he is the wonderfully named vicar of the bishop of Rome, Cardinal Camillo Ruini. In the middle of the stone bench around the apse behind the altar there is a medieval marble chair for the chief celebrant. It is reserved for when the pope or the titular cardinal of the church is visiting on special feasts; on these occasions the chair is covered in red cloth, and embroidered hangings decorate the lower apse.

The altar and ciborium are raised on a platform with two steps, around which is a low marble balustrade that was once graced by ten bronze lamps in the shape of split pomegranates. These were stolen in modern times; they were last mentioned in 1824. The one remaining pomegranate is now in the canonry chapel, where it is used as a sanctuary lamp. Marble balls bearing lights, of the same size as the pomegranates, have replaced them.[13]

The pomegranate is an ancient symbol of fruitfulness. The hard red and yellow skin of the fruit, once broken, reveals that it is packed tight with glistening, juicy red seeds: the skin, unassuming outside, bears riches within. Out of its "death" new life is born—hundreds of seeds, each potentially a tree to bear a thousand pomegranates. In the Christian view, the fruit represents both the superabundance of life in the world and grace "abounding," as Paul put it—more than enough to destroy the death which is sin.[14] The juice surrounding the seeds is the "blood" of Christ and of his imitators, the martyrs. Agnes, brutally cut open by the sword, was innocent and filled with faith; her death revealed to everyone the savagery of her murderers. And so her blood calls forth response in others—outrage, insight, resolution, conversion, determination never to forget. "The blood of the martyrs," wrote Tertullian, "is the seed of the Church."[15]

Next to the altar stands one of the most precious objects in the church, a Greco-Roman candlestick in creamy white Parian marble. Sant'Agnese's once possessed five of these man-sized, exquisitely carved candlesticks. Four of them were taken to the Vatican Museums in 1772; they now grace a gallery there, which is called the Galleria dei Candelabri after them. The candlestick remaining at Sant'Agnese's has a triangular base with rams' and winged sphinxes' heads at its corners, and on each of its three surfaces a cupid whose lower limbs metamorphose into swirling tendrils and flowers. Acanthus leaves sheath the column, which is in three curving sections and supports a broad and magnificently carved shallow cup. The original intention would have been for it to hold olive oil with a floating wick. The candlestick is used now to support a bronze cross bearing the sanctuary lamp, which is a red light customarily kept burning near the tabernacle in any Catholic church. The lamp is there to show people where the consecrated host, known as the Blessed Sacrament, is kept. It also provides continuing physical evidence of the faith and love of believers; in this respect a sanctuary lamp is similar in meaning to a candle left burning in a church.

Directly behind the altar is a statue of Saint Agnes, fashioned out of an ancient Roman work of yellowish oriental alabaster shot through with agate. It is now known to be an ancient copy of a female figure found at Herculaneum and kept today in the Dresden Museum.[16] Nicholas Cordier, a French artist working in Rome and known to Italians as "il Franciosino" (the little Frenchman,) was asked by Pope Leo XI in 1605 to turn this fragment of a statue into an image of the saint. Cordier added a head to the alabaster body, and hands, feet, and the lower part of her garments, all in bronze. She wears a crown of roses on her tied-back long, curly hair, and carries a tiny lamb as her attribute, together with a palm (added later).[17] In 1855 the bronze parts of the figure were gilded to match the yellowish alabaster more closely; the statue must have looked a lot more peculiar before that. But the mixture of shining stone and gleaming metal, of classical and Renaissance styles, still has an enigmatic strangeness. The Anglican clergyman Conyers Middleton was sufficiently unnerved by this figure to be convinced, in 1729, that it represented Dionysus, who, he believed, continued to be worshipped in Rome under cover of the name of Saint Agnes.[18]

A LITURGICAL PROBLEM

During the Second Vatican Council (1962–1965) the Roman Catholic Church decided to return to a very early custom, and have the priest say Mass facing the people. He would henceforth stand behind the altar; the tabernacle would be placed in a prominent position on the wall behind the altar, or in a side chapel set aside for private prayer. The main altar would be reserved for the ritual performance of the Mass, which imitates Christ's action at the Last Supper and follows his command, "Do this in memory of me."[19] Before the recent changes the priest would stand with his back to the congregation, facing the altar, the tabernacle on the altar, and the apse if there was one. The arrangement emphasized the theme of the "journey" of the people, with the priest "leading" them.

Nowadays the preferred model brings the priest down to the people's level and face to face with them. The symbolism stresses sharing and dialogue. To the idea of movement and the journey forward (which continues to be expressed by the spatial disposition of the church and by the congregation facing the apse) it adds the opposite and complementary concept of stillness; the celebration of Mass is "a pause on the way," with the group temporarily resting, talking, listening, reflecting and contemplating, re-enacting the Last Supper together.

The statue of Saint Agnes behind the altar—where the priest should stand—looks splendid, but from a liturgical point of view is now in the way. The tabernacle would also come between priest and people if he stood behind the altar, and would obscure the clear view of the ritual that is now demanded. Accordingly, the priest still says Mass at Sant'Agnese's with his back to the people, although he turns to face them whenever he appropriately can. Because of the arrangement of the altar, this church is one of the last in Rome where Mass is still said partly in the old way.

Discussion and disagreement about this has gone on for years; the congregation acquired a Web page, initially so that people could express their opinions on this thorny subject. Any change to the church's structure must have the approval of the Belle Arti, the branch of the state that watches over Italy's enormous artistic heritage. At present it has been decided—almost—that the statue and the tabernacle will be moved, the tabernacle to a side altar, the statue perhaps to the apse wall under the mosaic, where it would look a good deal less impressive and detract from the perfection of the plain marble and porphyry decoration there. Alternatively, the statue may be placed to one side of the chancel. As Sant'Agnese's is a small church, there is not much room for manoeuvre on this point. There was a suggestion from the congregation that the Renaissance balustrades around the altar be removed, but it has not been accepted. The altar must stay where it is because of its position over the saint's grave.

COMMUNION

The altar where the Mass is said, together with the bread and wine of the Eucharist itself, combine to express Christ's death—and his life. It is in order to remember that death that the Eucharistic table in a

Catholic church is referred to as an altar, and is frequently made in the shape of one. (The Eucharist, in fact, does not require an altar, or even a table—any surface will do.)

The idea of sacrifice—of killing a creature in order to achieve both human togetherness and an encounter with the divine—has been found everywhere on earth; a raised slab on which a sacrifice is performed is known as an altar. Sacrifice may be as old as religion itself, and almost as old as the hunting and killing by human beings of other animals for food.[20] Christianity, however, rejected blood sacrifice; this was in its time one of the most revolutionary aspects of the new religion. According to Christians, mediating sacrificial victims were no longer needed, for in the death of Jesus, God himself had become the victim, once and for all. It was the ultimate epiphany of his love: God had suffered as a victim suffers, and continues this solidarity with all victims. Christ's death at the hands of human beings definitively revealed the horror inherent in violence and made every subsequent act of violence an outrage. Scapegoating and violence continue in the world, but never again can they escape the light that reveals them for what they are.

The altar used as a Eucharistic table in a church is symbolic. It remembers, first of all, the ancient sacrificial altar at the Jewish temple. We saw earlier that the exterior columns of classical Greek and Roman temples became interior columns in a Christian basilical church. The altar, which stood outside both a pagan temple and the Jewish temple, is brought right into the centre of a church like Sant'Agnese's. It becomes the Christian holy of holies, the point of encounter between God and the group of people seeking him, between God and individual human beings. In Sant'Agnese's the domed ciborium standing on four columns above the altar recalls the *debir* or inner sanctum of the Jewish temple.

In earlier centuries curtains were hung between columns such as these; they were closed and opened at appropriate times during the ritual of the Mass. For the climactic moments the curtains were closed, in respect for the mystery. (Today, in Orthodox Christian churches, there is a screen in front of the altar with doors in it that can be opened and closed, for the same reasons.) Curtains made the ciborium even more suggestive of the tent that once enclosed the Ark containing the Covenant. The Ark enclosed the mystery (the word "ark" gives us the adjective "arcane"); only the high priest, once a year, could enter the room where it was housed.

Catholic churches today, without renouncing the idea of mystery, prefer the opposite and equally important symbolism of the availability of God, his desire that human beings should approach him. They therefore prefer the altar, and the ciborium if there is one, to be curtain-free, screen-free, and open. In Sant'Agnese's the space under the dome, like the temple's *debir*, is in the shape of a perfect cube. Modern churches rarely have a ciborium, but there is usually some attention-drawing device suspended over the altar; this can take the form of a circle, in the same tradition as the halo, the crown, and the dome. The tabernacle or "small tent" in a Catholic church (although not the tabernacle on the altar at Sant'Agnese's) often has little curtains covering the door, or even a veil that covers all of it, to remind Christians of the tent that was the origin of the Jewish temple.

Jesus had been put to death, yet Christians believed that he remained with them in the sharing of the bread and wine, which he said were his body and his blood. The Eucharist—the central rite of Christianity—not only symbolizes but also enacts sharing in love. In this ritual a number of great oppositions are articulated and the barriers dividing them collapsed: God and humankind; the group and the individual; death and life; spirit and body; then and now; here, elsewhere, and everywhere; eternal and temporal; and even meaning and fact ("This *is* my body").

The first Christians met in private houses, around ordinary tables in dining rooms, needing only bread and wine for their central epiphanic ritual. The elements of the Eucharist are indeed simple—but the meanings encompassed are vast. The action is intended to express union with God: oneness with what is eternally beyond and greater than human capacity. Eating, even before sex, is biological evolution's first step towards transcendence in the animal species because it initiates physical openness to and need for the Other.[21] For Catholic Christians, the Eucharist is God's gift of himself to humankind; and the ultimate sacramental mystery of love again takes the form of eating and drinking.

The altar remembers the central belief of Christianity, that from Christ's cruel death, new hope and the possibility of liberation were born for humanity. It concretely embodies the psalmist's poetic metaphor, which Jesus took to mean himself: "It was the stone rejected by the builders that became the cornerstone," the stone upon which the whole edifice depends.[22] Simon, son of Jonah, himself nicknamed Peter, "the stone," was later to comment on the relationship between the crucifixion of Jesus (his "rejection") and his status now as "the corner-stone" of the new view of the world.[23] People who do not believe that Jesus is the Christ foretold will not think him a "corner-stone" at all, Peter wrote; they will find him a "stumbling-block."[24] The latter expression in Greek is *petra skandalou*, the origin of the English word "scandal"; it means a stone that people fall over. Every altar in a Catholic church must either be of natural stone, or contain a stone element in the top of it, in order to recall this scandalous claim.

In order to "say" all this, it is essential that nothing be forgotten—neither the pain and the blood, nor the death—even as life and hope are being offered and celebrated. A cross stands on the altar. Nearby, at the end of the left-hand aisle, is a life-sized bronze crucifix, an unusually fine modern work by Uno Gera, who also modelled the Stations of the Cross for Sant'Agnese's. It is there to be contemplated by visitors, and it always has offerings of flowers and lights before it. The nailed feet of the dark bronze figure of Christ have been worn golden by the kisses of people doing homage to him.

The Eucharist, also known as Communion, is believed to unite Christ and Christians. Each of the people present at the ceremony eats the consecrated bread, and may also drink the wine: in sharing it, many become one. In order to make this possible, however, the bread must first be broken: the one becomes many. This breaking is another version of Christ's death, and also of his continuing life, his Resurrection.

It is the role of Christians, having witnessed the epiphany, to hand on the story, and also to continue it.[25] At the end of the Eucharist the people are sent away, out of the church. The ritual's name is "the Mass," from the Latin *Ite, missa est*, "Go, you are sent," the words the priest uses when sending the people away. For the ritual now has to be completed in "actual fact," that is in the world outside, where what has been experienced must find its response. After the encounter with God, the other half of the Christian's business remains to be done: the living with other people, and endeavouring to love them. As John's First Epistle bluntly put it, "We are to love, then, because he loved us first. Anyone who says, 'I love God' and hates his brother is a liar, since a man who does not love the brother that he can see cannot love God, whom he has never seen."[26]

The right Christian response, and the paradoxical way in which true love of God bears fruit, may be illustrated by a story about the four-teenth-century mystic Catherine of Siena. She was once enraptured by a vision of Christ, who at the climax of her ecstasy gave her his own cloak as a precious memorial of what had happened to her. No sooner had Catherine come to her everyday senses than she heard a knock at the door; a beggar stood there, in rags. Immediately, Catherine gave him the cloak.[27]

APOCALYPSE

A church is a physical expression of the saying of Jesus, "I am the way, the truth, and the life."[28] A Christian life is a "following" of Jesus along the "way"; but here Jesus goes further, saying that he himself *is* the way (and the truth and the life), just as he is "the door" or the way in.[29] The way of Christ is also the way of the cross. In one extraordi-nary metaphor in the Gospels, every human life becomes a potential road to Calvary, a Stations of the Cross: the "follower" of Christ is asked to take up his or her "cross" and walk the road.[30] Here, the cross symbolizes a life—or rather, everything in life that is not what the person living it would have chosen. Indeed, the Cross, the instrument of the death of Jesus, was an object in the shape of a human body, an obscene joke about the lot or fate of a human being. It had been contrived by ancient Greeks accustomed to stories in which a person's unavoidable fate could be symbolized by an object, cruelly alien but "to be borne."[31]

Sometimes human beings seem to achieve the all-important, impos-sible Christian goal of not merely trying to follow Christ, but actually imitating him in the way they live their own lives. These people would almost certainly deny this achievement, because they themselves are in a position to know just how far they have failed. But the opinion of such a heroic being is all but irrelevant: it is the opinion of other people that counts. Such a person is a hero, the Christian term for which is a saint. From the beginning it seemed to Christians that somebody who went so far as to die for the Christian ideal was especially faithful to the model. This type of saint is placed in a special class and called a martyr—a "rememberer" and a "witness." The most basic and natural response to the death of a martyr was remembrance too—the decision never to forget, made by others also trying to follow "the way." This memorable person had very literally imitated Jesus, who for Christians is the original martyr, the non-violent witness of God's love.

In the church of Sant'Agnese, the altar is placed directly above a coffin containing the remains of not one but two young women who died the death of the innocent victim, at the hands of people who were powerful, benighted, self-righteous, and ruthless. Agnes died by having her throat pierced with a sword, Emerentiana by stoning. Neither of these punishments was crucifixion, but these two girls reflected in their victimhood, and in their faith, hope, love, courage, and acceptance, the death of Christ. They were killed because they were his followers.

On the ceiling of the passage down into the church are late sixteenth-century frescoes depicting Christ holding the world in his hand, Saint Agnes, and Saint Emerentiana. There is also a symbolic design: the Cross, three crowns (for Christ himself and for the two young women who faithfully imitated him in their lives and their deaths), palms (symbols of the victory achieved in martyrdom), lilies (for innocence), crossed swords (referring to the sword that stabbed Agnes), and stones (representing those that struck Emerentiana). On a flying white ribbon is written, *Tollat crucem suam*, "Let her take up her cross."

Saint Emerentiana, buried with Agnes below the main altar, is the patron saint of another church a few city blocks away from this one, in the Piazza Sant'Emerenziana. It is a plain, barnlike twentieth-century brick building, deliberately designed to remind us of an early Christian basilica, a very much larger one than Sant'Agnese's. It possesses a huge and powerful modern mosaic designed and made by Ugolino da

Belluno in 1968,[32] covering the entire wall behind the altar. Twelve tons of mosaic pieces went into covering the 523 square metres of its surface.

The mosaic depicts God as Trinity (Christ in the centre of a giant cross, the Holy Spirit as fire and dove above him, and God the Father in the Hebrew letters for God at the top) and the people of God: a modern crowd advancing, and the Church's bishops clustered in a group at the foot of the cross. The mosaic is a pictorial depiction of the decree on the Church that was issued as the central document of the Second Vatican Council: *Lumen Gentium*, "The Light of the Peoples." The decree emphasized, as does the mosaic, that all of the bishops in the Roman Catholic Church, including the pope, must work together in "collegiality." And all people of good will—that is, all of the people of God, including (but not limited to) the members of the Roman Catholic Church—make up "the pilgrim people of God," ever learning, ever moving, in spite of failures, sinfulness, and difficulties, towards the light. The mosaic includes the animals of the earth and the stars, as representatives of the non-human world; the human crowd is made up of people of all races. Emerentiana herself, with Mary (here entitled "Mother of the Church," the title given to her by Pope Paul VI), is shown praying not only for but also with all humanity.

The design, profoundly traditional despite its modern style and theological significance, is very like that used by faraway Basque stonecutters for tombstones. The trapezoidal base represents what is of earth, here the Church; the oval aureole or mandorla[33] enclosing Christ, like the disk that stands at the top of a Basque gravestone, means "eternity" and "heaven." On either hand of the resurrected Christ ("He who is supreme, the first to return from death to life" says the inscription in Italian below) are Emerentiana and the Virgin Mary, supported by vigorous angels, swooping upward. The four signs of the evangelists—the Man of Matthew, the Lion of Mark, the Bull of Luke, and the Eagle of John,[34]—appear below Christ's feet, because it is they who have recorded his words on behalf of humanity as a whole. At the bottom of the design are handprints signifying the dead, who are also members of the "Communion of Saints," united with Christ. The mosaic depicts not only the Church in time, but also the apocalyptic end of the world and the revelation of the Heavenly Jerusalem, where all will be one in the final epiphany of God.

The burial of Agnes alongside the via Nomentana gave rise eventually to the church named after her. Emerentiana, who was Agnes' foster sister, was originally buried in the much larger, adjoining catacomb[35] called the *Coemeterium Maius* ("Bigger Cemetery"), to distinguish it both from the "smaller" *Coemeterium Minus* nearby, and from the catacomb of Saint Agnes. The modern church of Saint Emerentiana is situated over the underground Coemeterium Maius, the entrance to which is now in the via Asmara, some distance from Sant'Emerenziana's and near the via Nomentana. In the ninth century Emerentiana's body was taken from the Coemeterium Maius to Sant'Agnese's and buried with the bones of her foster sister inside the altar. This was the structure broken into in 1605 by an excited cardinal engaged in checking for himself that the bones were actually still there. Fragments of ninth-century, crudely chiselled stone transenne, some of which may have come from this altar, can be seen in the passage down into Sant'Agnese's, on the left near the cosmatesque fragments at the bottom of the steps. The bones of the two saints are not contained inside the present altar, but were placed in a silver casket directly below it.

The idea of doing such a thing—of constructing an altar over a martyr's grave and then saying Mass there—arose very early, although we cannot know exactly when, because records of Christian practices before their religion was sanctioned by Constantine are necessarily scarce. But from the late second century onward Christians used to meet from time to time at the catacombs (we have already seen that their regular meeting places were within the walls of the city); there, they honoured not only family members but other Christians who had died as well. One of Christianity's revolutionary ideals was that of caring intimately about people who were not kin.[36] It was, and often still is, especially in societies with close kin patterns, an extremely difficult requirement, one that had to be consciously and assiduously practised.

Somebody hit on the idea—in the context, perhaps, of sharing a meal, known as a *refrigerium*, in which the dead person was thought in some sense to participate—that it would be deeply meaningful to celebrate the Eucharist over the grave of someone who had been put to death for being a Christian. These were the mortal remains of a person whose soul was now at home with Christ, of one who had walked the road and reflected the model in his or her own life, and so had shown the rest of the people that it could be done. In the apocalyptic visions or Revelations of John (probably written in about 95 A.D.), the Lamb of God (Christ) breaks open seven seals affixed to a scroll in which are written the events to come in the last days of the world. Each seal reveals a different vision. "When he broke the fifth seal," John wrote, "I saw underneath the altar the souls of all the people who had been killed on account of the word of God, for witnessing to it."[37] Certainly, John's revelations refer to martyrs' souls rather than to their bodies. But for the living, the bones of the dead were the physical aspect of souls who were now enjoying God's presence "face to face."[38] The Revelation of the Fifth Seal was later adduced in support of the idea of altars being erected over martyrs' bones; it might also have helped to introduce the practice.

Naming a church after a saint is a custom that derives ultimately from these early churches built over martyrs' graves, or at the place where the martyr was thought to have been killed. (Saint Agnes has two churches named after her in Rome: one in Piazza Navona, the traditional site of her martyrdom, and this one where she is buried.)[39] The custom of calling churches after God or after saints continues to this day. The saint or the particular aspect of God gives a church individuality and character; the choice is always made for a specific reason, so that another layer of meaning is added to the building. And the custom neatly avoids naming a church after, say, a rich person or group that gave the money for it. A saint, for one thing, becomes a saint only after he or she is dead. Sainthood is perhaps the only honour accorded a person without consideration of physical beauty or prowess, wealth, birth, political power, intelligence, fame, or talent; a saint is admired, and considered exemplary, entirely for being good. When such a person becomes the "patron saint" of a church, the building then remembers the inspiration given, and proposes it to others. The trick for a Christian contemplating the story of such a figure is to turn his or her own unique circumstances and character into a new Christian configuration, an original way of following Christ.

In Prudentius' lines quoted on the arch preceding the church's apse, Agnes had given a wholly new example; she was "a glory unknown before." But the story people told about her resembles at many points the stories of other saints—there are saintly "types," in spite of the individuality that each saint invariably expresses. All these people follow one model, Jesus Christ; it is naturally felt that sanctity, although it must be various and appropriate to its time and circumstances, is in some sense always the same. And then, saints are not only people; they are also myths. We shall look at this fact in more detail later.

CANOPIES

The altar at Sant'Agnese's is anchored, as we have seen, to the place of her burial. Sheltering it is a domed ciborium or canopy. The word "canopy" means in Greek a mosquito net, from *konops*, "mosquito." Canopies, as practical objects, are protective devices. They may be portable roofs, carried to shelter people from sun and rain, or they may be built structures, providing cover for shrines, fountains, or graves. But sitting under a canopy—provided nobody else has one—can make a body extremely conspicuous in a crowd. Clearly, a person deemed worthy of such extravagant protection must be estimable, important, precious. Umbrellas have often been held over honourable people in crowds; in such cases mere onlookers have frequently been forbidden to use umbrellas or canopies because they might detract from the singling-out effect.

In ancient Rome it was common for the emperor's throne to be situated under a canopy—or under an apse in a basilica. Statues of the gods were similarly honoured. In a Christian basilica a canopy is also an honorific device: it marks out the altar as the most important place in the building. The altar is isolated and enhanced by the covering, just as the columns, the arches, the "road" of the nave ineluctably draw the eye to this focal point.

Canopies appear to have honoured tombs, and also the bodies of the dead during funeral rites, in the ancient Roman world.[40] In the catacombs it was possible for a family of means to have an arched structure excavated in the tufa over the burial place; this type of burial arrangement is known as an arcosolium. Like a canopy in a crowd, an arcosolium takes up more space and makes a greater effect than a simple slot for a body, a loculus. The business of such an honorific device is simply to point: what is being distinguished becomes thereafter the focus of attention, and must be deciphered. It is then up to the spectator to decide how to respond. We remain perfectly free, of course, to prefer the more egalitarian spirit expressed in the earliest catacomb galleries, where everyone received a similar and very summary loculus. The same effect is given by the extremely simple cemeteries of religious orders today.

The first canopy in a church in Rome seems to have been at St. Peter's, where an arrangement of arching ribs crossed over the Apostle's grave; from it a lamp in the form of a ring or corona was suspended. The arches rose from four twisted columns.[41] These were replaced thirteen centuries later by the giant columns of Bernini's masterpiece, the canopy over the altar in the new St. Peter's, created between 1626 and 1633. Bernini's columns are also twisted to recall the ones that had supported the earliest canopy. In Jerusalem, what was believed to be the Holy Sepulchre—the rock tomb where the body of Jesus was laid—was also turned into a shrine and surmounted by a canopy. These two extremely influential examples demonstrate how the combination in a church of tomb and altar provided a double demand for an honorary canopy.

SQUARE AND CIRCLE, CUBE AND SPHERE

Because a circle is a line without beginning or end, and the surface of a sphere is similarly "endless," circles and spheres represent eternity. The ancient Greeks thought that a sphere was so perfect a shape, it seemed obvious to them that the world must be spherical. To the philosopher Parmenides, even "being" could be thought of as round, "complete on every side like the body of a well-rounded sphere." And since being and truth for him were one, he could imagine truth as resembling a giant ball.[42] The semi-"spherical" ciborium or canopy in Sant'Agnese's is made of eight sections and its base is octagonal. A symmetrical eight-sided figure shares in the significance of a circle or a sphere, with the added meanings of the number eight.

The heavens that stretch over us from horizon to horizon seem like an immense dome, a star-studded vault. Accordingly, a dome or half sphere refers to the heavens resting on the earth's circular horizon. Judeo-Christian symbolic geography designates heaven as "where God is"; the heavens are infinitely vast, orderly, distant—yet familiar. All of this is implied in the essential Christian prayer, that Jesus taught to his disciples, where God is addressed as Our Father, who is nevertheless "in heaven," beyond us and invisible to us. The prayer also expresses the wish that the world of human behaviour should be as God wants it to be, "as it is in heaven."

An ancient basic image for the earth is that of a square or its three-dimensional counterpart, a cube. A square or a cube, like a circle or a sphere, always has the same shape, no matter what its size. A square or a cube has a definite centre, although that centre is not equidistant from the whole of the outline as is the centre of the round figures; circles and spheres are thought of as "perfect" partly for that reason.

A round periphery "moves." For example, in order to draw a circle you need a pair of compasses, with one arm stationary on the central dot and the other sweeping round it ("periphery" means literally "a carrying around"). The outline of a square or the surfaces of a cube, on the other hand, are "unmoving"; nobody would be foolish enough to create a square wheel. To human senses, the earth feels not only solid but also unmoving, and therefore a cube in its stability is a traditional symbol for the earth. (Ancient Greeks could also think of the earth as a flat disk with a periphery that was circular like the horizon. The spherical cosmos was "all there is." Earth as a cube was earth as immobile, and less than "all.")

Ancient Jews pictured earth as covered by a vast dome, fixed and steady (in English it is called "the firmament"). Under earth's flat surface were waters that welled up and broke through as rivers, lakes, wells, and the ocean (there was only one ocean); above the firmament there was also water, which fell as rain. Earth, like the firmament, was immobile and stood firm upon "pillars." Deep below the earth lay Sheol, the abode of the dead.[43] Such images of the universe reflect, of course, prescientific and poetic world views. They are, however, recognizable even today as symbolic systems, because they point to aspects of the way human beings feel and think about the world.

The domed ciborium at Sant'Agnese's represents heaven (the dome) resting upon earth: the four porphyry pillars supporting it form a perfect open cube. On the pillars rests the entablature, which in turn supports a square marble slab, and upon this slab rises the dome. This ensemble shelters the altar and the tabernacle, which in this church is covered by a small dome identical in shape to that of the ciborium. This domical form, which rises out of an octagonal base, is created out of eight segments, double the number of sides in a square. The eight sections of the ciborium are emphasized by double ribs, white on its pink and grey surface.

Eight sides surmounting four is a stage on the way to turning a square into a circle, a cube into a dome. Eight in this sense "mediates" between square and circle, between a symbolical earth and heaven, between four and infinity. Eight, in a structure such as this one, stands for Christ, who is a figure both heavenly and earthly, divine and human, the means of earth's approaching God, in conformity with God's will that the world be "as it is in heaven." Eight is also a common symbol of Christ's Resurrection, which happened on the "eighth day," the morning after the Sabbath, the last day of the seven-day Judaic week.

The eighth day, the first day of a new week—which pagans had already assigned, among their seven planetary days, to the Sun— became for Christians a weekly celebration of light conquering darkness, through Christ, "the light of the world,"[44] rising from the night of death. Sunday (*Sonntag* in German) is called "the Lord's day" in European romance languages: *domenico, domingo, dimanche, diumenge*. It is named for the epiphany of the Resurrection: every Sunday is for Christians a mini Easter. Eight also meant something both more than "all" and more than perfect—that is, greater than the world, and, as we should now say, beyond both space and time. Since Sunday is not only "the day after the last day," but also the first day (the day on which, according to the Book of Genesis, God began to create the universe), it also signifies the Christian belief that a new age dawned when Christ died and rose from the dead.[45]

At the summit of the domed ciborium is a small cylinder with vertical markings on its surface, holding, as in a cup, a sphere surmounted by a cross. A simple child's toy, available cheaply in traditional markets selling wooden playthings, consists of a cupped shape on a stick with a ball attached to the handle by a string. The game consists of jerking the ball into the air, then attempting—and occasionally managing—to catch it in the cup. The toy derives from the same system of ideas as the sceptre and orb of a monarch: in the hands of a king, the meaning is more obviously the world "as it should be," under the rule of order. The sceptre and orb of the king are separate objects, but they can be depicted as united, with the sphere balanced on top of the wand like a successful conjunction of cup-and-ball. At a deeper level this toy is an ancient and intentional metaphor for the profound experience of psychic satisfaction that is part of the meaning of epiphany. It is a metaphor that speaks to us in the finial of this dome.

The soul is open, longing for fulfillment of its desire, for what its very configuration demands. The objects of psychic desire could be, for example, truth (which Parmenides felt was "well-rounded" like being or the universe itself) or justice, a wholly supernatural concept that is not to be found in nature, but that every human being seeks and hopes to find. Psychic desire can be for understanding, for faith, for God: "Thou hast made us for thyself," wrote Saint Augustine, addressing God, "and our hearts are restless until they rest in thee."[46] The simple game of cup-and-ball can symbolize the human soul seeking for the moment of "getting it," of seeing things as they really are, of meeting God.

The sphere caught in the cylinder atop the ciborium stands also for "all there is," as it does for Parmenides, and as it also does in the vision of Julian of Norwich, who saw "all there is" lying in the palm of her hand, "the size of a hazelnut . . . round like a ball."[47] This symbol of the cosmos again has the "perfect" shape, a sphere. It is here surmounted by the sign of the cross. The meaning is that Christ is God, and greater than created matter. Having penetrated the world, revealing to it God's love, the cross now rises, and draws the world with it, to a higher level.[48] The shape of the cross as a geometrical figure—a horizontal bar intersecting with a vertical one—achieves the convergence of earthliness with heavenliness. Standing on this high place, on top of "the world," the cross expresses the vertical aspiration of the horizontal church building, its "heavenward" direction.

The ciborium ensemble also describes in its structure another of the central paradoxes of Christianity: that the one God is at the same time plural. God is one, but God is threeness, or Trinity. As Trinity, God is relationship itself, among three "persons": the Father (the creator), the Son (Jesus Christ), and the Holy Spirit. God the Father is expressed in the cosmic symbolism of the ciborium. And in the apse above it God the Father appears again, symbolized in mosaic as a hand reaching out of the circular heavens, the "hand" that made the universe. The Son is present in the Eucharist, and called to mind by the cross on the altar and by the culminating cross on top of the dome. The Spirit appears as a dove with wings outspread, sculpted in the square slab under the dome; the dove looks down upon the altar and the tabernacle.

The dove expresses the Spirit of God as love and as movement, a bird on the wing. It is a gentle bird and inhabits the air, which as wind is also an image of the Spirit. (The word "spirit" means "breath," as in "respiration"—as its Hebrew equivalent, *Ruah*, also does). "The wind blows wherever it pleases," Jesus said. "You hear its sound, but you cannot tell where it comes from or where it is going. That is how it is with all who are born of the Spirit."[49] Before the creation of the world, the Book of Genesis tells us, "the earth was a formless void, there was darkness over the deep, and God's Spirit hovered over the water."[50] God's "hovering" is thought of as being like that of a bird. And at the epiphany of God in the baptism of Jesus, the Spirit was experienced as a bird, flying out of heaven and resting upon the Son, as the Father's words sounded: "You are my Son, the Beloved; my favour rests on you."[51] The altar in a church represents epiphany for every human being. It echoes the epiphany of God's love in the Crucifixion and Resurrection, and it also recalls the epiphany at the baptism of Jesus in the Jordan river, which was another revelation of God as Trinity—Father, Son, and Spirit.

The structure—martyrs' tomb, altar, tabernacle, ciborium, cylinder, sphere, and cross—is static, mounting upward yet rooted deep in the earth. It is a Christian version of the ubiquitous religious symbol known as *axis mundi*, the vertical shaft around which everything revolves. But as an image the complex is, at the same time, dynamic. The ciborium or canopy remembers the tent that housed the Ark of the Covenant, carried by the Jews during their Exodus journey, the long struggle for liberation. As a tent it also expresses the Christian Church's view of itself as a band of people "on the move," searching for the liberation of the world from oppression, wayfarers seeking and getting lost, trusting in the promises and not giving up but struggling onward, on an exhausting journey that it seems, at times, will never be completed.

5

WORLD WITHOUT END:

Apse

....

The apse enfolds the altar and its canopy. Its rounded, expanding hollowness provides an "endless" end to the wayfarers' journey represented by the nave. In the mosaic covering the quarter-sphere above, Agnes and her two companions stand out against a field of plain, gleaming gold, signifying eternity and the Heavenly Jerusalem that is the world's destiny.[1] For each visitor to the church, this flood of gold is the *lux perpetua* that Christians hope all will enjoy beyond death: *Requiem aeternam dona eis Domine: et lux perpetua luceat eis*, "Eternal rest give to them, O Lord; and let perpetual light shine upon them."[2] Beneath the altar lies the body of Agnes; her soul is depicted in the apse mosaic above, already with God. She stands tall and regal, an adult rather than a child.

In the century after Agnes' death, details of her life were recalled, invented, elaborated upon, and finally written down as constituting her passio.[3] A passio is an account of a martyr's death or "passion," recalling as it always does Christ's Passion. (The word "passion" meant "suffering" before it came to mean "overpowering emotion.") In early times the lives of saints were also known as *gesta* or *acta* ("doings"), but only martyrs' stories are called passios. According to her fifth-century passio, Agnes had aroused a burning desire in the son of the Roman prefect, who had seen her coming home from school. Agnes was twelve or at most thirteen years old, the age at which Roman women could be engaged to be married. He begged her to marry him, offering her houses, riches, and luxury, as well as the power of being a member of the prefect's family, if she would agree.

He did not stand a chance. Agnes replied that she was engaged already, to someone far better than he, and who loved her more. "He has dressed me in the robes of a princess, in cloth of gold with borders, and has adorned me with enormous necklaces [*immensis monilibus*]." "He has placed on my right hand a priceless ring, and circled my throat with precious stones. He has given me earrings of glorious pearls and covered me with glowing, shimmering gems. He has placed his sign [the sign of the cross] on my forehead, and I shall have no other lover."[4] She had chosen Christ over the son of the Roman prefect.

Of course, "this world" would have its revenge. The law gave Agnes a fiendish choice if she would not marry: either to be made a vestal virgin and spend the rest of her life sacrificing to Roman idols, or to be exposed naked (spite, and more than spite, for the "priceless jewels") in a brothel. She chose the brothel, but was miraculously saved from rape. In the end she was stabbed in the throat—a merciful death, because of her age, and indeed stabbing is symbolic rape. The story also tells us that they tried to burn her alive because she would not change her mind, but the flames "divided" and went out. Throughout her ordeal, this fierce little twelve-year-old stood her ground.[5]

She stands now in the apse of the church, eternally with God, wearing the beauty with which Christ had decked her soul: Agnes is dressed in gorgeous Byzantine costume, in jewels and robes of purple. Her head is crowned; her earrings and the jewels at her throat are magnificent. There is at present no ring, but from photographs and in viewing the mosaic from a distance, there seems to me to have once been a ring on the fourth finger of her right hand. In the passio of Agnes, she is said to have appeared to her parents among "a whole army of virgins," *exercitum virginum*, a week after her death. The women were surrounded with light and wearing gorgeous robes; this heavenly apparition is doubtless also part of the inspiration for the mosaic in the apse.

She wears a tunic with narrow embroidered sleeves, and over it a long, soft gown of murrey (cloth dyed mulberry purple), with embroidered and jewelled stripes and borders. On top of this she has a magnificently jewelled garment, in cloth of gold with a white border embroidered with red flowers. This overgarment, a cross between a shawl and a scapular, hangs down in two panels at her front and back. It crosses over at her breast and descends to below her knees, and is held in place with a belt—apparently an unusual feature of her costume. Around her neck she wears a jewelled collar rather than a necklace. It was called a *superhumeral*, literally an "over-the-shoulders"; it is very like the jewelled collars worn by ancient Egyptian royalty. Her feet are shod in scarlet slippers.[6]

She stands with her weight resting slightly on the left leg, producing in spite of her robes an asymmetry, what the French call *déhanchement*. A swaying movement is introduced into her stance by the back panel of the heavy overgarment swinging out to her right, as though she has just taken a step; the strip of it that shows behind her is made artfully more distant than the brilliant panel in front, by means of duller mosaic cubes. Her whole body, and most delicately her right side from bent arm to ankle, is outlined with one row of dark *tesserae* (the tiny cubes that make up a mosaic). Her red-slippered left foot bears the weight of her body, while the right one points right, very unconcernedly close to the flames beside her. Agnes is standing on the instruments of her martyrdom: a long sword lies under her feet, and the fire "divides" into a ball of flame on either side of her. Hanging from her left arm is a broad white scarf with a beautiful embroidered motif on it, and in her long white fingers she holds a scroll sealed with a cross: the Scriptures.

Her face is extraordinary. It has been made in stone, whereas the rest of the mosaic is in glass. The tesserae of her face are also somewhat smaller than those used anywhere else in the work. The faces of the two popes, one on either side of her, have been created of tesserae like those everywhere else in the mosaic. Agnes' face stands out, therefore, white and intense. She has huge eyes which she raises slightly; her head is lowered by the apse curve, and from this position her eyes return the viewer's gaze with calm but piercing directness, as though she is looking up from a slightly bowed head. Her cheeks are reddened in two patches,[7] making her face look rather like her embroidered white scarf. It is a solemn, ghostly face, softened by its oval regularity, with a straight nose, level brows, and a small, sensitive mouth. There is a careful distinction made between the flesh of her beautiful, gently modelled neck, and the stiff, massively jewelled collar clasped around it.

THE PHOENIX AND THE PALM

Embroidered on her purple robe is a red-encircled gold roundel known as a *segmenta*, inset below the knee of her relaxed right leg. Inside the circle appears an exotic bird, which early Christians loved to borrow from classical mythology: the phoenix, here depicted in blue with a white tail and red legs. The Greeks themselves had learned of the phoenix from the Egyptians. Its name is a corruption of Bennu, the name of the god of the sun that dies every night and rises again every morning. The phoenix, as an aspect of the sun, lived for the span of a Great Year, which the sources variously report as lasting 500 years, or 540 years, or 1,461 years.

When this long age was over and the phoenix was about to die, it returned to the Temple of the Sun in Heliopolis ("Sun City"), Egypt. It arrived accompanied by thousands of other ordinary birds, following out of sheer curiosity because they had never seen anything like the phoenix before. Herodotus says that paintings of the phoenix showed it to be gold and red in colour, and like an eagle in appearance and size. On the altar at Heliopolis the great bird proceeded to make itself a nest out of twigs of cassia and frankincense. It had brought with it a great ball of myrrh, which it shaped like an egg, then hollowed out; it buried its "parent" inside. The nest completed, the phoenix became hotter and hotter and redder and redder until it turned to ashes; a new phoenix then emerged from the egg of myrrh. The process took three days.[8]

This fabulous bird lived alone in the universe. Like the sun, there was none like it; it was *monos, singularis, unicus*. There was no way it could generate offspring, because it had no mate; it had therefore to renew itself out of itself. The tale recounted by Herodotus and Tacitus, of the "parent" enclosed in the egg, indicates that the myth included in some way the idea of new life breaking out of the "tomb" that is an egg's shell. But the phoenix had no parent; it was its own parent. In a more complete version than has come down to us, the story must have involved the ashen phoenix returning to the egg—an egg of myrrh, the scented gum resin with which dead bodies were anointed and embalmed.[9] From the death-egg it re-emerged into life, as the Great Year began its new cycle.

For Christians the phoenix was a symbol of the resurrection of Christ from the dead on the third day.[10] (Christians were often to picture the Resurrection as like the hatching of a bird from an egg, an "Easter egg.") In Christ's Resurrection they see the dawning of a new era of consciousness on the earth; the former "Great Year" has passed. It means, too, the promise that human beings will also rise from the dead and live in a reality outside the limits of space and time. The risen Christ, wrote Saint Paul, is "the first-fruits" of the resurrection of all humanity.[11] "First-fruits" are a part of the whole crop, offered to God before the rest is shared out to human beings. The phoenix embroidered on Agnes' robe means that she, like Christ, is risen and is now with God forever. It means too that Agnes, like the phoenix, did not know sex; she died a virgin. And also that she "consumed herself" in the fire of her love for God.

The word "phoenix," apart from the bird and its origin in the name of the Egyptian god Bennu, means three things in Greek: the colour red, a Phoenician, and a palm tree. Phoenicians are thought to have derived their name from a Western Semitic term for the red dye we call madder. "Phoenicians" would be "those who work with and sell cloth dyed red."[12] The bird's redness suggested blood—the blood of martyrdom. The fiery nature of the phoenix reminded Christians of love and intensity, and of the Holy Spirit, who inspires and strengthens, as on the day of Pentecost, when there was a sound "like that of a strong driving wind, which filled the whole house where they [the disciples of Jesus] were sitting. And there appeared to them tongues like flames of fire, dispersed among them and resting on each one."[13]

Phoinix, the Greek word for "palm tree," only accidentally resembles the name of the bird, but for people who understood Greek the similarity was poignant. A phoenix is traditionally included in Christian mosaics showing the coming of Christ at the end of the world, and the eternal epiphany of the Heavenly Jerusalem. In such compositions[14] the sacred bird, symbol of the Resurrection, sits in a palm tree, an ancient symbol of the abundance of life. Perched on a shoot of its namesake, the phoenix signifies "life eternal."

Furthermore, a palm branch was widely understood in the ancient world as a symbol of victory and of explosions of communal joy.

(Modern fireworks often resemble rapidly growing palm trees.) The citizens of Jerusalem waved palm branches when Jesus entered the city in triumph; the event is remembered in the feast called Palm Sunday.[15] But Christians had learned to differ from ancient Romans in what they meant by "victory." For them the symbol of the palm most especially belonged to men and women who died for their beliefs, in those days most often at the hands of the Roman state. The phoenix on Agnes' dress in the mosaic is a symbol of her victory in death, her virginity, her love of God, and her life with God forever.

A HALOED HEAD

The head of Agnes in the mosaic is surrounded by a huge gold halo, descending to her shoulders and outlined in white and then dark blue. (The popes on either side of her have no such distinction.) Her clothing, and this type of halo, are sufficient to mark this mosaic as a distinctively Byzantine work. A halo (from Greek *halos*, a "round threshing floor," therefore a circle) or nimbus (from Latin *nebula*, "cloud") is like an aura radiating from a person's head. From an artist's practical, compositional point of view a halo makes that head remarkable, partly by isolating it from its background and partly by making it bigger. Like a canopy or a ceremonial umbrella, a halo points out a figure in a work of art. "This," it says, "is someone special." And then the picture asks, "Who do you think it is?"

Sometimes people have been depicted as wrapped entirely in a nimbus, but it is far more common for a halo to encircle only the head. For millennia people in the cultures of the Mediterranean and in Europe generally have believed that the head contained a person's soul, life force, or genius. Even before people caught on that we think with our brains (Homeric heroes, for instance, think and feel and rage with their chests), they knew that the head—the exclusive seat of four of the five senses and carried at the summit of the human body—was pre-eminent. Cut off the head, and the body dies. The brain, it was suspected, must be the seat of the life force, and in men was probably the source of semen.[16]

Ancient Romans and Hellenistic Greeks used halos in art to mark out people filled with power, such as gods and divine emperors. In very early Christian art, the meaning of a nimbus was still simply "power," so a demon, an emperor, or a Greco-Roman mythical hero could be shown haloed. Later, in keeping with Christianity's favouring of the saintly, it was Christ and the saints who alone could wear the halo; Christ was distinguished from saints by a nimbus quartered by a cross. Symbols could be haloed to make their meaning clear: the Lamb of God, for instance, or the symbols standing for the four Evangelists, or the dove representing the Holy Spirit. The dove that hovers over the altar at Sant'Agnese's is nimbed with a sunburst.

There are examples of halos for Christ and the saints in art from the Roman catacombs, but they are unusual and late. It was Greek Christians who loved halos first, and the introduction into Western Christian art of the halo as a widely received convention seems to have begun under Greek influence during the sixth century, less than a hundred years before the mosaic at Sant'Agnese's was made. Only by the ninth century did halos become *de rigueur*; but after that they remained so for a thousand years. Whenever art subsequently became realistic, however—in the Gothic period, for instance—use of the halo died down. It disappeared almost completely in modern religious art, in the new distrust for designating anyone as self-evidently admirable in the opinion of everybody. We are far more interested in feet of clay than in aureoled heads.

The newly awakened taste for Eastern icons, however, is reintroducing the common depiction of halos to Western religious art. The modern mosaic in the church of Sant'Emerenziana, for example, includes small halos for the dove of the Spirit, the angels, the Virgin Mary, Saint Emerentiana, and the symbols of the four Evangelists. Christ himself has a mandorla surrounding his entire body.

Saint Agnes' halo "says" that she is in heaven with God. She is immortal now: the halo's ring is that "unending" line we have noted before (the circle is assumed to be completed behind her). The whole nimbus, area and line, is light emanating from her soul and honour bestowed upon her by God for her courageous faithfulness. At the top of the apse the "hand" of God appears, holding out to Saint Agnes a crown, the crown of martyrdom. The meaning of a crown—a circle that surrounds the head—is similar to that of a halo, except that it tends to lack volume; royal crowns are often made tall to overcome this disadvantage. A crown is something "extra," a finishing touch of glory: honour for the honourable, triumph "crowning" success. Ancient Greek and Roman champions at the games were rewarded by being crowned in the sight of the admiring crowds. This moment of glory was for them a religious epiphany, and often depicted as such: the Greek goddess Nike ("Victory," the embodiment of winning) is shown flying down from heaven to bestow the crown. A crown could also symbolize a life now complete. The road is over, the race complete, the finishing line crossed, the victory won.

In the mosaic, the hand of God—symbol of God the Father, whose "hand" created the universe—reaches out of the white empyrean holding the wreath that is Agnes' crown. Only a segment of this circle of whiteness appears because the apse is only half a dome.[17] As suits the empyrean (the word means "fiery"), little burning red clouds spin in the light like flames—the flames, perhaps, of God's Spirit. Enclosing this uppermost region (although from earth's point of view the empyrean encloses the air) is a blue band, and then a dark blue one, presumably denoting air by night and air by day. Both zones are sprinkled with huge white stars, like lacy frost-flakes.[18] And above the saint's head, between her halo and heaven's vault, is her name, called aloud perhaps by God himself: "Sancta Agnes," abbreviated as SCA AGNES.

Photographs cannot express the beauty of this apse, and in particular of the figures depicted in it. To begin with, a photograph's flat surface cannot show the bend forward that is given to the body of Agnes by the curving hollow of the apse. (Photographs taken at the wrong angle often make her look dumpy, which she most emphatically is not.) The three tall figures stand on a green strip stretching around the bottom of the cupped space, a dark green band and then a light green one, parallel to the zones of blue above. The whole hollow in between is covered in gold, with the figures isolated against it, and well apart. The people who stood in the gallery of the church would have beheld the mosaic at close to eye-level. It twinkled in the light of votive lamps that were kept burning at the grave. At ground level the aspect of the apse changes as the spectator moves, especially as he or she moves forward: the totality of the concave half-dome gradually discloses itself, and the glitter shifts across the encrusted surface. Mosaic art plays with texture and with light.

MOSAICS: HISTORY AND TECHNIQUE

In the catacomb of Pamphilus, beneath the via Salaria to the west of Sant'Agnese's, it is possible to see, still imbedded in the tufa, a round image, only a few inches wide, of Saint Agnes. She wears a halo and beautiful robes, and stands with arms stretched out, palms up, in the ancient attitude of prayer. There are stars in the background, and doves on pillars on either side of her. The symbolism of doves (prolific birds) on pillars is similar to that of palm trees with their feathery leaves. In addition, white doves represent innocence, purity, and souls (which are often depicted as birds) alive in heavenly bliss. Agnes is standing in heaven, accompanied by the souls of the blessed, just as, in her passio, she was seen after her death in a vision accompanied by a whole procession of saintly women. Her name, AGN-NES, is divided about her head at the top. The image is in gold leaf. If you look closely, you can see that this roundel is in fact the bottom of a glass vessel, whose sides have been deliberately broken off to leave intact the base containing the gold picture imprisoned within it.

More than five hundred of these "goldglasses," with wide-ranging iconography, have been found in the catacombs, rifled though the cemeteries had been even before an archaeological interest in them began. Pagan examples of the type are also known, but they are much rarer—and often of a much higher quality. Most examples of goldglass that have come down to us show Christian subjects. Either Christians were especially fond of such glasses (perhaps some of their number were involved in the making of them), or the simple fact that they stuck them into catacomb walls caused proportionately many more Christian examples to survive. The glasses could have been wedding gifts, or anniversary or New Year's presents, treasured thereafter by their owners. It is conjectured that at a Christian funeral a glass, perhaps a favourite possession of the deceased, may have been used as part of the ritual feast, and then deliberately broken as an initiatory act to mark the passing of the dead person to eternal life. (Smashing something is a common ritual in initiations, where the old has "died" to give way to the new.) The decorative and still solid part of the vessel was then used to mark the simple grave.[19]

The technique of making goldglass bottoms began with a thick glass disk, often coloured. Onto this disk a cut-out in gold leaf was affixed and then engraved. A thin layer of colourless glass was then poured over the top, and the whole heated in a kiln. The resulting fusion of the glass held the gold leaf securely in place, and also greatly enhanced its brilliance.

It was exactly in this manner, but using plain gold leaf on thin sheets of coloured glass base, that the components of gold mosaics were prepared. Once the glass imprisoning the gold was cold, the sheet was cut with a hot iron tool into tiny cubes or tesserae, varying in size and sometimes less than a quarter of an inch per side. For the ordinary colours in a mosaic like the one at Sant'Agnese's, opaque coloured glass was cut into tesserae.

The pieces were stuck onto the surface of a wall prepared with layers of mortar: first a coarse layer keyed into the wall by means of large broad-headed nails, then one or two layers of fine mortar. The little cubes were pressed into the top layer of mortar while it was still wet; the mortar had therefore to be prepared in patches just about the size that could be finished in a day's work. (It is often possible to see from the layout of the tesserae just how large a patch was done on one particular day.) An underdrawing or a rough painting was sketched onto the wall to guide the artists in the placing of their tesserae. Irregular tesserae were made as well, for details and special effects. The iron tool often tore the gold leaf in cutting the tesserae. This was entirely desirable, as was the frequently spare use of gold: modern mosaics often look flat and loud just because they are too regular and too rich.

The earliest mosaics were made not of glass but of stone, even of uncut pebbles, such as the magnificent designs at Pella, the childhood home of Alexander the Great. Marble, in all the variety of its colouring, was a stone easily adapted for mosaic work, for cutting first in sheets and then cubes for reassembly. In the classical period, mosaic work was often thought of as a form of painting in stone. The virtuosity implicit in such an endeavour was part of its appeal, as was the durability and preciousness of stone as compared with paint. The cut marbles were set as closely as possible together to form a picture, then polished and buffed: the best mosaic was one in which it was hardest to detect that the design had been made in stone at all. There was also a glass technique, where fine rods of coloured glass were packed tightly together to form the design, rather as in a modern glass paperweight. Their ends were then ground down to a perfectly flush surface. Greek and Roman floors were of rougher mosaic work. (Roman floors are what have survived, we must remember, rather than walls and ceilings.) The pieces that made up the design were visibly tesserae, but again the point was to create a smooth floor surface.

The creators of Christian mosaic work, as it developed in the centuries before Sant'Agnese's was built, saw the technique very differently. Mosaic for decorating walls was enjoyed as such, for its crustiness and glitter. It lent itself to *pointilliste* effects, where pure points of colour merge into pictorial form when seen from a distance; the viewer's eye and mind "complete" the work, the coming together of colours to create vibrant form. We have quite recently relearned how to enjoy this technique through the art of the Impressionists, and especially through the work of Seurat and his followers.

Mosaic patterns in Christian art became sheaths, flexibly covering architecturally created surfaces such as arches, walls, domes, and apses. Once mosaics were accepted and admired as such, artists could relax into accepting the given surface, no longer creating figures in volume or pictorial compositions in depth, but preferring the flat, the decorative, the linear. They began to choose subjects that worked well in mosaic (jewelled dresses are a good example), and to love broad, simple areas of colour. Expanses of gold mosaic in particular became a stunning enhancement of pure architectural form. Shining gold worked especially well on curving surfaces. Furthermore, gold enhanced by a glass covering reminds us of Saint John's vision in the Apocalypse: the Heavenly Jerusalem, he wrote, was a city of "pure gold, like translucent (*katharō*, which is spotless or clear) glass."[20]

Although it was more costly than fresco decoration, mosaic was apparently not considered a particularly expensive medium, despite the gold. Contemporary accounts of Constantine's churches describe with wonder the gifts of gold and silver vessels that he made to these basilicas, and stress the richness of the marble slabs covering some of the walls—but they never mention the mosaics. The gold and silver disappeared during the many invasions of Rome, and the marble panels have almost all been stolen over the centuries. The mosaics, however, survive, unless the very walls under them have fallen. Even the gold, when gold backgrounds became important in later centuries, was of little monetary value to looters, being thin and glass-coated and in tiny cubes.

Finally, mosaic can be extremely practical: it is very durable and easily repaired because it is made of small pieces. (The principle holds good for street pavements in cities like Lisbon or Barcelona. The pavements are made of small pieces so they can be repaired exactly where and when necessary; there is no need to tear everything up in order to fix a damaged section.) Provided attention is paid to maintaining a mosaic, it can last for centuries—indeed, indefinitely. In fact, of course, many mosaics have been neglected, and repaired only when great patches had come away from the wall and needed replacing; the restored result may have seriously altered the intentions of the original artists. Often patches were painted in as a temporary measure before they could be repaired in mosaic. We know that after the seventeenth-century restoration of Sant'Agnese's church, patches filled in with painted plaster were left in the apse mosaic. These spaces, and new weak spots in the fabric, were repaired in 1842. Areas of restoration are visible, especially in the gold background.

The setting of mosaic cubes, especially over the curving surfaces of arches and vaults, has sometimes achieved great mastery. Artists have been able to set the pieces turned slightly outward and downward, at precisely the right angle to catch and reflect light: tesserae were set quite far apart from one another, exactly at a distance and an obliquity that melded them into a seamless but twinkling surface when seen by a viewer standing on the floor below. Artists in mosaic had to know exactly how much plaster should fill the interstices, and how to colour it correctly. This technique could save as many as half of the mosaic pieces that would have been needed had the surface been completely covered—and at the same time it actually increased the brilliance of the total effect. (Saving on the gold involved could mean a lot. The great church of Hagia Sophia in Istanbul, subsequently a mosque and now a museum, was once decorated throughout with mosaics; the area covered is estimated in acres, a great deal of it gold.)[21]

The gold background of the seventh-century mosaic at Sant' Agnese's has been deliberately dulled. The gold sandwiched between glass layers is scant, and the tesserae may also have been reversed in many cases, so that the thicker layer of glass is uppermost, reducing the gold's brilliance.[22] A further refinement of gold mosaic technique has to do with the colour of the glass base, which could be greenish, brownish, yellow, red, grey, or colourless; the effect desired governed the colour chosen.[23] Most of the gold tesserae at Sant'Agnese's seem to employ grey or green glass. There is no angling of the pieces, but depth of tone is achieved with irregular tesserae shapes and changing interstices between them.[24] The effect is carefully designed to set off and enhance with dull greenish gold the purple robes and the greens and blues that make up most of the rest of the design.

The face of Saint Agnes in the mosaic, with its marble tesserae, may have been made separately in a workshop and then transferred in one piece to the vault. In the apse of the cathedral of St. John Lateran there is a mosaic head of Christ that has twice been remade. According to tradition, the original head had been of supernatural origin: it miraculously appeared one day in the church. During work on the mosaic in the thirteenth-century, it was discovered that the portrait had been assembled on its own independent bed of travertine marble. Clearly, it had been made separately in a workshop. Suddenly it arrived, all in one piece, and the people of Rome have never forgotten their amazement.[25]

A LITTLE RED STONE

In November of 1887, Thérèse Martin, aged fourteen, was visiting Rome in the company of her father and her sister Céline. The family made a point of going to Sant'Agnese's church. It had a special significance for them because Pauline Martin, Thérèse's second-eldest sister, could not come. She was a Carmelite nun who had taken the name Soeur Agnès when she entered the convent. Pauline had become, when Thérèse wrote this account eight years later, Mère Agnès; and indeed Mère Agnès it was who asked her sister to write the story of her life. The section of what was later the book called *Histoire d'une âme*, (The Story of a Soul), in which this account appears, was dedicated to Mère Agnès.

Thérèse, the future saint, describes praying to Sainte Agnès in the church in Rome, and begging her for some memento of the visit for Soeur Agnès, Agnes' name-child. Thérèse must have wanted to take something from the church, and may have been told that she couldn't: she says she did everything possible—perhaps meaning that she did more than pray—to take away "one of the relics," and that it was forbidden for her to take what she wanted. And behold, "a little red stone" detached itself from a "rich mosaic" for Thérèse to take back for her sister. She interpreted this as a special gift from Sainte Agnès herself, whom Thérèse regarded as a "childhood friend," eternally of an age not much younger than she then was herself.

Where did the stone come from? Thérèse believed that the mosaic from which the tessera fell dated back to the time of Agnes, and that the saint "must often have looked at it herself." The stone would not have actually dropped out of the apse, since the central figure in the mosaic, with her name clearly written over her head, represents Saint Agnes herself; Thérèse can hardly have thought that Agnes gazed at it while she was on earth. The red stone could have come from one of the cosmatesque fragments now in the passage down to the church, the decorated bands of which are in red and gold mosaic; some of these are even now in a shattered condition. These fragments, however, are said to have been discovered only in the early twentieth century.[26] Perhaps the stone she found was not from a mosaic at all.

I have thought this small incident from the journals of Saint Theresa of Lisieux worth relating because it shows how very differently a church is experienced if the visitor is a pilgrim rather than a tourist or an art historian. Thérèse knew almost nothing of the history of the church, or of the history of mosaics or cosmatesque art. And really, she would not have cared more than mildly if she had had access to the scholarship. Her attention was focused on Agnes, whose story she knew intimately,[27] and her sister in the convent in France. She reacted directly and intensely to the church building. Expecting a miracle, she prayed—and got one.

HONORIUS, THE FALLIBLE POPE

Standing at Agnes' right hand in the apse mosaic is Pope Honorius I (625–638), under whose authority this church was built. He was a pope famous for having made an error in a matter of Church doctrine. He was condemned for doing so, at the Third Council of Constantinople, 680–681. During the First Vatican Council (1869–1870) the mistake of Honorius was used as an argument against the formulation of the Catholic doctrine of papal infallibility.

The Roman Empire was split when Constantine founded "New Rome" at Byzantium and named it Constantinople in 324. Subsequently, he governed the empire from the new capital, while the popes in Rome continued to lead the Church.[28] By the early 600s the capital of the empire was threatened by Persian advances towards the Bosporus, while the Arabs, newly converted to Islam, were conquering with their armies province after province of the empire in the south.

Rome, meanwhile, had recently benefited from the outstanding leadership of Pope Gregory I, the Great (590–604), who had strengthened and regulated the social organization of the city, and improved the health of the Church. Gregory's pontificate was marked by the Gothic Wars, waged by the emperor of Constantinople, Justinian I, in order to gain imperial control of the Italian countryside. Meanwhile, the Germanic Lombards had entered Italy in 568 and continued moving south. They laid siege to Italian cities and terrified the population; thousands of refugees flooded into Rome and had to be fed and lodged. The advancing Lombards finally invaded Rome's outlying districts. Gregory paid them off to keep them from further violence, agreed to continue paying a yearly ransom, and then adroitly negotiated peace; his aim, the pope said, was not to fight with the Lombards but to convert them.[29] The independent settlement caused rage in Constantinople.

Rome, increasingly dependent upon the papacy for actual government as well as religious leadership,[30] would continue to face barbarian invasions. But equally difficult and dangerous were its relations with the imperial court in Constantinople. The government there viewed religion as a social factor that could either divide or unite the empire. The need, as the Emperor Heraclius (610–641) saw it, was for unity in the face of Moslem advances. He therefore decided to impose unity of Christian belief upon his empire.

Christianity is a religion, as we have repeatedly seen, that rests upon a series of mighty paradoxes. At the core of the whole system of belief is the matter of Jesus Christ's being both utterly human and utterly divine. This central dogma or belief is a tension between opposites that the papacy has always considered it to be its duty to uphold. But it is always difficult to keep the two ideas in balance. At times in the Church's history, a leaning to one or the other idea has caused a fury of rejection of—and by—the other side. Once any argument becomes emotionally charged, it is easily manipulated for political ends. Even more sinisterly, political pressures, hatreds, and ambitions are then allowed to disguise themselves as religious disagreements.

In the 600s much of the Eastern part of the empire was Mono-physite.[31] As a theological position, Monophysitism held that Jesus Christ had one nature (*monos physis* in Greek). This formulation seems innocuous enough. But there was disagreement about what the Greek word *physis* meant: was Jesus one person (the Second Person of the Trinity, the Word of God,[32] Son of the Father) or did *physis* mean the quality or character of his person—his humanness, his divineness? Out of this difference in the definition of a word arose a great theolog-ical battle. It was both encouraged by the increasing hostility between East and West, and used to exacerbate that hostility. The East insisted that Jesus was one person; the West argued that he had two natures, divine and human. In fact, Christian doctrine might be agreed to contain both positions. But as is so often the case, intellectual argument was fuelled by political rigidities. The paradox therefore split in two.

A previous attack on the paradox had been far more significant. It had earlier been claimed by certain Monophysites that Christ was only divine, his human nature having been absorbed by his divinity. Under Pope Leo I, the Great (440–461), this idea had been condemned as a heresy. What was at issue—and the Church of the 600s had not forgot-ten it—was the doctrine of the Incarnation, in which it is believed that God (Christ) became human or "took flesh" ("flesh" is *caro, carnis* in Latin). God, as Christians believe, has complete solidarity with the human race he came to redeem; human nature is involved in the ongoing process of salvation. The heresy that Christ is only divine (not really suffering, for example, in his Crucifixion) caused Pope Leo the Great to give the clearest expression to that date (449) of the doctrine of the Incarnation. (From the Church's point of view, heretical ideas have always been indispensable, as occasions for the clarification of doctrine: they cause agreement to be reached on what it is that is *not* part of the faith.) "For he who is truly God," wrote Leo, "is the same who is also truly human."[33] And the pope explained this by saying that Jesus Christ had "two natures."

The Monophysites, interpreting the word *physis* differently, objected: to them it seemed as if this formulation must mean that there are two Christs. The Council of Chalcedon in 451 reaffirmed the paradoxical belief that Christ is both human and divine, "one person in two natures"—and repudiated Monophysitism. The council also formally rejected the belief of the Nestorians, that Jesus Christ was both human and divine, but that Mary gave birth only to the human nature and not to the divine. At the Council of Ephesus in 431 Mary had been declared to be *Theotokos, Dei Genetrix* in Latin, "She who gave birth to God." With this, the mother of Jesus was recognized as essential, not only humanly but also theologically, to the entire system of belief.

The repudiation of Monophysitism was received, in the East, as an outrage. Politics seized its opportunity. As academic arguments proliferated, Monophysitism increasingly assumed the role of apparent differentiator between Rome and Constantinople, between pope and emperor, even between West and East. Ordinary human beings trying to be followers of Jesus Christ would almost certainly have been baffled by the intellectual formulations of either side. While Christian scholars worried at the chestnut, the religion of Islam arose out of Arabia.

The seriously perturbed Emperor Heraclius demanded an end to Christian arguing; he wanted political unity.[34] Sergius, the patriarch of Constantinople, was ordered to find an answer. He made a new formulation, one whose weirdness is explicable only in the context of the time. It became known as Monothelitism ("one-will-ism") or Monenergism ("one-energy-ism"). Let us drop, said Sergius, the argument about whether Jesus had one or two *natures*, and ask whether he had one or two *wills* (one human, one divine) and one or two *energies* (one human, one divine). Having put the problem this way, Sergius concluded that it was silly to imagine Jesus having two wills and two energies; he must have only one of each. Sergius then wrote to Pope Honorius, setting out his propositions, and asked him what he thought. Obviously unaware of either the doctrinal subtleties or the wider political implications of the question, Honorius wrote back saying he thought Sergius was right: Jesus had only one will.

The emperor and Sergius were elated. A decree was promulgated in 638, known as the *Ekthesis*, which declared that Christianity was one and the faith was fixed: Honorius, the pope himself, had agreed. Very soon afterwards Honorius died. But theologians in the West, looking over Sergius' formulation, rejected it. The formulation seemed to them (and quite possibly was) a cunning attempt on the part of Sergius to impose Monophysitism on the universal Church. Furthermore, and more important, the Christian faith was not something to be set by the emperor. Constans II, the new emperor, then issued a decree in 648 forbidding anyone even to discuss the question of whether Christ had one or two wills. To debate the matter was to be deposed if you were a bishop, to have all your property confiscated if you were a nobleman, to be tortured and exiled if you were an ordinary citizen. Christendom was to be unified, at all costs, in the face of Islam.

The papacy responded in 649 by calling a synod at the Lateran, refusing the doctrine of "one will, one energy" and excommunicating the patriarch of Constantinople. Furthermore, the new pope, Martin I, was made first bishop and then pope without Rome asking the emperor's permission. For a century the emperors at Constantinople had insisted that all popes be investigated by the imperial government before being allowed to take office.

The exarch Olympios was ordered by the emperor to go to Rome, arrest Pope Martin, and bring him to Constantinople for trial. On arriving in Rome Olympios instead proclaimed himself emperor of the West, with a co-emperor named Valentinian. Olympios was killed fighting the Arabs in Sicily two years later. The pope, bedridden with gout at the time, was seized and smuggled out of Rome. At Constantinople he was condemned, not for religious beliefs, but because of the Olympios disaster. (Modern historians agree that the pope was made the scapegoat in this political affair.) He was publicly stripped of his vestments, dragged through the streets in chains and flogged, then taken to Chersonesos in the Crimea, treated very harshly, and finally starved to death in 655.

Meanwhile, Maximus the Confessor, a widely admired Eastern theologian, had written fierce condemnations of the emperor for usurping papal authority. He and his companions were also sent into exile in 655. Refusing under pressure to recant from his position that the emperor had no right to decide what Christians should believe, he and his followers had their tongues cut out and their right hands cut off, so that they should neither speak nor write again.

In 681, at the Third Council of Constantinople, the letter Honorius had written to Sergius, apparently supporting what had come to be called Monothelitism, was condemned by the Church as erroneous. The new formulation, later promulgated by Pope Leo II, was that Jesus Christ "is our true God" and "his two natures shine forth in his one hypostasis." *Hypostasis* ("substance"—the two words mean literally "what stands beneath" in Greek and Latin) was a sidestep from the noun *physis*. It was to have a long theological future.

In 1870, at the First Vatican Council, the Church formulated the doctrine of papal infallibility. This doctrine means that the Holy Spirit remains with the Church until the end of time and will not allow her, over time and in the end, to deviate fundamentally from the truth of the Gospel message, from her mission to bring about God's kingdom, or from her life of faith in Christ.[35] And therefore, on the very rare occasions when the pope as leader of the Church tells the world what the Church believes, and that only in the areas of faith and morals (the expression is *ex cathedra*, "from the chair" of Peter), then what he says will be the truth. (It does not mean that the truth of the Gospel is adequately expressed by doctrinal definitions: formulations are admitted always to be limited by culture, by history, and by language. No formulation—including that of the doctrine of infallibility—is ever the last word on the subject.)

When the First Vatican Council made the formulation, opponents brought up Honorius. Honorius, the pope, had been wrong! Following this objection it was stated that infallibility does not refer to what the pope himself thinks, says, writes, or even publicly announces. It is the Church as a whole that counts when it says what it believes; this point was insisted upon at the Second Vatican Council (1962–1965).[36] According to Catholic belief, the pope, speaking on behalf of the bishops and the people of God, is infallible only when he proclaims what the Church believes. And the Church had rejected Honorius' opinion.

Modern theologians have tended to exonerate Honorius entirely, saying not only that he was not speaking *ex cathedra*, but that what he wrote is, in fact, utterly unexceptionable.[37] The incident, and its use in 1870, did however serve to clarify the formulation of the concept of papal infallibility.

HONORIUS, THE BUILDER

Pope Honorius I was apparently not a man of theological sophistication, but apart from the incident of the letter to Sergius, he does appear to have been a practical and efficacious leader. His pontificate stands near the very beginning of what would later be called the Middle Ages; although, according to another evaluation of those times, it immediately precedes the early Dark Ages. Born in Campania, Honorius was the son of a Roman consul and a fervent admirer of his older contemporary Pope Gregory the Great, whose work he vowed to continue. He laboured to achieve peace in northern Italy, inducing the schismatic states of Istria and Venice to be reconciled with Rome, and further reached agreements with Spain, Sardinia, and Epirus. He continued the policy of Gregory the Great in the evangelization of Britain, and created two archbishoprics in England; the first to hold office were Honorius of Canterbury and Paulinus of York. The Anglican Church still has two archbishoprics in England, Canterbury and York; the archbishopric of Wales was created in 1920.

Honorius was one of the great building popes.[38] Still standing today in Rome are two churches he founded: Sant'Agnese fuori le Mura and San Pancrazio. The latter basilica was rebuilt in the Middle Ages and restored in 1609 (at about the same time as Sant'Agnese's), but suffered serious damage and looting in 1798 and again in 1849. The church stands outside the walls near the via Aurelia Antica, a highway historically of value for armies approaching Rome from the west. The apse of San Pancrazio's, despite later accretions, is still the one Honorius built.[39]

Underneath San Pancrazio's survives a semi-annular crypt, also provided by Honorius. This was an arrangement for ordering pilgrim crowds and preventing unseemly jostling at the grave of a saint. Pilgrims would walk along a semi-circular passageway underneath the church's apse in order to approach the saint's grave. From the centre of the half-circle a short, straight corridor led directly to the tomb underneath the altar; each person in turn could look down the corridor and see the tomb, and then had to move on. The semi-annular crypt at the grave of San Pancrazio's is the second-oldest example of its kind after that at St. Peter's, which had been created by Gregory the Great, the man upon whom Honorius modelled himself.

Near the traditional site of Saint Paul's martyrdom outside the city walls to the south, Honorius founded a church in 625 at the monastery Ad Aquas Salvias ("at the saving waters"), now known as "three fountains," Tre Fontane.[40] In the 650s a monastic congregation arrived at this monastery in Rome from Bethsaloë in modern Iraq, bearing with it the head of the Persian martyr Anastasius, murdered by King Chosroës II in 628; the monastery's church was called St. Anastasius by the eighth century, and Saints Vincent and Anastasius after 1225, when the relics of the Spanish martyr Saint Vincent were brought to Rome.[41] Over the centuries this church was entirely rebuilt; the one we see today was completed in 1221.

THE GIFT HE BEARS

In the apse mosaic at Sant'Agnese's, Pope Honorius I is the figure portrayed as founder,[42] carrying in his arms (both they and his hands decorously covered by his cloak) a model of a church. It was long thought that this model was a purely conventional representation of a generic church, with curtains at the front door as was the custom of the time. When Sant'Agnese's was restored (1956–1958), the medieval plaster that covered the outside walls was removed.[43] The restorers discovered with excitement that the model in Honorius' arms is, in fact, a fairly exact copy of the part of the building that stood above ground level in the seventh century. The pope's purple mosaic cloak covers up the buried lower half of the church.

The two black rectangles on the side of the model can now be seen as bricked-up areas behind the pepper pot turrets of the chapels on the side of the church along the via di Sant'Agnese. They were doorways that once led directly into the upper galleries in the church from what was then ground level. The original wooden lintels are intact. A small window with its lintel (not shown on the model) has also been revealed. The façade of the church had previously appeared to have four small rectangular windows, rather than a doorway and one window on either side as in the model. Today, facing the front of the building, we can see that originally there were indeed two windows and a door, as the model shows. The threshold of this door, high above the present entrance, shows us exactly where the floor of the gallery lies: this was the door that the model shows hung with draperies, leading into the galleries of the church.

The present roof is higher and more sloping than the original one depicted in the model; the roof was presumably altered, and a frontal with a round window (an *oculus*, or "eye") was added, in approximately 1000 A.D. (There are three windows below the oculus, rather than the two on the model.) Behind the triangular frontal inside the building, a fresco portraying peacocks with garlands was found, dating to the twelfth or thirteenth century. Peacocks symbolize immortality in Christian art; they create their own small epiphany every time their tails open out into a brilliant wheel filled with eyes.[44] They appear on either side of the round window, which is thus made to signify eternal light. The fresco cannot be seen today unless one climbs into the space above the church's seventeenth-century ceiling.[45]

PALLIUMS, AND THE CEREMONY OF THE LAMBS

The ecclesiastical clothing of Honorius in the apse, and of his companion on the other side of Agnes, shows us that she has been given a kind of sacerdotal dress,[46] but far richer than earthly priests' vestments. The popes are wearing white dalmatics, and over them purple cloaks known as *planetae* or chasubles. A planeta, literally a "floater," was a thin and costly version of a chasuble. The latter word comes from

Latin *casula*, a diminutive of *casa*, a hut: a cape or cloak was thought of as a shelter, in the same class as a primitive house. The original chasuble was a serviceable poncholike cape with a hood, which gradually became ecclesiastical dress; the hood was abolished for church vestments in 438. Chasubles are still worn by Roman Catholic priests saying Mass.

The jewelled overgarment Agnes wears has become, on the two men, the papal *pallium*, which is what marks them as indisputably bishops of Rome. In their case, the pallium has become a narrow white band, fringed at the ends and embroidered with small black crosses. Like Agnes' garment, this pallium is crossed in a V in front, and strips hang straight down, front and back. The pallium has been worn by bishops of Rome ever since the fourth century.[47] Even earlier than the fourth century in the Eastern church, a cloaklike forerunner of the pallium, in Greek an *omophorion* ("worn over the shoulders"), was ecclesiatical dress, as it still is in Orthodox churches. A pallium very similar to the two in the apse mosaic is worn by the pope and by his fellow archbishops today. The style has changed, but not the colour: the modern pallium is round rather than V-shaped, and the straight pieces front and back are usually only about a foot long.

The symbolism of the white woollen pallium is that its wearer is an earthly "shepherd" of the Church. The wool symbolizes the faithful as "lambs," which shepherds used to carry on their shoulders when they were in special need of care. One of the earliest sculpted images of Christ shows him as a young shepherd in a short tunic and buskins, carrying a lamb on his shoulders in an attitude well known in ancient Greek and Roman art: Jesus had called himself "the good shepherd."[48] After his Resurrection, Jesus spoke to Peter, giving him an opportunity to make up for his triple betrayal of his master in the time of trial before the Crucifixion. Three times Jesus asked Peter, "Do you love me?" and each time, after Peter had declared his love, Jesus said, "Feed my lambs," "Feed my lambs," "Feed my sheep."[49] According to Catholic Christendom, the pope's leadership of the Church is inherited from Peter; and the wearing of the pallium over the pope's shoulders is in memory of the injunction to Peter to become the "shepherd" of Christ's "sheep" and "lambs."

The duty extends also to all Christians, but in a very specific manner to clergy, to bishops, and to their superiors, the archbishops. In the Roman Catholic Church every archbishop is granted the wearing of the pallium. It is a favour the archbishop has to petition for, within three months of his appointment. Asking for and receiving the pallium expresses the jurisdiction he is granted by the pope, and also his allegiance. When Pope Honorius I appointed the first two archbishops in England, he did so by sending them these insignia; and the arms of the Anglican archbishopric of Canterbury still include the pallium. In modern times, a Roman Catholic archbishop usually goes to Rome to receive his pallium. He wears it only in his own diocese, because only there does he have jurisdiction. The pope, in contrast, can wear the pallium anywhere on earth—and he does so whenever he wears priestly vestments. He puts it on last so that it is always clearly visible, just as it is on the two popes in the apse mosaic at Sant'Agnese's.

Each pallium-bearer gets his own personal pallium, and he is buried wearing it, in recognition that ecclesiastical office is never to be hereditary. Before anybody can receive a pallium, however, it is traditional to petition Saint Peter himself to bless the sign of authority. The newly woven palliums are laid inside a silver-gilt box and placed in a special alcove at the *confessio* of Saint Peter—as close as possible to the spot where Peter is believed to have been buried, and over which the enormous basilica of St. Peter's is built. The palliums remain there for the night before the feast of Saints Peter and Paul, June 29. On that day the pope invests new archbishops in a ceremony called the Mass of the Rings; in addition to a pallium, each archbishop receives a ring, which, like a wedding ring, symbolizes binding promises.

But even before the palliums are woven, the entire process begins at the church of St. Agnes outside the Walls. On the feast day of Saint Agnes every year (January 21), two live lambs are brought to the church, placed on the altar, and blessed. They are crowned, one with red roses and one with white roses; these are attributes of Saint Agnes, in her double status as martyr and as virgin, respectively. The lambs are symbolic of innocence and purity, and also of Christ as the lamb,[50] whose death Agnes has imitated in her martyrdom. The name *Hagnes* means "pure" in Greek; the word *agnus* ("lamb" in Latin) turns her name into a pun. A lamb is therefore the attribute of Agnes, together with the palm for her victorious martyrdom.

The lambs come from the Trappist priory of Tre Fontane, outside the walls to the south of the city, traditionally the place where Saint Paul was beheaded. The original church at this site was, as we saw, founded by Pope Honorius himself. Every year a monk who is a shepherd at the community's fellow monastery at Val Sereno near Pisa chooses the two best white lambs from their flock and brings them to the Trappists in Rome. The custom is for the two youngest monks at the Roman monastery to take them, on the appropriate date, to the pope to be blessed in the Sala Clementina, a hall for private audiences with the pope at the Vatican. Vatican staff then wash and brush the lambs, and crown them with roses. By custom one lamb has the letters SAV in gold paper stuck to its wool, and the other SAM: Sancta Agnes Virgo and Sancta Agnes Martyr.[51] Until the advent of cars, it was the custom for a crowd to process through the streets of Rome and out along the via Nomentana accompanying the lambs, lying on cushions in baskets that were carried on the backs of flower-decked donkeys. By the feast day of the saint the almond trees in Rome—always among the first fruit trees to flower in the Mediterranean region—are often in bud and a few in flower: the feast is also a spring festival.

Today, the lambs arrive at Sant'Agnese's by car. They are kept briefly in an annex of the church on a table covered in flowers, and then taken in procession through the ranks of the congregation by bearers carrying them on leafy palanquins, still on their cushions in their baskets. Loud baas usually delight the crowd. After they have been placed on the altar and blessed, they are returned to the table outside, where people are allowed to see them and pat them when the service is over. They are then whisked off to the pope's residence at Castel Gandolfo in the Alban hills, to join the flocks kept there. When they have grown, they are shorn and their wool woven, by the Benedictine nuns at the church of Santa Cecilia in Trastevere, into palliums for archbishops. (Obviously, the wool of two sheep is no longer sufficient for all the palliums bestowed, even though palliums are quite small; it is said, however, that care is taken that some wool from these particular sheep is included in each one.)

The age of the custom is uncertain; the earliest reference so far known is a document dated 1442,[52] when Benedictine nuns inhabited the monastery buildings at Sant'Agnese's. It is still Benedictine nuns who do the weaving. There are many descriptions of the lamb festival, especially by travellers to Rome, from the sixteenth century to the present.

WHO IS THE OTHER POPE?

The two popes, one on either side of Saint Agnes in the apse of the church, are wearing identical seventh-century ecclesiastical dress, and constitute valuable evidence, for historians of costume, of apparel at that date. They are both tonsured. It is common in all cultures and religions for monks' heads to be shaven, either partly or completely. The styling of head hair is, culturally speaking, an individualizing physical attribute, and men in groups (including soldiers and other aggressive collectivities) often forgo their hair as an expression of determination, equality among their number, and brotherhood. It is a macho sign: long hair is often regarded as "feminine," and in any case locks can be a nuisance when men have intensely physical work to do. Hair styling can signify humility, however, and a desire to renounce gentility and mainstream fashions: ascetic men often either wear long hair (as in conventional depictions of Jesus) or shave their heads bald. Christian monks have often partly shaved their heads. Among Celtic monks, all hair was shaved off from the forehead as far back as a line extending over the head from ear to ear. The Catholic tonsure (from Latin *tonsura*, "shearing") shows obedience, and engagement in a group—but also humility. It leaves a fringe all round, in memory, it is said, of Christ's crown of thorns. The custom began about a hundred years before this mosaic was made.

Who is the second pope, the one carrying a Bible with a cross on its cover? No one, in modern times at least, has been sure. The *Liber Pontificalis* says that Pope Symmachus (498–514) restored the apse at Sant'Agnese's.[53] Most writers have therefore taken Symmachus to be the other figure: who more deserving of recognition when Honorius had the apse mosaic made? Scholars have even speculated that two figures, one of them Symmachus, might have been portrayed accompanying Agnes in an earlier apse mosaic; Honorius had the overall design copied, but he himself took the place of Symmachus on Agnes' right. Which begs the question of the identity of Symmachus' companion in the earlier design.

But only very recently the architectural history of the church of Sant'Agnese has been shaken to its core: the entire background of the church has had to be rethought. Symmachus repaired an apse here— but it may well not have been the apse of this church. We shall look at the truth of the matter in Chapter Eight when we move outside the building. Since Friedrich Wilhelm Deichmann, the archaeologist, made his momentous observations in 1946, the Symmachus theory seems questionable. But most writers on the church still repeat it, *faute de mieux*.

Another theory has suggested that this mysterious figure is Pope Liberius (352–366), because he is known to have set up a marble altar over the grave of Agnes in 358.[54] A further candidate for the other pope is Silvester (314–337), under whose pontificate "Constantine built a basilica to the holy martyr Agnes, at the request of his daughter [Constantina], and also a baptistery in that place, where his sister Constantia and [his] daughter were baptized by bishop Silvester."[55] Other scholars speculate that the second pope is included in the mosaic only for the sake of symmetry—a sort of generic "other pope." But this seems unlikely, given the importance of the figure and the tendency of churches to opt for meaning.

Although I have not seen or heard the idea mentioned, I like to believe that the pope whom Honorius made his partner in the apse mosaic is Gregory I, the Great. In spite of the fact that five papacies intervened between Gregory and Honorius, only twenty-one years had passed between the death of one man and the beginning of the pontificate of the other. Gregory was an older contemporary of Honorius, and a man Honorius greatly admired and tried to emulate. Like Gregory, Honorius was probably himself a monk, which might explain the tonsures. Both Gregory and Honorius were noblemen. Both abjured personal possessions and turned the papal residence into a monastery. Being a pope who supported monks was to take sides in a rivalry between pro-monastic and pro-diocesan clergy. Only Pope Boniface IV (608–615), among the five popes between Gregory and Honorius, had been pro-monastic. The epitaph on Honorius' tomb described him as "following in the footsteps of Gregory."[56]

LIGHT AND LIFE

Underneath the apse mosaic, Honorius placed an inscription in strange and corrupt seventh-century Latin, gold on a dark blue ground. (It may be that later restorers—or even the original mosaicists themselves, who were almost certainly Greek—had trouble with the Latin.) Corrected, therefore, and translated, the inscription says something like this:

> This picture stands up aloft, golden with neatly cut cubes of metal.[57] Here daylight itself is embraced and enclosed—as if Dawn, arising out of snow-cold waters, breaks through torn clouds and irrigates the fields with dew; or as if Iris, the rainbow, spreads her colours, glittering like the fiery peacock. He whose power fixed the boundary between night and day[58] has expelled darkness from the tombs of the martyrs. Look up! With a glance take it all in! Bishop Honorius has given these votive gifts—you can tell him by his clothing, and by what he has made. He shines; his aspect shows the generous heart he bears.

Whatever the accuracy of the text and its interpretation, it is clear that light and colour are what enchanted the seventh-century viewer of this mosaic. The dew at dawn, rainbows, and peacocks' tails were what it was expected to bring to mind.

Under the arch in front of the apse we have a very earthly depiction in mosaic of flowers and fruit growing out of two pots, each decorated with coloured stripes and standing on either side at the foot of the arch's curve. The two garlands, a traditional element of apse mosaics, include leaves, grapes, white roses, pomegranates, lilies, red roses, pears, pine cones, and more lilies. They meet at the top of the arch, in a silver cross on a blue circle outlined in white: earth's beauty lifts up the crowning apex of the cosmos, the Cross, where earth meets God. In the Cross, the vertical intersects with the horizontal in the shape of the human form. Christians believe that God, becoming human, suffered the worst that human beings could devise. And through his submission and forgiveness, Christ transformed the instrument of pain and infamy into a revelation of love and hope. An early Christian sign put it this way:

$$\phi$$
$$\zeta\omega\eta$$
$$\varsigma$$

The vertical line of the cross is *phos*, Greek for "light"; the horizontal line is *zoë*, "life." God's loving light strikes down from above, illuminating all of life with its transcendent glory.

6

LIVING STONES:
Chapels, Left Side

....

Whenever Christians want to rebel against the organized Church with its hierarchies and traditions, against the prestige inherent in beautiful buildings, against having to fit into structures instead of feeling free to create and expand into the new—then they tend to complain about churches. After a while, if they continue to meet at all, they prefer bare halls, basements, living rooms, and garages in which to pray together: in these they feel they are being purer, more energetic, approaching closer to their roots. It is a true and faithful option, and often a necessary one for those who choose it.

On the other hand, a well-made church that survives such times of purgation can offer almost limitless riches for the imagination, and therefore for the soul. It is, after all, entirely natural for human beings to find inspiration in direct contact with their past, with what has gone into creating their loves. And people who have access to a spiritual tradition commonly know at a profound (though not necessarily conscious) level how to "read" a church, and can respond to it instinctively. Deliberately to forego such pleasure and enrichment is an ascetic feat, and one to be undertaken only with full knowledge of the reasons for it and the risks and losses involved.

For anyone who is not spiritually allergic to churches, to walk into a beautiful church is to encounter understanding, to hear echoes of the soul's own experiences of epiphany. Such stimulus and concurrence need not involve anything theological. It can be a matter simply of sunlight striking through coloured glass and dappling the wall opposite, of the smell of flowers and lingering hints of incense, of the silent cold of stone, of movements of the soul that respond directly to columns, arches, domes, colouring and carving, or to the memory of the people who have filled this building in the past. I myself find it an invariable satisfaction just to see the dark entrance of a church (open!), even on a quick drive through an unknown town. It's a hole in the hard walls of the rackety everyday, a reassurance that, thanks to the care and attention of my fellow human beings, a place has been made ready for silent contact with something enormous, something present, for anyone who wants it.

Christians build, and love, and spend care on churches—yet they should need none. "The real altar of God," wrote Pope Gregory the Great, "is the mind and the heart of the just."[1] It is indeed impossible to appreciate a church without a sense of the extent to which it will not, cannot, do. The most beautiful Gothic cathedral is bound to fail in its endeavour to show forth God. How then must a Christian feel about a church that is just plain ugly? The answer has to lie in the basic admission that churches never have a hold on God—and also in an understanding that truth can exist within failure, and is always something other than "taste." The Jewish philosopher Simone Weil has described a mystical experience in which God communicated with her at length. He took her into a church: "It was new," she wrote, "and ugly"—there was no need for age or beauty to validate the encounter. He told her to fall on her knees before the altar. Afterwards, they climbed up together into an attic room and talked for a long time, "like old friends,"—and then he sent her away.[2] She had to return to the world, just as Catholic congregations are dismissed after Mass: *Ite, missa est*. "Go. The Mass is ended."

Church and world form a paradoxical pair, in which Christians are expected to be totally devoted to the world, yet not to be taken in by it, in both senses of the phrase. Christians do not believe that culture has the last word over morality—that all morality is "relative." Implicit throughout their Scriptures is the belief that, as the modern philosopher Emmanuel Lévinas put it, "Morality does not belong to culture; the former permits us to judge the latter."[3] Yet for Christians, culture is to be entered into and treated with respect because it is absolutely essential as a medium (though it is no more than a medium) for human self-expression; there is no such thing as belief unmediated by culture. An ongoing Christian project in recent times is that of learning to recognize and embrace the plurality of cultures, and to accept and learn from previously foreign cultures as mediums, expressions, and revelations of spiritual insights.

A further opposition is recognized and then collapsed: that between Church and church. It is no accident that one word denotes both building and people. "Church" is from Greek *kyriakon*, "house of the Lord." In Latin languages the word for "church" (*iglesia, église, església, chiesa*) is rooted in Greek *ekklesia*, "group of people."[4] In the first case the word comes from the building and is applied to the people; in the second the word refers to the people and the building is metaphorical.

The poetic link between people and building is made concrete in the ceremony for dedicating a church to God:[5] this liturgy treats the new temple as though it is a person, being baptized. The walls are sprinkled with water (as are the people attending the ceremony) and anointed. Individually, the members of the congregation are expected to "identify" with the church building, making the association with their own baptism and confirmation, when each person became "a temple of the Holy Spirit."[6] All around the walls of any Catholic church are the marks where it was anointed on the day of its dedication to God. These marks are twelve little crosses representing the twelve gates of the Heavenly Jerusalem, the twelve tribes of Israel, the twelve Apostles. The ones at Sant'Agnese's are particularly beautiful. They are white and rayed like sunbursts, the four ends of the cross's beams opening into lily flowers; each cross is enclosed in a brown circle and a green square.

Saint Paul and other writers of New Testament Epistles insist upon the way in which Christians themselves, this time as a group, are "the Church," symbolized by a building: "You are part of a building that has the apostles and prophets for its foundations, and Christ Jesus himself for its cornerstone. As the whole structure is aligned on him, all grow into one holy temple in the Lord; and you too, in him, are being built into a house where God lives, in the Spirit." Christians are to be "living stones, making a spiritual house."[7] Saint Francis of Assisi, soon after his conversion in 1205, experienced an epiphany in the little crumbling church of San Damiano: he "heard" Christ telling him, "Restore my church." Obediently he repaired the dilapidated building.

Only later did he understand what the command really meant: Francis was being asked not merely to fix a church building, but to save and reinvigorate the Church as a whole, the Church as a people.[8]

Christians are expected to have a lively ambivalence not only about church buildings, but also about the very idea of being part of a group of people. Christianity sets out to achieve something anthropologically and sociologically impossible, a contradiction in terms: to be a group without boundaries. In spite of many fallings-off down the centuries, the ideal remains and is clearly enunciated in Scripture: Christians have to try to shut nobody out. The Christian ideal is to transcend race and even family: every human being, and not merely "one's own," should receive unconditional favour. On one occasion Jesus was addressing an audience of people when his mother and his family (who are depicted as being at this point hostile to and embarrassed by his sudden missionary zeal) passed him a message asking him to leave the gathering and rejoin them—to return to where he "belonged." He refused. It was this crowd, he said, people who were thirsting for God, who were his real family.[9] As for "sinners" being unacceptable, Christ was repeatedly accused of preferring their company to that of the "proper."

The group of Christians, therefore, is to require no more than one simple step on the part of an individual who wants to join them. The ritual formalization of this step is baptism (literally "dipping") in water. Baptism is called a sacrament; it is a physical sign of a spiritual fact and a personal decision.

The baptismal initiation rite at Sant'Agnese's takes place outside the church itself, in a nineteenth-century annex to the church and canonry. The finely weathered orange stucco façade of this building makes up one side of the courtyard that visitors pass through in order to descend into the church; its door is fitted into a large glassed-in arch. Inside is a rectangular hall; it is here that the lambs are brought before the blessing on the feast of Saint Agnes. The baptismal basin or font (for pouring water, not immersion) rests on a small and ancient pagan altar that was found on Rome's Oppian Hill; it has wreaths and amphorae carved on its four marble sides. (One shudders to think what early Christians would have had to say about baptism being performed over a Roman sacrificial altar.) Over the marble basin for the water is a bell-shaped copper lid surmounted with a cross. The whole is surrounded by wrought-iron protective fencing.

Christian families baptize their babies because they intend to bring them up as Christians. Later, each child will make up his or her own mind about whether to remain in the Church or not. (The "walls" of the Church are completely permeable: people can leave, at least from a formal point of view, just as easily as they can enter.) After baptism at the font at Sant'Agnese's, the baby is taken down the steps into the church—just as he or she has been taken into the Church, a "living stone" to help create the community. During the nineteenth century, baptism at Sant'Agnese's was conducted in the passageway down; there is a niche in the left-hand wall where the font once stood. An engraved cross appears on its curving wall as *axis mundi*, the Tree of Life, bearing flowers and approached by doves (human souls). The cross stands on a mound of earth with four streams pouring out of it, denoting the four Evangelists, the four rivers of Paradise, and the waters of baptism.

Many churches stress the initiatory aspect of baptism by placing their baptismal fonts inside the church, but near the front door—often in a side chapel dedicated to Saint John the Baptist. Every baptism recalls the moment when Christ—who, as God, was sinless—nevertheless entered into the waters of baptism and so initiated his public ministry. The other possibility is for the font to be placed in front, not far from the altar itself. This position emphasizes both the centrality of the ceremony to all of Christian life, and the importance of the community: when the font is in front, baptism can be performed before the assembled congregation, often during Mass. The baby, baptized and anointed with the oil of the Spirit,[10] is held up by the priest to be applauded by the welcoming community. He or she is then dressed in new white clothes and presented with a candle, lit from the tall Easter candle—a symbol of Christ as "the light of the world"— that stands near the font. (One of the child's godparents "stands in" for the baby in order to hold this small candle.)

Often the priest walks down the nave afterwards, sprinkling the congregation on either side of him with water. For this operation he uses either a special ritual sprinkler or a bunch of leaves dipped in the water, as each person consciously renews the commitment made at his or her own baptism. This action is called aspersion and the sprinkler an aspergillum, from the Latin translation of the psalm, *Asperges me*: "Sprinkle me with the hyssop, and I shall be clean: wash me, and I shall be whiter than snow."[11]

GUILT AND SHAME, FORGIVENESS AND REVENGE

At first, Christians performed the initiatory action of baptism in rivers and streams—as when John the Baptist, at the Jordan River, invited people to purify themselves and begin a new life, giving physical affirmation to their enlightenment by means of the sign of water. Later, Christians constructed tiled baptismal pools, with steps down, into which neophytes would walk and be submerged in the waters, rising again into a life of following Christ. Many Christians still prefer the full drama of totally entering into the water to be baptized. But because the water is a symbol, it has been possible to reduce the quantity needed. A splash of water poured over the person's head is often thought sufficient—a part standing for the whole.

Like the bread and wine of the Eucharist, the water of baptism is as simple as could be. But again the symbol reverberates throughout the entire system of belief. The water means washing, of course—cleanliness, purity. It refers to grace and enlightenment as the life of the soul, as water is necessary for physical life. It both points to and expresses one of the most characteristic of Christian demands: that of forgiveness. The Christian practice of nonviolence begins with forgiveness— not with one person's forgiveness of another, but with the prior forgiveness of the person by God. Baptism signifies that the Christian's new life begins with an awareness of having been himself or herself forgiven: "The Lord has forgiven you; now you must do the same."[12]

It is knowledge of that original mercy that is to result in Christians striving to forgive other people who have done them harm. Pardon— real pardon, not the hateful power ploy that makes an act of "forgiving" crush the offender—happens in the soul of the forgiver. It is an exquisitely difficult giving up and letting go of the past, and a concentration on the present, on one's own (and not another's) "journey" of the soul. To forgive is to forgo revenge. The guilty person, on the other hand, needs first to face the truth and feel guilty, and then to try to express regret and make what reparations are possible.

If it becomes possible for a wronged person to forgive, then he or she will be freed from the self-inflicted damage that arises from resentment. Forgiveness is a gift, as the word itself implies, as does the word "pardon," from *donare*, "to give." The meaning is that forgiveness can never be demanded—it has to be freely proffered. To forgive is not, therefore, to "lose" anything. Only the freedom inherent in giving, and ultimately the ability to love—after having given up hating—somebody who has harmed you, defines forgiveness. It is an immensely difficult and demanding ideal, even to wish one could pardon. And no law can prescribe forgiveness—it has to come from the individual heart.

But if no one will forgive, then human beings have no recourse but to a shame/revenge mechanism. Here, people are defined by what they have done, or by what other people have done in their name. They may even be defined by what has been done to them, as when a raped woman is considered to be "spoilt property," to have been "shamed" and so to have "brought shame on" her family. A society that uses shame rather than guilt as a regulating device usually believes also in fate, which, as we have seen, Christianity rejects. Instead Christianity advocates forgiveness, which enables human beings to feel guilt rather than shame for the wrong they have done—guilt being preferable to shame precisely because guilt, unlike shame, can be forgiven. Revenge, which is indispensable for the recuperation of honour after its loss through shame, can be renounced if guilt replaces shame. This is the meaning of Christ's difficult demands that his followers "turn the other cheek" rather than strike back, and forgive others over and over again.[13] But forgiveness is possible only when people feel that they themselves have received mercy. Mercy "in the beginning," from God, is a further meaning of baptism.

The Catholic Church has a sacrament of forgiveness, where the contrite sinner confesses his or her sin to a priest, who absolves the guilt in the name of the Church. Admitting to another person the wrong one has done is the beginning of the possibility of change. This sacrament, called confession or reconciliation, may (though it need not) take place in a confessional. This is a wooden stall with a seat for the priest, a kneeler for the person confessing, and a screen between them, so that the sinner need not be face to face with the priest. The priest, or confessor in this situation, is not merely himself but a representative of the Church as a whole. There are two confessionals in Sant'Agnese's church, standing inside two of the side chapels. Both are modern, and it must be admitted that they are depressingly ugly examples of their kind.

Baptism (which is related to confession in that it is the first time a person is sacramentally forgiven for sin) is also an initiation rite; unlike confession, it can happen only once. As an initiation it symbolizes the neophyte's "death." Initiation always entails the death that is inherent in any change: one "dies to" whatever status or way of thinking is being left behind. (One "dies to" hate when one forgives.) Christianity is a religion of transformation, of conversion both sudden and ongoing, of change. Death itself is believed to be an initiation into life with God. The founder of Christianity underwent death—forgiving those who killed him;[14] but Christians believe that he lives. Baptism signifies, therefore, death in the waters and then resurrection to new life for each person who chooses to undergo it. This new life involves associating oneself with the group of people who have also decided to follow Christ.

Christians are individuals—in a group. They are a group, and initiated as such—but must strive to avoid creating barriers between themselves and others, "judging" them[15] and "defining" themselves against them. Once again the paradoxes are evident, and very difficult to keep in balance. In the modern Western world, in fact, Christians feel they must fight for community—the apparent opposite of individualism—since individualism, for reasons that include a strong impetus from Christianity itself, has so triumphantly conquered the field. The "community" that Christians now strive for does not mean the Christian community only, but the very idea of solidarity as part of the common good. As always in the Christian view, whenever one of the opposites becomes rampant at the expense of the other, things fall apart.

THE PASCHAL CANDLE

A paschal (Easter) candle several feet tall stands beside the baptismal font at Sant'Agnese's. There is one in every Catholic church, near the altar or near the baptismal font. It symbolizes the close connection of baptism with Christ's Resurrection, a relationship that is celebrated during the climactic liturgy of the Church year, which takes place at about midnight on Easter eve. The service begins with a bonfire being built and lit outside the church—new fire, light in the dark night. (The past two nights and days have been for Christians the darkest time of the year, beginning with the memory of Christ's horrifying death and continuing in the bleak silence thereafter.) From the Easter fire the big paschal candle is lit, and from it all the people present, each holding his or her own candle, spread the light by handing it on to each other.

A procession with lighted candles follows, the people entering the dark, empty church, the priest leading with the burning paschal candle, which symbolizes Christ, "the light of the world" that "shines in the darkness and the darkness does not comprehend it."[16] The priest sings three times, each time at a higher register, "Christ our light!" On this candle has been written the number of years since Christ's birth—in countries influenced by Christianity, this means the date—and into the wax have been pressed five lumps of incense, for the wounds where Christ was pierced, in his hands, his feet, and his heart. The incense signifies that Christ's body, still bearing its wounds, lives now in glory.

The service then launches into the Exsultet, the great ninth-century hymn that is sung by one person, standing beside the paschal candle. Its flame is the only light in the church—the people blow out the candles they have been carrying. The song remembers the bees who made the candle's wax. Unlike resin, which is "forced from pine-trees by fire, or wept like tears from cedars suffering the strokes of the axe," according to the Ambrosian liturgy for blessing the candle, wax is given freely by the bees, just as God gave himself freely to us. Bees were believed not only to provide their wax without recourse to violence, but also to produce offspring without sex; in this they were symbols of the Church, married to God alone and prolific in its children and in the graces it provides for them. "The heavenly throngs of angels exult. . . . The Earth rejoices in the light; she comes to life in the passing of the dark. . . . The Church [this church] shines in the brilliance of this great light, these walls resound with the voices of a great people. . . . This is the night! This is the night when the Israelites passed through the Red Sea to salvation; this is the night in which Christ broke the chains of death! . . . Oh necessary sin of Adam, which brought us Christ, black death's destroyer! Oh happy fault, that caused our knowing so great a saviour! Let hatreds flee away, let peace come in, let worldly power bow down."

During the ceremony that follows, with the church lit still with the Easter candle alone, a number of the stories of salvation history are read from the Old Testament. Several of them are directly connected, in the Christian view of things, with baptism: Genesis ("Beginning"), with the Spirit hovering over the waters of chaos; Noah and all the creatures in the ark floating on the waters of the Flood; Abraham being told that he will be "the father of a multitude of nations"; the story of Isaac, who for Christians is the "type" of Christ; the miraculous passage of the Israelites through the sea to safety; the prophecy of Isaiah inviting "all who thirst to come to the waters."[17]

After these readings, gradually advancing in time as they do, the church, usually shortly after midnight, is made suddenly to blaze with light, to symbolize Christ's Resurrection on Easter morning. At this point the Easter bells ring out (bells have rung seldom or not at all throughout Lent,[18] and not at all during the two preceding days). The members of the congregation may also bring with them their own dinner bells and ring them all together. The priest presiding slowly intones in song the ancient, majestic declaration: "Christ is risen, Alleluia, Alleluia, Alleluia!" and the congregation repeats it together. In Catholic churches the word "Alleluia" has not been heard during the forty days of Lent.[19] Sudden light and thrilling new sound also signify conversion as sudden insight and transformation, and the epiphanies each person experiences in his or her own life. The "opposites" of instantaneity (the sudden light and sudden sound) versus duration (the long story of the gradual conversion of each person and of all humankind) receive ritual expression.

Later, the baptismal font and the water ("this holy and innocent creature") are blessed. The priest may plunge the paschal candle's base into the font: fire uniting with water, vertical intersecting with horizontal, Christ entering the waters of Jordan at his baptism, the fiery Spirit "making the water fruitful." The gesture insists on the conjunction of opposites, and creates an image decidedly sexual. Oil is poured on the water too—another symbol of the Spirit of Peace. During the service on this night, adult catechumens—people who have been studying the Christian faith during the weeks of Lent and who have decided to become Christians—are baptized. Every other baptism, throughout the year, will also involve lighting a candle from the Easter candle, to symbolize new life as a Christian, being "lit" from Christ. At every funeral the paschal candle will burn beside the dead person's body, a symbol of faith that Christ will take this soul to himself forever.

MARY

The many symbols for the Church, often physically depicted in church buildings as well as used in prayer and poetry, include the tent and Ark of the Covenant; a fountain (lifegiving water, baptism); a lamp; a city built on a hill and therefore visible to all; a vine (Jesus said, "I am the vine—you are the branches," and Israel saw itself as "God's vineyard");[20] a tree (the Tree of Life, the Cross); Noah's ark; a ship with the Cross as its mast; Christ's body and the body of every human being; a woman, a bride, and most specifically the Mother of Jesus, the Virgin Mary. In Catholic churches Mary is always given important space, and she draws to herself complex symbolism on many levels.

Catholic Christendom considers Mary to be first and finest among all the people who have ever made up the Church. She was indispensable to the revelation, because she freely said "yes" to God's plan of entering into humanity. Response is what religion is all about. Mary is seen as the supreme example of one who responded to God, who let God act, who accepted God's gift of himself: she is the model disciple. In the Gospel story, she was told she would bear an "illegitimate" child, with all the stigma (shame more than guilt) that she knew she was liable to receive on that account. Not knowing what would come of it, she nevertheless agreed, and God then entered human history—beginning life in the world as one of the poor and as a child of "shame"—in a manner and with consequences she could never have imagined.

At three climactic moments in the New Testament story, the words "let your will be done" are spoken to God. Jesus said them when he realized in the Garden of Gethsemane that his own death was imminent: "Not my will but yours be done." They appear in the prayer that Jesus taught all Christians to say: "Thy will be done on earth, as it is in heaven." And they form Mary's *fiat*, "Let it be done to me according to your word."[21] Did Mary teach these words to her son? In any case, according to the story, she said them first.[22]

She also decided when it was time for Jesus to reveal his powers. It happened at the marriage feast at Cana, when the water was turned to wine: the physical was being divinized through the coming of Christ. He thought his time had not yet come; she knew he would not refuse to save the wedding party from being spoiled, and despite his protest, she prevailed.[23] And Mary—unlike nearly all the frightened disciples—stood by the Cross as her son died in agony.[24] To many Christians Mary is the one who knows what it is like to stand by, suffering helplessly, when a loved one—child, lover, parent, friend—is in pain. In Catholic countries during Holy Week—the week that culminates in Easter—people remember the Passion, the sufferings of Jesus when he was put to death. Always immensely important in the processions and other ceremonies recalling the Passion is the mourning Madonna: Mary who weeps for her son and weeps with every human being in pain. Mary is the patron saint, the understanding model, for anyone suffering in sympathy with and because of their own.

As his mother, she treated Jesus well, and Christians have felt that they, had they been living then, would probably not have behaved as she did—they might have joined the crowd, yelling for his execution. They suspect that they would have been no better than Peter (the "rock" upon whom the Church was built!), who denied knowing Jesus as soon as he felt himself in danger.[25] There is immense gratitude to her, for having been good to him and having stood by him as he died on the Cross. Christians have also felt, down the centuries, that he would be especially likely to listen to her, and that she would be forgiving and merciful to a repentant sinner no matter what he or she had done. It was women's role to be kind, where men were supposed to uphold justice and enforce it. And therefore many Christians have asked for Mary's help, often turning from God—from whom Christians are supposed to expect mercy—to her first. To think of God as just and not merciful is, in fact, a heresy, which involves the further heresy of thinking of God as "male" (and as such unlikely to be merciful). Today, it is easier to see how the "medium" of culture induced this kind of thinking; until recently it has not been easy.

Mary has supplied a powerful female presence within Catholic Christianity, which so far has been heavily overweighted with power in the hands of males. Yet modern women often find Mary irritating. She does not seem to have achieved much—apart from bearing and bringing up God, that is. And she appears to have been too quiet for modern taste. (We should always remember, of course, that the Gospels were written by men. It is perhaps remarkable that they did not feel they could leave Mary out.) Also, it is complained, she is impossible to imitate. According to two of the Gospels, she was both virgin and mother—a living paradox. Who could measure up to that? (Not that anyone apart from Mary has been asked to do so.) She has also been accused of presenting male clerics with a "safe" model for women, to keep them pure and humble, quiet, and content with motherhood alone. It should be remembered, however, that the very same clerics traditionally made much of Mary: in the references to her in the Bible they found signs of indisputable greatness. They proposed her as a model not only for women but for men, and most especially for themselves.

In Luke's Gospel Mary is made to express what she felt in one of Christianity's great prayers, perhaps the greatest after the "Our Father." She was a very Jewish girl (she probably spoke her world-shattering yes at about the age Agnes was martyred, in her early teens), and her prayer, the Magnificat, is an Old Testament-inspired hymn in honour of God's decision to reveal himself to the world through her.[26]

She is traditionally depicted as a veiled and cloaked figure, a sign, certainly, of her purity and modesty. But that cloak has also meant powerful protection. It is usually blue, the colour of mysticism, wisdom, peace, and loyalty, of the cosmic universality of the heights of the sky and the depths of the sea. A favourite medieval and Renaissance depiction of the Virgin shows her spreading her cloak over the members of the Church in all their variety—children, popes, old and young, girls and priests, bankers and millers, nurses and queens. Her cloak is like a sheltering church wall. Mary is often taken to be a symbol of the Church.

MARY AND AGNES

Martyrs were the first Christians to receive feast days, celebrated on the dates of their deaths. Christians, understanding death to be an initiation into eternity with God, called these days "birthdays," *dies natales* in Latin: each martyr on his or her annual "birthday" received honourable remembrance among the society of Christians.[27] It took a while for Christians to accept as heroes people who led more peaceful lives and died in their beds.

According to the tradition, Mary died a natural death, years after her son's crucifixion. We therefore hear comparatively little about her during the first centuries. During the second century her importance for the coming of Christ began to be emphasized, and the writers Ignatius of Antioch (martyred in about 115), Justin Martyr (killed in about 165), Irenaeus (died ca. 202), and Tertullian (born ca. 160) contrasted Mary and Eve: whereas Eve caused the Fall, Mary's acceptance of the Spirit brought the Messiah and redemption. The palindrome EVA–AVE (the latter being the first word of the angel's greeting to Mary, "Ave Maria!") came later to be used as a poignant figure for the revolution in which Mary was instrumental. And Mary, impregnated by the Spirit, was believed to have retained her virginity along with her state of motherhood.

As a non-martyr, however, she did not, to begin with, have a feast day of her own, apart from "feasts of the Lord" commemorating events in the life of Jesus, such as his feast of Manifestations, or Epiphany.[28] Agnes received more individual attention at first than did Mary, because she was a martyr. Her story seems also to have influenced the iconography of Mary. Prudentius' hymn to Agnes (ca. 405 A.D.) describes the girl saint set free from the bondage of the world by her execution. The soul of Agnes rises, laughing, towards heaven, and looks down at the whirling vanities of the world, still bound and struggling on the illusory wheel of fortune. She tramples on the serpent that tempted Eve: "But now he is subdued by a virgin's foot; he lowers the crests on his fiery head, and in defeat dares not to lift it up."[29]

Christians also interpreted God's condemnation of the serpent in the Book of Genesis ("there shall be enmity between you and the woman, between her offspring and yours") and read it together with the vision in the Apocalypse, of "a woman, adorned with the sun, standing on the moon, and with twelve stars on her head for a crown," whose child the dragon sought in vain to devour.[30] For them, the first woman was Eve and the second was Mary and her child, the Messiah: the tempter in the garden was overcome by the posterity of those he had seduced. At about the time Prudentius wrote his poem, belief in the Assumption of Mary (her being taken up at once into heaven by God) was beginning to grow. Pictures of Mary's Assumption (on the feast celebrating the anniversary of her "birthday" or *dies natalis*) show her rising, like Agnes in this hymn, towards heaven; as Mary Immaculate, "conceived without sin," her head is surrounded by stars like the vision in the Apocalypse, and she stands on the moon above us, treading the serpent underfoot.

THE CHILDREN OF MARY

At Sant'Agnese's two of the chapels that open from the left aisle are dedicated to Mary; the left aisle, from the point of view of the altar, is at the right-hand or honourable side. The chapel nearest the altar was once a place of special devotion for the world-wide organization of the Children of Mary, which began in the mid nineteenth century. I myself in my early teens, in Zambia (then Northern Rhodesia) in the 1950s, was a rather unsatisfactory member of this society: I took a very long time, I remember, to progress from wearing a mere round medal as an "aspirant" to being considered "mature" enough to drape myself in a much-coveted blue taffeta cloak and wear the oval medal of true membership. I have a group photograph of myself in Lusaka, Zambia, among the other Children of Mary, all of us standing in rows in front of a rock "grotto" containing a statue of the Virgin. The other girls are wearing blue cloaks. I, alas, am still in an uncloaked school uniform. The oval design on the medal I eventually achieved (I have it somewhere, stored with other mementos in a little wooden box) shows the Virgin Mary as Immaculate (without sin), trampling upon sin in the shape of a serpent: Mary as the new Eve, greater than sin's temptation. This figure, and the design on the reverse of the medal, had been seen in a vision by Saint Catherine Labouré in Paris in 1830; she asked for it to be struck as a medal and worn.

Saint Agnes is the patron saint of women before marriage and before their first experience of sex;[31] she is shown in her basilica's chapel presenting five Children of Mary, who like herself are about twelve years old, to Christ's mother, depicted as a girl in her mid teens. The girls are in white dresses with blue sashes; the idea of their wearing cloaks seems to have been a later development. Mary herself wears a blue cloak in the picture. The expectation is that she will lead them to her divine son; in a typically Catholic way of seeing things, Mary, like Agnes, is a human being who is able to help other people find God. Mary is depicted haloed with the apocalyptic twelve stars. Her feet crush the serpent, the apple of temptation still gripped in its jaws. Angels appear in the sky above. Agnes is accompanied, as ever, by her lamb, and there is a lily (for purity) lying in the foreground.

This picture, while an original work in oils and competently made, is not valued as art. It was painted in 1867 at the request of the parish priest at Sant'Agnese's, Don Alberto Passèri, who founded this branch of the Children of Mary in 1864. He was assisted in the initiative by the Marchesa Costanza Lepri, who had recently founded a girls' school nearby and wanted its pupils to become members of the society. Later, Sant'Agnese's church became the central seat for all the Italian branches of the Children of Mary. Passèri later became Abbot General of his order and is buried in this chapel—there is a carved portrait of him on the right-hand wall—which was completed in 1882 with donations from the Children of Mary. The chapel was created by opening up the wall of the church and building outwards, in the small space between the church and the road. Costanza Lepri is buried in the church of Santa Costanza nearby.

MARY AND BERNADETTE

In the piazza in front of Sant'Agnese's church is a replica of the famous grotto at Lourdes, built into the vertical wall of earth left by the excavation of the church's façade. (The "grotto" before which I stood as aspirant to the Children of Mary in Zambia was also, though less successfully, meant to represent the grotto at Lourdes.) It is a popular place for prayer, and usually has candles burning in front of a statue of Mary standing inside the grotto in an oval niche. She is dressed in white with a long blue sash. In 1858, at some distance from the French Pyrenean town of Lourdes, a desperately poor and illiterate girl of fourteen named Bernadette Soubirous was collecting wood beside a river.[32] She saw someone standing a little above her among the rocks—a girl, no older than herself, dressed in white with a blue sash and carrying a rosary[33] over her arm as girls in Bernadette's world commonly did. Not knowing who it was (*Aquéro*, she called the figure in patois, meaning "That person," "She"), Bernadette was caught up into a rapture.

She saw the figure on eighteen different occasions, and gradually the crowds grew, gathering to watch her in ecstasy; *Aquéro* remained unseen to everybody but Bernadette. The figure did not always appear to her, and seldom spoke; when she did, it was to ask Bernadette to tell the world to pray and be sorry for sins, and later she requested that a chapel be built and processions made to the grotto. On one occasion people were horrified to see Bernadette scrabbling in the mud, apparently in obedience to *Aquéro*. (Many were convinced that the visions were diabolical.) Bernadette said later that she had been told, "Go, drink at the spring and wash in it." She turned to the river, but the girl in white called her back and pointed to a muddy puddle. Bernadette scratched at it, but there was barely enough water to swallow, and her face when she washed it was covered in mud. In the course of the week that followed a clear stream broke out of the earth, and it flows to this day.[34]

Instructed by civil and Church authorities to ask what the apparition's name was, Bernadette did so, and the girl in white laughed. On a later occasion, however, she did say who she was, speaking, as she always did, in Bernadette's language: *"Que soy era Immaculada Councepciou"* ("I am the Immaculate Conception"). Bernadette said she had no idea what the words meant, but it was certainly clear to others who the only person was who could make such a claim. Just four years earlier Pope Pius IX had proclaimed the dogma of the Immaculate Conception: that Mary was conceived and born without sin or the propensity to sin, because she was to bear the Messiah.[35] According to Luke's Gospel, the angel who appeared to Mary had said, even before she accepted God's will and conceived the Messiah, that she was "full of grace" and that the Lord was with her.[36] The image of Mary *conçue sans péché* had already appeared on the medal of the Children of Mary, inspired by the visions of Catherine Labouré in 1830.[37] The mysterious *Aquéro*, then, was Mary herself.

People flocked to the grotto, first local people, then people from all over France, then Europe, and then the world. They washed in the stream Bernadette had uncovered in obedience to the young woman in white, and some of the sick, lame, and blind among them subsequently recovered; many more received spiritual healing and hope even if their sufferings continued. Today, Lourdes is still a place of massive international pilgrimage. People visit it in their millions, and, whether one believes these are miracles or not, many of those suffering infirmities are restored to health. It is a city of the sick, and of those who volunteer to help them.

"TASTE" AND THE LOURDES GROTTO

Sant'Agnese's, like many Catholic institutions all over the world, has its own Lourdes grotto, on the principle we have seen before, that pilgrimages are excellent, but that it is less important to go to some shrine than to respond in your own heart to what the sacred place means to you: if you want to go to Lourdes but cannot, then make your own Lourdes nearby. (In the Christian view, a sacred place that is utterly indispensable and unreproducible—that claims to be the only place where contact with God can occur, that must be fought over because possession of it is religiously essential—is an idol.) It can escape no one who visits Sant'Agnese's church that a lot of people pray at this grotto. It is rare to find no one standing before the ceramic statue of the Virgin in her ersatz niche with a little figure of Bernadette kneeling on the ground below her, no one lighting candles and leaving flowers. There are rows of votive plaques on the wall, too, with thanks to Mary inscribed on them.

Religious art is religious before it is art. Religious images often reflect first and foremost whatever people need, what they feel to be useful to their soul's journey. The meaning will count before skill or even artistic insight. "Usefulness," in religion, begins with focus; you cannot respond if you are not paying attention.[38] Popular art openly engages its viewer—and therefore annoys people who have no wish to be engaged. And to most people (the art that is thought to be in "bad taste" is usually popular art), it does not matter what it is that engages and concentrates the mind, just as long as it does the job. If taking some water home from the famous spring at Lourdes is your aim, then buy one of the bottles on sale (plastic is cheap and won't break in your luggage); you could choose one in the shape of the Virgin Mary to remind yourself of who revealed the source. What looks ridiculous to some seems ingenious to others.

MOTHER OF GOD, MYSTICAL ROSE, HOUSE OF GOD

The shifts over time of taste and sentiment are perfectly exemplified by the vicissitudes of the altarpiece in the next chapel, the middle or second one off the left aisle. The chapel was built in the seventeenth century; in the early nineteenth century a fresco of the Virgin breast-feeding Jesus was moved from the canonry into the space over the altar in the chapel, which was then dedicated to Mary. By the late nineteenth century it was thought preferable to hang a painting of the Madonna of Pompeii[39] on top of the original fresco and inside its ornamental frame, either because the new image had a greater popular appeal, or because the picture of Mary openly breastfeeding may now have seemed less than suitable in a church, or both. (The fresco had decorated a wall in the priests' living quarters without causing offence for nearly four hundred years before it was moved into the church.) Five years ago, however, the painting that had covered the fresco for a century was banished to storage in the gallery of the church, to be brought out twice a year when services are held to venerate Mary under the title of the Madonna of Pompeii. The fifteenth-century fresco once again has pride of place.

She is sitting on a cushion on a medieval white marble throne; on closer inspection the throne looks very like an altar. She wears a ruby red cloak with a green lining over a green-grey tunic, and looks out at us as though interested to hear what we have to say, in spite of the all-important function she is performing. (This Virgin, like figures in modern "holy pictures" in "bad taste," looks directly out at the people who contemplate her.) Her exposed breast is not very convincing anatomically, but her body is solidly seated and she holds her child with one competent arm as she gives him her breast with her other hand. The baby places his little hand on hers.

Under her feet is a large octagonal wooden platform. This is a symbolic expression of her child's humanity, indissolubly united with his divinity: as noted before, an octagon is thought of as both square (earthly and human) and circle (eternal and divine). The number eight is also, as we have seen, a symbol of the Resurrection and there-fore of salvation. The white throne with its altarlike seat has a high back and sides, pierced with church-window-like openings. There are small rose windows on either side, recalling Mary's title "Mystical Rose": she it was through whom God passed to become created matter, even as light passes through a rose window's petal-like sections. The white marble throne represents a church, as does Mary herself, who once "housed" Christ.

On either side of this fresco hang two large oval paintings by an unknown eighteenth-century artist; they show the birth of Christ and Mary's Assumption into heaven. Both of these are competent, if not especially original, works of art. Their oval shapes ingeniously suggest to the casual viewer that they are actually round and only look oval because seen from the side—they create the illusion, therefore, that the chapel is deeper than it is. This chapel once held the gorgeous Greco-Roman candlestick that now supports the sanctuary lamp beside the altar, and the much admired marble head of Christ, which is now in the chapel opposite, on the other side of the church.

The chapel off the left aisle nearest the front door is slightly larger than any of the others. It was built in 1866–1867 by the Confraternity of the Sacred Hearts of Jesus and Mary. Like the chapel next door, it is provided with a pepperpot dome to let in light from above. In it is a limp pastel picture of Jesus in pale pink and blue, with his heart in a blaze of light on his chest. The golden tabernacle door, positioned below the picture, also has on it a flaming heart in relief. Each of two oval paintings, one on either side wall, shows a disembodied heart emitting rays of light and floating in the sky. The fleshy hearts—they are neither symmetrical nor abstract—are surrounded by symbolic signs. That of Jesus, on the right-hand wall, is on fire, wounded by a spear, and both bound with thorns and encircled by a crown of thorns as by a halo. It is accompanied by a cross, a cup catching the blood dripping from the heart, and doves drinking from the cup. Mary's heart opposite is also alight with flames and wounded by a sword,[40] but circled with roses, tendrils, flowers, a wreath, a crown, and again two white doves: in both cases the doves represent Christian souls. These two hearts, of Jesus and Mary, also appear on the "miraculous medal" seen in a vision by Catherine Labouré, and worn, for example, by the Children of Mary. They express burning love, and the willingness to endure pain rather than commit any violent or unloving act.

Nothing in the church or the surroundings of Sant'Agnese's is likely to seem as strange today as do these nineteenth-century images of hearts. It is not merely that we reckon them slight as paintings— although there is indeed nothing ambitiously artistic about them.[41] The level of draughtsmanship and the painterly skill shown in the eighteenth-century pictures in the chapel beside this one are immeasurably higher than in these nineteenth-century works. But even somebody repelled by the "heart" pictures can see that they are far more deeply felt than the older paintings. I believe it is the sentiment itself that many people today would find most distasteful.

The idea of emphasizing the heart of Jesus in devotion to him arose first in the East, within Syrian and Byzantine Christianity. From earliest times the heart has been thought of as the seat of human courage

("courage" comes from Latin *cor*, "heart"), and equated with human identity (the heart, though not centrally placed in the body, came nevertheless to be synonymous with "centre"). The heart, which beats faster when a person is in an emotional state, seemed also to be the organ that registered emotions. Christianity values love above all feelings, and the heart seemed self-evidently its seat.

In the West the Carthusian and Cistercian orders were the first to spread devotion to the Sacred Heart of Jesus, during the twelfth century. This was when Christians were beginning to shift their focus from the omnipotent aspect of Christ to that of his humility and love. (The message, of course, was always there. One of the sources for the devotion to the Sacred Heart is the saying of Jesus: "Learn from me, for I am gentle and humble-hearted."[42]) For a thousand years Christians had insisted on the divine half of the great paradox of Christ's simultaneous divinity and humanity; from now on the mystery of God's love, of his insistence upon entering into the human condition, would receive the greater share of Christian attention. The process began with meditations upon his human heart. Key writers on this subject were Bernard of Clairvaux in the twelfth century, and Bonaventure, the contemporary of Thomas Aquinas, in the thirteenth. The idea of God's infinite love was the main point; the natural human response would be gratitude and hope.

In the 1670s the French saint Marguerite-Marie Alacoque experienced visions of the Sacred Heart of Jesus, which led to a much greater emphasis upon this devotion within the Catholic Church. Attention was focused anew upon the idea of Jesus as Man of Sorrows, the suffering figure depicted—prophetically, as Christians see it—in the Book of Isaiah.[43] God gave human beings his love and their liberty, and in doing so risked—and received—rejection and worse. The conjunction of God's love and his suffering was richly and extravagantly expressed by the heart of Christ rendered not only visible, but also on fire and bound with thorns. It was a shocking and upsetting sight, and it was meant to be. The image arose out of and encouraged an anguished longing to comfort Christ and ease his pain. Such feelings are an inevitable aspect of Christian faith, as anyone who knows the story of the life and death of Jesus can imagine.

The seventeenth century, however, was the very one during which William Harvey discovered the circulation of the blood. In the scientific view a human heart was no longer to be thought of as the seat of courage and emotion, let alone of love: Harvey had revealed it to be nothing more than a mechanical pump. People were beginning to feel the first onslaughts of that aspect of science that tends to reduce everything to a matter of practical efficiency. If hearts were to remain symbolic—and they did, as the modern metaphorical usage of words relating to "heart" attests—awareness that such hearts were "merely" symbols was henceforth unavoidable. The rift was beginning to widen between "science" and "religion," "objective" and "subjective," "rational" and "spiritual."

By the nineteenth century images of the Sacred Heart, because of their enormous popularity, had become banal. By the twentieth, devotion to the Sacred Heart could look, especially to intellectuals, increasingly like a lamentable breach of taste. The demand made by figures of the Sacred Heart for a subjective response in love appeared too insistent, excessively sentimental. It did not help, either, that people were becoming more and more separated from the sources of their food; consequently, the idea of even glancing at "innards," such as dripping hearts, became revolting to many who thought of themselves as "civilized." Devotion to the Sacred Heart tended to remain strong among people less squeamish, less "refined."

In reaction to nineteenth-century sentiment, there was also by the twentieth century a new coldness in the culture, a reluctance to express blatant feeling. We all of us undergo nowadays the pressure to be "cool," which mostly means unmoved, unimpressed, flint-faced— apart of course from occasional explosions of rage or triumph. For one thing, openly to show one's feelings is to make oneself vulnerable to the abuse of others. We call people who are soft, soppy, and unrealistic "bleeding hearts," and those who wear "their hearts on their sleeves" (as the Sacred Heart appears outside the robe of Jesus) are likely to receive considerable condescension. In any case, the hearts in the chapel at Sant'Agnese's seem far too realistic to be symbolic: hearts meaning "love" have now become flat symmetrical shapes, about as emotive as traffic signals.

Today, there is a powerful impulse among Catholic Christians not to abolish the message given by their traditional pictures of the Sacred Heart, but to investigate it more deeply and restate it in different language. Jesus looking predictably and complacently sweet, together with any merely masochistic dwelling on his sufferings being "my fault"—these, many feel, have got to go: nineteenth-century attitudes towards the Sacred Heart can seem very out-of-date. It is not, however, that the Sacred Heart has less to say to Christians—it is that contemplation of this symbolism demands far more from them now than before.

After the twentieth century's repeated confrontations with horror and the triumph of evil—from the Holocaust to the Rwanda massacres, from the Gulag to Pol Pot's regime, from the Chinese Cultural Revolution, to devastating wars and social breakdown in Africa, Latin America, Asia, and Europe—Christians feel called upon to take more seriously than ever before their own doctrine that God is not merely omnipotent. He has also chosen to be one with the victims, the marginalized, the weak. God, therefore, is experienced very directly as pure love, which means that in "this world" he is wounded, in pain, without shelter, without help, without attention. God "is," in this view, the man who "fell among thieves" in the parable of Jesus[44]—the one beaten up and robbed, whose need was ignored by the selfish and, in particular, by the "churchly," pedantic in their merciless insistence on "purity" and avoidance of the afflicted.

Christians feel that the Gospel is inviting them, here and now and with a fresh intensity, to "help God," especially in the poor and suffering of this world. Jesus said, "Whatever you do to these my brothers and sisters, especially to the least powerful of them—the hungry and thirsty, the poor, the strangers and refugees, the sick and handicapped, the despised and marginalized, the imprisoned—you do it to me."[45] These words are implicit in the notion of the Sacred Heart. To ignore them has become intolerable to modern thinking and committed Christians.

In reconsidering the image of the Sacred Heart, moreover, it cannot be denied that Christianity is a profoundly bodily religion. Christ's becoming human is called "incarnation," God literally "becoming flesh." The image of the Sacred Heart recalls the fact that, after his bloody death, Jesus was pierced by a spear, "and out of his side ran blood and water."[46] No, Christians cannot get away from the body: as fact and symbol, as medium and foundation, as necessarily the way to God. The bodily pain, famine, thirst, and homelessness of others demand relief; such sufferers are the very person of Christ. Christians, perhaps modern ones especially, cannot simply avert their eyes from images of the Sacred Heart.

PICTURES, STATUES, AND CANDLES

On any day at Sant'Agnese's church most of the candles are lit before the Sacred Heart and outside at the grotto. Candles symbolize some or all of the following: the length of a human life (the number of birthday candles signifies the number of years lived); the tiny but indomitable light of life; a longing for a life "consumed" by love, as a candle burns itself away; a desire for simplicity, purity, and uprightness; a determination to remain awake and ready for Christ's coming, like the wise bridesmaids with their lit lamps in the parable;[47] human vulnerability to death or being "snuffed out"; illumination that can be "handed on" to others; memory and vigil on the part of a crowd witnessing an event or peacefully resisting an injustice. Candles carried in processions at night—at Lourdes, for instance—give people an idea of their numbers, and express faith and hope in the darkness. When people light votive candles in a church, they are representing themselves, their yearnings, their lives. They have prayed, and now must leave; they wish they could stay and continue praying. Candles remind others of the prayers, and therefore of the needs, of people who have stood or knelt in the church before them.

Christians are supposed to strive to remain consciously present to God in every moment of their lives. Many so-called devotions are attempts at maintaining this awareness; lighting candles is one example. A Catholic church like Sant'Agnese's provides candle-racks, candles, matches, and a money box for paying for a candle—or (again a horror to aesthetic sensibilities) it might provide a rack of electric lights, one of which turns on when you put in a coin. Electric lights have advantages—they are cleaner, easier, cheaper, safer—but they are also "commoner" and newer. They lack the flickering charm, the archaic associations, the physical symbol of length representing time, and the many other symbolic resonances carried by candles. There is now, in candles, even a powerful uselessness, that helps keep them purely symbolic.

One of the ways you can tell, in a Catholic church, which saint or devotion to God is most popular is to count the candles and notice the quantities of flowers. These might be most numerous in front of some great work of art, but if they are, you may count on it that that is a mere coincidence. The work is only a representation of something entirely other than itself; it is that other reality in honour of which the candles are lit, no matter how lovely—or how dreadful—the art. If that were not so, the work would be what Christians think of as an idol, like the Emperor of Rome, to whom Christians in early days were asked to burn incense. Their heroes refused to do it; they preferred torture and death.

Roman Catholics often like touching and even kissing pictures and statues when praying. This does not mean that they think the representation is anything more than a representation: people often kiss photographs of people they love, with the same symbolic intent. Often beloved images—crucifixes, for instance—will be worn down and rubbed smooth by kisses and touches, as are the feet of the big bronze crucifix at Sant'Agnese's. Another example in this church is the picture near the door of Saint Antony, which is worn away in three places by people who touch it and pray before it, often just before they leave the church.

There has always been a strong anti-representational tradition in Christianity. Jewish Scripture warns repeatedly that images are not to be worshipped; Protestant Christendom is often fiercely opposed to pictures and statues. Catholics themselves may dislike the lighting of candles before images, feeling that to do this is to lean towards idolatry. All this caution is salutary and worthy; it keeps alive a wariness of idolatry.

But on the other hand, people are usually more intelligent than judgemental others give them credit for. It must be rare for a candle to be lit at Sant'Agnese's by someone who thinks that the ceramic figure in the grotto, say, really is the Mother of God, or that the statue somehow vibrates with its very own power. Idolatry is far more dangerous and insidious than that: its real meaning is turning from God out of preference for some earthly object or attainment. An idol is much more likely to be money, prestige, or even "good taste" itself, than a depiction of Jesus or a saint.

7

ONE BODY:

Chapels, Right Side

....

Once you have turned left after the chapel of the Sacred Heart, and crossed the narthex to walk up the right-hand aisle, you encounter three chapels that open out of the southern flank of the church, all of them built during the seventeenth century. But first, near the foot of the staircase leading down to the church, is a small door, normally kept closed. Behind this is a narrow spiral stairway that leads up to the medieval complex next door; it was built as a private entrance to the church for the community of canons.[1]

The chapel beside the door is dedicated to Saint Augustine,[2] venerated here as the father of the Congregation of the Canons Regular of the Lateran,[3] who now occupy the monastery buildings and have run the church for over five hundred years. An eighteenth-century fresco in the chapel depicts Augustine, pen in hand, in a bishop's vestments: cloak and mitre. There is a jewelled band round Augustine's head, holding his mitre in place, and one of two infulae, (broad ribbons that hang down from the back of the hat) falls over his left shoulder.

Augustine's mitre is a smaller, eighteenth-century version of the headdress still worn for ceremonial liturgical functions by Christian bishops in the West. It is useful for marking out the bishop in a crowd. Mitres are known to have been worn by Roman clergy since the ninth century; they have been reserved for bishops since the eleventh century.[4] The Church has long thought of the mitre (Latin *mitra*, meaning "headband" or "turban") as being an imitation of the headdress of Jewish priests, as prescribed by Yahweh according to the Book of Exodus 39:28. The mitre's two points allude to the two rays of light that issued from the head of Moses when he received the Ten Commandments; in addition, they are symbolic of the Old and New

Testaments. The hat also evolved from the Greek diadem (literally "tied-around"), which was a band tied round the head, with the knot behind and the two ends left dangling (hence the mitre's infulae). It was worn in ancient Greece by persons considered sacred, such as priests, and by champions at the games.

Augustine's saintly attribute is usually a heart held in one hand because he speaks often in his writings of the longing of the human heart for God. But here he is depicted as composing, in a book, a set of regulations for community life—those forming the basis for the rule followed by the resident Congregation of the Canons Regular of the Lateran. After his conversion in 386 A.D. Augustine lived with circles of friends, first in Milan, then in his hometown of Thagaste in modern Algeria, then in Hippo. He did not write a monastic rule, but we know that his community tried to base itself on the behaviour, as it is reported in the Acts of the Apostles, of the earliest Christians in Jerusalem: "The whole group of believers was united, heart and soul; no one claimed for his own use anything that he had, as everything they owned was held in common."[5]

In the early sixth century Caesarius of Arles provided a set of rules to a community of women who asked for his help; this document survives in a seventh-century version. The first part of it is called "The Rule of Saint Augustine," although only the second part, advice to women in religious life, is now believed to be by Augustine himself. The Rule is a very brief list, not really enough to guide a community in any detail—which is perhaps why it has been chosen down the centuries as a basis of behaviour by a number of religious orders or congregations, including the Augustinians, the Dominicans,[6] and various groups of canons. Each has added to and adapted the Rule in ways it has seen fit. Augustine lived in community but in town, associated with a church and not retired from the world, which is why canons base themselves on his Rule.

Rule Three of this list (partly taken from the verse in Acts) reads: "One soul and one heart, turned towards God." In the fresco this is what Saint Augustine has just written in Latin in his book, which he holds turned to face us so that we can read it. His eyes are looking up, almost squinting with the effort of concentration; if we follow his gaze, we see that it is trained on the carved ceiling of the chapel, above the picture, where a dove with wings outspread appears in a sunburst, within a roundel supported by angels. It is a typically Baroque conceit to make figures in a painting or a sculpture interact with features of the building outside the work; the strategy fits well into church iconography, which in any case always points beyond itself. Here, Augustine looks out of his picture frame at the dove, which in turn symbolizes the Holy Spirit, the creative and inspirational Third Person of the Trinity.

STEPHEN OF JERUSALEM, LAWRENCE OF ROME

Next to the chapel of Saint Augustine is the chapel of the Saviour, built by Pope Leo XI, who spent less than a month in office (April 1–27, 1605): he caught cold while visiting the monastery of Sant'Agnese, and died of it. (Another pope caught his death of cold at the church: Paul V, who said Mass at the Sant'Agnese's on the saint's feast day and died of pneumonia a week later, on January 28, 1621.[7]) A monument to Leo XI is on the left-hand wall of the chapel, with a worn painted portrait medallion and an inscription noting his many benefactions to the church when he was its commendatory abbot;[8] these included the restoration of the building beginning in 1600, and the clearing away of the catacombs before its front façade.

The Cathedral of the Lateran, the "mother house" of the canons, is dedicated to Christ the Saviour, so in this chapel the priests have again made their imprint on the building. The white marble bust of Christ on the altar came originally from a chapel in the canonry built by Giuliano della Rovere, later Pope Julius II, the powerful patron of Michelangelo. The canonry chapel was embellished many times by cardinals who loved going out to spend time in these buildings among the fields and vines. The chapel, which was described in 1776 as frescoed all over and containing several works of Renaissance sculpture and painting,[9] was destroyed during nineteenth-century renovations to the canonry. The head of Christ is no longer thought to be by Michelangelo, but attributed to Nicolas Cordier, who created the figure of Saint Agnes that stands behind the main altar. It is an outstanding early sixteenth-century work, at once delicate and forceful.

The altar itself in this chapel was created out of the most complete remaining piece of the cosmatesque altar complex, destroyed in the early seventeenth century. What is now the altar front was discovered face down in the canonry kitchen, forming part of the paving of the floor. It is composed of eight slabs of porphyry and precious marbles, divided by bands of red and gold mosaic in tiny pieces, set in starry patterns. The back or reredos of the altar has two statues carved in high relief out of fine white marble: Saint Stephen and Saint Lawrence. The Canons Regular are especially interested in these two saints because they are models of the early Christian behaviour that their order sets out to emulate.

Stephen is revered by Christendom as "the protomartyr," the first martyr after Christ.[10] Stephen was one of seven men chosen to be deacons (*diakonoi* means "servants" in Greek) to feed the poor and the widows out of the shared wealth of the Christian congregation. The Greek of the passage in Acts literally says that they were to "wait on tables" in Jerusalem, relieving the Apostles of this duty so that they could concentrate on preaching. Despite his Greek name, Stephen was Jewish. Arrested and asked to give an account of his beliefs, he did so in a speech describing the ancient story of the Jews: the Covenants, the Exodus, the Ark, and the temple. He upbraided the Jews for not accepting Christ as the Messiah they had so long awaited and, looking up, cried out that he could see Jesus "standing at the right hand of God." This was blasphemy to unconverted Jewish ears, and Stephen was taken outside the city walls and stoned to death. He died praying for forgiveness for the people who killed him.

The men who stoned Stephen had taken off their cloaks and left them at the feet of a young man named Saul, "who entirely approved of the killing." Saul was the future Apostle to the Gentiles, who changed his name after his conversion to Paul (*Paulus* means "not much" in Latin; it was also the cognomen of several Roman clans). The execution of Stephen set in motion a persecution of the Jerusalem Church, in which Saul took an important part. The survivors fled, but preached the Gospel wherever they went. In this manner Stephen's blood proved to be "seed" for the Church.[11]

Lawrence was a third-century martyr, also a deacon, who worked in

Rome. The Spanish claim that he was born in Huesca, Aragon, although the Spanish-born poet Prudentius, who wrote a magnificent hymn in honour of Lawrence,[12] does not mention the Roman martyr's being originally one of his countrymen. Third-century Rome had seven deacons in charge of feeding, clothing, and befriending the poor, in imitation of early Christian practice in Jerusalem. In 258, the second of the Emperor Valerian's anti-Christian decrees condemned Christian clergy to death unless they rejected their faith, beginning with the bishop of Rome, Pope Sixtus II. Four of Lawrence's fellow deacons refused to recant and were executed; Lawrence was spared for a few days because, as head of the group, he was thought to know the whereabouts of the "secret treasures" of the Christians.

Lawrence was probably beheaded. Later legend, which he shares with the martyred deacon Vincent of Saragossa, has him roasted to death on a gridiron; in art this became his attribute. Prudentius describes Lawrence as *ludibundus*, "playful"; there are three jesting stories attached to his name. In the first, the prefect of Rome orders Lawrence to hand over the Church's treasures. Lawrence gathers together all the lame, the blind, the sick, the poor, the widows and orphans, and brings the prefect to see them: "These are the riches of the Church."

The enraged prefect orders Lawrence to be tortured on the gridiron for this impertinence. While Lawrence is being roasted, he asks his torturers to turn him over: "I'm done on this side." And then, "Try some: do I taste better raw or grilled?"[13] (Many stories of martyrdom have a hideously culinary aspect to them.) And much later, when the relics of Stephen arrived in Rome via Byzantium in the fifth century, they were placed beside those of his brother deacon Lawrence in his grave underneath the church of San Lorenzo fuori le Mura. It was said that Lawrence's bones rolled over again, as he had rolled over on the gridiron, this time to make room for Stephen. Lawrence was affectionately known after this as "the courteous Spaniard."[14]

In 330 the Emperor Constantine founded a splendid basilica beside Lawrence's tomb outside the walls of Rome. A church over the tomb itself, in the catacombs of Cyriaca on the via Tiburtina, was later erected by Pope Pelagius II (579–590). Pope Honorius III (1216–1227) added a second church onto the Pelagian one. At San Lorenzo fuori le Mura, it is possible to get an idea of what Sant'Agnese's looked like in the Middle Ages, for there the gorgeous cosmatesque ambones still survive, the left one for reading out the Epistle and the right for the Gospel. The stately pillared medieval ciborium on its four porphyry columns is also still there, as is the sumptuous marble mosaic floor.

Guillaume des Perriers ("William of the Pear Trees") was a French lawyer, born at Condom in Aquitaine in about 1420. He worked in Rome as auditor of the Roman Rota[15] for twenty-four years, and died in 1500. In his old age, des Perriers liked to donate marble altars to churches in Rome, ordering them always from the sculptor Andrea Bregno and his school of assistants. Eight of these altars, known after him as *de Pereriis* altars, have survived, seven of them in Rome.[16] Part of one of them now forms the reredos of the altar in the chapel of the Saviour at Sant'Agnese's. It was made for San Lorenzo fuori le Mura, which is why it shows Lawrence with his fellow deacon Stephen; it was once one of seven altars that stood behind the choir there. The Canons of the Lateran long served at San Lorenzo's, and during their tenancy they decided to take this altar for Sant'Agnese's when the excavations of the church were being done in about 1600. Agnes, Lawrence, Paul, and Peter—martyrs all—are the four main patron saints of Rome; their bodies lie roughly north, east, south, and west of the city.

The reredos bears the inscription *Guillermus de Pereriis. Auditor. M.CCCCXC* (1490). The donor's arms—three pear trees tied together with a ribbon on which is written the letter G—appear twice, beside the two saints' carved names. Between the names is a Eucharistic chalice and host (a cup and circle of bread), an expression of the altar's function. Stephen and Lawrence wear dalmatics[17] because they are deacons.[18] The dalmatic is an over-tunic with open sides and wide, straight-set sleeves, which give it the shape of a cross. It is decorated either with two stripes or (as here) with two inset embroidered panels and two tassels; both forms of decoration represent the love of God and of one's neighbour.[19] The colour of a dalmatic matches the liturgical colour[20] which the priest or bishop is wearing at Mass.

Stephen has a stone striking his head and Lawrence a gridiron behind him: objects that identify the two men while reminding us of their deaths. During the Middle Ages Saint Stephen was appealed to for the curing of headaches and Saint Lawrence was patron saint of cooks: saintly patronage often has a humorous side. Both carry Bibles and palms for the victory that martyrdom has won; the palm-bearing right hand of each is displayed with the fourth and fifth fingers curled in, leaving three straight fingers, an ancient symbol of the Trinity. They are standing on little platforms in niches. A semicircular scallop shell arches over each neatly haloed head; such a shell creates a tiny apse, signifying eternity, where they now dwell. Stephen and Lawrence are flanked by three exquisitely carved pilasters with capitals and classicizing Renaissance motifs (vases, leaves, tendrils). The two heroes are very different, but strikingly similar as well; their stories are meant to contrast with and reflect each other in the viewer's mind as he or she "reads" the iconography. Now that they have reached this church, they are also to be thought of as male companions to Saint Agnes, and may be compared and contrasted with her.

SAINT EMERENTIANA

The third chapel on the right, beside the altar, is dedicated to Saint Emerentiana. Emerentiana, according to legend, was Agnes' "milk sister." Agnes came from a Roman family rich enough to have its own burial plot along the via Nomentana, called in the sources their *praediolum* or *agellus,* possibly with a hypogeum or underground burial chamber. Such a family might well have provided a milk sister for one of its offspring. Rich mothers down the centuries in Europe have often preferred to delegate other women to nurse their babies for them. A poorer woman, who herself had borne a child and so had milk to provide, would breastfeed a second infant, for a fee; the two babies were then considered to be part kin, "milk brethren." The nurse and the two children, despite class differences, would commonly maintain this link through life.[21] Sometimes milk brethren would become servants in the households of their rich milk kin. (The nurse is part of the earliest narrative of Agnes' martyrdom. Probably figuratively in order to emphasize her youth, Damasus wrote that the girl ran away "from the arms of her nurse" to confront the Roman authorities.)

In the sixth century, a third chapter was added to the fifth-century

Latin passio of Agnes. It tells of the funeral of Agnes after her death by the sword, of the martyrdom of her milk sister Emerentiana, and of the miraculous healing, after prayers to Agnes, of Constantina, daughter of Constantine. Constantina was baptized, and decided to build a basilica in honour of Agnes.

Emerentiana, says the passio, was an extremely holy virgin. Like Agnes, she would have been about twelve years old. She was a catechumen, still preparing herself and studying the Christian faith in preparation for baptism, when her milk sister was murdered. One day, not long after Agnes was buried in her family's *agellus*, a crowd of pagans, who had been waiting in hiding, attacked a Christian group who had gone out along the via Nomentana to visit the martyr's grave. Some of the Christians were struck by stones; everyone but Emerentiana fled. She stood, "constant, intrepid, without moving," and shouted at the crowd, calling them superfluous, pathetic, out-of-date savages[22] who killed innocent people for worshipping God. The furious crowd stoned her to death; she died praying, next to Agnes' tomb. After that, the narrative continues, there was an earthquake and some of the crowd died of fright. Visitors to the tombs of the martyrs were subsequently left in peace. Agnes' parents came in the night and took away Emerentiana's body; they buried her at the edge of their own burial plot, *in confinio agelli*.

"There is no doubt," the passio concludes, that the as-yet-unbaptized Emerentiana "was baptized in her blood": she had died for what she believed in. Her story is a heightened instance, a dramatization, of what Christians call "the baptism of desire": when the real object of desire is God, no matter how unknown God may be, then wanting it is having it. As Saint Bernard of Clairvaux once said, "It is God alone that can never be sought in vain, not even when he cannot be found."[23]

THE BODY OF EMERENTIANA

As far as archaeology is concerned, Emerentiana was one of several Christians, revered as martyrs, who were buried close to one another in a catacomb adjoining the one at Sant'Agnese's. There is epigraphical evidence confirming the existence of the graves that pilgrims were accustomed to visit: inscriptions mentioning (in this order) Victor,

Felix, Papias, Emerentiana, and Alexander. Another martyr, Maurus, was said to have his grave in the vicinity, and a transenna has been found with his name on it.

Pilgrims to Rome in the seventh century would be guided by itineraries, telling them where the martyrs' shrines lay in the countryside beyond the city's walls.[24] According to these guidebooks, pilgrims who had visited the catacombs of Priscilla on the via Salaria should walk next, in a clockwise direction, towards the via Nomentana. On the connecting road, on their left, they would see the church of Emerentiana (it may not have been a very large building, perhaps no bigger than an oratory), standing above ground. They could take the steps from it down into the "bigger" catacomb, the Coemeterium Maius, where Victor, Alexander, Felix, and Papias were buried. Next they would walk on to the via Nomentana, turn right, and soon find themselves at the tomb of Agnes.

The *Acts of Saint Marcellinus* (fifth century) say that Papias and Maurus are buried near the via Nomentana "at the waters of Saint Peter, where he baptized." There is a tradition—unprovable—that Saint Peter lived outside the walls on this side of Rome, that he preached to soldiers in the praetorian camp not far from the Nomentan Gate, and that he baptized in the waters of a stream that flowed past the site where Agnes was to be buried about 250 years later. The stream, now built over, was known during the nineteenth century as the Marrana di Sant'Agnese. Within the Coemeterium Maius several seats have been discovered, carved out of the tufa walls of the catacomb. These used to be called "Peter's chairs," but it is clear that they were made, in fact, for Christian meals eaten on anniversaries at the graves of their dead. In 1876 the archaeologist Mariano Armellini reported finding a crypt in the Coemeterium Maius containing a "chair of Peter." He believed that Emerentiana's tomb was in the apse. This is no longer thought to be a verifiable fact, although it is clear that some martyrs were venerated in the crypt.[25]

In the early twentieth century the small church of San Salvatore de Pede Pontis in Trastevere—near the ruined ancient Roman bridge Ponte Rotto near Tiber Island—was pulled down. In the debris part of a fourth-century marble slab was found, which the great archaeologist of the catacombs, Giovanni Battista de Rossi, recognized immediately:

it must once have been inside the church of Saint Emerentiana, because on it were some lines from an inscription that the *Martyrologium Hieronymianum* (fifth and sixth centuries) recorded as being there. The name of the huge catacomb near Sant'Agnese's had been called many things: the Cemetery of Agnes (it was long believed to be a continuation of the one at Sant'Agnese's), the Cemetery of Emerentiana, the Ostrianum, the *ad Nymphas*, the *Fons Sancti Petri*, and the Maius. This inscription gave what must be the earliest version of the name Coemeterium Maius, by which the catacomb is now invariably called. The rest of the slab was subsequently found in the catacomb itself; it names Emerentiana and her fellow saints, Victor, Felix, Papias, and Alexander, and it records the removal of relics from the catacomb into the oratory above ground.[26]

We know that Pope Paschal I (817–824), taking the passio of Agnes into account, had the body of Emerentiana brought to the present church of Sant'Agnese and enclosed it in a marble altar with the bones of Agnes. He removed the skull of Agnes and sent it to the Sancta Sanctorum at the Lateran.[27] That of Emerentiana was given to the church of San Pietro in Vincoli on the Esquiline, where it still is today; one of her finger bones is at the church of Santa Maria in Campitelli. The church/oratory of Emerentiana, last restored by Pope Hadrian I (772–795), was left to fall into ruin; no trace of it remains. In 1605 Cardinal Paolo Emilio Sfondrati broke open the ninth-century altar in Sant'Agnese's church, and in it he found the headless skeletons of two small bodies lying side by side. After removing several bits of them, Pope Paul V had the remains enclosed in a silver coffin and buried, in 1615, underneath the new altar and ciborium that he had ordered to be made for the church. There they remain. In 1901 the coffin was uncovered and is now visible in the crypt, under the main altar of the church.

In 1255 an altar described as *totum tessellatum*, "all covered in mosaics,"[28] was made in honour of Saint Emerentiana, and placed near the present chapel, on the spot believed to be where she was stoned to death—as the passio says, beside the grave of Agnes. Three new altars were dedicated in the church at this time; the other two were for John the Baptist and John the Evangelist. A fourteenth-century fresco in the canonry reflects the existence of these three altars, depicting as it does the two Johns and Emerentiana, together with Agnes. The altars were inaugurated by Pope Alexander IV on March 17, 1256; the commemorative inscription, now in the passageway down into the church, says that Lucy the Abbess was present (at that time the monastery buildings were occupied by Benedictine sisters), together with Theodora the Prioress, and the Lady Jacoba.[29]

By 1620 the altars had disappeared, and the present chapel for Emerentiana had been built. In it was a copy of a painting by Guercino, the original of which is now in the Galleria Colonna in Rome, showing Emerentiana being stoned. In 1895 the Rev. Louis-Emérentien Le Bourgeois (born in Le Mans in 1860) was living in Rome. He was much devoted to his patron saint, and gave money for the Italian artist Eugenio Cisterna (1862–1933) to paint three pictures in the chapel: a portrait of Emerentiana for the altar, and depictions of her martyrdom and her funeral on the two side walls. Cisterna was chosen because he had recently decorated in fresco some of the walls in the crypt below the church of Sant'Agnese in Agone, in Piazza Navona. A new altar was also installed; when the old one was removed, two inscriptions came to light, one referring to Terentia Chryse and the other identifying the gravestone of Inportunus the Subdeacon.[30]

As her attribute, Saint Emerentiana holds the stones of her martyrdom in the folds of her dress. Perhaps because of a clumsy depiction of this, in faraway northern France during the Middle Ages the stones were read as Emerentiana's entrails pouring out of her body, and her martyrdom was assumed to have been disembowelment. She was therefore invoked for stomach ailments.[31]

THE CHRISTMAS CRIB

Every year at Christmas Sant'Agnese's church presents a "crib" (*presepio* in Italian): a three-dimensional reconstruction of the scene of the birth of Jesus as it is described in the Bible. It is traditionally placed in the chapel of Saint Emerentiana. The idea of creating a representation of the Nativity goes back to a memorable celebration of Christmas Eve that Saint Francis of Assisi staged in 1224. It happened at Greccio, where a landowner named Giovanni Vellita had given

Francis a wooded mountainside outside his village; there, Francis had founded a small hermitage.

That night he turned the hermitage into a stable, with a real ox and an ass (for centuries an ox and an ass had been part of the iconography of the scene).[32] People came from their houses for miles around in procession, bearing torches and singing. At midnight Mass was said on top of a stone container for straw, a "manger"; the people present believed that they saw Francis holding the Christ child in his arms just before, as deacon, he chanted the Gospel. Mass continues to be celebrated at midnight on Christmas Eve throughout Catholic Christendom. The Christmas crib, still customary in churches all over the world, is called in French a *crèche*; it is often thought that the word (etymologically related, in fact, to German *Krippe*, "crib") recalls the place name Greccio.

Christmas cribs often depict the scene—with the newborn Jesus in the stable, his mother and Joseph, the angels, the shepherds, the star, and the visiting magi[33]—as taking place locally, in the fields or in the town or city surrounding the church. A crib is a ritual made solid; its making and embellishing, its setting out, and the visiting of it to contemplate what for Christians is the Good News (God's gift of himself to humankind), literally "takes place" every Christmas: a place is made for the crib inside the church. Like all rituals, every time it recurs it happens in the new place and in the new time; on every occasion, people are invited to see in the crib Jesus born for them, personally.

Cribs can be made and set out at home, or in public squares (a life-sized Nativity scene is placed in the centre of St. Peter's square every year in Rome), or in churches. In Rome churches vie with one another for the creation of the most magnificent crib scene; for weeks before and after Christmas people visit church after church, bringing their children with them, to see the baby Jesus in the *presepio*. In Piazza Navona a Christmas fair is held where crib figures, and also moss and cork and dried plants, can be bought for the making of cribs at home. The scene commonly includes local monuments and genre scenes of ordinary people, especially poor people, living their normal lives as the miracle occurs in their midst.[34]

The yearly crib at Sant'Agnese's is made afresh and differently every year, under the supervision of the Di Lazzaro family. Gabriele Di Lazzaro is a local doctor who is fascinated by the long, popular Roman tradition of making *presepios*. Members of the community assist the family in the work. The crib always includes Roman monuments in the background against the night sky, such as the dome of St. Peter's, the Castel Sant'Angelo, Bernini's Bridge of Angels across the Tiber. The people in the scene, apart from the humble figures at the stable proper, are dressed in a generic nineteenth-century costume, for today's cribs usually maintain an element of nostalgia. We see women peeling vegetables, neighbours chatting or leaning on balconies or walking their dogs, a stall selling roasted chestnuts, somebody knitting on a bench. There are lighted street lamps and lights behind window-panes, and plenty of snow (although it rarely snows heavily in Rome). The buildings are the old brown and ochre apartment blocks of Rome, with astonishingly accurate depictions of the little bricks, the worn and flaking earth-toned plaster, and the arches and window ledges of stone. Viewers examine every detail and have at first to search for the representation, often under some arch and off to one side, of the event that was to change the history of the world.

AN ACCIDENT AND ITS AFTERMATH

Above the columns of Sant'Agnese's nave, painted in roundels, are the heads of a number of the popes who have been involved in this church's history. The series begins with Liberius (352–366), the first pope to offer financial support for the shrine of Saint Agnes, and ends with Pius IX (1846–1878). (A plaque in the wall near the entrance on via Nomentana recalls that Pius XII (1939–1958) lived in the canonry as a seminarian in his teens.)

The most famous exploit of Pius IX at Sant'Agnese's occurred not in the church but in the canonry beside it, and is depicted in a large and exuberantly ludicrous painting by Domenico Toietti that hangs in the hall where today baptisms are celebrated, next door to the church. On April 12, 1855, the pope went on pilgrimage to the recently discovered church and catacomb of Sant'Alessandro on the via Nomentana. On the way back he visited Sant'Agnese's, and after lunch held a reception and audience for 102 people, including 76 students for the priesthood, in a large room on the first floor of a building that stood where the hall is today. The ground floor was used for storage. During the proceedings the upper floor collapsed and the entire company fell into the store-room below. No one was injured. When everybody had safely emerged, the pope immediately led them all up into the gallery of Sant'Agnese's church, where they sang the Te Deum[35] in thanksgiving.

In the painting the accident is depicted as resulting in a miracle. Saint Peter in a blaze of light personally supports the teetering pope in his white robes and red velvet shoes, as the Virgin, standing on clouds and implored by Saint Agnes to help, watches over the safety of pope, clergy, and students. Pius IX's chair topples over, beams crack and fall, a torn red rug descends to drape a broken rafter and two huge wine barrels in the storage room. Students and clergy sprawl on the floor while a canon in his habit hangs helplessly kicking his feet at an upstairs window; gestures of horror and wonder enliven the composition.

Pius IX never forgot this event. He immediately set about restoring the canonry buildings, so clearly in the process of collapse. Most of the structures dating from the time of Julius II, including the Renaissance chapel, were pronounced unsafe and pulled down. The Sala Giulio II remains, however, high and nobly proportioned, with a ceiling of massive wooden beams and a fifteenth-century fireplace. The first six verses of Prudentius' poem in honour of Agnes are painted on the cornice running under the ceiling. The Sala is now used for parish parties, lectures, and other functions. Encased in one wall is the front of a magnificent second-century Roman sarcophagus, dug out of the ground near Sant'Agnese's church during the seventeenth century. The Roman matron carved in the middle of the front of the sarcopha-gus—her portrait held up by two enormous winged Roman genii, with river gods below and images of Cupid and Psyche on either side—was once taken to be Agnes herself; this was thought to be her original tomb. Her attributes, a lamb and a palm, were carved into the marble beside her. When the mistake was pointed out by modern archaeolo-gists, the lamb and palm were removed.

The pope's chosen architect, Andrea Busiri Vici, also managed to conserve several fine fourteenth- and fifteenth-century frescoes in the canonry. These include a magnificent Annunciation, dated by its inscription 1454; the Virgin and Child with saints Agnes, Emerentiana, John the Evangelist, and John the Baptist; the Persian physicians Cosmas and Damian, who are the patron saints of doctors; a young man wearing a dalmatic and carrying a chain and handcuffs, who might be the patron saint of prisoners, Saint Leonard; and the Virgin and Child with the apostle to the Sienese, Saint Ansanus, in an elegant cloak. Ansanus holds in his left hand his attribute, a windpipe and lungs: he was one of the saints invoked against respiratory diseases. (If we recall that two popes died from catching cold at Sant'Agnese's in January, Ansanus might well have been an appropriate saint for the monastery's devotion.)

On the orders of Pius IX, a new two-storey building of no architectural distinction was erected for the priests, and the hall in which the accident happened was rebuilt in the form it has today, with wall space—handsomely decorated in mauve with golden scrolls—large enough for the commemorative painting and two plaques listing the people involved in the accident. The wall on the cloister side is glassed in. The bas-relief in the triangular frontal outside the hall shows Saint Peter and Saint Agnes presenting to Christ the people of five continents, all of which had been represented among the guests at the reception on the memorable day. Two terra cotta statues of angels flank the scene; their wings are now missing.

The pope then turned his attention to the church of Sant'Agnese. Its ceiling was gilded and painted with considerable skill and sensitivity. The walls were frescoed with geometrical designs, crosses, the papal portraits in roundels, papal arms complete with tiaras and crossed keys,[36] the figures of virgin martyrs, and over the apse the scene of Agnes' martyrdom. The eighteenth-century brick floor of the nave and the stones paving the aisles were removed, and the whole surface repaved. In the gallery, the seventeenth- and eighteenth-century soffits gave way to vaulting, and the seventeenth-century balustrades were replaced with the transenne we see there today. Beautiful gilded bronze candlesticks were presented to the church for use on special occasions. Finally, Pope Pius IX had himself painted into the lunette under the arch at the entrance to the complex from the via Nomentana; the picture, now faded and difficult to make out, shows Saint Agnes presenting him to the Virgin. In the background is the church of Sant'Agnese.

TWO GENTLE MEN

At the back of the church, near the door, is a round painting in a square frame of a man in a religious habit, kneeling down with a baby in his arms. Heaven opens and angels swirl about, looking down, gesturing, pointing. The picture shows the kneeling figure undergoing a mystical experience or epiphany. At the front of the church on the right, after the chapel of Saint Emerentiana and next to a doorway marked *cripta* (for beyond this door it is possible to take some steps down to the tomb of Agnes) is another round picture in a square frame. It, too, is a nineteenth-century painting, and it shows a bearded man in brown holding a baby. These two people lived 750 years ago and two thousand years ago respectively; but never have they been more popular as saintly heroes than they are today.

Ferdinand, the man portrayed in the back of the church, was Portuguese.[37] He was a brilliant linguist and more learned than most men of his time; he became in the opinion of many the greatest preacher of the Middle Ages. Deeply pious from his youth, Ferdinand at fifteen became one of the Canons Regular of Saint Augustine, and led a studious life for ten years at the university city of Coïmbra. The heroes he admired, however, were not the scholars but the martyrs of the Church, and when he heard of the possibility of martyrdom in his own world—the Mediterranean region in the early thirteenth century—he longed to go to where the action was.

The new Franciscan order was at the time proposing a return to Christian ideals, including renunciation of the violence represented by the crusades. Franciscans wanted dialogue, not war, with Islam. They were willing to risk death rather than protect themselves with the sword. Canons Regular, however, cannot leave the church to which they are attached, so Ferdinand changed his order. He took the name of the patron saint of the chapel in which he received the Franciscan habit.[38] He would be called Antony, after the third-and-fourth-century Egyptian hermit.

He set off for Morocco, from where the bodies of assassinated Franciscans had recently been brought to Portugal. In Morocco he immediately became ill (he was to die ten years later of dropsy) and had to be shipped back to Portugal for treatment. On the way the ship was blown off course and stopped at Messina, Sicily. Antony, recovering, heard that a General Chapter of the Franciscans was taking place in Assisi, and two months later set off on foot for the gathering, hoping to take part in it. (Antony was to walk immense distances, all over northern Italy and southern France.) Francis himself was present at the assembly of several thousand members of his order. Antony was silent, unknown—probably busy learning Italian. An ordination of Franciscans and Dominicans took place, the Franciscans expecting the Dominicans to preach and vice versa. No one was prepared. Francis asked the new unknown to say whatever the Holy Spirit put into his mouth. Antony preached—and astounded everybody with his ability and his learning.

He was of medium height and fat, with powerful legs, a round face, big dark eyes, and charismatic presence. Vast throngs of people would travel to hear him; his sermons took place in piazzas and fields because churches were too small to hold the crowds. He travelled in the areas where Catharism[39] was powerful, to Montpellier, Toulouse, Le Puy, Brive, as far north as Limoges, always on foot. His preaching was so compelling that, it was said, the fish poked their heads out of the water to listen to his voice, just as flocks of birds gathered to hear Saint Francis. He preached poverty according to the spirit of the Gospels, and comforting and caring for the poor; he denounced dissolute churchmen and the rich. He always spoke to the people, much to their amazement, in whatever was their own dialect or patois.

There were hundreds of miracles. One day at Limoges a novice (a friar in training) ran away with Antony's book of psalms. He prayed; the novice saw a terrifying apparition and came running back to Antony with the psalter. This is the story advanced to explain why it is that to this day Antony is invoked by people who have been robbed, or who have simply lost things. One night he was staying at Châteauneuf-la-Forêt near Limoges. His host looked in at the window when Antony was at prayer and saw him standing, his arms held as though he were carrying a baby; he was in ecstasy. (It may be recalled that Saint Francis, too, had in ecstasy carried the child Jesus in his arms during the first Christmas midnight Mass at Greccio.)

Antony returned to Italy and eventually settled at Padua, where he became a famous peacemaker, somebody who was consulted in all kinds of private and political crises. By 1231 he was seriously ill with dropsy and living for the summer in the country outside Padua. He saw an enormous walnut tree, and decided that he would avoid the heat and be closer to God and nature by spending his days in the tree (he had often preached to his congregations standing in a tree). His friends placed planks on six spreading branches, and every day helped him hoist his huge weight up into the tree. His nights were spent in a small cell nearby, which still stands. In this cell he was again observed through a window, this time sitting before an open book on which stood a small child. The observer knew that it was the child Jesus. When he was close to death, Antony was transported by ox cart back to Padua (the people of Padua desperately wanted their saint to die in their town). The cart did not quite make it; Antony died at Arcella, outside the walls of the city. He was thirty-six.

Today, Antony of Padua is honoured as the patron saint of Portugal and of Brazil. Apart from his advocacy in finding lost objects (Antony is one of the most solicited of saints), he is also, as a result of his life history, the patron saint of seamen, the shipwrecked, the victims of other transport accidents, and the poor. In many churches the box for donations to the poor is placed near a representation of Saint Antony, as it is in Sant'Agnese's. Ironically, perhaps, he is buried at Padua in one of Italy's most splendid cathedrals; however, several million pilgrims visit this church every year, so the building fulfills an undeniably popular purpose.

Antony has been portrayed by many great artists, including Donatello and Titian. The representation that has been chosen for the narthex of Sant'Agnese's church is in the tradition of the paintings of Murillo. Painted on marble during the nineteenth or early twentieth century, it could easily be dismissed as merely a mawkish depiction of a man carrying a baby. What people today love about Antony, however, is not his extraordinary intellect, nor his oratorical powers and linguistic skills, but the fact that he was a man who loved Jesus as an infant. The gentling of the male is always one of the most urgent aims of civilization; people in the modern West tend to focus upon this universal human enterprise with uncommon zeal. The image of Antony as one to whom God revealed himself as a baby reflects this social fact. In any case, the revelation of the omnipotent God as a helpless and needy baby is one of the great paradoxes upon which Christianity is founded.

The second picture, which hangs in the right-hand aisle at the front of the church, shows a man who, although he was not the baby's father, nonetheless accepted the child Jesus as his own. He took responsibility for him, suffered on his behalf, and did not reject his mother, as he could easily have done when he found out that she was pregnant, and not by him. Joseph receives the ultimate accolade, that of Scripture itself, which calls him "a just man."[40] Yet for most of Christianity's history, Joseph was almost ignored among Christians searching for heroes to inspire them; Mary took the limelight. (Joseph was always part of Nativity scenes, of course, and of depictions of the Holy Family.)

In the Middle Ages Joseph was often a rather ridiculous figure, a man "cuckolded" by God.[41] Folklore and superstition surrounding Joseph still include affectionate but rough badinage: his statue may be planted head down in somebody's garden until he answers prayers to do with fixing the house; the child Jesus may be stolen from the arms of his statue until prayers are answered, upon which the child is returned to him. He is depicted as elderly because it is clear that by the time of Jesus' death, Joseph was no longer at Mary's side. Presumably he had died by then, although that does not necessarily mean that he was old.[42] A legend has Joseph contend with eleven other suitors for Mary's hand; he is revealed to be the correct suitor when his staff breaks into flower.[43] All that remains of this story in the modern iconography of Joseph is the lily that he carries, for example in the picture at Sant'Agnese's. This white lily signifies also his pure heart, that of "a just man."

The possibilities of Joseph as a Christian hero began to be widely appreciated during the sixteenth century; Saint Teresa of Avila and the

Jesuits were his most effective advocates.[44] He was made patron saint of Mexico in 1555, of Canada in 1624, of the universal Church in 1870. In 1955 May Day was made for Christians the feast of Joseph the Worker. People thought about Joseph's death, and imagined that he must have had both Jesus and Mary at his bedside: he became the person to whom one prays for a happy death. He is the solid, understanding, responsible, faithful husband and father, dependably competent and working at a useful trade. But most important, he was a man who took care of the child who appeared in his life, a man with a baby in his arms. Joseph the loving "non-father," it was then realized, heroically fulfilled one of Christianity's most demanding ideals: that of being a father (a brother, a sister, a mother) to somebody who is not your kin. Saint Joseph is also, for this reason, the patron saint of priests: Fathers/non-fathers.

Countless Catholic boys are called Joseph, José, Giuseppe, Joe; girls are Josepha, Giuseppina, Josephine. His popularity is now such that Pope John XXIII decided, in 1962, to insert his name into the Canon of the Mass.[45] The two ancient lists of saints in the Canon, unchanged for over a thousand years, include Agnes; they did not include Joseph.[46] Who could object to the addition of Joseph's name? Arousing not a murmur of disapproval, Pope John did a hitherto unthinkable thing: he made a change in the Canon, the central, most important, immutable part of the Mass. With the help of Joseph's irreproachable name, the renewal of the Church in modern times had begun. The Second Vatican Council opened the same year.[47]

THE COMMUNION OF SAINTS

At Sant'Agnese's, above the roundels containing portraits of popes come the galleries with their columns and the arches that carry the clerestory walls. First, there is a band of simple squares and oblongs. Above this band and between the windows, placed as high as possible just beneath the ceiling, is a series of nineteenth-century frescoes of young women—yet more saints. These are the martyred "companions" of Agnes, chosen as such because of the similarities between their stories and hers. They all lived during the first eight centuries of Christendom, and most of them are the heroines of passios, stories that fascinated their late antique and medieval listeners. We see Victoria, Lucy, Agatha, Barbara, Cecilia, Martina, Bibiana, Emerentiana (who, because she died a catechumen, is placed over the narthex of the church), Rufina, Columba, Julia, Apollonia, Flora, Catherine, Susanna, and Candida. Cecilia appears again, with Constantina and Agnes, in the ceiling.

These figures, and those honoured in the side chapels of the church, are only a tiny representative selection out of all the hosts of saints available to the people for whom this church was built. They are fellow Christians, believed to be now with God, who are thought of as ready and willing to offer inspiration, support, company, a sense of history, and even simple narrative interest and variety, if it is desired. They are the forebears, who have now reached the fullness of life promised in Christ's Resurrection. They have been through the mill and have made a heroic stand for the invisible Transcendent, for loving and helping other people as the real expression of authenticity in people of goodwill.

It is by no means necessary for a Christian to pray to saints or in the company of saints, to remember them or celebrate them—nor is it required that saints be depicted in churches. Many Christians are repelled by any attention paid to saints, and many Christian churches are chastely saintless. Sant'Agnese's church, indeed, is particularly *kataphatic*: it rejoices in the imagination. The opposite, and equally valid, way of praying is also valued in the Christian tradition. This is *apophatic* prayer, the deliberate shunning of imagining, the emptying of the mind so that God can enter and fill the soul. (*Kataphatic* and *apophatic* are Greek words that refer to gestures meaning "yes" and "no" respectively. To this day Greeks nod to say yes, lowering their heads—*kata*- means "down." In order to say no, they do the opposite, jerking their heads up rather than down—*apo*- means "away from" or the opposite of a nod.)

Some people object—fairly enough—to the wild imaginings that often make up saintly legends, to the strange superstitions that sometimes surround saints, to vulgar and sentimental representations of saints. Sant'Agnese's, however, has no such scruples. This is a church that expresses interest in these people; it has plenty of saints. They crowd the walls and the chapels and the ceiling. The ring of virgin martyrs around the top of the wall is a visual counterpart of a prayer known as a litany (from the Greek word for "prayer"), where saint after saint is invoked by name, and the congregation answers, "Pray for us" or "Pray with us" after each name. Such litanies remind Christians of how many saints there have been in the course of two millennia. The congregation thinks, during these prayers, of their multifarious history, and of the cost that has been paid down the centuries for keeping Christ's message alive. The pieces of marble on the walls of the passage down into Sant'Agnese's constitute a similar visual litany, albeit of people whose stories have been lost to us. Christians believe, however, that their destinies—like ours—are known in detail to God.

The virgin martyrs between the windows and the portraits of the popes form a kind of procession, which we have already noted as a favourite ritual action at a church like Sant'Agnese's. Processions, both of the living and of the lined-up-and-remembered dead, recall the continuous but itinerant character of Christianity. The Church is experienced as a huge crowd of people, past as well as present, on the march, pressing on towards the day when God's kingdom will reign upon earth. For more than 1,350 years the procession has been passing through the little church of Sant'Agnese. People have come wearing everything from togas to frock coats, veils to wimples to feathered headpieces to baseball caps, cloaks to tippets, crinolines to miniskirts. Men in skirted tunics, men in stockings, men and women in shorts: the church has seen it all. Many visitors come with no specifically spiritual intention, but simply as part of a tour of Rome that goes beyond the obvious highlights. They may or may not stay to observe the people using the building, or to look on at the ceremonies.

Worshippers in this church down the centuries have stood through the services; some of them have been made to stand in the narthex; the congregation has been more or less shut out of the sanctuary by marble screens; people have sat in chairs with kneelers, and in pews. They have groped their way down the passage in semi-darkness to get into the church, they have entered by doors into the galleries to look down at the altar, and they have walked in procession through the newly created front door and out to the church of Santa Costanza a short distance away.

There seem to have been cloistered women here, living nearby and serving the church, as early as the fifth century; after that, there is a reference to nuns (order unknown) in the early ninth century. By the tenth century Benedictine monks had replaced them; they themselves were reformed by the great Abbot Odo of Cluny in 936. Then came a group of secular priests of unacceptable behaviour: they were replaced by Benedictine sisters in the twelfth century; these in turn were succeeded by the monks of Saint Ambrose of Milan in 1480. The Augustinian Canons of the Saviour arrived from Bologna in 1489 and have remained ever since, having merged with the Canons Regular of the Saviour at the Lateran in 1823.[48]

In the course of the history of Sant'Agnese's church, the clergy have been enclosed monks and nuns, "guardians of the tomb," who would enter the church via the spiral staircase leading down from their monastery over the passageway; they have performed elaborate liturgies upon cosmatesque pavements inlaid with porphyry circles showing them where to stand; they have processed to the altar in billowing incense through marble choir screens filled with chanting clergy; they have sat on the bench around the lower apse behind the altar with the celebrant enthroned on the marble chair in the centre. They have preached from inlaid marble pulpits and from little wooden stands. The liturgy has simplified, and moved recently from Latin to the Italian vernacular.

Today, the priests are in charge of a parish,[49] and there are too few of them. In the canonry buildings they host parish classes and dinners and other social events. The large and busy congregation must be content to run most things themselves, led by their elected parish council: from scouts (both male and female), to Bible study groups and lectures by invited scholars, to visits to artistic and religious sites, to picnics and a polyphonic choir, to confraternities to help the poor and the sick, to organizations to welcome influxes of immigrants and refugees (the Roman embassies of some of the world's most embattled and desperate countries are situated in the neighbourhood of the church), to the popular sports club, bowling alley, and playing fields in Sant'Agnese's grounds. The modern lay Christian community of Sant'Egidio[50] prays every fortnight at Sant'Agnese's church. At the end of the service, while they are still singing the last song, they briskly move out of the church, expressing in this their resolve to get on with their work of teaching disadvantaged children, with befriending the poor and the sick, the old and the lonely, and with their peacemaking projects.

Hundreds and hundreds of Easter vigils have been celebrated in this place, hundreds of thousands of baptisms, hundreds of thousands of Masses. In 1959 Pope John XXIII made Sant'Agnese's one of the station churches of Rome: station churches used to have to be inside the walls. In the past the pope would visit a church ("stop" or "station" at it) on its special day during Lent, and also on great feasts such as Christmas. People would follow him, walking in procession, and join the church's own congregation waiting for him there for Mass.[51] Today, Sant'Agnese's has its own stational feast, the fifth Saturday in Lent, when people from all over Rome come to special services in this church. A huge influx of visitors arrives every year to see the Ceremony of the Lambs on January 21, and to join the procession through the catacombs that takes place a few days later. On a big, touristy day such as these always are, the parish likes to have a ceremony of its own in the evening, usually followed by a party in the Sala Giulio II: people feel a need to take back their church, and celebrate in it as a family. Sant'Agnese's has a famous resident cook, who prefers not to be named in a book. She lives in her own house over the entrance to the catacombs. She has presided over many memorable parish parties, and is said to outdo herself on ceremonial occasions.

8

ETERNAL REST:

Outside

....

In the grounds of Sant'Agnese's is a small round church, one of the most beautiful and influential buildings in the city. It dates from the years immediately following the death of Constantine in 337, and is among the oldest Christian buildings to have survived almost complete; it is still in use as a church. We saw in Chapter One that the congregation at Sant'Agnese's uses this church, Santa Costanza's, as a symbolic destination for processions and for special liturgies. The rotunda is also a prized venue for the celebration of marriage services. Small gilt chairs sometimes crowd the space inside, and there are often spectacular flower arrangements, left over from weddings. Outside the hours of services, a visit to Santa Costanza's is included in the tour of the catacombs underneath Sant'Agnese's.

To reach Santa Costanza's you take one of two paths, starting either from the top of the descending passageway to Sant'Agnese's or from the present front door of the basilica. The first path passes through the vaulted space underneath a powerful medieval tower, part of the monastic complex, on the left as you leave the top of the passageway. The tower is of flat, dark Roman bricks pierced by a few irregularly placed windows. It has ancient white and coloured marble fragments gleaming here and there on its surface, like charms in a chunk of Christmas pudding. Leaving the tower behind, you take the straight, cobbled avenue, which often has motorcycles parked along it. The path turns right at an orange building, which seems to be part of a school complex. You continue along the path with the building on your left. On your right is a sports complex, with pear trees in bloom in the spring. You walk 110 yards in all to reach the church of Santa Costanza on your left.

The second route starts from the excavated piazza in front of Sant' Agnese's. Leaving the candle-smoke-darkened walls of the Lourdes grotto on your left, you climb some steps and follow a rising path between dense green bushes and clipped hedges (you are returning gradually to the original ground level from the excavated piazza), to approach Santa Costanza's from the front. Below this path on your right is a tangled nursery garden. Just before reaching the round church, if you look over a low wall on your right, you will see a broad green field, bounded at one end by a massive, ancient semi-circular wall.

Santa Costanza's[1] was built as a mausoleum for Constantine's daughter, who wished to be buried near the grave of Agnes. The building today has a plain brick exterior. All embellishment, including a columned portico that used to circle the outside of the building, has long ago been stripped away. But the exterior of the mausoleum may never have been very showy: we have seen that early Christian buildings tended to be deliberately unassuming outside, reserving decoration mainly for their interiors. Santa Costanza's has arched windows and a belt of small white marble consoles or projecting blocks—the only remaining decoration—below the circular tiled roof. A flat brick façade reaches halfway up the cylindrical body of the building. It is pierced by a marble-framed door with two deep niches (they once held sarcophagi) sunk into the wall on either side of it. Two curving walls project from the corners of the rectangular front like a pair of brackets; the clergy at Sant'Agnese's used to keep their beehives in the right-hand curve. These walls once formed part of a round-ended covered forecourt to the building.

A PORPHYRY SARCOPHAGUS AND ITS SETTING

You enter the church via a widening aperture, through a deep stone portal and a wall five feet thick. The space inside is cool, broad, restful, and mysterious. A sense of numinousness is aroused by the light. The building's plan is circular, with a low vaulted ring round the circumference, and a series of twelve pairs of columns set in a circle about a tall cylindrical space topped by a hemispherical dome. The outer ring has a barrel vault covered with mosaics, which are low enough to be closely examined if you raise your head. The light in the ambulatory ring is diffused, and passes into it from between the dark verticals of the columns. The source of illumination is twelve windows set high up in the structure's central cylinder. Light streams down from above, into the heart of the building.

At some time after the mausoleum's completion, seventeen small windows were let into the barrel vault. They are irregularly placed, but angled so that the source of light is concealed unless you are is standing directly opposite one of them. Crude as these windows are, their makers knew that no openings should be visible in the ambulatory—light must appear to come only from the building's centre.

The columns are of granite, all of them grey except for two pairs of pink ones that distinguish the two main points on the building's circumference: the entrance and the niche opposite the entrance. All the columns have white marble Composite capitals, the outer ones smaller than the inner ones, creating a subtly centrifugal effect. Arches spring from elaborate entablatures that link the pairs of columns and add lightness and height; the cylindrical drum and its dome appear to be lifted with effortless grace. The columns and their acanthus-leaf capitals are thought to be of the second century:[2] ancient Roman buildings were already being raided for columns.

The effect of the ambulatory is to entice the visitor to follow its curve. Your steps are slowed because this space is a circle, not a purposeful rectangle. The mosaics, set in panels overhead, beckon you on: as you move forward, the panels become more and more richly decorated. The designs cunningly stretch to cover the shapes allotted them, which both arch upward and are shorter on the inner side of the wheel than at its circumference. Bands of delicate spirals divide them. The colours of the panels are predominantly a cool green with a background of white, offsetting the dimness of the light. This is a pre-Byzantine building; it was not yet common for mosaic backgrounds to be golden.

At the middle of the perimeter, opposite the door, is a niche containing a large red sarcophagus. This is a plaster copy of the original one in porphyry, which is kept today in the Vatican Museums. A small square turret with three more windows in it rises from the ambulatory's ceiling in front of the tomb. Over the niche containing the sarcophagus is an arched vault, once covered with dark blue stars crowded over a white sky, with the chi-rho sign like a golden sun in the middle of it. Only a patch of this decoration remains. The two letters of the Greek alphabet, X (chi) and P (rho), are the first two letters of the word XPI ΣTOΣ, "Christ." The superimposition of one of these upon the other produces a design like a wheel with spokes: a monogram of Christ.[3]

It was said that Constantine was shown this sign in a vision before the Battle of the Milvian Bridge in 312 A.D., and that a voice was heard proclaiming: "By this sign you shall conquer." Constantine won the battle, a victory that had enormous consequences for the history of Christianity. After the battle and the subsequent granting of freedom of worship to Christians, the sign stood for the triumph of Christianity in Rome. It is still a favourite Christian symbol, signifying Christ; in modern Christian minds the monogram rarely recalls Constantine.

Red porphyry, from which the sarcophagus was made, was the most precious building stone of the Romans. It was associated with the power and prestige of the emperors, who wore clothes dyed with the expensive colouring (similar to that of the stone) derived from huge quantities of purple-yielding sea snails. The Greek word *porphyreos*, from the name of this mollusc, *porphyra*, is the root of "purple" in English, but in the ancient world it could mean deep red, or purple, or russet; it also included the idea of a gleaming darkness, and as such could be used to describe the sea.[4] Redness evokes both fire and blood; the stone's name refers to its colour and its sheen when polished.

The Romans obtained almost all of their finest porphyry from a single mountain in Egypt, which they called the *Mons Porphyrites*, and also *Mons Igneus*, "fiery mountain," perhaps because of its store of porphyry. After the Arab conquest of Egypt in the seventh century, the whereabouts of the mountain were lost to the European world, until Richard Burton and George Wilkinson rediscovered the porphyry caves in the early nineteenth century. By that time the mountain had become known in Arabic as Gebel Dokhan, "smoking mountain," perhaps because of the earlier Roman name for it.[5]

The Santa Costanza sarcophagus possibly came from Alexandria, Egypt.[6] Its decoration is stiff and lifeless in spite of its vigorous subject matter (porphyry is extremely hard and therefore difficult to carve), with huge acanthus volutes and grapevines, and little winged genii (the ancestors of Italian *putti*) picking and packing grapes. A fat-tailed ram and two peacocks appear below. On the short sides of the sarcophagus three of the winged boys tread the grapes for wine, and the juice runs out of a lion's-head spout into three round pots. The heavy lid of the tomb has a carved head and two garlands on each of its sides. The fact that the decoration covers all sides of the stone chest has made some archaeologists think that it did not originally stand inside the niche, but in front of it, below the small turret that rises between the last two mosaic panels in the ambulatory. From there it could have been seen from all four sides and would have received extra light from the turret's windows. The red granite slab laid in the floor between the two pairs of columns opposite the niche would have been the place marked out for it. The starry vault, however, convinces others that the niche is where the tomb was always intended to stand.

Its contents, which almost certainly included jewels, were rifled during an early barbarian invasion of Rome. In 1467 the Venetian Pope Paul II moved the sarcophagus out of the mausoleum and placed it in the square outside the Palazzo San Marco, now Palazzo Venezia in central Rome, in order to add distinction to the palace ensemble. It stood out in the open as a public monument for four years, until Pope Sixtus IV, yielding to complaints, restored it to Santa Costanza's. In 1790 Pope Pius VI had it removed again, this time for safe keeping in the Vatican Museums; when he did so, forty oxen were required to drag it there.[7]

MOSAIC TAPESTRIES OVERHEAD

Whether you turn right on entering Santa Costanza's, or left, a similar set of mosaic panels covering the vault above you will accompany your steps round the ambulatory towards what is at present a plaster copy of the tomb. These mosaics have been repaired and restored with considerable success: when filling in damaged patches, the restorers could use the similar panel opposite as a model.[8] First, you will see, faintly glittering (unless the electric lights are turned on, in which case the effect is brilliant instead of dim), a panel filled with Greek (equal-armed) crosses, octagons, and hexagons drawn in red, green, and blue-green on white. The strategy is, in part, to move from abstract geometrical shapes to lifelike representations. Next, you will notice lozenges formed into crosses decorated with oak leaves, and star shapes each enclosing four dolphins, heads together as they attack octopi. Then comes a series of roundels large and small (straight lines here give way to curves). These are linked, and filled with crosses, dancers, naked flying genii,[9] sheep, and birds: ducks both flying and standing, storks, peacocks, a heron, a blackbird, a swan.

You will then see a trellis of vine leaves with blue naked boys climbing about, and birds pecking at bunches of grapes. Fully depicted vintage scenes appear at the short and long sides of the two corresponding panels. There are oxen pulling carts loaded with fruit. Two shed roofs shelter troughs in which men in loincloths crush the grapes with their feet while waving staves—sticks with curved ends for pulling down the grapes from the high vines. They look as if they might be dancing in time to music, perhaps to their own song. It is the same scene as the one that appears on the short sides of the sarcophagus. In the middle of this panel, and the middle of its counterpart on the other side, is a portrait bust: one of a woman and the other of a man. These may represent Constantina and Hannibalianus, the first of her two husbands.

Following this fourth panel comes the fifth, a carpet of roundels filled with busts of youths, flower designs, and standing figures male and female, dressed and undressed. And finally, nearest the sarcophagus, are the two most luxurious panels, the only ones to be heightened with discreet touches of gold. They are covered with fruiting and flowering boughs of bay, apples, pine cones, grapes, quinces, pears, and pomegranates, with large, carefully depicted birds: partridges, pheasants, ducks, and peacocks. These panels follow the tradition of floor mosaics for dining rooms, called *asaroton* ("unswept" in Greek), where fishbones, peelings, and other remains of the meal appear to litter the floor; such pavements give us an idea of the table manners of the Greeks and Romans.[10] Here on the ceiling, however, is a collection of pretty objects, far from being intended as litter: drinking horns, a bowl with doves drinking from it, *phialai* or flat dishes for libations, and water containers, such as fluted vessels, *aquamaniles* (vessels used for handwashing before, during, and after meals), vases, pans, and jugs. Greenery, fruit, flowers, birds, and plenty of liquid meant pure delight.

Although the building is round and the light comes from its centre, it nevertheless contrives to suggest a specific direction. The two halves of the ambulatory hold the centre in their embrace, while the succession of mosaic panels gently but unmistakably lead "up to" and then "down from" the sarcophagus opposite the entrance. The resting place of the dead person is in the richest, best, and happiest spot.

THE DOME'S GREAT LOST MOSAICS

The wall of the cylindrical drum was once covered, below and between the windows, with coloured marble slabs; nail marks are the only traces left of them. A modern sensibility, however, is able to enjoy contemplating the beautiful brickwork in and of itself. The powerful pairs of brick arches within the fabric of the clerestory walls hold up the weighty cylinder and dome. They are entirely functional, and yet they create radiating, decorative patterns that lighten the whole and direct the eye upward. The windows in the drum were made smaller at some unknown date: people apparently came to want less light in the central cylinder and more in the ambulatory.

The dome itself was decorated with a magnificent Hellenistic mosaic, which was in a very bad state of disrepair in the early seventeenth century; in 1620 it was destroyed and replaced with the fresco now in its place.[11] Because of the loss of the mosaic, never has a fresco stood as little chance of approval as this one. (The work remains, perhaps fortunately for its author, anonymous.) Actually, it is not at all a bad fresco, although expressing dislike for it has become *de rigueur*; its colours have largely faded away. It shows Christ with his saints (including Saint Agnes) sitting in a circle in heaven, conversing.

Descriptions were written and drawings were made of the dome's famous mosaic decoration during the fifteenth and sixteenth centuries, before it disappeared. The most detailed of the drawings, those by Francesco de Hollanda who lived in Rome from 1539 to 1553, were rediscovered in the library of the Escorial, Spain, in the 1870s. From them we can see that a river or sea flowed round the base of the dome, and on it baby genii darted about in boats and rafts, played with swans and other aquatic birds, and pursued fish and octopi with nets, rods, and harpoons. Greeks and Romans traditionally thought of the earth as a flat disk surmounted by a heavenly vault; the ocean, as a river, circulated around the perimeter of the disk. In thirteenth-century Rome river scenes like this one were imitated from ancient models; examples can be seen at Santa Maria Maggiore and at the cathedral of the Lateran. We are reminded of the water that poured out of Ezekiel's Temple and created a paradise out of the desert.[12]

Above this scene the blue dome, representing the heavens, was divided into twelve compartments, like a wheel with spokes, by golden caryatids supporting on their heads shafts sheathed with acanthus leaves; wild beasts crouched at their feet. The shafts resembled the Greco-Roman marble candlesticks that once stood inside Santa Costanza's; one of these is now the support for the sanctuary lamp in Sant'Agnese's church. In the dome's compartments were scenes from the Old Testament: the sacrifices of Cain and Abel, Moses striking water from a rock, the sacrifice of Elijah on Mount Carmel, Susanna and the lascivious old men, Tobias with his fish.[13] All the stories that we can decipher from the drawings of the mosaic—or that we know from travellers' descriptions were once depicted here—concern prayer, faith, divine concern for humanity, and their dramatic consequences.[14]

By medieval times the building had become a church. The earliest extant reference to its being dedicated to "Santa Costanza" dates from 865, when Pope Nicolas I reinstated Bishop Rothad of Soissons, who had been deposed without the pope's authority by Hincmar of Reims: for some unknown reason Santa Costanza's was chosen as the appropriate place for the ceremony.[15] An altar, probably not the first one, was constructed here in 1256 by Pope Alexander IV; it was broken open in 1605 as "research" into relics, and a new one was provided in 1620. The medieval altar had stood in front of the sarcophagus niche, under the turret with its extra windows, but it now seemed obvious where the new altar of such a church ought to go: in the middle of the central space. This is the altar in use today. It is similar in style to the one in Sant'Agnese's church. Costanza Lepri, founder of the union of

Children of Mary at Sant'Agnese's, was buried at the foot of the altar in the church of her namesake in 1867.

BACCHIC REVELS

During the sixteenth century, when all things classical were the rage, it became fashionable to believe that Santa Costanza's was not originally Christian at all, but a Greco-Roman Bacchic temple. The vines and the pressing of the grapes appear not only in the ambulatory mosaics but on the sarcophagus itself; the sarcophagus was accordingly thought to be the tomb of Bacchus. The depiction of tiny dolphins in two of the ambulatory panels, and the mosaic "sea" scene round the base of the dome, were taken to refer to the story in which Dionysus, attacked by pirates while on a sea voyage, turned his molesters into dolphins. The importance of vine and wine symbolism in Christianity[16] was therefore set aside, as was the well-known Christian symbol of the fish,[17] and that of the "living water" pouring out of the city in the vision of Ezekiel.

A group of seventeenth-century Dutch artists living in Rome formed a club called the Bentvogels (which means "members of the Academy" in Dutch), dedicated to drinking and revelling in honour of Dionysus. They initiated new members by first drinking all night in a nearby taverna, then sneaking into Santa Costanza's at dawn, where they celebrated "baptism," with many a libation, in or over the sarcophagus (the original porphyry one). Their names may still be seen as graffiti scratched into the plaster of the niche.

Santa Costanza's is, in fact, a very early Christian building. When it was designed and decorated, however, the creation of a distinctive Christian iconography was still in its infancy. Christian artists—or the pagan artists hired by the very newly Christianized (I avoid the word "converted") imperial family—naturally used the art they knew; pagan motifs were inevitably adopted, their meanings simply changed where necessary.

Certainly greenery, especially vines, and the pressing of grapes were images used to express Dionysiac themes. Fish—less frequently—might appear in a temple to Bacchus. But the mediating culture into which Christianity was born was imbued with the same Mediterranean tradition and choice of phenomena—bread, wine, dolphins, pines, peacocks, Roman silver and ceramics, octopi, vines, pomegranates. It is no wonder that the mausoleum employs these motifs. When it was built, barely twenty-five years had passed since Christians were first permitted to produce public art. They had, however, been decorating the galleries of their underground catacombs with imagery very like that at Santa Costanza's for 150 years.[18]

There was never any doubt about the Christian content of the mosaics in the two apsidal recesses to the left and right of the church's entrance. Some have thought them later additions to the mausoleum. Those who believe that the building was made into a baptistery some time after its completion think that these mosaics were added then. They cannot have been made very much later, however, because they have white, not gold, backgrounds: they are rarely thought to be later than the second half of the fourth century.[19] Unfortunately, both mosaics are in very bad shape, having been poorly restored more than once. The garlands of grapes and pomegranates underneath both compositions are probably the best-preserved sections.

The left-hand picture may well be the earliest surviving example of what became a favourite iconographical scheme.[20] A youthful Christ wearing a halo stands above (probably originally on) a mountain out of which pour four rivers (only three of which remain, but this detail as well as others is known from a number of similar examples). The mountain symbolizes the Church, the rivers the four Evangelists. Without excluding this interpretation, we can also read the scene as depicting paradise regained, at the end of time; the four streams then represent the four rivers of Paradise,[21] and the mountain represents Paradise itself, transfigured.

The palm trees on either side are for life, fruitfulness, joy, and victory at the end of time. Approaching the waters are four white sheep, two on either side: the followers of the Good Shepherd, eager for the water of life.[22] Sheep in scenes like this, representing either the Apostles or Christians in general, are all alike: they are meant to show that for Christians, family ties are not as important as the new notion that every believer (today Christians would say every human being) is to be thought of as "family." On either side of Christ are Peter and Paul, Peter receiving a scroll on which is written *Dominus pacem dat* (The Lord gives peace) and Paul being blessed by Christ's raised right hand. Behind the two Apostles are two houses that, as we know from other examples of the scene, represent Bethlehem (behind Paul) and Jerusalem (behind Peter). Bethlehem, the goal of the journey of the Magi—foreigners seeking truth—represents the Church of the Gentiles; Jerusalem, behind Peter, is the Church of the Jews.[23] Christ's blessing of Paul shows that Christianity welcomes people not of the original chosen race.

The mosaic opposite shows a haloed and bearded figure sitting, holding a book, on the globe of the world. He is approached by a single figure, who is receiving, with hands covered in his cloak, some object that is impossible to make out. Ten palm trees surround the two figures; some claim that one palm tree, the little one in the middle, is a restorer's addition. This mosaic is often said to represent Christ again (an older Christ, very different from the depiction opposite—but this might be the result of over-restoration). He could be giving the Keys of the Kingdom to Peter.[24]

The first scene is usually said to represent the New Covenant, or *traditio legis*, "the granting of the law," to the followers of Jesus; in other examples of the scene, the words on the scroll read *Dominus legem* (rather than *pacem*) *dat*. If this is correct, then the right-hand scene would almost certainly represent God (as a bearded, older man) giving the Law to Moses: the Old Covenant would be facing the New. If the palms originally numbered ten, as they do today, then they could refer to the Ten Commandments.

However, it is possible that *Dominus pacem dat* might be correctly written on Peter's scroll in the left-hand mosaic. In that case Christ standing on the mountain of the Church between figures representing Gentiles and Jews would be the reconciler, bringing peace: "But now in Christ Jesus," says the Letter to the Ephesians, "you [the pagans] that used to be so far apart from us [the Jews] have been brought very close, by the blood of Christ. For he is the peace between us, and has made the two into one and broken down the barrier which used to keep us apart."[25]

Santa Costanza's, because it is round with an ambulatory, is like a church surrounded by its narthex, or like a basilica with its nave wrapped around its sanctuary. The centre, here, is the "end." The source of illumination is from "above," which signifies the transcendent, "where God is."

The idea of a journey of the soul around a central space is extremely old; it recalls ancient Greek ideas of *moira* or fate, where a person walks his "road of life" and yet must see his fate as his "portion": an "area" or part of a whole that is "apportioned" to him. The underlying spatial metaphor for a life lived in time is easily translated into the shape of a round building; it is one of the strands of meaning at Santa Costanza's. From this point of view, to die is to link one end of the "line" of life with the other end. An "area" is created thereby, filling out the line; and together, portion and line are the person's fate. The porphyry sarcophagus at Santa Costanza's stands where the "roads" to it end. The ambulatory "creates" the space within it.

The design of Santa Costanza's is to be "read" as expressing the destiny of a soul enjoying fulfillment and peace at last. It can simultaneously evoke intimations of such a state of soul in a visitor. There is no Dionysian fury or drunkenness about the expressive features of this building, not even in the iconography, with its vines and winepressing. Joy is there, certainly. The objects depicted in the culminating mosaic panels in the series—the greenery in profusion, the fruit, the silver and gold vessels, the colourful birds—should be understood as the late antique world's shorthand symbols for paradise eternal, the garden of endless bliss. The wine being pressed may mean the eternal reward, the "harvest" of a life completed. The round shape of the building expresses eternity in the "unendingness" of its circular outline, and totality in its perfection.[26] The illumination from the windows is the "perpetual light" shining upon a soul resting in peace.

The light-filled centre, however, is the beginning as well as the end; it is the hub of the wheel. As such, it can be felt to correspond to the soul's core, in anyone who visits Santa Costanza's with the intention of responding to the building's meaning. It refers us to the part of ourselves that receives and remembers mystical experience; it is this "place" that empowers the following of the dim "road around" it, the journey that will define who we are and what is our deepest intention.[27] The centre of the soul is the abode of God: "The Spirit of God," as Paul put it, "has made his home in you."[28] Line and area, centre and circumference express fundamental oppositions which, in the language of spiritual insight, are paradoxically "the same."

In spite of its circular form, Santa Costanza's is also subtly cross-shaped: the columns, on closer inspection, are regularly spaced except for four points at which they stand farther apart; the arches they support spring higher at these places too. The larger spaces at these four points correspond to the entrance, the sarcophagus opposite, and the two large niches in the outer wall, to left and right as you enter, each with a mosaic-filled apse, as we have seen. There are also twelve other regularly placed niches in the wall, square in plan alternating with curved, but all arched overhead;[29] these are smaller than the four main radial points. The cross that is superimposed on the circle is a sign evoking stillness.

The design of Santa Costanza's creates a series of paradoxes: movement (the wheel's perimeter) and the cross, a four-square design that is immovable, like the four cardinal points of a compass. The building is one, a unified circle, resting in itself—but it also expresses two[30] (the columns standing in pairs, and the two enticing hemispherical "journeys" of mosaic panels). The points of the cross create a square in the circle. The building is a rotunda, but also has direction and a destination; it is a Christian building, and as such converts fate into destiny. The central space is a hub for the turning circumference, and also a stationary circle containing the intersection of the unmoving cross. The still weight of the building is as solid and as grounded as the earth—but at its core is a flood of light from the heavens.

OF ROUNDNESS AND BAPTISM

Ancient Roman mausolea were often round. The mausoleum of Hadrian (now known as the Castel Sant'Angelo) and the mausoleum of Augustus are two spectacular examples that survive in Rome. The vast Roman baths also contained circular structures.[31] From the mid fourth century, and especially from the fifth century onward, Christians made their baptisteries round.

The associations were not only with bathing and water (both "round" and "water" belonged together, both of them "female," "of birth," and "of the soul" in the ancient lists of opposites), but also with death. In baptism, as we have seen, Christians are initiated by "dying" and rising again, being reborn out of the waters. "Have you forgotten," wrote Paul to the Christians in Rome, "that when we were baptized into union with Christ Jesus we were baptized into his death? By baptism we were buried with him, and lay dead, in order that, as Christ was raised from the dead in the splendour of the Father, so also we might set our feet upon the new path of life."[32]

The first public baptistery in Rome, built by Constantine at the Lateran, is octagonal in shape, an octagon being to ancient minds "like a circle." The walls of Constantine's baptistery still stand; the interior was remade by Pope Sixtus III (432–440) and redecorated in the seventeenth century.[33] It originally had a low vault over the ambulatory, as at Santa Costanza's. It still has eight huge porphyry columns and steps down into the central, circular pool area for baptism by immersion; an octagonal entablature supported by the columns is inscribed with a poem on baptism, by Sixtus. Above it is another series of eight columns, and a dome in eight sections with the dove of the Spirit in the centre of it, "hovering over the waters."[34] The figure eight, as we have seen, signifies Resurrection, new life, and the new age inaugurated by Christ.[35]

The Lateran baptistery stands apart from the cathedral nearby: it had special requirements for the provision of water. Furthermore, catechumens were baptized before entering the Church: their solemn entry into the church building, after the ceremony in the baptistery outside, symbolized the beginning of a new "path of life." Separate baptisteries have often been customary ever since. Even the simple arrangement at Sant'Agnese's, with baptism in the hall next door, continues this tradition.

In Rome, during the first years after Constantine's victory, baptism was administered only once a year, on the eve of Easter and in the presence of the bishop of Rome himself, in the baptistery of St. John at the Lateran. A great many people would be baptized at once. After the solemn rites had been accomplished in the baptistery, a procession of neophytes newly robed in white would move to the cathedral proper, where the faithful awaited them; the building would have been filled with light, to celebrate the light of Christ and the enlightened state of the Church's new members. There Mass would be said, and the newly baptized would receive Communion for the first time. Today, adult Christian converts still try to receive baptism on the eve of Easter. In churches where catechumens are not excluded from the central part of the Mass, baptism before the united faithful takes the place of the drama of the entry into the church. Some modern parishes, however, have re-adopted the old method of initiation: catechumens leave the church before the central part of the Mass begins, until the day when they receive baptism and are admitted to the mysteries for the first time. In both cases, much is made still of the splendour of light after darkness.

In Jerusalem a huge basilica was built by Constantine on what was believed to be the hill of Golgotha, the site of the Crucifixion. Nearby, and separate from the basilica, stood the Anastasis, a round building over what they thought had been Christ's tomb; *anastasis* means "resurrection" in Greek.[36] This rotunda had an ambulatory around the central space inside, like Santa Costanza's. Later, the shrines of martyrs were often round, like the Anastasis. In Rome, for instance, the round church of Santo Stefano Rotondo was built in honour of Saint Stephen, the First Martyr after Christ.[37] We saw in the case of Emerentiana, who died while still a catechumen, that martyrdom could be a "baptism of blood." A round (or octagonal) building could—without contradiction—serve Christians as a mausoleum or a baptistery. Mausoleum, baptistery, martyrium: all were buildings with meanings that predisposed them to a circular shape; and they were often buildings separate from their churches.

There are references to baptism in early times at Sant'Agnese's. The *Liber Pontificalis* says that Constantina had a baptistery built there, "in the very same place," *in eodem loco*, where she had been herself baptized, together with her aunt, Constantia. If this is correct, the two women were presumably baptized in some unassuming place in the grounds of the catacombs; a stream flowed nearby until the nineteenth century. Appended to the account of Constantina's baptism in the *Liber Pontificalis*, and probably copied from archival sources, is a list of gifts made to the basilica she founded, in order to support its running costs. These goods include donations of land, and gold and silver lamps and altar vessels, among which is "a gold lantern with twelve wicks, above *the font*" (my emphasis).[38]

In 419 Pope Boniface I, unable to reach the Lateran because it was in the hands of the usurper Eulalius, "celebrated the baptism of Easter in the basilica of the blessed martyr Agnes, with all the customary rites." However, the Latin record could well mean that it was baptism at Sant'Agnese's that was customary.[39] Perhaps when Pope Liberius took refuge at Sant'Agnese's in 357–358, he chose the place not only because it was outside the walls, but because he could properly baptize there (he was there for Easter), in spite of the anti-pope Felix's being in possession of the Lateran.

It is perfectly understandable that people have wondered, down the centuries, whether Santa Costanza's was built to be the baptistery mentioned or hinted at in the sources: true, it is rather far away from the church, but being separate was normal for baptisteries. It has the right shape. When the floor of the building was excavated during the nineteenth century, a small cistern was found beneath the middle of it. Some maintain that the cistern was only for collecting rain water, via a complex system of conduits running down from the roof of the rotunda into the cistern; from there, a single pipe carried the water down the hillside.[40] Others think that the mausoleum was turned into a baptistery soon after its completion, although the archaeological evidence does not support the existence of an excavated pool. If the sarcophagus was moved into the niche from its original position on the red granite slab in front of it, a new use for the building as a baptistery, perhaps with a large basin instead of a pool, could explain why.

CONSTANTINA THE GOOD

Two codices of the poet Prudentius (ca. 348–ca. 405) transcribe, together with his hymn in honour of Saint Agnes, a poem proclaiming that "Constantina, a worshipper of God and devoted to Christ, has dedicated a temple to the victorious virgin Agnes. By the will of God and thanks greatly to the help of Christ, she has with a devout heart paid for everything." This temple is greater than all buildings, the poem goes on, religious and profane buildings alike, tall and glittering with gold though they may be. It celebrates the name of Christ, the only one who, though human (literally "sharing the name of Adam"),[41] has been able to rise from the blind night of death and triumphantly enter heaven. The verses end with the desire that the building should keep alive for centuries the name of Agnes, who offered herself for Christ. The poem is an acrostic: the first letters of its verses make up the words CONSTANTINA DEO, "Constantina, to God." The commentaries in the codices tell us that this poem was inscribed on marble and displayed inside the church Constantina founded. In the seventeenth century a fragment of the inscription was still to be seen in the church of Sant'Agnese; it has since disappeared.

Constantina was later believed by Christians to have been a saint, probably in large part because of this inscription, which would have said all that most people knew about her, apart from her founding a basilica and a mausoleum, and the fact that she belonged to Constantine's family. The acrostic poem says in the first line that she was *Christo dicata*, which seemed to proclaim that she was a dedicated virgin; "dedication" had come to mean most obviously a vow of celibacy. Her name was suggestive too: constancy must have been her virtue. (People were expected to live up to the names given to them: one was to take one's saintly namesake as a model, or at least to live the virtue expressed by one's name.)

And so an inspiring legend evolved, which made her its heroine; Constantina came eventually to be known as "Santa Costanza" in Italian. Before we launch into the tale of Constantina, it is worth pausing to consider the ease with which confusion can arise out of the names of the Emperor Constantine's family. His father was Constantius. Constantine had three sons called Constantine, Constantius, and Constans; one of his daughters was Constantina, also called Constantia, and his sister's name was Constantia.

In the story told about her in the passio of Agnes, the heroine is called not Constantina but Constantia (which is closer to "Costanza").

She was a queen and a *virgo prudentissima* (which meant that she was not yet married, and was therefore a young, if precociously wise, girl). She became afflicted with a virulent scrofula: sores erupted all over her body. Advised to try praying for a cure at the grave of Agnes, Constantia went there at night, though a pagan, and besought the saint's help. She fell asleep, and in a dream Agnes appeared to her, exhorting her to courage: "*Constanter age Constantia!*" ("Be constant, Constantia!") Then she added, "Believe that Jesus Christ, the Son of God, is your Saviour,[42] the one who will heal you." The voice itself woke Constantia, and she discovered that the sores had vanished from her body. She returned to the palace, and her father and brothers rejoiced.

According to the *Liber Pontificalis*, she was baptized a Christian near the shrine of Agnes, together with her aunt, Constantia. And not content with that, the passio adds, she decided to become a consecrated virgin, a condition that in the late antique mind epitomized constancy. She also asked her royal menfolk to build a basilica dedicated to Agnes, and demanded that a mausoleum for herself be placed next to it.

However, there were vicissitudes to come. In a different passio, that of the Roman martyrs Gallicanus, John, and Paul,[43] Constantina plays an important role. Here, we are told that her father the emperor had given her as the future bride of a widowed general, Gallicanus,[44] in reward for military services. Her fiancé was away at the time of her conversion, subduing Thrace. Constantina approached her father with her plan of remaining a virgin. She was not afraid of defying him, and successfully wrung from Constantine his consent to her avoidance of marriage to the worthy Gallicanus—or to anybody else. She even persuaded Gallicanus' two daughters, Attica and Artemia, first to become Christians and then to remain virgins too. By this time Constantina had 120 virgins ready and willing to join the community she was creating in the palace. But what to do about Gallicanus?

Constantina sent her faithful eunuchs John and Paul[45] to the general, who was suffering reverses at the hands of the Thracians. John and Paul told Gallicanus about Christianity, and he promised to become a Christian if he won. An angel appeared on the battlefield and led the army of Gallicanus to victory. When he returned to Rome to celebrate his triumph, the general was told that his betrothed had been cured of the scrofula, but that he could not marry her: she was, it was explained, already wedded to Christ. Far from enraged at the news, Gallicanus happily agreed to renounce her, sought baptism, and vowed to live in continence himself. After working for the poor for many years, he eventually became a hermit in Egypt, and was beheaded for his faith.

CONSTANTINA THE BAD

To leave the world of Christian romance and turn to the annals of the last important historian of the Roman empire, Ammianus Marcellinus (ca. 330–ca. 400), is to receive quite a shock. Ammianus, it should be noted, was a supporter, though a critical one, of Julian the Apostate;[46] and Roman invective against political opponents was invariably savage. Constantina, in his account, was no pure virgin. She was first married, aged fourteen, to Hannibalianus, the son of one of Constantine's own brothers. (The Piazza Annibaliano lies below and behind Santa Costanza's church today; from it, you can see the sign for the Sant'Agnese Tennis Club.) Constantine made Hannibalianus ruler of Pontus, Armenia Minor, and Cappadocia, in 335. After the death of their father in 337, the sons of Constantine murdered their potential rivals, including Hannibalianus, their sister's husband. Fourteen years later Constantina married another of Constantine's nephews, Flavius Claudius Constantius Gallus, who had been a child at the time of the killings and therefore escaped them; Constantina was five years older than her second husband.

He was made Caesar in 351 and sent to rule at Antioch; Constantina went with him. Gallus, says Ammianus, was guilty of bloodthirsty crimes. "And his wife was a serious incentive to his cruelty," he adds, "a woman beyond measure presumptuous." She is accused of agreeing to have a man killed because his wife, lusting for her son-in-law, wanted him removed. Ammianus calls her "a Megaera [that is, one of the Furies] in mortal guise, one who assiduously inflamed the savagery of Gallus, being as insatiable as he in her thirst for human blood." "The pair became ever more expert in doing harm," he goes on. " They fastened upon innocent victims false charges of aspiring to royal power, or of practising magic . . . The queen pushed her husband's fortunes headlong to sheer ruin."[47] The Emperor Constantius II decided to recall his sister from Antioch, and Constantina died on the journey home, in 354. Then Gallus was summoned to Rome. Although he blamed Constantina for his wickedness, the Emperor had him beheaded. He was twenty-nine years old.

It happened that Constantina's sister Helena was married to none other than Julian the Apostate. When Helena died in 360, Ammianus tells us, her body was sent back to Rome and interred "near the city, on the via Nomentana, where also her sister Constantina, formerly the wife of Gallus, was buried."[48] Apart from Constantina and Helena, we have heard of Constantina's aunt Constantia, an apparently blameless woman who was baptized together with her niece. Some have wondered whether this aunt Constantia—and not "the Fury" Constantina—was, in fact, the "Constantia" of the passio of Agnes. Perhaps she was buried with Constantina as well as baptized with her. The bones now inside the altar at Santa Costanza's are those of three women and two men;[49] it has been suggested that the men might originally have occupied sarcophagi in the two niches outside, in the front of the building.[50] It is tempting to imagine three sarcophagi inside for the three imperial women, one for each of the three main niches in Santa Costanza's.

Clearly, the facts about Constantina's morality, or lack of it, are simply not available to us. Her story has always been overshadowed by the lives of her male relatives and her husbands, as well as dramatized and fictionalized by the vituperations of Ammianus—and the equally passionate desire of the authors of the passios to make her, because she had founded a church, into a saintly virgin. Ammianus gives us a few nuggets of historical accuracy, no doubt. But who would bother to look into a passio for factual information? And yet, as we shall see, it was the passio that held the clue to the real nature of Constantina's basilica dedicated to Saint Agnes.

DETECTING THE SECRET FROM A SYLLABLE

The tomb of Agnes, who died in 305 A.D., lies underneath the altar of the present church of Sant'Agnese, built in the 630s. An earlier basilica, which probably replaced a small shrine, had been built over the grave in the late fourth or early fifth century. Archaeology has established that this earlier basilica had no aisles. Its length was the same as that of today's church; its width corresponded to that of the present building's nave. It lay in a position very slightly oblique with respect to the existing structure, and had a smaller apse, the foundations of which are underneath the present one.[51]

Behind the altar and in the apse the eighty-five-year-old Abbess Serena was buried in 514, and in the catacomb gallery in the same area an inscription was found which is datable to 349,[52] approximately when Constantina's basilica was being built: Constantina was living in Rome at that time. The present church façade has retained fourth-century brickwork, as has the lower left side of the passageway down into the building. Constantina's fourth-century basilica, then, would seem to have been a disappointing affair: narrow and not very long, despite the claims of her grandiose inscription. Her mausoleum was some distance away; if it was ever used for a baptistery, the procession of neophytes would have had to walk some distance from there to the church after the ceremony.

Christians were interred in the catacombs around Agnes's burial place and beneath the little basilica; they are also known to have been buried in the field near Santa Costanza's.[53] The enormous hemispherical wall that stands today at one end of this field delimited what was apparently a cemetery *sub divo*, "open to the sky." Pagan hypogea and a pagan *columbarium* (a burial building with little alcoves for incinerated remains) were also found in the field; they were there before the wall was built.

In 1946 Friedrich Wilhelm Deichmann published an article that revolutionized modern ideas not only about Sant'Agnese's, but also about the first big public buildings built by the Christians in Rome.[54] On reading the passio of Agnes, he was struck by the prefix to one word. "Constantia [as the passio calls Constantina] asked her father and her imperial brothers to build a basilica to Saint Agnes, and she placed her own mausoleum next to it." The word is *collocavit: con* (*col-*) means with, and implies close proximity. What if the legendary passio pointed to a physical fact?[55] What if Constantina's mausoleum really was *collocatum*, "attached," to her basilica?

Deichmann looked at the front of Santa Costanza's. He considered the big hemispherical wall marking the end of the field to his right. The wall, he realized, could be one end of a building enormous enough for Constantina's mausoleum to cling to one side of the structure, to a wall no longer standing.[56] One widely held suggestion had been that the field in front of Santa Costanza's had been an open-air cemetery in the shape of a circus, with long straight walls and at least one rounded end. He looked again at the wall. Staring everybody in the face for centuries, without any real attention being paid to it, was a simple and obvious fact: the wall has windows in it! It is pierced by a row of rectangular openings and a round window in the middle. And that must mean that it originally supported a roof, or windows would not have been needed.[57]

The archaeologist realized that Constantina's basilica was not a meagre structure built over Agnes's tomb, as everyone had assumed, but rather an enormous roofed basilica, now in ruins, to which Constantina's mausoleum was directly attached. When Constantina exclaimed in her inscription about the "greatness" of her church, readers had thought she must be referring to the greatness of its purpose, of honouring Christ and remembering Agnes. If Deichmann was right, she was also extolling the vast dimensions of the building she was dedicating to Christ and to the saint.

Eight years after Deichmann published his article (which was received with considerable scepticism by the scholarly community),[58] excavations began. They proved him resoundingly right: the basilica of Saint Agnes that Constantina built lay under the ground in front of and beyond Santa Costanza's church. It was about a hundred yards long and forty yards wide, with an atrium the same width and a further sixty yards long.[59] Within the perimeter of its walls today are a substantial empty field, a ball court, a sports club, and an area marked out for playing *calcetto* (five-a-side football).

The church was what has now been named a funerary or cemetery basilica. It had side aisles that curved round the huge back wall to form a continuous ambulatory, which was presumably used for processions. (Modern funerals are also celebrated with processions. Even now, a line of cars following the coffin—its length is important—is a formal ritual, and a mark of respect and friendship for the person who has died.) Within the central body of the church was a small area with an apse, perhaps for an altar where Mass was said. The aisles were formed by square pillars rather than columns, which suggests that there were arches rather than an architrave above them, supporting the clerestory walls. If this theory is correct, the beautiful columns in Sant'Agnese's church today would not, as it is sometimes claimed, have come from this building.[60]

The entire floor of the big funerary basilica would have been literally paved with the graves of people who were not buried in the catacombs, but who wanted nevertheless to be laid to rest near the body of the martyr Agnes. Christian families would visit their dead here, on the anniversaries of their deaths. The family would walk or ride out of Rome on the *dies natalis* of the dead relative, bringing food and drink for a feast. Inside the cemetery basilica they would gather at the graveside. The basilica was not for ordinary church services, but for these family celebrations, and for enormous concourses of people on the "birthday" of Agnes herself.

It was here that Gregory the Great twice delivered sermons on the feast day of Saint Agnes[61]—and not, as used to be thought, in a small church over the grave. We can imagine him looking out over the packed crowd as he remarked on "the disappointment any Christian in Rome must have been feeling if he or she had not been able to come." Constantina's mausoleum was the largest and finest tomb at the site, but it was still only a tomb, attached to a cemetery basilica. When the *Liber Pontificalis* said that Pope Liberius stayed "in the cemetery" of holy Agnes because the anti-pope Felix had usurped his place in Rome, it did not mean that he took refuge in the catacombs: it meant that the pope temporarily lived at, or even in, the cemetery basilica. (The picture of the pope living "in the cemetery," when it was believed that the only cemeteries in this area were an open field and the catacombs, was the kind of idea that had helped give rise to the modern myth that early Christians routinely hid in the catacombs during the persecutions.)

Why was the cemetery basilica built so far away from the grave of Agnes? The answer is simple: it wasn't. Its remaining foundations establish that the basilica was so immense, in fact, that the passageway down into the present church of Sant'Agnese leads from what was a corner of the atrium of Constantina's building. The big basilica faced via Nomentana, whereas the present church is oriented in the opposite direction, with its back to the road. The two pathways now taken from Sant'Agnese's to Santa Costanza's pass either diagonally across the giant basilica, or along the front of its atrium and then along part of its side. The mausoleum was added after the cemetery basilica's completion, by means of a so-called forceps atrium: the two curving walls in front were once covered with a roof that collected rain from the large building as well as the small one, and ran the water off and away from the walls, perhaps via the cistern inside Santa Costanza's. As catacombs continued to be built under the area, one late gallery was dug underneath the basilica to join up with the spiral staircase inside Constantina's mausoleum.

ANOTHER, AND ANOTHER, AND ANOTHER

People find, on the whole, what they are looking for; conversely, if they do not suspect the existence of something, they may not see it even if it lies in front of them. After the discovery at Sant'Agnese's, other giant cemetery basilicas started to come to light outside the walls of Rome. It was soon realized that one such basilica was, in fact, still standing: its central nave is today the church of San Sebastiano, along the via Appia, at the site where underground cemeteries first received the name "catacombs."[62]

San Sebastiano's had always been a puzzle because there was nothing, architecturally, quite like it, with its piers and arcades instead of an architrave, its U-shaped ambulatory, now outside the present church,[63] its tombs covering the floor and stacked along the walls both above and below ground, and the mausolea clinging to the outside of the building like limpets.[64] The building can now be identified as perhaps the oldest of the cemetery basilicas so far discovered at Rome; Christians might even have begun to build it before Constantine entered the city.

Constantine was known to have founded a basilica beside the mausoleum of Helena, his mother, in the grounds of the present church of Saints Marcellinus and Peter on the via Labicana southeast of Rome;

inside Constantine's ruined rotunda stands a small seventeenth-century church. The porphyry sarcophagus of Helena, taken from this mausoleum, is now in the same room as Constantina's sarcophagus in the Vatican Museums. It has carvings on it of a battle, and was probably originally intended for Constantine himself, before he left Rome to found Constantinople. When Helena died in 330, her body was brought back to Rome and laid in the sarcophagus, within the massive brick rotunda. The mausoleum stood before the atrium of what we now recognize was once a huge cemetery basilica. Catacombs spread out all round the site, as at San Sebastiano's and Sant'Agnese's; the shrine of the martyrs Marcellinus and Peter[65] remained a chapel inside the catacombs, with steps down to it.

Another cemetery basilica was found alongside the present church of San Lorenzo fuori le Mura to the east of Rome. It was separate from, though situated alongside, the shrine in the catacombs, to which there was a descent by means of steps; the present church was later built over the grave. Along the via Prenestina a rotunda known as Tor de'Schiavi has recently been found to have yet another cemetery basilica nearby; the mausoleum lies behind the building's apse. So far, no written sources have been discovered about the building—we have no idea what saint might have been venerated there, or who was buried in the mausoleum. There are two catacombs in the area.[66] An epitaph found in the floor of San Paolo fuori le Mura in the sixteenth century, and now in the Lateran collections, proclaims that one Eusebius had repaired "the entire cemetery," including fixing its windows; it seems as though here was yet another a cemetery basilica, still unexcavated.[67]

The great apse at the end of the field stretching away from Santa Costanza's church stands at the extreme edge of a hill. The hilltop was levelled for the basilica's foundations, and the surface then extended with filling to support the apse. The walls of this apse reach to the bottom of the hill and shore up its flank. The enormous earthworks can best be appreciated when you stand behind and below the structure, in the Piazza Annibaliano. Great supporting buttresses have been added. They were obviously needed, given the precarious site of the apse. The entry for Pope Symmachus (498–514) in the *Liber Pontificalis* says, "This man restored the apse of the holy Agnes, which was threatening to fall into ruins, and the entire basilica."[68] It is for this reason that the mysterious pope accompanying Pope Honorius in the mosaic of Sant'Agnese's apse today is commonly said to be Symmachus. But it seems likely that Symmachus restored the cemetery basilica and its teetering apse, not the present church of Sant'Agnese.

Even in Symmachus' own time, Rome's funerary basilicas were being gradually abandoned. Christians had ceased digging catacombs, and soon the catacombs themselves would be forgotten. It was the memorials of the martyrs, and the churches built over them, that would continue to be remembered. A hundred years after Symmachus, Pope Honorius decided to leave the cemetery building to its fate and concentrate on beautifying the shrine of Agnes; he pulled down the church over the grave[69] and replaced it with the present basilica of Sant'Agnese fuori le Mura. Sant'Agnese's cemetery basilica was the largest and the last to be built, in the series known to us. Thanks perhaps to Symmachus' restoration, the apse walls have withstood the wear and tear of fifteen centuries, most of them without a roof.

It has now been proven that Constantina's mausoleum was added on to a huge Christian basilica.[70] Perhaps that fact might help allay scholarly doubts as to whether the building was meant to be Christian or not. And as for the elusive baptistery: if it was not the present church of Santa Costanza itself, then perhaps it awaits discovery somewhere nearby, possibly within the perimeter of the cemetery basilica's enormous atrium or "paradise."

9

FINER THAN GOLD:
Road, Crypt, and Tower

By 9:30 a.m. on the morning of September 20, 1870, after four hours of incessant firing, Italian nationalist troops finally succeeded in tearing a gap in the Aurelian Walls of Rome. They poured through the breach—*la breccia* as it is called in Italian history books—and they made for the Quirinale Palace, which since 1592 had been the official summer residence of the popes.[1] On the way they met the last resistance by papal troops and easily defeated them. The pope, Pius IX, fled to the Vatican. The Quirinale Palace was handed over to King Vittorio Emanuele.[2] Italy had at last completed its unification as a nation state, with Rome as its capital.

La breccia was blasted through the walls a little to the west of the city gate called Porta Pia; after the wall had been repaired, a commemorative column surmounted by a bronze embodiment of Victory was set up to mark the spot. At first the army, under General Raffaele Cadorna, had attacked the Porta Pia itself. A photograph of the event survives. The Bersaglieri (the Gunners) stand proudly atop a massive earthen mound before the gate. Their guns are cocked, their legs astride. The battlemented walls are pocked with bullet-holes. On either side of the columns and damaged pediments surrounding the gateway are niches containing statues, both of them now broken and headless. One had represented Saint Agnes, the other Pope Alexander I.

PORTA PIA, VIA PIA, VIA NOMENTANA

We may be grateful that it was the exterior façade of the gateway that bore the brunt of General Cadorna's attack. The part of the gate facing into the city was designed by Michelangelo, in 1561–64. It is the artist's last architectural creation, a work both monumental and full of imaginative verve, almost Baroque rather than Renaissance. It is decorated with stylized dishes and towels—a reference to the Medici family's origins as barber-surgeons—and has Pope Pius IV's arms flanked by angels above the powerfully ornamental pediment. The gate was intended to be a climactic ending, closing the vista created by the long, straight via Pia; both road and gate were designed under and named after Pius IV (1559–1565).

It is difficult for us today to appreciate the revolutionary nature of long, straight, broad roads, striking through old, established cities full of narrow, twisting alleys. Via Pia, an ancient traffic artery that Pius IV widened, straightened, and levelled, was one of Europe's earliest and most successful experiments in this form of urban planning, an ancestor to such monumental ways as the Champs Élysées (Paris), the Passeig de Gràcia (Barcelona), and the Malls of London and Washington. The love of axial city vistas began at a time when the new science of perspective was revolutionizing the pictorial arts. Military science also came to appreciate straight streets, for parades and for the speedy entry of armies into cities—Karl-Marx-Allee in Berlin is an example. After passing through the breach in 1870, the Italian nationalist army quickly rejoined via Pia and marched along it straight to the Quirinale Palace at its other end. The road is known today as "20th September Street," via XX Settembre.

The street still starts, as Pius IV's planners intended, at the giant ancient Roman statues of the Heavenly Twins, the Gemini, flanking an obelisk from Emperor Augustus' mausoleum; the street ends seventy-five metres west of the Nomentan Gate, which was closed and bricked in when Porta Pia replaced it.[3] Via Nomentana itself, a road at least twenty-five centuries old, became a continuation of via Pia, starting at the new gate. Today, the ancient part of the road—considerably more winding and lying up to two metres beneath the surface—joins up with the modern road at the nearby Villa Torlonia, where Mussolini lived from 1925 until July 1943. Under the villa's grounds are two Jewish catacombs, discovered in 1918.

Before the Aurelian Walls were built, the road left the city at the so-called Servian Wall[4] (dating back to 378 B.C.—a stretch of this wall survives beside Termini Station) and led to the town of Nomentum, fourteen Roman miles from Rome.[5] The ancient Nomentan Bridge still crosses the river Anio, not far north of Sant'Agnese's church. The bridge was built in the first century B.C., damaged by the Gothic King Totila in 549 A.D., restored by the Emperor Justinian's General Narses in 552, and repaired again by Pope Hadrian I in the eighth century. Medieval additions were also made. The bridge, now closed to traffic, is perhaps the most picturesque in Rome, and is set in a park full of old pines, a reminder of what the countryside used to be like along the road and around Sant'Agnese's church.[6]

If you take a 308 bus going north on the viale Adriatico and stay on it, passing through green countryside outside Rome on the way, you will reach a point where you can still walk along a short stretch of the ancient Roman via Nomentana, which runs beside the modern road. Its smooth, rounded stones are picked out by the green grass growing between them. A gas station services the modern road and marks the end of this uncovered portion of a route built for carts and for people walking on or beside it. Appropriately enough, the gas station's emblem is the ancient badge of pilgrims, a scallop shell:[7] the via Nomentana was for many centuries a pilgrim road.

The Italian army that marched down the via Nomentana to reach Rome was only the latest of many: the roads leading to Rome have often seen armed hordes advancing upon the city. The via Nomentana has not always been thought very useful for this purpose; the vias Flaminia and Salaria have made more military sense. Roman armies often marched as well, of course, in the opposite direction. Cadorna's troops, passing by Sant'Agnese's in September 1870, dropped a cannonball through the building's roof—damage that was later repaired. Fourteen soldiers were killed in the area at the time. A memorial for them stands in front of the church of Santa Costanza.

The side of the Porta Pia that faces out from the walls of Rome was designed by Virginio Vespignani in 1853–69; it was completed just before the battle that took place in front of it. Between his façade and the one designed by Michelangelo lies a courtyard surrounded on four sides by rooms that now house the Museo storico dei Bersaglieri, created in 1932. The Fascist government also erected a monument raised on a small mound outside the gate. It has a huge bronze statue of a soldier racing towards the wall, bayonet and trumpet at the ready. Among the friezes on the stone base is a representation of the storming over the *breccia*.

Inside the museum are mementos and relics of battles: there are clutches of spears and sabres, and arrows set out in radiating patterns; flags, statuary, saddles, bayonets, trumpets, uniforms, helmets; and medals in glass cases. Photographs and paintings cover the walls, and there are momentous letters, framed. A small room is dedicated solely to September 20, 1870; it is decorated with pictures, especially of soldiers triumphantly leaping through the breach. *Hic vivunt homines superstites sibi* is the Latin motto of the dead Bersaglieri: "Here men live on: men who have survived themselves." We need not imagine that either relics, or the desire for relics, have died out.

AT THE CATACOMB OF SAINT ALEXANDER
ON THE VIA NOMENTANA

The damage to the outside of the Porta Pia was repaired after 1870, and the two statues of Agnes and of Alexander were carefully restored. These two saints had been chosen for the gate because the via Nomentana led, and still leads, to their shrines. (The old Porta Nomentana had long been known as Porta Sant'Agnese and Porta de Domina, "Gate of the Lady," meaning Agnes.)[8]

Alexander I, whose pontificate lasted from 109 to 116 A.D., is said in the *Liber Pontificalis* to have been beheaded, and then buried at the seventh mile from the city along the via Nomentana.[9] The statue on the Porta Pia portrays Alexander as elderly, bearded, and papal. But the *Liber Pontificalis*, especially in its early entries, can be an unreliable chronicle. In 1854, during excavations at the site of the ancient Roman town of Ficulea, Alexander's burial place was accidentally rediscovered. However, according to the altar inscription and other evidence found at the site, a totally different person of the same name, not the pope Alexander, had been buried there: a boy in his early teens, murdered under the Emperor Diocletian in the first years of the fourth century, along with his tutor Eventius and a man called Theodulus.[10] A medieval passio survives about Alexander and his companions; owing perhaps to the confusion in the *Liber Pontificalis* between

Alexander and the pope of the same name, the passio simply assumed that Alexander was made pope at a very young age (about the age of Agnes!), since he was murdered with his tutor.[11] The burial arrangements for these martyrs give a good idea of what the earliest shrine for Agnes must have been like.

The archaeologists discovered the remains of a half-buried church like that of Sant'Agnese, with eighteen steps going down into it. When the excavations were completed, the church building was reconstructed over the site, so today it is possible to celebrate Mass again at the spot. The three martyrs were buried inside the galleries of a small catacomb that had begun to be hollowed out during the third century.[12] After their deaths, probably in 304 or 305 A.D., during the same persecution in which Agnes was killed, their graves attracted not only pilgrims but also burials: people wanted to be buried near the martyrs, and the catacomb grew considerably. (It was never very large.)

Later in the fourth century a roughly square room was created around the single sepulchre for Alexander and Eventius[13] so that groups of visitors could stand around the site. Existing catacomb galleries were cut away to make space. The grave of Theodulus was a little distance away; around it, too, an area was cleared. The shape of the room containing the graves of Alexander and Eventius was governed by the remaining galleries around it. The graves were not centrally placed within the room, nor was the structure later built over them made parallel with the walls. This lopsided arrangement was not corrected by moving the martyrs' remains. Other bones had been carried away, but these graves were not even turned so as to lie on axis within the walls of the shrine.[14]

In the course of the fifth century the small oratory was given a narthex, placed so that the two shrines shared it. The staircase with eighteen steps leading down into the catacomb was broadened. Next, a hall for worship was added onto the narthex, extending away from one grave and at right angles to the other. It was independent of both shrines, even as the big Constantinian basilica was different from, though connected to, the shrine over the grave of Agnes. Again, catacomb galleries were destroyed to create more space. The building that resulted was a small, half-buried basilica; the upper portion of its reconstructed apse is what you see from the via Nomentana today. The little church turns its back to the road, as does the church of Sant'Agnese. In the complex thus created worshippers came down the steps and turned left into the basilica, or right into the square oratory, or walked straight on towards the grave of Theodulus. The vestibule or narthex was now common to all three.

Inside the square shrine a man named Delicatus dedicated a new marble altar, placed directly over their bodies, to Alexander and Eventius.[15] A section of his inscription survives on a stone frame surrounding the frontal of the altar, which has now been re-erected. It was first set up between 401 and 417, or thereabouts. We know this because Bishop Ursus is mentioned in the inscription as having consecrated the altar; this man is also named in an extant letter that is datable because it was written by Pope Innocent I. Ursus was buried in the catacomb nearby, as were Bishop Adeodatus (fifth century) and another bishop, his name missing in the inscription, who died in 596. Junia Sabina, called *clarissima femina*, "a most distinguished woman," lets it be known in another inscription that she provided for the erection of the ciborium over the altar.

In the middle of the altar's frontal with its wavy transenna pattern is a rectangular opening known as a *fenestrella* ("little window"). This had a very specific function. People who had walked this far to visit the bones of these saints were not content with merely praying near their graves: they wanted a memento, and this had to be a physical object. The custom had arisen of touching the bones (or rather the coffin enclosing them) with a small object, often a strip of cloth (known as a *brandeum*). The pilgrim, or some attendant, would lower one of these down on a string, like a bucket into a well, so that it rested on the grave and could then be pulled back out. The pilgrim went away carrying in his or her own hand something that had actually been in contact with the box that contained the bones of Christian heroes.

THE PRAYING GIRL

In 1883 Mariano Armellini, remembering earlier discoveries of ancient artifacts underneath the staircase leading down into Sant'Agnese's church, approached the then titular cardinal, Charles-Martial Lavigerie, archbishop of Algeria, for permission to lift the marble slabs forming the steps and look for inscriptions written on the other sides of the stones. (Rome had an ancient tradition of reusing not only columns but also blocks of ready-cut marble.) Cardinal Lavigerie not only gave permission, but offered to pay for the research himself. The archaeologist was rewarded, in the summer's work allowed him in 1884, by finding a large number of previously unknown pagan and Christian inscriptions and sculpted fragments. Then came a completely unexpected discovery. Three marble slabs had been turned face down and used, for nearly three hundred years, as steps. Together they formed three sides of a rectangular box-like altar decorated with pseudo-transenne, very like that over the grave of Alexander and Eventius, which had been rediscovered thirty years earlier. Instead of a fenestrella, the front of the altar had a figure roughly three feet high, carved in bas-relief between two more transenne.[16]

A young girl is praying, her arms raised to shoulder height, palms open, and eyes lifted. Her left leg bears most of her weight, so that her body shifts slightly out of alignment, giving subtle movement to her stance. She wears a narrow-sleeved tunic, and over it a light, simple, but very full cloak that totally envelops her body and is sewn up the sides, leaving wide openings for the arms; the fabric is made skilfully to outline and enhance the shape of her body. She has a round, almost chubby, very young face. Her wavy hair, parted in the middle, falls to chin-length; on the top of her head it is drawn into a small and elegant bun. This figure almost certainly represents Agnes. The sculpture dates from the mid fourth century, about fifty years after the martyr's death.[17]

The girl's attitude in prayer is an extremely ancient one. It is described in the Old Testament;[18] in the Greco-Roman world, as well, people stood, raised their arms, and lifted their eyes towards the heavens to pray.[19] Christians prayed with the same bodily movement, adding their own meanings to those of supplication, adoration, and self-offering that already existed in the ancient world: in praying thus, they were showing themselves to be open to God's grace. The gesture simultaneously reminds Christians of the Crucifixion.[20] Further, raising the eyes to heaven is a symbolic direction of one's prayer to God as transcendent.

Modern Christians sometimes return to this early attitude for prayer, with its stress on openness and exultation; and Catholic priests use it as part of the ritual of the Mass. But for centuries the custom has been to prefer the opposite—and equally appropriate—"containing" attitude, with hands together, knees bent, and eyes closed. Here what is being expressed is the inwardness and intimacy of individual prayer, and the speechless adoration that consciousness of God naturally evokes in the spirit.

Early Christian art frequently depicts figures praying as the young girl is doing on the altar frontal. They are called *orantes* ("people praying") and are most often female figures, although the oldest examples represent personages from the Old Testament, and these are usually male. Sometimes a female "orant" clearly represents a male. For example, in the catacomb of Calixtus, the tomb of a man called Faustinus has a female orant painted on it; and on a medallion the burned body of Lawrence on the gridiron has a female orant rising from it.[21] She is then an embodiment of his soul: *anima* and *psyche*, "soul" in Latin and Greek respectively, are feminine nouns. Christians liked adopting the Greek legend of male Eros ("love and desire"), and female Psyche ("soul") as an allegory of the love of God for every human soul. Sometimes an orant is depicted accompanied by Christ as the Good Shepherd, with a similar meaning.[22]

An orant could also be a quasi-abstract representation, an embodiment of the whole Church, living as well as dead, in constant prayer to God. Or she could represent a single soul, a person now dead and therefore "standing before God," praying for the living, as one member of the Communion of Saints. These meanings are neither exclusive nor cut-and-dried; they must have intermingled in the minds of the creators and the viewers of these figures.

Early Christians—like modern ones—were not sure what happened to a person when he or she died. They said (and still say) that they believed in "the resurrection of the dead."[23] When would that be? Immediately after death? Or at "the end of the world"? This ancient idea—that souls are united with God as soon as they die, but that all must await the resurrection of the dead—further articulates the pair of opposites frequently encountered in Christian belief: already, but not yet.

Before the fifth century Christian burial grounds were commonly known by the Greek term *koimeteria* (the root of our word "cemeteries"); they were only later called catacombs. *Koimeteria* means "resting places" or "dormitories," where the dead wait to rise again. A room among the galleries that contained a number of graves was called a *cubiculum*, which also means literally "a place for sleeping. " In the cemeteries the bodies of the saints lay waiting for the Last Day; their souls, however, lived already in heavenly bliss. *Orantes*, then, would be depictions of souls (they are often shown sumptuously dressed, like Agnes in the apse mosaic of this church) already with God, but awaiting the resurrection of the bodies they had left behind on earth. It was these bodies, thought of as bound for glory, that pilgrims visiting the graves of the sainted dead regarded with such awe.

What, then, does the orant on the fourth-century altar front at Sant'Agnese's represent? She is positioned the way a portrait of the deceased was customarily placed on a sarcophagus, in the middle of the three sections of the frontal. The bas-relief certainly depicts a young girl. All the other symbolic ideas called up by the sight of a praying woman, an orant, are doubtless present; but this simple and touching figure really does seem to be intended to portray Agnes herself. If so, this bas-relief is one of the earliest examples of an orant who represents not any Christian soul, or an embodiment of the Church as a whole, but a specific saint, a martyr.[24]

The dating of the rediscovered altar coincides with the pontificate of Liberius (352–366), who is said to have lived "in the cemetery of holy Agnes" (meaning, as we now know, at the big cemetery basilica built by Constantina) on his return to Rome from exile in 358. An antipope, Felix II, had meanwhile been installed at the Lateran.[25] The emperor insisted that Liberius should rule jointly with Felix, but the people of Rome came out to meet him in crowds, chanting, "One God, one Christ, one bishop," and Felix fled. Perhaps in gratitude for the asylum he had found near the grave of the saint, Liberius decided, when he returned to the city, to have a new marble altar built over her grave. "This Liberius," continues the *Liber Pontificalis*, "adorned with marble slabs the sepulchre of holy Agnes the martyr. "[26] There is every reason to believe that the slabs now encased in the wall of the passageway down to the church were the very ones erected by Pope Liberius over the tomb of Agnes.

A little farther down the staircase, and also set into the wall, is a large marble slab (roughly 11 feet by 3 feet) bearing a Latin inscription executed in magnificent lettering. It, too, was found upside down and being used as part of the pavement, this time inside the church. It had been laid there by the builders of Pope Honorius during the seventh century. Giovanni Marangoni, the archaeologist in charge when the church was being refloored in 1728, scraped away some of the accretions of lime that had adhered to the underside of the stone, and recognized first the calligraphy and then the inscription. With great excitement he set the slab aside; it was broken in three and a small piece at one corner was missing, but otherwise it was entire. In his absence, his workers almost sliced the marble up into tablets for reuse; they were prevented from doing so just in time.[27] The inscription, which gives us a poetic eulogy of Agnes, was probably meant originally to go over an arch surmounting Liberius' altar, itself sited directly over the saint's grave.

On or near martyr shrines around the city, Damasus I (366–384), the pope who succeeded Liberius,[28] placed inscriptions like this one. He had composed all of them himself, and had them carved in an alphabet invented especially for the purpose by the illustrious calligrapher Furius Dionysius Philocalus. About sixty of these epigraphs have survived, from manuscript copies made during the Middle Ages. This particular poem, copied from this stone, had previously been known only from manuscripts of Prudentius, where it was appended to his "Hymn to Agnes"; Marangoni had found the original carved version. It is one of only four Damasus inscriptions to have survived complete in marble. Otherwise, only broken marble pieces have come to light— sometimes mere fragments with a few Philocalian letters on them— and archaeologists have had to fit them together and fill them out with the help of the medieval manuscripts.[29]

The Agnes eulogy is exceptionally heartfelt and dramatic: other Damasus inscriptions are more sober and restrained in tone. The poem does not try to narrate the story of Agnes; it assumes that the pilgrim visiting this grave knows it already. Damasus alludes only to a few scattered moments of the girl's martyrdom. What happened to her, the poem declares, is known from people who had it from the testimony of her family. The prosecutor wanted to burn her alive, but, little as she was, she defied him. Indeed, she had run away from home to seek out the representative of the Roman state and tell him she was a Christian, although the law had announced a renewed persecution of Christians.[30]

In rushing to her martyrdom of her own accord, Agnes was going against a principle that the Church was to state repeatedly: martyrdom is never to be actively sought.[31] However, the idea of running away to be martyred has remained tempting. Saint Antony of Padua, as we saw, was inspired to become a Franciscan when he heard of the Franciscan martyrs. Twelve and a half centuries after Agnes, the future saint Teresa of Avila relates with irony how as a child she decided that martyrdom was definitely the way to go. "We used to get together to read the lives of the saints," she wrote in her autobiography (the passio of Agnes, always a favourite, would doubtless have been one of these stories of Christian heroes). "It seemed to me that the price these people paid for going to enjoy God was very cheap, and I greatly desired to die in the same way." She and her little brother decided "to go off to the land of the Moors and beg them, out of love of God, to cut off our heads there. It seemed to me the Lord had given us courage at so tender an age, but we couldn't discover any means. Having parents seemed to us the greatest obstacle. . . . Then, when I saw it was impossible to go where I would be killed for God, we made plans to be hermits."[32]

The eulogy of Damasus memorably informs us that Agnes hid her naked body, "the temple of God,"[33] with her hair. This does not necessarily mean that Agnes was naked when she died; it has been suggested that her dress was ripped open to make way for the sword. But Damasus does not actually say—as others did—that Agnes died by the sword; he mentions only burning. The Roman prosecutor, Damasus writes, "wanted" (*voluisset*) to burn Agnes alive. Possibly, this was only a threat and not carried out. Jugulation (throat-cutting) was a far more likely form of execution. (The bones in the grave below the high altar at Sant'Agnese's show no signs of burning.)

But the belief that she was burned persisted, possibly because of the opaque language and scattered allusiveness of this very poem. Later, the Latin passio of Agnes would say that the Romans first tried to burn her but the flames miraculously went out, and then they stabbed her in the throat. A Greek passio and the Syriac version of it say she was burned to death. In the apse mosaic in the church, Agnes stands upon the sword, with fire "divided"—as the Latin passio puts it—on either side of her.

THE SHRINE IN THE CATACOMB

The parents of Agnes are said to have buried their murdered daughter in their *agellus* or burial property beside the via Nomentana. It might have been a private family hypogeum among the galleries of the already-existing catacombs, about ten metres below the level of the road. In order to make room for the many groups of people, more and more of whom were coming to pray at her graveside, a space was cleared around the grave, as was done at the tombs of the martyrs Alexander, Eventius, and Theodulus. This earliest oratory was almost entirely buried in the flank of the hill.[34] Probably at this stage, Pope Liberius donated to the shrine a marble altar, similar to the one for Alexander and Eventius. Damasus, the pope who succeeded him, wrote the poem in praise of Agnes, mentioning a few well-known incidents from her story, and placed it above the tomb.

Soon more space was needed for the pilgrims to the site, so the top of the hill was dug away and the oratory extended. By the early fifth century a church had been built, the length and width of the nave of the present basilica. It had no aisles, again as at Sant'Alessandro's, except that here there was only one altar over the single grave. People longed to be buried close to the martyr—a feeling related to that of wanting to touch the hero's bones—and the catacomb grew. Soon the area behind the altar inside the church itself was filled with graves.[35]

We have no idea what lay around the grave site before space was cleared to accommodate crowds. All that remains is a crooked little room with a tufa vault at the end of the right-hand aisle of the present church. It has only recently been plastered and painted. This room lies one catacomb level above Agnes' tomb, and might have been part of the hypogeum in which she was buried. Visitors today may pass through this room to enter or leave the site of the burial underneath the church.

We ourselves will be taking the route through the catacombs, continuing our journey by traversing the galleries to the spot where Agnes was buried. There, we shall find the coffin containing her relics and those of Emerentiana. But before we do so, let us pause to consider why relics have fascinated people in the past and still continue to do so.

INSIDE OUT

Soon after 155 A.D. the Christians of Smyrna (modern Izmir in Turkey) wrote to the Church at Philomelium to tell people there about the death of their aged bishop. He had been arrested by the Roman authorities, and was made to stand in the stadium before the crowds who had gathered for the games; the proconsul then ordered him to abjure Christ. Bishop Polycarp replied, "I have served Christ for eighty-six years and he has done me no wrong. How can I blaspheme my king and saviour?" He was condemned to be burned alive. Near the end an official circus "dagger man" finished him off. Later, the Christians came and took up his bones, which, wrote the scribe, "are more precious to us than jewels, and finer than gold." The letter continues: "We have laid his remains in a suitable place where, the Lord willing, we may gather together in gladness and celebrate the birthday of his martyrdom."[36]

A martyr whose soul was believed to be with God soon became much more than a wept-for daughter, father, niece, or uncle: he or she was a hero, and therefore belonged not only to the family but to everyone in the Christian community. Such a person united the entire social group in mourning and in joy, in awe and in gratitude. Christians flocked to the graves of their martyrs, and built shrines, oratories, and basilicas there. In the end they slowly but inexorably turned what had been the antithesis of a city—impure places, for the dead not the living, polluted by corpses and avoided except by the families of the dead—into pilgrimage goals and the occasional setting for enormous assemblies of people. The martyria outside the city walls sometimes became as important as the churches and the bishop's headquarters downtown.

By the mid fourth century, after the age of persecutions had ended, many felt called out into another "non-city," the uninhabited, uncultivated desert. (The word "hermit" comes from Greek *eremos*, "emptiness" or "desert.") They were no longer in danger of being killed for their faith; they could, however, be witnesses (the literal meaning of the word "martyrs"), concentrating totally on God by living their lives in prayer and contemplation. They became known as "desert fathers" and "desert mothers." Athanasius, bishop of Alexandria, hyperbolically claimed that so many people followed the example of the pioneering hermit Antony of Egypt (251–356) that "the desert was turned into a city." And "the city," wrote Jerome, "has changed address."[37]

Ancient Roman sensibilities were outraged by what pagans saw as uncivilized behaviour ("civilization" originally meant something that came from living in cities, *civitates*). In remembering their martyrs the way they did, in particular, Christians offended the city's gods and polluted the living with a filthy love of bones. Julian the Apostate, emperor from 361 to 363, who tried in vain to bring back the religion of ancient Rome, railed against "the carrying of the corpses of the dead through a great assembly of people, in the midst of dense crowds, staining the eyesight of all with ill-omened sights of the dead. What day so touched with death could be lucky? How, after being present at such ceremonies, could anyone approach the gods and their temples?"[38] From an anthropological point of view, or a political one, the Christians were creating a social revolution by reversing the value system of the establishment, and turning a pollution-system on its head.

BONES ON THE MOVE

After Christianity had become the official religion of the Empire, the Christians who had lived in secret and in danger seemed holy and heroic to the comfortable, safe souls who came after them. The cult of the martyrs arose as the danger of martyrdom itself receded— although people who spread the faith to the edges of the known world continued to meet bloody deaths.

Newly converted peoples—the Gauls, the Germans—wanted to share in the enormous togetherness that honour for a society's heroic dead always produces. They wanted relics like the ones Rome had. For a long time Rome resisted removing bodies from their graves; the old custom prevailed that far. In a letter dated 594 to Constantina, wife of the Emperor Maurice, Pope Gregory the Great refused to grant her request, which was for the head of Saint Paul, or at least a piece of his body and the cloth that was wrapped round his head. It was not Roman custom, Gregory wrote—his tone is one of indignation and disbelief—to divide up bodies, or indeed even to touch them. Such an act could be dangerous: the saints would not like it at all.[39]

We wonder today whether Gregory believed these stories he told about saints harming people who tampered with their bones. (Such legends survive to this day: those who uncovered Tutankhamen's tomb in the 1920s, for example, are said to have all died mysterious deaths.) Gregory was, after all, very effectively defending Rome's treasure of relics and preventing a rush to get hold of more and more bodies of the saints. In the event he sent Constantina some filings from the chains that reputedly once bound Saint Peter;[40] relics (the word is from Latin *reliquiae*, "left behind") can be objects that resonate because of their association with great events and the famous dead, as well as actual bones. Other people were sent, on request, cloths that had touched martyrs' coffins, handfuls of dust from special places, or little bottles of oil taken from the lamps that burned at martyrs' shrines. (In the time of Gregory a bottle of oil from a lamp near Agnes' tomb was sent to Queen Theodelinda at Monza; the bottle has disappeared, but the record of it survives.) The recipients were doubtless content, as the people presumably were who carried away pieces of the Berlin Wall.

Constantina had thought she could ask for the head of Saint Paul because, in the Eastern Empire, the moving, division, and distribution of the bodies of the saints had been going on for more than two centuries. The first known movement of a saint's body took place at Antioch, and was ordered by none other than Gallus, the husband of Constantine's daughter Constantina, who built the basilica at Sant'Agnese's. As ruler of Antioch in 351, he ordered the body of

Saint Babylas to be taken from its grave and buried a few miles away at Daphne, in a newly constructed church intended to replace the local shrine of Apollo.[41] Gallus' action was possible in Asia Minor as it would not have been in Rome.

Eventually, however, beginning in the second half of the seventh century, Rome was to capitulate. Relics began to be sent to churches all over the spreading Christian world. People wanted their local church to include the body (or a bit of the body—it came to seem the same thing) of a saint, if possible a martyr. As well, they wanted to affiliate themselves with the "mother Church" in Rome, so relics from Rome, once they became available, were especially popular. Having a church with a saint or saints buried in it became a *sine qua non*. In 787 the Second Council of Nicaea made this custom into law: the consecration of a church was always to include the placing of relics in it. Churches, in the form of martyria, had once moved out into the cemeteries. Mass was celebrated there; tombs became altars. Now it was the saints' bones that began to move: they were taken to churches, and placed in or underneath the altars.

Because of the barbarian invasions, the popes eventually decided to bring the bones from the catacombs inside the walls of Rome for safekeeping. Soon the loculi were mostly empty—rifled by invaders or cleared out by command of the pope himself—except for odd corners and galleries, and catacombs like that of Sant'Agnese, which had filled up with mud. Archaeologists have found only one martyr's body intact in its original loculus. Inside the catacomb of Sant'Ermete on the via Salaria, a loculus never before opened was discovered in 1845, low down in a small gallery; the slab that closed it was inscribed "DP [*depositus*] III IDVS SEPTEBR YACINTHVS MARTYR." Hyacinthus was the name of a well-known saint who died in 258.[42] Inside the grave were charred bones; Christians never cremated their dead, so the story of Hyacinth's martyrdom by fire was confirmed. A stone slab for Hyacinth's brother Protus was also found nearby, but the grave had been emptied.[43]

In a few places the martyrs' bones were left in situ, where their shrines were protected by monasteries attached to them. These included the martyria of Sebastian, Lawrence, Pancras, Valentine, and

Agnes.[44] Pilgrims continued to visit these places and to celebrate festivals there. During the ninth century, when most "translations" of bones from the catacombs into the city took place, and when the division of bodies had finally become established practice in Rome, the body of Saint Emerentiana was taken from her oratory and placed with that of Saint Agnes in a new altar-grave.

Mortal remains of saints, once they began to travel, helped in unquantifiable ways to spread Christianity across Europe. Any town or village could become a "little Rome" complete with its own saint; all that was needed was a piece of bone, sometimes a mere splinter of one, with assurances of its saintly provenance. Other people would come on pilgrimage to visit the site; relics were good for business too.[45] The famous half-cloak of Saint Martin (he had sliced it in two and given the other half to a beggar) was visited by thousands. It was kept in a small room, named after the cloak (*cappella* in Latin, *chape* in French), leading off the saint's cathedral at Tours. The piece of cloak is said to have given rise to the word "chapel."[46]

Bones and teeth survive when people die. Bones are divisible; jaws hold many teeth. Value attaches to these remains entirely by virtue of the honour granted to the dead person by the living. Bones in themselves are uninteresting. But Christians felt that, because of the identification of certain bones with Christian heroes and because of what the lives of these heroes meant, they were "finer than gold." These were the bodies of people already "in heaven"; they were bodies that would rise again to be reunited with their holy souls on the Last Day. The great insights of Judeo-Christendom travelled throughout Europe along with these little scraps of bodies. There were so very many pieces; they helped to ensure that Christianity did not become a religion centred in only a few privileged places.[47]

LURID LEGENDS

A lot of Christians nowadays, and that includes many Roman Catholics, are embarrassed by the existence of relics, even genuine ones, and by their history. Relics were symbolically central in the revolution brought about by sixteenth- and seventeenth-century Protestant reformers, who smashed reliquaries and dumped bones into rivers with righteous fervour. (One Protestant friend of mine says his "toes curl up" when he thinks of relics.) The cultural matrix in which the idea of Christian relics originally took form—the first persecutions, and the revolutionary changing of the urban and religious landscape of imperial Rome—has long fallen away. Moreover, relics have often been the locus of rampant abuses. Long lists can be made of superstitions related to the seeing, touching, and owning of relics over the course of the centuries.[48]

The bones of saints, for instance, were often believed to have intrinsic power (in other words they could work magic), and were kept like fetishes. The saints became "helpers" rather than models, and were thought to aid particular people or cities or armies lucky enough to possess bits of their bones. Many people were duped by fake relics, in part because it is very difficult to keep relics securely authenticated over centuries. Some people claimed to have "found" the graves of previously unknown martyrs—a case of supply keeping up with demand. Some stole or bought relics, and occasionally reassured themselves that the saint must have wanted to change proprietors or would not have moved; others were astonished when a set of little dry bones suddenly seemed too heavy to lift, because the saint wanted to stay put. It was long customary in Europe to swear oaths on saints' bones; and many a saint's relics were treated with pointed disrespect until a request was granted. Some Christians demanded to be buried near a holy grave in the hope that its occupant would put in a good word for them on Judgement Day. Relics were known to bleed, or to move of their own accord. A little cloth that had touched a coffin, like the ones let down onto the graves of Alexander and Eventius beside the via Nomentana, would return to its owner feeling eerily heavy.

Objects said to be the actual things mentioned in Scripture counted as relics, or objects used in the course of famous incidents, like Saint Martin's cloak. When Christians visited the Holy Land, longing to see where Jesus lived and where the great events related in the Old and New Testaments had taken place, they were all too easily taken in by people who allowed them to see—for a fee—the amphorae used at the wedding at Cana, the ring of Solomon, Mary Magdalene's comb, the dish on which John the Baptist's head was carried in to dinner. The list, as everybody knows, gets better: we have reports that people believed they saw, or even owned, the crown of thorns; that they jubilantly carried off little bags of white powder, the (of course now dried) milk of the Virgin. They saw the very place where Jesus sat when he composed the Our Father; considered with awe a stone that had struck the protomartyr Stephen; and, of course, marvelled over thousands of splinters of the True Cross—enough, John Calvin complained, to build a ship, or to constitute an entire fleet.[49]

For a thousand years at least the Church appears to have permitted its members to entertain unconscionable quantities of superstition in this area.[50] There has always been, however, a tradition of opposition to and mockery of excessive credulity and relic-mongering. We hear, for instance, of an abbot who, in 707, successfully besought his abbey's saint to stop performing miracles, and of monks who sent their relics away so that the crowds of pilgrims would go elsewhere and leave them to pray in peace. As early as the mid third century the martyr Fructuosus of Tarragona appeared in a vision to his brethren and told them to put his relics back at once where they had found them. The Egyptian monk Schnoudi demanded caustically whether any bodies other than those of martyrs had ever received burial, since every uncovered corpse was at once declared a martyr and therefore a trove of relics. The medieval abbot Guibert of Nogent-sous-Coucy fought for reason in this area, objecting, for instance, to a "milk tooth of Christ" and to the several heads of John the Baptist. And it is certain that even in the most credulous of times there were people who could ridicule absurdity, as when Chaucer describes his Pardoner as keeping "pigges bones" in a glass, as well as a pillow made of Our Lady's veil and a piece of the sail from Saint Peter's boat: "And thus, with flattery and suchlike japes, he made the Parson and the rest his apes."[51]

On the whole, it was the people who demanded relics, and plenty of miracles to go with them. The clergy would try to contain and redirect their fervour—or shockingly take advantage of it by keeping the miraculous objects and then orchestrating relic mania for their own benefit. It is also clear that a great number of the reports of wonder-working relics and the tales involving them were what we would now call urban legends, or constituted a medieval version of the modern sensation-mongering press. Interestingly enough, it is still quite impossible to write on this subject without bringing out a string of legends and bizarre instances of relics: the appeal of these narratives is as irresistible today as it ever was, although some of the reasons for this have changed.

A BONE AND ITS STORY

Relics have always been one of the "special extras," as Ronald Knox called them, of the Catholic part of the Christian spectrum, along with rosary beads, holy water, candles, incense, sanctuary lamps, dog collars for priests, and so on. These are physical objects to be used, if helpful, for spiritual ends; they are part of a powerful cultural nexus, but none of them is essential to Christian faith. All are liable to be rejected, and even excoriated, by Christians who demand a total purity of intention—a purity that often ends up being hostile to the body, to embodied action in religion, and to symbolism in general. For symbolism is not "pure." A symbol, unless it is deliberately reduced to being a defined and therefore lifeless sign, is a resonating thing, making suggestions and connections, pointing in many directions at once; it can never be captured entirely, whether by classification or by analysis. Relics are both concrete and particular—they are actual bodies, or real objects associated with specific people—but they also point to the whole complicated matter of the stories told about people who are believed to have done something important, and what those stories mean to others.

Many people nowadays, Christians included, have a particularly hard time with relics because water-tight proof of their veracity is so often lacking, and because of a modern reluctance to be reminded of death. We still have relics, however. People line up to see Marilyn Monroe's shoes, visit the wonderfully named Graceland because of Elvis, peer at the medals and bayonets of the Bersaglieri in their museum. The body of the Unknown Soldier, underneath the flame that proves we remember him, resonates because his remains are distressingly particular—and simultaneously general, because anonymous. The body therefore both symbolizes and *is* Everyman, killed in war. The body parts of the (long) dead, however, are now subject among modern Westerners to a mild form of taboo.

It is still possible for us to understand without much difficulty the powerful pull of place. There is something moving, even now, about "the very place where" an event of importance happened: Stonewall Inn in Greenwich Village where the gay rights movement took off; the site of the Bastille; the column 202 feet high because it stands 202 feet from the shop where the Great Fire of London began. The same can still be said of the grave of a hero, a person whose life story means a great deal, for whatever reason, to other people.

Any heroization of a human being (a process that is performed not by the hero, but through the opinion of other people) is completed only when the person in question is dead. Heroes tend to die young, and often violently. It is normally only when they have gone that other people begin fully to realize their value, and to "think through" what their story means. Little is left for us to contemplate, by this stage, but the hero's tomb. All through history, the tomb has been an important locus for the expression of honour and remembrance for those dead whom we admire and love. A grave is tangible and very specific, like the bones within it. It can be seen, touched, visited; offerings of flowers can be brought. People may decide to travel a long way to get to such a tomb, or to a particular and significant place; their journey then becomes a pilgrimage.

Much more meaning may accrue to a pilgrimage than the thought of whose bones these are, or what significance we attach to a place. The journey can take on the symbolism of the traveller's own life; and even, perhaps, of all humanity on the move, of a long march to escape from oppression, of ideals to be followed, goals to be striven for. People leave home in order to strike out into unknown territory, both physically and spiritually; they travel with others doing the same, and feel one with them in the *communitas* of people who find themselves temporarily outside the boundaries set by normal, everyday living;[52] they take time out of their lives in order to see their affairs in spiritual perspective. For centuries Christians have turned such journeys into trajectories of the soul. The destination often was, and still is, the site of a holy event or epiphany, or the tomb of a saintly hero; it is up to each Christian to make the journey meaningful in terms of his or her own life.

One way of understanding the power of bones, and of relics in general, is to consider their paradoxical nature. The Christians who gathered up the burned bones of Polycarp, bishop at Smyrna, said they found them "finer than gold." The bishop had chosen to die rather than reject Christ; his bones were physical embodiments of that choice. People could look at them, and remember both the loyalty and the conviction, and its price. The soul of Polycarp, they believed, was now with Christ and in eternal ecstasy: he had not flinched, had not denied his master.[53] He had not let someone else's cruelty force him to denounce what for him was the truth. To value his charred bones more highly than refined gold was, at some level, to make the same choice oneself.

A martyr is one who has shown greatness of soul in the leaving of his or her life. But Christianity is a religion that insists not only on souls but on bodies and bodiliness. The contemplation of a martyr's bones reminds people that these heroes lived bodily lives, were human just as we are: would we be able to do what they did, if we were put to the test? Bodily remains may seem worthless, pathetic, even loathsome—yet to somebody who knows their story, they become endlessly meaningful. The very gap between a bone and its story, and the effort needed to bridge it, can increase the significance of both narrative and relic.

Relics are often tiny, and can resonate the more for being minute. One bone is very like another, and looks just as unimpressive; the value with which bodily relics are charged owes nothing to material gratification for the beholder. (This is one of the many reasons why the use of relics for material gain is so offensive.) It is an essential Christian paradox that it is the person who is "small" and unassuming who is truly great, that humility (which for Christians is an aspect of honesty) primes grandeur. The placing of little bones in magnificent reliquaries is intended to make riches and skill "kneel down" and serve something neither imposing nor consequential in "this world."

Where relics resonate, it is with the apprehension of greatness in smallness: the little grey thing and the glory it points to; the symbol of death itself and its direct contact with eternal life; the bones in the dark grave, buried, and the heights in which this person now lives in the light that will never die. Where the story of a saint's life is known, a relic or a grave can supply the other half of an opposition, in the body that lived that life: text and object, time and place embrace. In relics, earth and heaven meet. The particular and the general, the concrete and the transcendent coincide.

THROUGH THE CATACOMB TO THE TOMB

In the left-hand aisle of Sant'Agnese's church, opposite the passage-way down, is a doorway marked *Catacombe*, which leads into a large room, added to the church as a sacristy in 1667. (The previous sacristy had been the tiny, ancient tufa room at the end of the right-hand aisle and under the bell tower. In the 1950s a new sacristy, or room where the priest vests for Mass, was built at the end of the left aisle.[54]) From one corner of the old sacristy, which is where catacomb visitors meet their guide, pay for tickets, and buy books and other objects, a door opens onto steps down into the underground galleries of the early Christian cemetery.

A modern tourist group crowds in after the guide, but soon people find themselves walking in single file, at most in couples: these galleries were dug not much wider than was necessary for bearers carrying, at the head and at the foot, a wrapped body on its bier. The people at the back find it increasingly hard to follow what the guide is saying up front, and soon most of us are left to our own devices, star-ing round while taking care not to be left behind. Graves, almost every one of them empty, are dark rectangular slots, as regularly spaced as mailboxes, dug into and parallel with the surface of the earthen walls. We wonder how bodies could have fitted into them. They are shallow (no room for anyone fat), and short.[55] A few are still intact, with tiles covering the openings; some are little, for children and babies. Corri-dors lined with many more grave-slots fork off at intervals; the elec-tric light penetrates a little way along them and then dies in the dark. We feel no temptation to stray.

At Sant'Agnese's the soil in which the galleries have been excavated is an unpleasant liverish colour. Tiny slivers of stone and minerals trapped in the tufa glitter silently in the heavy walls. Sweating marble inscriptions, irregular in shape because mostly broken, provide patches of white, sometimes with the original red in the grooves of the lettering, to facilitate reading the inscriptions. At intervals along the route finds of interest have been displayed: a simple sketch, cut into stone, of a balding man (who should, according to the iconographic tradition, be Saint Paul[56]) has the word PETRUS engraved over it. There is a sign depicting a ham in relief and inscribed *perna*, "ham"; it once marked the grave of a pork butcher.

On half a broken stone slab a vivid figure peers out, his outline scratched with childlike simplicity: a jug-eared man, in a short tunic and with a band tying back his hair, holds a pick from which speckles representing lumps of dirt fall into a bucket. He is a fossor or catacomb-digger; his trusty lamp would have been at the other side of him, most likely at the end of a stick. He would drive the stick into a tufa wall in order to leave his hands free for digging.[57]

The catacombs of Sant'Agnese are famous for the number of graves in them that have never been rifled. Early in the Middle Ages fine silt seeped into the galleries because of the stream and wetlands nearby, and finally blocked most of the passages altogether; only modern excavation has been able to clear them. Water still seeps into the galleries; it is very difficult to keep it at bay. Perhaps because of the mud, there are no surviving frescoes in the catacomb; there may never have been any. However, there are plenty of paintings in the adjoining Coemeterium Maius, and some were seen in the Coemeterium Minus.

Many inscribed marbles have been found here, however, including some in the excellent lettering of a family of calligraphers who lived and worked at the Coemeterium Maius and at Sant'Agnese's. Other finds include a bronze plaque with Peter and Paul on it, glass perfume vases, a figure carved in obsidian, a slab with a portrait of the deceased, extremely rare because it is in ivory and enamels. There were lamps, finger rings, one outstanding goldglass bottom and other goldglass fragments, coins, bone plaques, and other objects.

One of these is a white marble chi-rho or monogram of Christ, with alpha and omega ("beginning and end") on either side of it, all drawn within a capital letter omega, for God as the end of all things; it is about five inches in diameter and set off with coloured enamels. On it are written the words said to have been proclaimed to Constantine and accompanied by a vision of this sign. But this time the words are addressed to a man who died and was buried in the catacomb: "By this sign, oh Siricius, you shall conquer." Clearly, "Constantine's sign" could refer to something very different from the outcome of an armed conflict.

The regular guided tour of the catacomb takes us through a section of the oldest part of it, which stretches underneath the alleys of the parish bowling club, beneath via di Sant'Agnese, and northward towards a large, ancient Roman *pozzolana* quarry. Christian catacombs, as we have seen, often began in association with the ready-made tunnels of such quarries. This region has been dated to the middle of the third century. A second region, from the third and fourth centuries, continues the old area northward, and also lies as a warren of galleries underneath via Nomentana and on the other side of it. This is the region contemporary with the period of Agnes' death. The galleries around the saint's grave were soon cleared to make room for visitors.

Two separate regions of galleries were created after Agnes' martyrdom and burial had made the area famous. One extends for some distance to the right of the present church, some of it lying under the passageway down and some under the canonry. The other region tunnels out underneath the area that was once the atrium of the huge cemetery basilica. One of this region's galleries reaches as far as Santa Costanza's church; a spiral staircase, now closed, inside the round mausoleum and a little to the left of its doorway, formed an exit from or an entry into the catacombs.[58] Ten pagan *hypogea* or ancient Roman underground burial precincts were found in this area. One of these, a three-storey structure, may have belonged to devotees of Apollo: an inscription was found nearby listing favours accorded them by the Emperor Septimius Severus (193–211 A.D.).

This relatively small catacomb has other underground passages, some of which have never been explored. When the church of Sant'Agnese itself was built, and, much later, when the ground that had buried the front of the church was cleared, some ancient galleries were removed. Many more were probably destroyed during the twentieth century, as the vineyards that had surrounded Sant'Agnese's monastery and church for many centuries were quickly built over; they had covered this catacomb, the Coemeterium Maius, and the little-known and now perhaps irrecoverable Coemeterium Minus. Tourists today are normally led through only a small fraction of the network of known galleries at Sant'Agnese's catacomb.

This journey—short, safe, and well lit (unless in error we wander off the route)—ends as the group crowds into the small space around the bones of Agnes and Emerentiana, where they rest in a tarnished silver casket behind a marble screen and an iron grating. Bunches of flowers and a lamp stand before the grave. Tiny winged dragons and crowned eagles in silver are appliquéd to the edges of the coffin's silver casing, and the papal arms of Paul V, whose symbols the eagles and dragons are, fill the centre of the front panel. A vainglorious gesture this seems to modern eyes, in spite of the splendid workmanship employed. It should be borne in mind, however, that the silver coffin was buried in 1621 and not meant to be visible to the public.[59] It was uncovered during excavations in the apse of the church, in 1901. On one half of its frontal is the dedication in Latin, "To Saint Agnes, Virgin and Martyr," and on the other, "To Saint Emerentiana, Virgin and Martyr." The casket gleams softly, enigmatically, in the dim light. Inside it are bones, crumbling gently into dust. We have reached the centre of the labyrinth.

A church labyrinth, however, is not like the Cretan one: what potentially awaits us here is not a monster, but an epiphany. From the Christian point of view, this grave is not a "dead end," but a source of light and hope. It can allow us a glimpse, if we are ready for it, of what Agnes and Emerentiana believed was worth dying for. The architectural disposition of the church building is itself designed to express, not exactly what each individual will see thanks to these two martyrs, but rather the experience of "rising again," which is the consequence of a "leap of faith." Immediately above the grave stands the main altar of the church; it supports the tabernacle containing the Eucharist. Above that rises the dome with its pinnacle, a cupped sphere surmounted by a cross. Beyond this and arching over it springs the glittering apse depicting Agnes in glory, under the Hand of God. Outside the church the upward movement continues, as the tower, lifting its bells, points to the heavens.

BELLS

The church tower at Sant'Agnese's can be thought of as like a plant, springing from the buried "seed" that is the tomb of the saints and the memorial of their heroic faith, hope, and love. It "grows" up and out, to stand as a reminder, a witness, and a beckoning sign to the world outside. The church holds the martyrs' grave like a secret, deep within; at the same time its tower indicates to everyone just where the bodies lie.

Like most church towers, Sant'Agnese's brick campanile "flowers" into lightness and complexity at the top. It has two storeys of gracefully arched windows with white marble insets, each window split in two by white columnar dividers. In a row beneath the top floor of the tower, like small coloured blossoms, are turquoise ceramic dishes and porphyry crosses, set into the brown brickwork. The tower also holds three more "flowers," which are its bells. Nowadays these are set ringing by means of an electronic device. Bells in a church tower add sound to sight, lending the building a voice.

Other methods of summoning the faithful preceded the use of bells. After the First Council of Nicaea (325 A.D.), Christians—newly permitted to proclaim their faith openly—called congregations to prayer by rapping on a two-metre-long wooden board, called a *semantron*, Greek for "signal." It is thought that knocking might have been used as a semi-secret Christian calling device before Constantine. Knocking on wood has strong reverberations in the Christian imagination: it recalls the nailing of Jesus to the cross, for example; or God "knocking at the door" of the human heart, in hope of a response.[60] The knock was traditionally double, a short and a long beat, reputedly to remember how God called Adam in the Garden of Eden: "Adam! Adam!"[61] During the three days preceding Easter Sunday, from Holy Thursday night until the feast of the Resurrection, the bells in all the churches go silent in memory of Christ's sufferings; a frenzy of ringing breaks out when Easter has come.[62] In Spain and Portugal the *matraca* may be brought out to take the bells' place in the days of mourning. This is a descendant of the semantron: a wooden contraption that may take various forms. It produces a dire, doleful rattling sound when swung or shaken—the absolute opposite of a ringing bell.

Ancient Romans clashed cymbals[63] or struck gongs to open and close the games, and to announce that the water was warm at the baths; such public signals were, of course, forbidden to Christians in the first centuries. Drums, gongs, tambourines, and cymbals were all precursors of the percussive bell. Saint Paul thought of the whole family of booming and clashing instruments as producing merely meaningless noise: he reminded the Corinthians that "If I speak in the tongues of men or of angels but am without love, I am but a sounding gong or a clanging cymbal."[64]

A bell[65] is a gong or cymbal ingeniously wrapped around its clapper, unless it has a hammer to strike it from without. "Ringing" a bell is achieved by swinging it; "chiming" is striking the bell's stationary sides. In the East bells are usually chimed rather than rung. It is said that when, in an early movie, Russians first saw the Western method of agitating the entire bell instead of just the clapper inside, the audience burst into gales of laughter at what seemed to them our monumentally stupid waste of effort.

Bells have been known in China since at least the eleventh century B.C.; and Buddhist and Hindu traditions long preceded Christianity in their use of bells and gongs. Ancient Jewish priests wore tinkling golden bells sewn onto their vestments.[66] In the West bells are believed to have been developed in Egypt, and certainly used in Christian church services there first. The other early users of bells in the West were the Irish. Their bells were hand-held, and forged and hammered rather than cast; they were first used as sheep bells (and still are) and then adopted by the Church.

It was the Irish, after their conversion in the fifth century, who, in helping to spread Christianity, spread with it the use of bells across Europe. Their name for a bell is *cloc*, which is the root of the words *Glocke* in German, and *cloche* in French. (*Cloc* also gave rise to the English word "cloak" for a bell-shaped garment.)[67] Small hand-held bells began to be used regularly inside churches in Rome, to mark high points of the Mass, under the pontificate of Pope Sabinianus (604–606), who may have been carrying out the wish of his predecessor, Gregory the Great.

Bells hung in towers outside churches were to become part of monastic life, calling monks and nuns to prayer at regular times throughout the day. People in the countryside around a monastery came to rely on the bells to know what time of day it was. Eventually, city-dwellers made their own bells for secular use. In medieval towns they woke people up, opened the markets, signalled lunchtime, ended work, warned that the city gates were closing, and finally told the townsfolk to cover their fires and retire for the night. (The word in French for this last sounding of the bells was *couvre-feu*—"cover the fire!"—which became "curfew" in English.)

In each bell tower a man would take turns with others on a team to watch a klepsydra (a water clock) or sundial; he would strike or ring the bell at regular intervals. His attention to this duty simultaneously proved that he was alert and watching, from his tall look-out, for possible danger, whether from fires or from attacking armies. When mechanical clocks were invented, beginning in the fourteenth century, automata in the shape of men (known as "jacks," as in jack-in-the-box) often automatically struck the bells when made to do so by the clocks. The creation of jacks moved by "clockwork" was an early and poignantly dramatic instance of the replacement of human beings by automation.

As cities grew, they provided themselves with bigger and bigger bells: a city "was" that area that could be reached by the sound of its bells. The man who struck the bells, his job, and each period of time marked out for the whole community were all called by the same word: "watch." This is the origin of our name for the timepiece we now wear on our wrists. The mechanical clock took its name from the word for "bell": *cloc, Glocke, cloche,* and (Flemish) *klok.* Public clocks still chime the hour with the appropriate number of strokes.

A bell that is cast in one piece out of a particular proportion of tin to copper, carefully shaped, and then tuned by filing, has always been thought to produce a very special sound, unlike any other. Buddhists and Hindus think of each bell as containing a potential manifestation of the harmony of the universe. The power is hidden until it is released by the clapper's blow. A struck bell therefore rouses the soul to attention and meditation, to the possibility of epiphanic experience.

But bells speak to communities as well as to individuals. In European cities people have always known their bells intimately: each has its own inimitable timbre. Christians often name their bells, even "baptizing" them before hanging them. An inscription on a bell is often in the first person, as if the bell is speaking the written words with its "tongue" and its "mouth": "I awake the living, I mourn the dead" is a typical inscription, or "You love my voice because I announce that dinner is ready."

A set of bells is known as a "ring. " The largest and deepest-sounding bell in the ring is usually the most widely known, and often given a masculine name: Vienna's Pummerin "the Growler," Big Ben, Great Tom. The other bells are usually thought of as female. Two at the cathedral of Saint Stephen at Sens are named after the two men who brought the Gospel to the town and were martyred for doing so: Savinienne after Savinienus, and Potentienne, after his disciple Potentienus. The cathedral of Barcelona recently received a new bell, whose name was voted for by the people visiting the church. (The bell stood outside waiting for her name to be given so that she could be raised up into the tower to join the others there.) It was eventually agreed that she should be called Montserrat, a common girl's name that is also a title of the Virgin Mary at her shrine among the tall fingers of rock that rise from the Catalans' holy mountain, Montserrat.

Bells are often classed as "the opposite" of their cousins the "male" drums; while drums generally mean "war," bells signify "peace." (This meaning is included with "joy" and "community" in the symbolism of wedding bells, and bells on Christmas cards and other decorations.) Cannons used to be cast in the same workshops as bells, and bells were frequently destroyed to make weapons; melting down bells to make cannons, therefore, was the reverse of "beating swords into ploughshares."[68] In any case, to destroy a town's bells was to attack both its sense of community and its security. The Nazis melted down 150,000 of Europe's bells to make weapons, and also to crush morale.

Bells, like organs, generate vibrations that pass through people's bodies if they are standing nearby, and create "thrilling" sensations. (The word "thrill" is cognate with "through.") The very sound of bells, as we have seen, has long been said to have something strange or "supernatural" about it. The reverberation of bells has been analysed in modern times, and found indeed to be peculiar—no more to be found in nature than is a cast bronze bell itself. There are five partial tones to a Western bell's ring: three notes in octave, one a perfect fifth above the "fundamental" or middle octave, and the last—the strange one—a minor third above the fundamental, giving the bell's "voice" its complexity and unique plangency.[69]

Sant'Agnese's has two eighteenth-century bells and one modern one. The largest, installed in 1707, has an inscription that puns on the Latin word *fundere*, "to cast" a bell and also "to pour out or diffuse." (The English word "cast" has a similar double sense.) The previous bell had cracked; its recasting was paid for by the congregation of the downtown church of San Pietro in Vincoli, Saint Peter in Chains. The inscription also plays on the conceit of Saint Peter's being freed from his chains,[70] as his church has made available or "freed" the sum of money needed. The bell says: "Jesus! Maria! Agnes! Constantia! I ring out [*fundo sonum*] since the chains of Peter are loosed [*cum solvunt Petri vincula*] to pay for me. The names printed on me will diffuse [*fundent*] virtue. " And at the bottom it adds, "Giovanni Giardini cast [*fundit*] me in A.D. 1707. "

On the smallest bell is written, "Jesus! Maria! Agnes! Emerentiana! A.D. 1769." The inscription on the middle bell, hung in 1973, records the blessing of the bell on the feast of Saint Emerentiana (January 23) by Cardinal Ugo Poletti, Vicar of Rome; its installation, after the restoration of the campanile, by engineers of the Italian state; and the name of the foundry, Lucenti of Rome. The bell's exclamation in Latin is, "Whiter than snow!" This is a quotation from the passio of Agnes, describing the lamb, her attribute and a figure of her Christlike innocence. The reference is also to Psalm 51, a great plea to God for forgiveness, in confidence that he will grant it: "Wash me," the psalm implores, "and I shall become whiter than snow!"

THE BELL TOWER

The Italian word for a bell tower is *campanile*, and for a bell, *campana*, after the Italian province of Campania, because the best bronze foundries were once to be found there. Campaniles were rare in Rome until the twelfth century; between 1100 and 1250, however, nearly a hundred of them were built.[71] Many of these survive, all of them different, yet with a strong family resemblance among them. They are still one of Rome's most characteristic features, rising like exclamation marks at intervals across the city's skyline.

The twelfth century was an age of what the Church called *renovatio*: it was a renaissance, a period when the Church made efforts to return to its roots, to the purity and determination that always seem, to later ages, to have characterized the exemplary "early Christians." The architecture of the period reflected this admiration: new churches were built in deliberate reference to early Christian styles, and mosaic decoration returned, after centuries of preference for sculpture and frescoes. Old churches were remodelled: the Quattro Coronati, for example, was given a false gallery in imitation of the churches of Sant'Agnese and San Lorenzo fuori le Mura. Religious orders were reformed; the liturgy was both purified and enhanced.[72]

But there was no precedent for the bell towers. They appeared, apparently fully developed in design, all at once. The building material is unplastered brown brick, and they rise in storeys, each one clearly underlined by cornices (the demarcation of the constituent parts of a whole is typical of Roman architectural tradition), to "flower" at the top with arched windows in white marble with colonnettes. Very early on campaniles were decorated with *bacini*, large and colourful ceramic bowls set into the brickwork. Many of these are of Arab origin, although they also came from local producers, or from Sicily, or southern Italy. The colour of ceramic glazes lasts indefinitely, so unless these dishes have broken or fallen off the walls (which is, unfortunately, often the case), their effect is as vivid today as when they were first installed.

Rome added to these its own unique decoration, known as *specchi* (literally "mirrors"). These are polished stones, of porphyry, green serpentine, or *verde antico*, taken from ancient Roman ruins. Porphyry columns were sliced like salami to form red disks to decorate campaniles; stones were cut into lozenges, or in the shape of crosses. The little white columns in the top windows of the towers were often ancient Roman as well. But by the twelfth century ancient Roman stones were no longer lying plentifully about for the taking: these "spoils" were rare and expensive, yet they were used in the decoration of the newly fashionable campaniles, largely because they reminded people of early Christian architecture.

The bell towers had an important function in the twelfth-century *renovatio*: they were there to carry the bells that called the faithful to prayer. Monks and nuns were also summoned by bells to sing the Office,[73] several times a day. Many churches, and every one with members of religious orders attached to it, received brand new bell towers. One such church was Sant'Agnese's. The original campanile (there had not been one before) is thought to have been built under Pope Paschal II (1099–1118). Sant'Agnese's monastic buildings were at the time inhabited by secular priests, whose behaviour in the new climate of reform was considered unacceptable. Paschal replaced them with Benedictine sisters under the Abbess Adeleita in 1112. The campanile was probably added to the church to mark this occasion, the regular ringing of bells all over Rome being intended to proclaim a renewal of order, discipline, and fervour.

This twelfth-century tower forms the lower part of the present one; it is not made all of bricks but is a rustic version, of tufa blocks interspersed with rows of broken bricks. Its remaining windows, two rectangular and one arched, are now bricked up. Chunks of marble form part of the fabric; they protrude awkwardly from the walls. The tower was in very bad shape by the sixteenth century, when it was repaired by Cardinal Giuliano della Rovere (later Pope Julius II). He added the two storeys with double-arched windows at the top. Of the eight *bacini* underneath the final storey, one is broken, with only the letters "Christ-" remaining on it; three others are missing, as are two of the *specchi*.

Two of the bowls still in place are inscribed with words from the "Blessing of Saint Agatha," patron saint of bell-founders. (This blessing, often in abbreviated form, is also written on many bells throughout Europe.) Agatha, who was martyred during the third century in Catania (a town that lies at the foot of Mount Etna) is patron saint of Sicily, and her protection is traditionally invoked during volcanic eruptions, lightning storms, fires, and earthquakes. She is depicted wearing or carrying a veil with which she smothers fires.

The passio of Agatha claims for the saint a martyrdom commensurate with her responsibilities. She decided to remain a virgin in order to dedicate her life to Christ. But Quintinian, an evil Roman administrator, tried to seduce her from her purpose. She adamantly refused to have anything to do with him, whereupon she was sent to a brothel, but was miraculously preserved from being raped. Quintinian then set about torturing her. In the end, she was hauled over coals until she died, but not before Quintinian had had her breasts hacked off. In paintings Agatha is shown with her fire-fighting veil, carrying a pair of pincers and—most unforgettably—a dish with her two breasts on it, side by side. (Her compatriot, the martyr Lucy of Syracuse, was also sent to a brothel, and then had her eyes gouged out. She was burned at the stake and finally finished off by being stabbed in the throat. Lucy's saintly attribute is her eyes, which she, too, carries, either on a plate or threaded on a skewer.[74])

Agatha's patronage of bell-founders has to do with the molten copper and tin that are poured, like lava from a volcano, in the casting of bells. It is also believed that bell-founders chose her because her breasts look like small, round bells. During the Middle Ages her breasts were represented in loaves, cakes, and cheeses (many Mediterranean cakes and cheeses today are made in the shape of breasts), and on her feast day, February 5, breast-shaped delicacies are still eaten.

In her sixth-century passio we are told that a mysterious youth (an angel) left on Agatha's tomb a tablet with a blessing written on it. Only the first letters of the words were supplied: MSSHDEPL. It was decided that the words must be *Mens Sancta Spontaneus Honor Dei Et Patriae Liberatio*: "[She had] a holy mind. [She gave] spontaneous honour to God. And [she asked for and obtained] liberation for her country. " This blessing could also describe the work of bells themselves. Bells have often been used to proclaim messages and call the people together for "patriotic" reasons; bells "spontaneously" release sound when struck in God's honour; and bells recall the holy to people's minds.

10

VIRGIN MARTYR:

Tomb

....

Agnes is buried at Rome—
mighty girl, famous martyr!
Lying in sight of the city's towers,
the virgin watches over the Romans,
preserving their safety.

When the Spanish-born poet Prudentius visited Rome in 402 to 403, he travelled out along the via Nomentana to pray at the grave of Agnes; soon after, while still in Rome or perhaps back in Spain, he wrote a hymn in her honour, and this was how he began it. "The Hymn to Agnes" was one of fourteen poems he dedicated to martyrs who had been put to death in Spain and Italy; his purpose was to praise them as Christian heroes. Prudentius, a former civil administrator who had held a position at the imperial court, was steeped in the culture and traditions of the Roman empire. His Christian poetry sang a new theme in ancient Roman verse; and when he told of the heroic deeds of Christians, insisting on the utter difference of the new ideals from the ones being superseded, he nevertheless spoke of a greatness of soul that any ancient Roman could admire, even if unwillingly.

This is always the way with the stories of heroes: they tell of unexpected and extraordinary deeds, but they must do so using at least some of the old terms of reference. For without these, the audience will not feel closely involved in the story—will not see for themselves the extent of the discrepancy between old and new that heroes always demonstrate. For a hero is "made" by the rest of us: other people (we) must agree that he or she is great. Prudentius, as poet, is charged with the important role of showing how and why this heroic individual has

come to be so highly valued. He has to communicate with his reader-
ship; otherwise, he cannot express for them their own admiration.

Standing outside the shrine built over the small grave, and near the
great cemetery basilica erected by Constantina in honour of Agnes,
Prudentius looked back at the world's most splendid and powerful city
and saw the massive walls encircling it. They had been built by the
Emperor Aurelian (271–275 A.D.) and finished under Probus
(276–282); a mere ten years it had taken to complete them. There were
nearly twelve miles of walls; prodigious engineering and organizational skill had gone into the constructing of them, and millions of
perfectly laid bricks. Three hundred and eighty-one tall rectangular
towers projected from the walls, every one a hundred Roman feet
from the next, except for the stretches along the riverbanks. There
were seventeen gates, each flanked by massive semicircular towers;
they included the Porta Nomentana, through which Prudentius had
passed to travel to Sant'Agnese's. During the very years Prudentius
was in Rome the walls were being doubled in height, to more than
forty feet. In spite of enormous damage done in the past hundred
years, considerable sections of the walls still stand. One of these is the
stretch of wall Prudentius would have seen from Sant'Agnese's.

But the point of Prudentius' poem was that Rome did not depend on
these massive battlements for its eternal safety. Greater far than this
staggering display of power was the choice that had been made by a
twelve-year-old girl: what had inspired her and then sustained her as
she was murdered for her convictions. She had faced threats of torture
at the hands of her persecutors, but refused to sacrifice to idols. She had
been punished for her obduracy by being dragged off to a brothel.
Miraculously, she had been preserved from rape. Agnes was and is
Rome's hero but, the poet tells us, she also listens to strangers like him:
Agnes in death has become more than a local manifestation of this new
energy abroad in the world. And her glory is twofold, "a double crown"
of virginity as well as martyrdom. Agnes is glorious—and intact.

VIRGINITY, AND THE SAFETY OF THE CITY

Virginity for a female is the state of being intact, unviolated. In the
ancient world a woman "pierced" by sex was laid open to the male: if

married, she was in many ways his property; if unmarried, she was spoiled goods, and marriage was henceforth out of the question. If a woman lost her virginity outside marriage, or had extramarital sex, whether consensual or not, it was a matter of shame rather than guilt. Her "fault," if any, was grave, but in the end incidental: whether she had willingly complied or had been forced, the result was the same. "My body only has been violated," said the Roman heroine Lucretia after she had been raped. "My heart is guiltless [*insons*], as death shall be my witness." She goes on to add, in the manner of Oedipus before her: "Though I acquit myself of the sin, I do not absolve myself from punishment," and she plunged the knife into her heart.[1] Neither Oedipus nor Lucretia was to blame. He, however, had indeed committed parricide and incest and so polluted Thebes; and she had—no question—ceased to be "a chaste wife." To be "shamed" is less a crime than a state of being; shame, unlike guilt, cannot be forgiven.

A woman, ancient Romans easily saw, was very much like a city. If her purity—her walls—had been successfully assailed, she was delivered over to the rule—or simply the power—of men. From time immemorial men have besieged cities, and after battering down the cities' defences, they have celebrated their victory with an orgy of raping women—partly because to do so insulted the defeated men, but also partly because one deed was reflected in and therefore readily led to the other. Men were raped too—"shamed" by being forced to submit to being treated as women. Rape continues in our day to be used as a weapon of war.

Ancient Romans, and Greeks before them, protected through cultic observances the walls around their cities. A group of female virgins, devotees of Hestia (Roman Vesta), tended the fire at the circular shrine of this virgin goddess of the hearth. The hearth of a house was often literally, and always symbolically, round; a circle is a quintessentially female sign. The hearth contained the utterly "male" element, fire. Hestia/Vesta was worshipped at the hearth (*focus* in Latin, a word that includes in its connotations what we now mean in English by "focus") that lay at the heart of every house. It was tended most especially by the still-virgin daughters of the family, women who continued to be devoted to their fathers, not having yet left home to join a husband's family. A woman taken away to share her spouse's "hearth and home" had to be sexually pure at marriage, and remain faithful thereafter to the man who would give his name to her children. His family's bloodline required her purity: everyone knows who is the mother of a newborn child, but a great deal of "culture" is required to be certain who is the father.

The virgin goddess Vesta was given a public cult, echoing private household worship, at her circular shrine, the city's "hearth" in its main square; the fire that constantly burned there was tended by six officially appointed, sexually pure women, known as vestal virgins. To let the fire go out in the cultic city hearth was severely punished: it meant that the vestals had placed the defences of the city in peril. The penalty for a vestal virgin caught copulating was to be scourged and then buried alive.

Ancient Greeks and Romans also created an embodiment of the good fortune, the beauty and tranquillity, the continuance in safety, of a city. She was Tyché or Fortuna, a comely woman serenely seated, wearing on her head a crown made of the city's walls unbroached.[2] Before the Aurelian Walls were built Rome was surrounded by the smaller periphery of the so-called Servian Walls. Just outside the Porta Collina in these walls (Porta Collina was where the via Nomentana originally began) was the temple to *Fortuna Publica Populi Romani,* the "Public Fortune of the Roman People."[3] As *Turrigera,* "Tower Wearer"—a reference to the virgin goddess's battlemented head-dress—Fortuna's statue stood in her temple at the gates of the earlier wall around Rome. The vestal virgins, on the other hand, attended the goddess Vesta at the centre of the city, in the Roman Forum. (The shrine's ruins, and those of the house the vestals lived in, are visible there today.) Virginity at the heart of the city, virginity at her walls: together they represented and preserved the city's integrity.

The Christian hero Agnes, who according to Prudentius now watches over and preserves the safety of Rome's citizens, died a virgin—or so it was said. Prudentius tells us in his poem that Agnes was given a fiendish choice by her persecutor: either to lay her head on the altar of the virgin goddess Minerva and beg her pardon for refusing to sacrifice to her, or to cease to be a virgin herself. Agnes again refused to commit idolatry. She was therefore stripped naked and made to stand at a public place, *publicitus . . . flexu in plateae*, as Prudentius put it.[4]

In Piazza Navona today rises the magnificent baroque church of Sant'Agnese in Agone.[5] Underneath it is a series of vaulted rooms that may still be visited. They are the remains of three parallel galleries of arcades that once lay beneath the seats on the outer periphery of the stadium built on this site in the first century A.D. by the Emperor Domitian. The Piazza Navona[6] espouses the outline of the stadium exactly. These vaulted arches, here and in other stadia, were known in Latin as *fornices*. So common were brothels and stands for prostitutes in such places that the word *fornix* came to mean "brothel," and is the root of the English word "fornication."

Tradition claimed that it was here that Agnes was exposed to the passing crowds; and this would indeed have been a likely place for such a punishment. Prudentius might well have heard that the event took place at this spot. Moreover, it was here that she was also generally believed to have been killed. An oratory dedicated to Agnes existed on the site in the eighth century and is mentioned in the Itinerary of Einsiedeln: "*Circus Flaminius. Ibi sca Agnes.*" (Domitian's circus was then known as the Circus Flaminius.)[7] Pope Calixtus II built a church on the site of the oratory in 1123. This building was in turn replaced in 1652–1657 by Rainaldi's and Borromini's church, which still stands.

Agnes, then, is the patron saint of two sanctuaries in Rome: one outside the walls, and one downtown; one for her virginal death in "the place of shame," and one for her burial. In the church of Sant'Agnese in Agone her skull is venerated; the rest of her bones are buried in her church outside the walls. Like the vestal virgins and the goddess Fortuna before her, the virgin Agnes came to occupy both the centre of the city and its periphery.[8]

HAGIOGRAPHY

Most Christian martyrdoms were, of course, never recorded. Many died—and still die—for their faith, and remain uncelebrated, "their names known to God alone," as Christians frequently remind them-selves. Concerning the martyrs who were remembered during the earliest centuries A.D., there was little that could be done to check the facts about their deaths, unless written reports had survived. *Fama refert*, says the Damasus inscription about Agnes: "Many people say . . . ." He is referring particularly to the girl's family, who were, presumably, in a position to know something about the circumstances of her death. Until Damasus wrote his eulogies, the martyrs' stories at Rome were handed on orally. There remained, of course, the graves of the heroic dead, and the fact that Christians, often at considerable risk, had continued to honour them at these burial sites, and in that manner remembered them.

But there is an important sense in which heroes—in this instance Christian saints—are not only real people; they are also mythic beings. Heroes must do deeds of heroism, and many of their actions will be "known to God alone." But they are heroes only insofar as their deeds are known to other people and their stories told, for it is other people who decide that someone is a hero. These "others" will often not scruple to alter the facts if they can, in order to shape the hero's actions into the story they want to hear. This tendency is powerful even today, when we have far greater means than ever before of recording, preserving, and checking "the facts." With heroes it is *the story*—what ancient Greeks called the *mythos*—that counts. Very often a myth—a trajectory of the soul—is told again and again, in different versions and with varying protagonists. It is the task of heroes to enact the story—on behalf of us, the audience.

The founding story of Christianity is the life of Christ. The Christian religion continues to consist of people's response to Christ's coming as the revelation of God's love: attention to his words; contemplation of his life, his death, and his Resurrection; and obedience to his desire that love of him should be expressed in love for other human beings—all of them: no one is to be dismissed. The liturgy of the Catholic Church includes a year-long "reliving" of the events of the life of Christ, one after the other, and a constant reminder of the stories of people who have paid attention to it, heroically.

Each Christian is called to aspire to sanctity. "Saints," as the word is used among Catholic Christians today, are those who, in the opinion of other people, have succeeded in this enterprise. The Roman Catholic

Church "canonizes" certain saints, placing them on a list (canon) of those given the seal of its approval, after long study and a process of discernment.[9] There are far more saints not in the canon than there are in it; and many a saint in the canon receives little or no veneration from people today: it is always the people who finally decide that someone is, for them, a hero. The Church understands that saints, their prayers, their lives, are for people on earth, and that sainthood, as an earthly honour, is not coveted by the saints themselves.

Every Christian saint's life is lived in emulation of the life of Christ—even though each new narrative is utterly different from all the others because it takes place with a new hero, in a new time and context; and it arises out of different circumstances. A saint's life is therefore always new and surprising—but always "the same." As hagiography, the life is recounted on behalf of the listeners, in order to clarify the issues for them, to inspire them, and to confront them with choices that only they can make, for themselves. And a story, like an architectural space, can both express and recall epiphany.

A "LITANY" OF VIRGIN MARTYRS

Early Christian martyrs must have been young girls comparatively rarely. Yet the figure of the female virgin martyr was one of those that most fired the Christian hagiographical imagination, especially from the third century to the early Middle Ages. The church of Sant'Agnese has a string of these virgins depicted in fresco on the walls above the gallery.[10] The women are all different, and from different places, but their stories strikingly resemble one other, and of course they recall the story of Agnes herself.

The first in the series is Victoria (whose *Acts* are a contemporary report). Aged about twelve, she jumped out of a window on her wedding day in order to avoid being saddled with a husband, and then refused to pretend to be insane in order to save her life; she died in a prison in Carthage. Lucy would not marry her suitor; she was sent to a brothel, but remained a virgin. Burning her failed, and she was then stabbed to death. (These events are the same as those told of the death of Agnes). Lucy's name (from the Latin for "light") is thought to have prompted the story of her eyes being put out; she is the patron saint of people with eye trouble. Agatha was sent to a brothel in vain, then tortured to death. The virgin Barbara (whose story is taken to be wholly mythical) struggled valiantly with her horrible father until he killed her, but she forgave him before she died. Barbara's story involves a tower, the windows of which she deliberately increased in number from two to three, in honour of the Trinity. She became the patron saint of architects and builders—and also of gunners.

Cecilia (who appears again on the ceiling of the church) was given in marriage to Valerian, whom she persuaded on their wedding night to drop sex forever. (Instead of paying attention to the wedding celebrations, she "sang in her heart to God," which made her the patron saint of music.) Valerian and his brother Tiburtius were beaten to death, and Cecilia condemned to suffocation in the saunalike bathroom of her own house; she finally had to be beheaded. Martina, another of the patron saints of Rome, was tortured and then killed by stabbing under the emperor Septimius Severus. Milk flowed out of her wounds instead of blood. Bibiana (Vivian) was first sent to a brothel "to have her mind changed," and when that did not work, she was beaten to death; two other young women died with her. Their bodies were exposed to be eaten by dogs, but the dogs refused to comply. (She, like Cecilia and Martina, is the patron saint of her own church in Rome.)

Rufina and her sister Secunda, daughters of a Roman senator, were engaged to Christian men who apostatized under threat. The girls, however, refused to renounce Christianity; they were scourged, tortured, and beheaded. The church in Rome dedicated to these women is now enclosed inside a convent; it is said to be at the site of their family house. Columba, aged sixteen, was condemned to be mauled by a bear before the crowds in the amphitheatre at Sens in France. The occasion was the visit to the city of the Emperor Aurelian (he who built the walls of Rome). The bear is said to have protected her from rape in the jail, and then to have refused to attack her in the arena.[11] Columba was later decapitated; as often happens in the stories of the martyrs, a fountain sprang up where her head was buried. Julia, after being sold as a slave, travelled with her owner on a ship and had many adventures before being killed by pirates who first tore her hair out and then crucified her. She is the patron saint of Corsica where she was killed.

Apollonia was not a teenager but an aged deaconess. A mob of pagans knocked out all her teeth, but she continued to refuse to blaspheme against Christ. She is the patron saint of dentists and sufferers from toothache. On being threatened with burning, she leaped into the flames of her own accord. Flora was beheaded by the Saracens at Cordoba; as she awaited her death, she was encouraged by Eulogius, who afterwards wrote a (surviving) narrative of the events. Catherine of Alexandria argued with a crowd of philosophers and converted every one—as well as hundreds of other people. Refusing to be married to a powerful man because she had already committed herself in mystic marriage to Christ, she was condemned to be torn on a spiked wheel (a "Catherine wheel"). But it flew apart, and she had to be beheaded instead. She used to be the patron saint of spinsters, the celibate clergy—and wheelwrights. Because her story is now believed to be completely mythical, she has been withdrawn from the canon.

Susanna refused to marry Maximian, son-in-law of the emperor Diocletian, but instead converted the emperor's go-between, her uncle Claudius, who was trying to arrange the marriage. Claudius and his brother Maximus, also converted by Susanna, were burned to death and the girl beheaded. The church of Santa Susanna in Rome has magnificent frescoes that tell her story, including the miracle of her protection, by an angel, from rape in prison. Her head on a dish is carved above the front door of the church. The body of Candida, the last of the procession of virgin martyrs and "companions" of Agnes depicted on the walls at Sant'Agnese's, was brought to the church of Santa Prassede by Pope Paschal I in 817; her name appears in close proximity to that of Emerentiana, on the famous stone inscription still preserved in that church, giving the names of the martyrs whose relics were brought for safety within the walls. There is a tradition that Saint Peter himself baptized Candida at Naples, together with Asprenus, who later became the city's first bishop. It may be recalled that Peter traditionally baptized near Sant'Agnese's when he was in Rome.

Most of these stories have large accretions of legendary material gathered around a small core of facts; some are entirely made up. The Gospel accounts of the life of Christ, as Scripture, could not be altered; but the authors of these "sacred biographies" felt free to indulge in what today we might call "creative fiction." The cultural traditions and expectations of the audience deeply affected what was said; indeed, it can fairly be claimed that the real authors of these accounts were to a large extent their audiences.[12] All of the stories can be read as deliberate reflections, in narrative form, upon Scripture.

Many of them must have been based on no more than names and places. The facts about Agnes are hardly more plentiful: we know of her "for a fact" only her name, the site of her burial in her family's plot, her extreme youth, the day of her death, and that she was martyred. The date of her death is likely to have been after the fourth edict of the persecution of Diocletian, which in March 304 ordered all Christians without exception to sacrifice on pain of death; Agnes probably died on January 21, 305. Even the manner of her death is told to us in several different versions: beheading, stabbing in the throat, and/or burning.

None of the early hagiographies says very much about the lives of the saints before their martyrdom. With modern martyrs—of which there are huge numbers: more Christians have been killed for their faith in the last century than in all of the previous nineteen[13]—it is very different. We have far more documentation about the lives of these people, and often more facts about their deaths, in spite of the preference for secrecy in modern methods of persecution. But with the early virgin martyrs it was an account of the actual death that the audience wanted to hear: horror unable to overcome innocence, conviction triumphant over seduction, the drama of brave faithfulness and purity of heart—and rape miraculously averted.[14] Another demand was for the telling and retelling of an ancient and archetypal heroic plot, one that was known to the ancient Greeks and Romans and valued to this day, wherever stories are told.

SINGLENESS OF HEART

The stories of virgin martyrs as "imitations" of the passion of Christ portray innocent victims, people done to death for their beliefs. The martyrs refuse to worship idols or to shift allegiances. As women, they express their heroism and loyalty by first exerting extraordinary sexual attraction, then turning down the advances of rich, noble, powerful Roman men: they proclaim that their allegiance has already been granted, to Christ. Female witness to Christianity was especially outrageous and jarring to Greek and Roman ears—but there were important precedents; the message could find a space for its telling.

Ancient Greeks are notorious for their misogyny, and yet their mythology includes stories of outstandingly powerful women, not to mention great goddesses. Strictly speaking, heroism was for men. It is about prowess, usually in public action. Women were by definition weak, themselves in need of protection by "heroes," and their role was wholly private. The heroic myth conventionally includes a journey, in the course of which prowess is demonstrated and adventures undergone: heroes almost invariably travel about. But women's place—and that included their religious and mythic space—was in the home. They stayed in one place; indeed, they were often the goal of the hero's journey. Greeks went so far as to make "movement" male and "immobility" female.[15] Women were under the control of men, on a lower level entirely. For all these reasons female heroes—Electra, Medea, Penelope, Alcestis—were highly paradoxical figures.

But all heroes to a certain extent break the heroic mould, and question it. Indeed, the difference between the official pattern or set of criteria for heroes, and the behaviour of any particular hero, is the very stuff out of which stories are made. An author telling us a story says, in effect, "You think that this character is unheroic—rowdy and lustful (like Heracles), much too clever—heroes are rarely allowed to be "smart"—(like Odysseus), or incapacitated by a terrible wound (like Philoctetes). But I tell you, this *is* a hero." And the narrative proceeds to show us that it is so. Heroic figures from other cultures and times range from the simple-minded Parsifal and the too-complicated Hamlet to the foppish or apparently colourless detective; from the cowboy with a crime in his past to a man confined to his apartment with a broken leg but who nevertheless saves the day. Disabilities are overcome, disadvantages and personal defects surmounted: they merely serve to help the audience understand how truly great the hero's qualities are.

Women, given their inherent inferiority within the cultural system, and given the love of paradox that is perhaps inseparable from the very idea of heroism, have always made excellent heroes, although there have traditionally been far fewer of them than of men. An outstanding Greek example is Antigone, who, in Sophocles' play of the same name, confronts the state, in the shape of her powerful uncle Creon (his name means "Powerful One," "Ruler"). Creon has decreed that Antigone's dead brother, a traitor to the city, shall not be buried, but will be left to be ripped to pieces by birds of prey.

Antigone buries him, knowing the danger to herself. For this, Creon decrees an appropriate punishment: she is herself entombed in a cave—alive. The result is not what Creon expected. The city is polluted—the birds themselves are revolted—because the king has been profoundly mistaken, as Antigone has not: he has "confused the upper and lower worlds," leaving the dead unburied and burying the living. Antigone hangs herself in her underground prison. Antigone's fiancé—Creon's son—commits suicide, and Creon's wife stabs herself to death. Creon is left alone, his life destroyed. (He does not die. Heroes die; Creon is merely bereft, condemned to a "living death.")

In this story Creon ought to have been the hero—king as he is, a powerful male, attempting to carry out "justice" on behalf of the state. But Creon is a mere politician—a manipulator of facts, a man of "common sense," a compromiser (he keeps changing his mind, which is fatal for the heroic "pattern" and unthinkable in Antigone). It is Antigone who is the hero. With heroic singleness of heart, she refuses to be disloyal to her brother. Nothing can sway her or frighten her. Antigone's name means "Born Against": she says no, accepts the consequences—and breaks Creon. The people of Thebes take her part. She has done what is right, they sing—and therefore she, and not Creon, is the hero. Even though Antigone's goals and thoughts are far from Christian, she bases her behaviour on a statement that could have been made by a Christian hero. She acted, she says, out of love for her brother, no matter what he had done: "I cannot share in hatred but in love."

The myth of Antigone finds many echoes in the story of Agnes, and of other Christian martyrs, male and female, as well. Antigone tells Creon that he has no right to forbid her to bury her brother; Agnes refuses to "render unto Caesar the things that are God's."[16] Antigone points out in the play that her allegiance to her brother comes first—it long preceded either the love of Creon's son for her, or Creon's decree. Agnes says she is already totally committed, to Christ. Both young women run away from home (their "place"), to complete against all the odds a heroic journey. Antigone refuses to hide the fact that she was the one who disobeyed the state's decree; Agnes cannot bear to keep quiet about her belief, knowing that Christianity is proscribed, and knowing that she will be put to death for speaking out. (Heroes must make their actions and convictions known. How else is society to see what they have done and, amazed, decide that they are heroes?)

Both Antigone and Agnes—and many of the other martyrs too— present their reasons for their actions in a confrontation with a person representing law and power. Such a scene is known in Greek as an *agon*, a struggle, one on one. Christian art has often portrayed the scene: the little girl (Thecla or Catherine or Eulalia), finger raised, confuting the philosophers, or fearlessly stating her case before the furious enthroned governor and his shocked courtiers. The fact that the confrontation has archetypal dramatic power does not mean that such "struggles" never occurred in real life: written reports of actual trials exist, where Roman officials questioned Christian prisoners, and the words used have come down to us. These court documents are every bit as dramatic as stories known to be legendary.[17]

Both Agnes and Antigone achieve what males alone, and few of them, are supposed to find possible: what the ancients called "a beautiful death." This is a death that is brave, famous, and honourable, one that demonstrates greatness of soul, and shows forth the strength and beauty of heroic commitment.[18] All these qualities are made manifest by Agnes, and also by Antigone, whose sister reminds her in vain that she is a mere woman, and "women do not do battle with men." A great many early Christians, given the choice between idolatrous worship of the emperor or death, had given in and abjured their faith. Agnes, a mere girl who courted confrontation with the edict and could not be broken in spite of her age, was admired as a marvel and a standing reproach.

Christianity adds to the heroic mythos its own special take on the greatness of the so-called weak. One of its foundation texts extols the blessedness of the gentle, the pure of heart, the poor in spirit, the persecuted, and those despised and hated because of Christ. It is a religion that eschews spiritual "technique" and "prowess" in favour of its first command: "simply" to love God with all your heart and all your mind and all your strength, and your neighbour as yourself. It insists that it is easier for those not bloated by possessions to get through "the needle's eye" into the kingdom of God; and Jesus thanked God that the truth has been revealed not to the learned or the brilliant but to "little ones."[19] In short, the ideal of Christian saintliness turns the entire concept of heroism on its head. That does not mean that it rejects, or even changes, the heroic picture: it keeps it, but reverses it, so that its heroes protest always that they are *not* heroes, not strong, not outstanding, not worthy, not able. The majority, of course, knows better: it makes such people its heroes. Saint Francis of Assisi, "the little poor one," *il Poverello*, is one of the greatest heroes—that is, one of the closest imitators of Jesus—in the Christian canon.

The *De virginibus* of Ambrose, the Ambrosian hymn *Agnes beatae virginis*, the "Hymn to Agnes" by Prudentius, and the passio of Agnes were all written in the closing years of the classical era. Christianity had arisen out of Judaism and become the official religion of the Roman Empire. The original *mythos*, however, remains forever unofficial. Antigone can be neither confined nor muzzled by Creon, although the battle continues. Prudentius fully understood the enormity of the paradox when he made Agnes, not the Aurelian Walls, the protector of the Roman people: "mighty girl, famous martyr!"

MIRACLE AFTER MIRACLE

But Agnes, unlike Antigone, apparently had to endure not only a martyr's death but also an attack on her sexual integrity, her virginity. This aspect of her story grew—we can actually see it growing—as the poems, sermons, and passios gradually elaborated upon the memory of the death of this little girl.

The Damasus inscription was probably the earliest written narrative. He says that even as she died, in modesty Agnes covered her body with her hair. And he ends with a prayer to Agnes, famous martyr, glorious in her *pudor* ("shamefastness" as it used to be called). For Damasus, she died modest to the last, like many a martyred heroine, both classical and Christian, before her. The hymn *Agnes beatae virginis*, probably by Ambrose, calls her a virgin but speaks only of the moment of her execution, describing her *pudor* as she drew her clothing around her after her executioner had stabbed her, and covered her face with her hand as she fell.[20]

When Ambrose alluded to the story in *De virginibus* (ca. 377 A.D.), he openly turned it into a eulogy of the virginity of Agnes, her purity, her perfection as a model for all virgins. Ambrose tells us, for the first time among the sources that have reached us, how the Roman prosecutor, whom he calls "the tyrant," desired her sexually, how he tried to seduce her by flattery and promises of marriage—but she refused him, having made her choice in advance. Ambrose avoids describing the actual blow that killed her, contenting himself with the calm and courageous behaviour of Agnes despite her age: "Intrepid, she prayed; she bowed her head."

"You have, therefore," he goes on, "in one victim a double witness [*in una hostia duplex martyrium*], of purity and of faith!" Ambrose concludes, "She both remained a virgin and achieved martyrdom: *et virgo permansit et martyrium obtinuit*." We shall look again at Ambrose's last sentence. But the "double crown" of Agnes, as Prudentius was to call it, remains a feature of her story down to the present day, with the *two* lambs at her yearly festival. The tradition has remained that Agnes was martyred, but died intact.

The fifth-century Latin passio amplified the story, devoting considerable energy to explaining how it came to pass that Agnes remained inviolate; in doing so, it sensationally exploited the sexual drama merely hinted at by Damasus and Ambrose. Symphronius, the Roman prefect, we are told, was the father of a young man who had been in love with Agnes, and whom she had resoundingly rejected. In revenge, he reported to his father that she was a Christian, and the prefect ordered her to appear before him. He threatened her, and tried to seduce her with sweet promises, but she remained adamantly faithful to her original commitment.

The prefect declared his determination to make her into a vestal virgin, who would be forced to offer idolatrous sacrifice to the goddess night and day for the rest of her life. He came off very badly, however, in the battle of words that followed. Enraged, he changed his tack and gave her the choice: either be a vestal virgin or be condemned to sexual slavery in a brothel. She chose the latter, convinced that her guardian angel would protect her, that Christ would be for her "an impenetrable wall." Symphronius commanded that she should be dragged through the streets naked, to the brothel.

The Damasus inscription had briefly alluded to her having "covered her body with her hair" out of modesty. The passio of Agnes, however, improved considerably on this detail. It says that when she was stripped of her clothing to be escorted by the military to the *fornix*, her hair suddenly grew so long that it became a veil and covered her body.[21] When she arrived at the brothel, a brilliant light shone about her, and as she prayed a beautiful white garment appeared before her. She put it on, and it was so white and fitted her so perfectly that everyone said it must have been ready made by the hands of the guardian angel who, as she had told the prefect, would certainly protect her.

The prefect's son with a group of his friends went to the brothel with the object of "insulting" her there. But as he stretched out his arm to touch her, he fell choking to the ground. The cry went up that Agnes was a death-dealing witch. The prefect himself came to the brothel on hearing the news. But Agnes prayed to God, and the prefect's son not only came round, but proclaimed his conversion to Christianity.[22] At this, the Roman priests stirred up the people, who even more angrily denounced Agnes as a witch. The prefect himself now wished he could save her from execution, but he could not go against the priests. (In this inability to act he resembles Pontius Pilate, in the Passion of Jesus.[23]) The vicarius or deputy of the emperor, Aspasius by name, now took charge. He had a fire built up to burn the witch. Agnes was thrown into the flames, but they divided in two, flew out, and burned the crowd instead. She stood there, her arms raised in a prayer of ecstatic joy ("Behold, what I believed I now see; what I hoped for, I have; what I desired, I now embrace"), and gradually the fire went out.[24] Aspasius, terrified that the people would rise up against him, stepped forward and plunged his sword into her throat.[25]

Prudentius' poem, which probably predated the passio, does not tell of the miracle of Agnes' hair. The crowd, he says, refused to look at the girl standing naked in the *fornix*: they were ashamed to do so. (Shame is a positive force as well as a negative one: it is supposed to *prevent* violations of the moral system.) But one man did look, and was struck blind by a thunderbolt for his baseness.[26] Agnes rejoiced because her virginity remained to her. She then prayed for the young man, and his sight was restored. She was applying the new heroic standard of virtue in forgiving her enemy.[27] But the judge, as he is called in the hymn by Prudentius, did not repent. Merely angered because the girl had won the struggle between them, he ordered that Agnes should die for not obeying the emperor. She bowed her head, and with one blow the executioner cut it off. The soul of Agnes rose heavenward; she laughed for joy. A "double crown," *duplex corona*, was hers as martyr and virgin; she had been killed, but never violated.

Because of the survival of several different documents telling the story of her martyrdom, the Agnes story is particularly revealing of how a virgin martyr myth evolved. The sexual theme (nubile girl totally at the mercy of a benighted and ruthless male ruler or judge) is fully dramatized. Yet it became clear, as the myth was told and retold, that Agnes must not, could not have been raped. Indeed, nothing in these documents suggests that she did not die a virgin. On the contrary: miracle after miracle occurs to ensure that Agnes remains inviolate. In order to be considered a hero, Agnes was apparently required to achieve both moral and physical integrity: to keep both her courage and her physical virginity intact. If that was so, then hers is still a Greco-Roman rather than a Christian myth.

RAPE AND VIRGINITY

It is probable that many, even most, early Christian virgins executed for their faith were, in fact, first raped. One of the most shocking incidents in the story of Agnes cannot be dismissed as a lurid invention: Christian women are known to have been punished by being forced into brothels. The equivalent for men was consignment to work in the appalling conditions of the ancient Roman mines. In a rhetorical address to Roman persecutors of Christians, Tertullian mentions a woman who was forced into prostitution. "In condemning a Christian woman to a brothel," he wrote, "instead of to death by being mauled by a lion, you were admitting that to us such a fate is more terrible than any punishment and any death."[28] During the trial of Pionios before his martyrdom at Smyrna in 250, Sabina, one of Pionios' companions, was interrogated by Polemon. The court secretary recorded the words spoken in the encounter. "Those who will not sacrifice are made to stand in the brothel," Polemon reminded her. Sabina's reply was, "God most holy will take care of that."[29]

Ancient Romans felt uncomfortable about killing—especially stabbing or beheading—a virgin. Their unease came from the violation of religious and social categories. In Greek and Roman myths women who commit suicide usually hang themselves, take poison, or leap off cliffs—anything rather than use the phallic sword, death by which was the quintessence of a gloriously "masculine" end, but for a woman symbolized rape. True, the mythical Roman heroine Lucretia had stabbed herself—an appropriate gesture in this case, since she had been raped; and moreover she was a wife, not a virgin. Eurydice, in the *Antigone*, stabs herself, but she is Creon's wife. When mythical virgin women are killed with a sword, it is a terrible affair, as the death of Iphigenia—and its reverberating outcome—shows.[30] Tacitus tells us that when the daughter of Sejanus was murdered, she was violated first by the executioner, then strangled, "because capital punishment of a virgin was unprecedented."[31] In practice it was safer, even perhaps more "aesthetic," first to change the virgin's status—and easily done.

To a modern sensibility, the fact that virgins were probably routinely raped before being put to death not only rings hideously true, but makes these martyrdoms more terrible—and more moving.[32] It seems very odd to us that tales of martyrdom should dwell in detail upon blood and pain, but always take care to insist that a female hero could never have been raped. (The insistence is continual: look over the short list of virgin martyrs painted on the walls of Sant'Agnese's, and see how many of them were sent to brothels but miraculously remained inviolate.) Death was different. Death in the passios of virgin martyrs can involve flaying by hooks, being rolled in barrels of glass shards, having breasts lopped off, or teeth broken; it often features whips and wild beasts, burning and dismemberment. These are described and (later) depicted. But rape? Never.

One reason must be that rape was still held, in the culture, to have the power to render a woman "shamed," and a "shamed" hero was a contradiction in terms. Female heroes, therefore, against every likelihood, had to maintain their virginal status. We know that thinking Christians accepted the implication of their faith, that a raped woman was in no way "polluted" or "reduced" by what had been done to her. Saint Augustine (354–430), for instance, spoke of "the chastity preserved in the spirit," which cannot be destroyed by the physical violence of a rapist.[33] When it came to the stories of the virgin martyrs, the myth was capable of accepting that a torn and mutilated body could paradoxically declare the extent of a martyr's psychic integrity. But sexual assault, even in brothels, is invariably and triumphantly warded off by these heroines. Presumably, popular thinking could still not accept that a woman who was the victim of rape might have kept her purity of soul intact, and so remained heroic: when people told her story for the admiration of others, they apparently felt obliged to make editorial improvements.

The endurance in a Christian setting of the very kind of thinking that the Christian revelation sets out to dispel is deplorable. We should consider, nevertheless, the historical context to which the virgin martyr stories belong. The martyr legends were told after the great persecutions had ended, among Christians who were much less likely to be called upon to die for their faith. The enthusiasm of the heroic among them was now channelled instead into asceticism. Some disappeared into the desert, for instance, to live as hermits. Some decided to stay at home without ever marrying. Others chose to live in community, leaving their natal family and giving up the possibility of a procreative family in order to help form new groupings of "brothers" and "sisters" whose ties were spiritual, not physical. To renounce family was to renounce sex.[34]

Hagiographical stories, therefore, stressed virginity: they were intended to inspire men and women living or wanting to live celibate lives. These were people who might not aspire to Agnes' two crowns, but could surely aim to achieve one of them.[35] When Ambrose, addressing in *De virginibus* an audience of celibate women,[36] spoke of Agnes' "double witness" and then said that these were virginity and martyrdom, he was assuring his listeners that their virginity too was a form of martyrdom—martyrdom in the sense of "witnessing" to faith. It is important to add that the stories extolling virginity also addressed the majority of people, who had no intention of aiming for the total devotion expressed in a vow of celibacy.

During the first Christian centuries, celibacy for both men and women had come to be considered an outstandingly virtuous choice in life. As we have seen, one of the paradoxes of Christianity is its demand for both community and individualism. At first, individualism was the revolutionary ideal. To renounce sex and choose virginity, especially for a woman, was to maintain one's "outline"—like a city that repels armies from its walls—and to avoid losing one's individuality in the creation of a family. It meant freedom from much of the control of men, and freedom from the constraints and commitments inherent in child-bearing.

Freedom is not only "from" but also "for": a choice of virginity could be (and still can be) in favour of living at the disposal of others, not necessarily those belonging to one's family. Living as virgins in community expressed the paradox perfectly: single individuals, living as a group, with everyone's attention turned towards helping all of their neighbours, both within the community and outside it. Such a life "witnessed" to this essential aspect of the Christian ideal as surely as dying for refusing to sacrifice to idols witnessed to one's revolutionary faith in the Judeo-Christian God. And the exceptional nobility of the calling to a celibate life "for the sake of the kingdom of heaven" had scriptural assurance in the words of Christ, together with the warning, "It is not everyone who can accept what I have said, but only those to whom it is granted."[37]

From the point of view of the pagan world, however, especially before 300 A.D., Christianity was a threat precisely because it lured women away from their ancient social role. It broke up families, and caused women to become recalcitrant and opinionated. It encouraged many of them to abandon their duty to the state and the family, which was the bearing of children and the creation of family alliances through daughters being "given away" by their fathers to men whom the family wanted to count as members of their clan.[38] The new Christian system gave scandalously high status to unmarried women and to widows—women outside the sphere where their usefulness might, in the pagan world, have been rewarded with honour.

Christians expressed their version of virginity as "marriage to Christ"; this meant that a heroic choice had been made, explicitly to prefer God to everything else. For centuries women have been initiated into religious orders in a ceremony that quotes the words spoken by Agnes in her passio when she refused the hand of the prefect's son: "With Christ alone do I keep faith; for him do I reserve my devotion. . . . And after this my wedding, many will be the children that I shall mother."[39] The vows of poverty, chastity, and obedience are still taken in religious orders, male and female—and to this day the three vows directly and totally reverse (with revolutionary intent) the powers, lures, distractions, and pressures of "this world." From a religious point of view, virginity is never merely biological.

But we must come back to the fact that martyred women may seldom have died virgins—except in the spiritual and metaphorical, but nevertheless real, sense that they remained faithful to their convictions, their souls undiminished. These women must often have been first raped and then killed: if so, they suffered a double martyrdom. It is this "double crown" that we wish the virgin martyr stories would acknowledge, and they do not.

Christianity changed human history when, taking up with renewed intensity a theme already present in the Jewish Old Testament, it insisted on a new view of scapegoat killings: *the victim is innocent.* This was one meaning of the crucifixion of Christ. Death on the cross was deeply shameful—a "double martyrdom" of pain and shame—so much so that the earliest Christians could not bear to depict their founder undergoing it. The nakedness of the victim was part of the shame. In the case of Jesus no miracles occurred to save him; he even shared the common experience of victims that they have been abandoned by God, crying out on the cross: "My God, my God, why have you forsaken me?"[40]

Even so, it is perhaps only now that we can honestly look at the virgin martyrs as representatives of female heroism. An insistence on literal virginity (as opposed to integrity of mind and soul) as essential to female heroism is no longer acceptable. In this respect we are certainly closer now to the original Christian revelation. Christians (unless they take a fundamentalist stance) experience the revelation proceeding from Christ's life and death as ongoing, always growing. The application of "shame culture" to women, which has persisted for nearly two thousand years after Christ's coming, is increasingly revealed for the outrage that it is. Human beings are better able now— at least in this respect—to endure the light.

THE SCAPEGOAT

The parents of Agnes, recounts the last chapter of her passio, after burying her milk sister Emerentiana, spent night after night in vigil at their daughter's grave. One silent midnight they saw a great light, and a multitude of virgins all clothed in gold appeared to them, moving in a long procession. Among them was their daughter. Her father and mother were amazed. Agnes asked for the procession to stop a moment. She spoke to her parents, telling them not to mourn for her but to share her joy, for now she lived among these marvellous companions, in total intimacy with the One she had loved on earth above everything else.

The scene is reproduced in the great mosaic that accompanies the nave on the clerestory wall of the sixth-century church of Sant' Apollinare Nuovo in Ravenna: it shows a line of women haloed and clothed in gold, each one wearing a jewelled pallium under her cloak and carrying in her veiled hands a martyr's crown. Agnes stands out among them because beside her walks a white lamb with a tiny bell around its neck; it turns and looks up at her. The lamb is Agnes' attribute or identifying symbol; she was one of the first Christian saints to have one.[41]

The lamb (*agnus* in Latin) is a visual pun on the girl's name. In Greek (her name is, in fact, Greek) *hagne* means "full of religious awe" (*hagos*). In ancient Greek religion, sacred people, places, or objects—those that were considered untouchable and "fenced-off"—

had, and aroused, *hagos*. Examples were the holy ground occupied by a temple, holy objects inside a temple, or, from a sexual point of view, close family members, sex with whom was utterly taboo. Such untouchable people, places, or things were protected by a curse, or gave rise to pollution if they were tampered with. It is not surprising that the myth of Agnes should have endowed her with sacred virginity, for such a quality was suggested by her name. Just as the "virgin" Constantia in her hagiographical tale was constant, so Agnes must have been virginal or sacrosanct: *hagne*. The son of the Roman prefect had indeed attempted the impossible.

The philosopher René Girard[42] has shown how the strategy of human sacrifice, masked by myths such as those of the Greeks, is fundamental to the birth of human culture. In moments of crisis human "togetherness" has been achieved—and still is, if we are not very careful—by the creation of scapegoats. A scapegoat is a person or a group of people blamed for the discord that periodically arises within human societies because of what Girard calls "mimetic violence." Once order has broken down, social groupings degenerate into a murderous chaos that people can neither fathom nor control. Escape may be found when a scapegoat is blamed for the trouble. The many unite against the one: a vilified group, or a person upon whom blame can be foisted, becomes intolerable and must be persecuted—wiped out, if possible. "Society" has its way. In the creation of a common enemy, concord is re-established, as by a miracle.

In ancient or primitive societies, once peace has been restored, the survivors are grateful. Just as they once relieved their hatred for each other by blaming their victim, they now offer gratitude to the one—or the group—who appears to have saved them by accepting death. They begin to worship their enemy.[43] The execrable has become its exact opposite: *hagios*, "holy." In Greek the word *hagos* is used to mean "expiation" or "sacrifice" as well as "awe," "curse," and "pollution."[44] The victim has been the cause of evil; now he or she is shown to have been its remedy. (The Greek word *pharmakos* means "a remedy" as well as "a purificatory victim"; it is the root of the English word "pharmacy.")

The sacrificial remedy cannot work, however, unless society is completely convinced that the one who must die is to blame for the faults of the people. Oedipus really did cause pollution in Thebes. Pentheus certainly provoked the rage of Dionysus and his followers. The beggar of Ephesus, whom Apollonius of Tyana persuaded the citizens to stone to death, "really was" a devil that had caused all the trouble they were undergoing.[45] For Girard, such myths mask the generalized violence afflicting the community, which was the true reason behind the deaths of all of these figures; the stories are there to camouflage the truth.

But Girard goes on to demonstrate how, in the Jewish Scriptures or Old Testament, a very different story began to be told. The Book of Job tells of a man who suffers. Other people believe that he must have done something wrong; his "comforters" try to persuade him that he must have deserved his misery. But Job refuses to accept that what has happened to him arose from his guilt. And—most important, for this is a story—the readers of the book are told the facts behind the hero's pain. *We* know that Job is innocent; he is suffering, but blameless. This understanding lies at the heart of the Christian revelation. God—Jesus—dies the scapegoat's death with all victims, and we know that he has done no wrong. "Don't you see," says the high priest before the decision to put Jesus to death, "that it is better for one man to die for the people, than for the whole nation to be destroyed?"[46] The Crucifixion reveals once and for all that the "scapegoat mechanism" is a lie: the victim is innocent.

THE LAMB

Christ, as the victim who reveals God's love for us, is symbolized by a lamb.[47] For Christians, he is the "lamb" described in the Book of Isaiah: "Harshly dealt with, he bore it humbly; he never opened his mouth: like a lamb that is led to the slaughterhouse, like a sheep that is dumb before its shearers, he never opened his mouth."[48] Lambs suffer violence; they do not inflict it. They are symbols, apparently in all languages and literatures, of innocence. And lambs have always been favourite animals for sacrifice. John the Baptist said of Jesus before his baptism, "Behold the lamb of God, who takes away the sins of the world."[49] John's meaning was that Jesus was the Messiah, he who in his life and death would reveal the true nature of God.

Sheep and lambs are symbolic in the New Testament not only of Christ but also of his followers; in these cases Jesus becomes the shepherd and they his flock. He searches for the lost sheep until he has found it, leaving all the "safe" sheep to look after themselves in the meanwhile. Peter, to whom Jesus entrusts the Church, is told to "feed" his sheep and lambs. Jesus sends his followers out into the world with no weapons, no money, no power—"like sheep among wolves."[50] They must not expect an easy time, but rather the "blessing" of being despised and persecuted. People who die for believing in the revelation, for not defending themselves by partaking in violence, imitate Christ. To be martyred is to be "like a lamb that is led to the slaughterhouse."

All these meanings, and more, are evoked by any representation of a lamb in Christian iconography. When we see Agnes accompanied by her attribute, a lamb, the animal represents Agnes, her death, her blamelessness: Agnes was an innocent victim. The lamb also links her sacrifice to Christ's: she, too, was a "lamb of God," *Agna Dei*. Included in her innocence was her inviolate chastity. However, insofar as the essence of that chastity is thought of in terms of physical inviolability, the Christian revelation is betrayed, because then Agnes is *hagne* in the Greek sense: a "space" untouchable, an "outline" protected by a curse (such as a thunderbolt ready to blind a man who would look upon her with lust). The implication is that if Agnes had lost her inviolability for any reason, including reasons utterly beyond her own choice or control, she would have been, permanently because in her very essence, shamed and "defiled." Saint Augustine in the fifth century had already denounced this kind of thinking, as we saw, yet it persisted, and it still exists.

But if the innocence of the "lamb" Agnes is understood to be an aspect of her soul, a purity of mind and singleness of heart, and her virginity in the story is an expression of that innocence, then she is properly a Christian hero; for the equation of physical sacrosanctity with purity is inimical to the Christian religion. Christ refused sacrosanctity for himself; his death shows it. The Eucharist, the supreme mystery of the Christian religion, does not distance God or fence him off, but makes him profoundly, even humbly, available.

As a saint, Agnes is a person who has imitated Christ. As a martyr, she died like Christ; as a virgin, she kept her faith, hope, and love alive even in the midst of horror. Hagiographically speaking, she is a version of Christ, even though when she died she was twelve years old, a female, and living in Rome not Jerusalem. The lamb—her attribute, her name—is a symbol of Christ himself. Agnes, because she is remembered, is continuing proof that imitating Christ is possible, in the specific circumstances of every person's own unique life.

THE LIGHT AND THE LIFE

After traversing the dim passage through the maze of catacomb galleries, a visitor today standing underneath the church before the grave of Agnes and Emerentiana may (if he or she wishes) consider many things, remember many a moment of insight. The silver coffin with the bones of two young women inside it can embody and recall, for example, a person's deepest desire, or a specific experience of grace in the life of the beholder at the end of a long "dark night of the soul." It can remind the visitor of seventeen centuries of faithful memory, of the long history of this place, and of the story of the death of Agnes.

It will certainly recall to Christians the words of Jesus: "I tell you, most solemnly, that unless a wheat grain falls on the ground and dies, it remains only a single grain; but if it dies, it yields much fruit."[51] Because of the story of Agnes, the little grave caused an oratory to be built, then a church, and then this basilica, just as the Christian community grew from small, poor, and unpromising beginnings. The whole building is rooted in this coffin, just as the Church lives still out of the spiritual conviction, the courage, and the generosity of its members—out of the choice, continually to be made by Christians just as it had to be made by Agnes and Emerentiana, of love over hatred, greed, selfishness, and violence.

This simple church provides a place where Christians can meet and pray, listen to the word of Scripture, and celebrate together the mysteries of their faith. It reminds each person of his or her own past intimations of the light, and it proposes a renewed approach towards what it was that inspired these two Christian martyrs, and thousands of others like them. The story of Agnes, like the church building itself, reflects Christ. Both church and saint, through spatial disposition and through narrative, refract the light and the life. "And that life was the light of men," wrote John the Evangelist.[52] "The light shines on in the dark, and the darkness has never quenched it."

NOTES

....

One: The Door Swings Open: Threshold

1. Leclercq (1924), I, 932–942.
2. This particular aspect of mystical experience is the one most readily expressed in language or indicated by a church building. A good introduction to the subject as a whole is Evelyn Underhill, *Mysticism*. New York and London: Doubleday, 1990. Originally published 1891.
3. Thomas M. Robinson, ed. and commentary, *Heraclitus: Fragments* (Toronto: U. of Toronto Press, 1987). Fragments 60 and 12.
4. Blaise Pascal, *Pensées*. Edition de Philippe Sellier (Paris: Classiques Garnier, 1999). Originally published 1670. Fragment 220.
5. For a simple treatment of the difficult subject of ritual, see Visser (1991), s. v., which treats as ritual performance the way human beings eat meals.
6. Aristotle *Poetics* 6.1449; 13.1452–14.1453.
7. The phrases "narrowing and flattening" and "deviation into the trivial" are Charles Taylor's, in *The Ethics of Authenticity* (Boston: Harvard U.P., 1991), 6, 57.
8. Matthew 24:42–44; Mark 13:33–37.
9. Exodus 3:14.
10. Julian of Norwich, fourteenth century. Modern version: *Revelations of Divine Love*, tr. and ed. Clifton Wolters (London: Penguin Books, 1966), chapter 73, p. 192, chapter 5, p. 68, chapter 26, p. 102. Original version: *A Revelation of Love*, ed. Marion Glasscoe (U. of Exeter Press, 1986), chapter 27, pp. 28–29, chapter 26, p. 28.
11. The word "mean" is from Old English *maenan*, "to recite, to tell." It means "to have in mind," with an intention of communicating; its sense, therefore, is both "to intend" and "to signify." In this context God is what Julian has in mind as her destiny. But the idea of God as "Meaning" is, I believe, not foreign to Julian's thought: God is already there, making sense of her life and giving it depth and direction.
12. Costantino Caetani, early seventeenth century. MS in the Biblioteca Alessandrina, cod. 91, fol. 306r–307r. Quoted at length in Frutaz (1992), 52–54.
13. In a Roman church *matroneum* is, strictly speaking, an incorrect term for this gallery. De Benedictis (1981) shows that in Rome a *matroneum* was a small area

of the right aisle near the sanctuary, on the ground floor and walled off by parapets, for the use of consecrated women. There was a *senatorium* on the other side, for consecrated men.

14. In *opus mixtum*, one (sometimes two) layers of *tufelli* (bricks made from tufa) alternate with two to four strata of broken clay bricks; this was the characteristic masonry of early Christian times. For the rest, the walls of the passage are medieval and built all of *tufelli*. Krautheimer (1937), 19, 23.

15. Virgil *Aeneid* 6. 264–268.

16. John 12:25; Matthew 10:39.

17. John 12:24.

18. For nearly three hundred years the steps led directly into the church's narthex. See Krautheimer (1937), fig. 10.

19. Costantino Caetani, early seventeenth century. Quoted in Frutaz (1992), 86. There are now nine windows, five on the left and four on the right.

20. Two of the ten bas-reliefs—*Endymion Sleeping* and *Perseus Rescuing Andromeda*—are kept in the Capitoline Museum; copies of them are in the Palazzo Spada. One of the bas-reliefs was found in the Piazza SS Apostoli and another on the Aventine, but they clearly belong to the same set. See Ashby (1906), 41–42.

21. Lanciani (1924), 261–267.

22. Krautheimer (1980), 66.

23. Romans 16:11.

24. Bacci (1902), 51–58; see Schmitz (1926).

25. *Liber Pontificalis* II, 24. The *Liber Pontificalis* or "Book of the Popes" is an ancient and medieval compilation of the lives of the popes, beginning with Peter and ending with Pius II (died 1464). It was begun in the sixth century, using earlier sources, and was continued thereafter by various hands. The edition used here is that of Louis Duchesne, vol. I (1886) and vol. II (1892).

26. Hebrews 12:1.

Two: Space and Time: Narthex and Ground Plan

1. The blessing, which is performed by a priest, dedicates the water to God and moves it from the secular or "profane" sphere into that of the church—both building and institution.

2. For the history of the sign of the cross, see Thurston (1953) and Sulzberger (1925).

3. The inner wall of the present façade of the church is three hundred years older than the rest of the building: it is of the same masonry as the lower left-hand portions of the wall in the passage down, which are datable to the fourth century. Krautheimer (1937), Plan IV and p. 25.

4. Hebrew "Eden," meaning "plain," is a word, like "Paradise," that has connotations of pleasure and ease: the Israelites found it wonderful to see rough places made plain. The Hebrew for "Paradise" in Genesis is *gan eden*.

5. Romans 5:20–21.

6. William Butler Yeats, "Lapis Lazuli," line 24.

7. The Christian doctrine of the Trinity is that God has three "persons." It expresses the belief that God "is" loving relationship. God's oneness is plural; God, being greater than any categories the human mind can devise, contains both one and many.
8. Isaiah 7:14, 9:1–7, 11:1–9; Matthew 1:18–25.
9. Exodus 25–31.
10. Exodus 36 gives a different version, saying that Moses built the structure only after the crisis was over.
11. Judges 18:31; 1 Samuel 1:3; 1:24; 3:3; 3:15.
12. 1 Samuel 4:3–11.
13. Isaiah 2:2–4.
14. See Frye (1981), especially 78–138.
15. 1 Kings 5:15–7:51; I Chronicles 22:7–10.
16. 1 Kings 8:1–9:25; 2 Chronicles 5.
17. 1 Kings 6–7; 2 Chronicles 3–4.
18. 1 Kings 7:23–39; 2 Chronicles 4:6.
19. 2 Kings 25:1–21; 2 Chronicles 36:17–21.
20. Ezekiel 40:1–48:35.
21. Hebrews 9:7.
22. Psalm 2:7–9; Isaiah 2:2–4, 9:1–7, 11:1–9, 61:1–2; Micah 5:1–3. The idea of the Messiah and this term to name him became common in post–Old Testament Judaism. See further R.E. Brown in Brown, Fitzmyer and Murphy (1990), 1310–1312 and bibliography.
23. Exodus 26:31–36.
24. Acts 2:46, 3:1–10.
25. Acts 26:28; I Peter 4:14–16; Tacitus *Annals* 15.44; Suetonius *Lives of the Caesars* 6.16.
26. See the Suffering Servant poems in the work of the "Second Isaiah," especially Isaiah 53.
27. Matthew 21:12–17; Mark 11:15–19; Luke 19:45–48; John 2:13–22.
28. Luke 2:22–24.
29. I owe this interpretation to Francesc Riera i Figueras, *Jesús, el Galileo* (Madrid: Narcea, 1992), 179.
30. Matthew 27:51.
31. Matthew 26:18–19; Mark 14:13–16; Luke 22:10–12; Matthew 14:13–21, 15:29–39.

Three: Trajectory: Nave

1. See, for instance, Matthew 5:1–12; Luke 6:20–23.
2. On the catacombs, see, for example, P. Brown (1981), s.v. "cemeteries"; Fasola in di Berardino, ed., *Encyclopedia of the Early Church*, I, 1992, 155–158; Fiocchi Nicolai et al. (1998); Frend (1996) passim (on the history of the rediscovery of the catacombs); Jeffers (1991), chapters 2 and 3; Luft (1990), chapter 29; Pietri (1976), 122–134, 659–667; Stevenson (1978); Tristan (1996), "Les catacombes."
3. Ugo Ventriglia, *La Geologia della Città di Roma* (Rome: n. p., 1971), Fig. 101, p.

174, gives a cross-section of the soil structure of the Catacomb of Sant'Agnese, which depicts an *arenaria* and two levels of galleries dug into the tufa.

4. Jerome, *Commentary on Ezekiel* XII.40.5–13.

5. See, for example, Prudentius, *Hymn to Hippolytus*, in his *Peristephanon liber* XI.194.

6. On the behaviour of ancient Romans, including Christians, at the cemeteries, and on the attitudes they expressed, see Barral i Altet (1988), P. Brown (1981), Delehaye (1933), Février (1977).

7. The Laterani were a patrician Roman family whose property had been confiscated by Nero. Constantine's wife, Fausta, was the sister of his defeated rival, Maxentius.

8. There is scholarly disagreement about the percentage of the population that was Christian before Constantine: estimates are necessarily hypothetical. For the tituli and church halls, see Krautheimer (1980), 18.

9. Constantine might have built on the outskirts and beyond the walls rather than in the centre of Rome because he did not dare, or found it impolitic, to disturb the city centre and so annoy still-powerful pagan interests. Nor did he convert pagan temples into Christian churches.

10. For Peter's death and burial, see Eusebius II.25 and Toynbee and Ward Perkins (1956). A monumental basilica was built over the bones of Saint Paul, outside the walls on the road to Ostia, in 384 –ca. 390. Most of it burned down in 1823, and was later rebuilt.

11. The bishop of Rome was known in early times as *Papa* ("Father"). The earliest known inscription calling a bishop of Rome *papa*, or "pope" in English, is that of Marcellinus in the Catacombs of Calixtus (before 304 A.D.); the title is abbreviated as PP. The term was in common use by the fifth century. "Pope," then, is very early popular usage for the correct title, which is " bishop of Rome."

12. Krautheimer (1980), 55–56, 80, 203, 226–227; *Corpus Basilicarum* 5 (Vatican City: 1977), 1–92. The papal residence sometimes moved, but the Vatican remained the most important ecclesiastical site in Rome.

13. Van der Meer and Mohrmann (1966), #489b.

14. By the seventh century the octave of the feast, January 28, was celebrated as well, and it still is. According to the passio of Saint Agnes, just one week after her death the girl's parents saw a vision of their daughter among a crowd of virgins in heaven. This vision is thought to have given rise to the second feast for Saint Agnes. See Frutaz (1992), 30–31.

15. See, for example, Swift (1951). The literature on basilicas, as well as the indebtedness of Christian basilicas to ancient Roman precedents, is enormous. The following is a selection: Andresen (1971); Armstrong (1967) and (1974); Deichmann (1983), chapter 6; Duval (1962); Krautheimer (1967), (1971), and (1986); Mathews (1971); Matthiae (1964); Ward Perkins (1954).

16. The medieval mosaics of the nave floor, and the reused marbles paving the aisles, had been replaced with a simple brick floor in 1728. Frutaz (1992), 65.

17. Glass (1980).

18. The Exodus is the central event in the Hebrew Bible. The promises to Abraham

inform the entire Torah or Pentateuch (the Bible's first five books), and the epic of the Exodus extends from the Book of Exodus to the Book of Joshua.

19. The Stations were made for this church in 1938 by Uno Gera, the sculptor of the life-sized bronze crucifix at the end of the left-hand aisle.

20. For the history of the Stations of the Cross, see Thurston (1906). The spread of the custom to churches outside the Holy Land seems to have occurred during the sixteenth century, and to have reached its full development as a popular devotion in the eighteenth.

21. John 14:6.

22. Apocalypse 1:8, 21:6, 22:13. See also Isaiah 44:6.

23. John 10:7–9.

24. Genesis 6:5–8:22.

25. Early Christian writings that use this imagery are the *Apostolic Constitutions* on the ordination of bishops, the Clementine *Homilies*, Asterius *Homilies* XX.19, and Hippolytus of Rome, *Christ and Antichrist* (before 236 A.D.). See Daniélou (1961), 58–70; Rees (1992); Rush (1941), 54–71; Stuhlfauth (1942).

26. Romans 8:31–39.

27. Vitruvius says that the name was in memory of the abject slavery to which the Greeks reduced the women of Caryae, as a punishment because the men of Caryae supported the Persians when they invaded Greece (*De architectura* I.1.5). But caryatids existed in the Near East a long time before they reached Greece.

28. Galatians 2:9.

29. The Letter of Clement was sent, in its own words, "by the Church of God dwelling as a pilgrim in Rome to the Church of God dwelling as a pilgrim in Corinth." The author is believed to have been Clement the bishop of Rome (88–97 A.D.), and also, traditionally, the person who donated to the Christians a building in Rome (a titulus) that lies underneath the church of San Clemente. The building can be visited. It is situated below a fourth-century basilica, on top of which is the present basilica, built ca. 1100. See Boyle (1989).

30. Apocalypse 3:12.

31. Pliny *Natural History* 36. 6. 45.

32. Paul Valéry, *Charmes* (Paris: Gallimard, 1922).

33. The Doric temple of Athena in Syracuse, now Santa Maria delle Colonne, shows what changes were necessary to turn a pagan temple into a Christian church. The peristyle was filled in; the arcades were created by piercing the cella walls so that the corridors between cella and columns became aisles. The partition between the cella and the enclosed section behind it, the opisthodomos, was broken down in order to create an area for the altar, which is now housed, because it is a Christian church, inside rather than outside the building.

34. The sixteen clerestory windows were originally larger than they are now, but still smaller than the gallery spaces. See Krautheimer (1937), 23.

35. One aisle would fit almost three times into the width of the nave; a much more common arrangement in Rome is a nave the width of two aisles. See Krautheimer (1937), 38.

36. Krautheimer (1937), 36.

NOTES TO PAGES 68–76

37. Deichmann (1941), 73–76.
38. On San Lorenzo fuori le Mura, see Krautheimer (1960); Krautheimer, *Corpus* (1962); Matthiae (1964).
39. In Byzantine churches, galleries were where women sat, apart from the men. This is why the gallery at Sant'Agnese's is sometimes referred to as a *matroneum*. But as we have seen, the gallery had a specific, and different, function in Sant'Agnese's. The same is true of the gallery in San Lorenzo's, which was built in the reign of Pope Pelagius II (579–590).
40. Frutaz (1992), 167, note 85; Lanciani (1924), 260.
41. "Composite" is a Renaissance term for these capitals; Romans thought of them as Roman Corinthian.
42. J. Onians (1990), 42–48.
43. Onians thinks that the galleries are given a status lower than that of the nave by means of the capitals: Ionic at the start, and merely Corinthian at the end. This, he says (p. 67), is because the gallery was for women only, as in Byzantine practice. But see above, note 39, and Chapter 1, note 13.
44. The present organ was built in 1931.
45. Sfondrati also had vaults made for the church's gallery, and in doing so covered up a series of medieval (mainly thirteenth and fourteenth century) paintings. These paintings were rediscovered in 1855, removed, and taken to the Vatican Museums. They include eleven scenes from the life of the virgin martyr Catherine of Alexandria, and eleven from the life of Saint Benedict. Frutaz (1992), 63, 252.

Four: Alpha and Omega: Altar

1. By Pietro Gagliardi, 1856.
2. Prudentius *Peristephanon liber* XIV.124–125. The title of the book is translated, in Vol. ii of the Loeb edition of Prudentius, as *Crowns of Martyrdom*. The painting above the arch illustrates Prudentius' poem.
3. The quotation, placed on the arch by Pope Pius IX in 1855–1856, replaces Pope Honorius' seventh-century inscription, which said in Latin: "The virgin's hall is resplendent with twinkling metals, but shines more brightly still because of her great merit." The "twinkling metals" referred to the gold mosaic in the apse.
4. By Virgilio Marchi, Emilio Tavani, and Silvio Mingoli, inaugurated January 18, 1940. Frutaz (1992), 74.
5. The Eucharist may also be kept in a small box called a pyx, originally an ointment box (Greek *puxis*), which was traditionally made of boxwood (Greek *puxos*).
6. The Pantheon was exceptional in being built with a giant dome: Roman temples were normally given a non-domed shape, which was for Rome traditional, even archaic. The Pantheon's outline contains the height and diameter of a perfect sphere, with the dome as its top half. See further MacDonald (1976).
7. For the complicated history of St. Peter's dome, see, for example, Lees-Milne (1967), chapters 5 and 6; and Lotz (1995), 98–101.
8. *Liber Pontificalis* I, 323.

9. The buildings next door to the church are those of a medieval monastery. They are now referred to as the "canonry" because the order of priests who live there are canons, not monks.

10. A broken gilded metal transenna was discovered in an oratory of the canonry; it, too, is thought to have been part of the medieval altar complex. Frutaz (1992), 70.

11. The broad pavonazzetto band above the horizontal strip of porphyry had two curtained windows, inserted into it during the seventeenth century to give light to the apse; they were covered over during the 1950s. The only signs of them now are to be seen outside the church from the road.

12. The original tituli are the ancient downtown churches whose buildings were donated to the early Christian community. They are known by the names of their original owners, who were later called saints. All the cardinals' churches at Rome are now called "titles." Cardinals are the most senior members of the Church hierarchy after the pope himself. The word "cardinal" expresses the importance of the office: it comes from Latin *cardo*, meaning "hinge" or "pivot."

13. Pomegranate lamps identical to the original ones at Sant'Agnese's may be seen on the altar balustrade in the church of Santa Cecilia in Trastevere, Rome.

14. Romans 5:20–21.

15. Tertullian (A.D. 160–240) *Apologeticus* 50. The mystical Spanish poet Saint John of the Cross (1542–1591) was especially fond of pomegranates and their imagery; see *The Spiritual Canticle* and his commentary on its meaning.

16. Grisar (1897).

17. Pressouyre (1984).

18. Middleton's Letter from Rome set out to show "the exact conformity between Papism and the religion of the Romans of today, which is derived from their pagan ancestors." See Frutaz (1992), 172.

19. Luke 22:19–20; Matthew 26:26–29; Mark 14:22–25.

20. Sacrifice is an immensely broad and difficult subject. A very short summary of the reasoning and meanings behind it may be found in Visser (1991), 32–37, together with a short bibliography, p. 361. Sacrifice remembers the death that gives rise to the life-giving comfort of eating. The Eucharist is a "sacrifice" in part because it remembers the death at the very moment that it gives rise to hope.

21. On this subject, see Leon R. Kass, *The Hungry Soul. Eating and the Perfecting of Our Nature* (New York: Macmillan, The Free Press, 1994).

22. Psalm 118:22–23; Matthew 21:42. See further Isaiah 8:14, 28:16; Ephesians 2:20–22.

23. Matthew 16:13–19.

24. Acts 4:11; 1 Peter 2:4–10.

25. Compare Colossians 1:24.

26. I John 4:19–20.

27. Wyschogrod (1990) provides a reproduction of a fresco depicting the event (see p. 2). It is by the Sienese painter Giovanni di Paolo (died 1482), and is kept in the Cleveland Museum of Art.

28. John 14:6

29. John 10:7–9

30. Matthew 10:38; 16:24–25; Mark 8:34; Luke 9:23, 14:27.

31. For example, in Greek myth the sadistic bandit Procrustes devised a hideous form of torture for his victims: he would forcibly fit them to a wooden bed, stretching them if they were too small, and lopping off any pieces of their bodies that extended over the edge of the bed, Plutarch, *Lives. Theseus 6.*

32. Fanano (1968).

33. "Mandorla" is from the Italian word for "almond," because of its shape. (Another term for a totally enclosing halo of this shape is *vesica piscis*, "the bladder of a fish," again descriptive of the outline.) An "aureole," from *aureus*, "golden," is an elliptical display of golden light completely surrounding a figure, unlike a nimbus or halo, which emanates from the head only.

34. The source of this symbolism is Ezekiel 1:5–14, where the prophet tells his strange vision of the four winged "beasts," each of which had four faces, of Man and Lion and Bull and Eagle. John's Apocalypse (4:6–8) describes four creatures, Man and Lion and Bull and Eagle, surrounding the throne of God. They were known very early thereafter as the "apocalyptic beasts," and taken to represent the four Gospel writers: Man for Matthew because he begins his Gospel with the ancestors of Christ; Lion for Mark, who starts with "a voice crying in the wilderness"; Ox, the beast of sacrifice, for Luke because he opens with the sacrifice of Zacharias; and Eagle for John, because he soars at once to the heights of heaven, with "In the beginning was the Word . . ."

35. Josi (1933); Fasola, (1954–55).

36. See, for example, Matthew 10:37, 12:46–50, 19:29; Mark 3:31–35, 10:28–30; Luke 8:19–21, 18:29–30.

37. Apocalypse 6:9.

38. First Epistle of John, 3:2.

39. There is another chapel dedicated to her, in the Roman seminary, or college for student priests, that occupies the Palazzo Capranica, in the piazza named after it. This Renaissance building incorporates a medieval chapel traditionally believed to have been built on the site of Agnes' family home. The street-level chapel now houses an antique shop, but the students have a chapel in honour of Agnes upstairs; she is regarded as their patron saint. See Caiola (1997).

40. Teasdale Smith (1974), 383, citing Dio Cassius. *Roman History*, Book 75, 166–167.

41. Teasdale Smith (1974), 381–382.

42. Parmenides Fragment 8 (DK 28 B 8), lines 42–49; Fragment 1 (DK 28 B 1), line 29.

43. For a drawing of the ancient Jewish picture of the world, see Boadt (1984), 115.

44. John 8:12, 9:5. See also John 1:7–9, 3:20–21.

45. For the history and meaning of Sunday, see Bradshaw (1996), 75–79; Rordorf (1968). For the number eight in its relation to baptism, see Chapter Eight.

46. Augustine *Confessions* 1.1.

47. Julian of Norwich. Modern version: *Revelations of Divine Love*, tr. and ed. Clifton Wolters (London: Penguin Books, 1966), 68 (Chapter 5).

48. Jesus said, "And when I am lifted up from the earth, I shall draw all people to myself." John 12:32, cf. John 8:28. Being "lifted up" refers to his death by crucifixion, adds John (12:33).

49. John 3:8; see Acts 2:2. The Spirit is also symbolized by water (John 7:37–39) and fire (Acts 2:4).
50. Genesis 1:2.
51. Matthew 3:16–17; Mark 1:10–11; Luke 3:22; John 1:32–34.

Five: World Without End: Apse

1. Jerusalem-made-perfect is for Christians a symbol of the end of all things, in the final epiphany of God. The ideal Jerusalem is described in the Book of Ezekiel, 40:1–48:35. In the New Testament the Heavenly Jerusalem appears in Hebrews 12:22–24 and Apocalypse 21:2–22:5. For the meanings of gold, see Averincev (1979).
2. 4 Esdras 2:34–35. 4 Esdras is a Christian addition to a Jewish apocalyptic text, and is dated about 100 A.D. The work belongs to the Apocrypha, meaning that it is not part of the canonical Bible; since 1590 it has stood as an appendix after the New Testament in the Latin Vulgate Bible. What has survived is a Latin translation of an originally Greek text.
3. The chief early sources for the story of Agnes are: the *Depositio martyrum* (336 A.D.), which is the first mention of the saint, giving her feast day as a customary celebration; the Damasus inscription at Sant'Agnese's, between 366 and 384; Ambrose's *De virginibus*, ca. 377; a passage by Ambrose in a letter, *De officiis*, 389–390; the Ambrosian hymn *Agnes beatae virginis*, fourth century (it is not absolutely certain that the hymn is by Ambrose, though most scholars now think it is); Prudentius' "Hymn to Agnes," published in 405 (Prudentius went to Sant'Agnese's in 402–403); the passio or *Gesta Sanctae Agnetis* in Latin, compiled by pseudo-Ambrose from traditional sources, early 400s, with chapter III added later; a shorter Greek passio derivative from the Latin one, and a translation of it into Syriac, fifth century.
4. God's love for the soul is frequently expressed in erotic language. This section of the passio of Agnes is written in the tradition of the Old Testament *Song of Songs*. Compare also Ezekiel 15:6–14, where the Lord covers Israel, as a woman, with his gifts. (The Latin word *vernantibus*, literally "burgeoning as in the spring," I have translated here as "glowing.")
5. Pseudo-Ambrose, *Gesta Sanctae Agnetis* (see bibliography, under Ambrose). In the Greek passio Agnes is burned to death. She is also described as a young adult, and this could well have influenced the mosaic artist.
6. For the costume and its history, see Houston (1931).
7. This is an early version of what later became a Byzantine convention. See Oakeshott (1967), 148, and the examples given.
8. Herodotus 2.73; Pliny *Natural History* 10.2; Tacitus *Annals* 6.28; Gregory of Nazianzus *Carmina* I.2.532–533; Van den Broek (1972).
9. The Magi brought as gifts to the infant Jesus "gold, frankincense, and myrrh" (Matthew 2:11). These, the wealth and perfumes of Arabia (cf. Isaiah 60:6), symbolize his kingliness (gold), his divinity (frankincense), and his redemptive death (myrrh).

10. The connection is made in the Letter of Clement, 25 (ca. 96 A.D).

11. 1 Corinthians 15:20–23. For more on "first-fruits," see Visser (1991), 34–35.

12. Canaan, where the Israelites settled, was inhabited by Phoenicians; in Mesopotamia the word "Canaan" meant "purplish red dye," and in biblical Hebrew the word "Canaanite" became the equivalent of "merchant," like one of the mercantile Phoenicians. Van den Broek (1972), 65.

13. Acts 2:1–18, especially 4.

14. Examples in Rome include the apse of the church of Santi Cosma e Damiano in the Forum, the apse of Santa Prassede, and that of Santa Cecilia.

15. John 12:13. (See above, Chapter One.) Mark (11:8) says the crowd waved "greenery" (the Greek word *stilbadas* means "what you use to strew the ground"). It is pointed out that palms were not native to Jerusalem, and the Jews imported them for the Feast of Tabernacles (2 Maccabees 10:7). Still, John calls the plants "palms" because of their well-known symbolism.

16. R. B. Onians (1951), especially Part 2, chapters 1 and 2.

17. The upper apse at Sant'Agnese's is actually less than half a dome, but the symbolism of a dome and a semidome is in no way altered by this fact.

18. Such a depiction of the cosmos in the hollow of a dome is called a "meniscus" or lens-shape, from the Greek for "little moon."

19. See Bisconti, in Fiocchi Nicolai et al. (1998), 80–81. On goldglass, see further Engemann (1968–69), Garrucci (1858), Morey (1959), Zanchi Roppo (1969).

20. Apocalypse 21:18.

21. Swift (1951), 134. On mosaic technique, see further Oakeshott (1967), Matthiae (1967), Sear (1977), and Milburn (1988), chapter 13.

22. Oakeshott (1967), 148.

23. Astorri (1934).

24. Matthiae (1967), 173.

25. Oakeshott (1967), 70.

26. Frutaz (1992), 71.

27. Thérèse wrote a *Cantique à Sainte Agnès* on the saint's feast day, January 21, 1896, based on the passio of Agnes, which she probably read in Latin.

28. For the following brief summary, I am indebted to Duffy (1997); various entries in the *Encyclopedia of Early Christianity* (1990); Krautheimer (1980); Mathieu-Rosay (1988); McBrien (1981), especially 835–842; McBrien (1997); Richards (1979); and Ullmann (1972), especially chapters 2 and 3.

29. Most Lombards were pagans, and the Christians among them Arians; Gregory initiated their conversion through their Catholic queen, Theodelinda, wife of two successive Lombard kings.

30. "The Church was the only efficient organization left to maintain the economic, social, and indeed the political fabric of Rome." Krautheimer (1980), 69.

31. See Robert Wilken, in *Encyclopedia of Early Christianity*, s.v. "Monophysitism."

32. John 1:1–5.

33. Leo I, The Great, *Tomē. Opera*, P. And H. Ballerini, eds., in J-P Migne, *Patrologia Latina* vols. 54–56.

34. Constantine had called the Council of Nicaea in 325 for the same purpose. Several

early emperors (when they were not Arians themselves) took steps to enforce orthodoxy.

35. Scriptural passages adduced include Luke 10:16, John 16:13–15, and Matthew 16:16–20.

36. 1 John 1:3 and Ephesians 4:5–6 were among the scriptural passages quoted.

37. See Mathieu-Rosay (1988), s.v. "Honorius I."

38. Honorius built churches "too numerous to mention," says the *Liber Pontificalis* I, 323–324.

39. *Liber Pontificalis* I, 324; Krautheimer, *Corpus Basilicarum Christianarum Romae* Vol. III (1967), 153–174.

40. A fifth-century legend recounts that when Saint Paul was decapitated at this spot, his head bounced three times, giving rise to a spring at each bounce. Legends of the saints often relate that saints' deaths, especially the deaths of decapitated martyrs, give rise to fountains. Fountains are beginnings—what we call in English "springs" or "fountainheads"; and Christians thought of the blood of the martyrs as the "seed," in Tertullian's phrase, of the Church. In Christian symbolism streams of water "mean" redemptive cleansing, and very specifically baptism; and we shall see that the idea of "dying" to the past is part of the Christian initiatory sacrament.

41. Jounel (1977), 217.

42. A hundred years later, according to Roman custom, he would have been given a square halo, as founder of a church and still living when the mosaic was made. A square halo does not denote a saint: people can be called saints only after their deaths. Honorius was not made a saint.

43. Perrotti (1961).

44. In the Middle Ages the meat of peacocks was said to be incorruptible; this notion derived from the symbolism of immortality already attached to the bird.

45. Perrotti (1961), 163.

46. Houston (1931), chapter 5.

47. For the pallium, see Noonan (1996), 359–363, and the illustrations.

48. Luke 15:4–7; John 10:1–16. Tristan (1996), "Agneau et Bon Pasteur," 122–141.

49. Matthew 26:69–75; Mark 14:66–72; Luke 22:54–62; John 18:15–27, 21:15–17.

50. John 1:29.

51. I owe these facts to my sister, Dr. Joan Barclay Lloyd, who got them from the prior of Tre Fontane, Father Ansgar Christensen, O.C.S.O. See further Frutaz (1992), 32–37.

52. Frutaz (1992), 136.

53. *Liber Pontificalis* I, 263.

54. *Liber Pontificalis* I, 208.

55. *Liber Pontificalis* I, 180.

56. G.B. De Rossi, *Inscriptiones Christianae* II, 127. Cited in Richards (1979), 179–180.

57. The translation of this sentence is Oakeshott's (1967, p. 31).

58. Genesis 1:4–5.

Six: Living Stones: Chapel, Left Side

1. Pope Gregory I, the Great, *Homily on Ezekiel* 19. Compare Jesus' words to the Samaritan woman, John 4:20–24.

2. Between pages 416 and 417 of Pétrement (1973), vol. 2, are photographs of Weil's original hand-written account of what happened.

3. Emmanuel Lévinas, *Humanisme de l'autre homme* (Paris: Fata Morgana, Le livre de poche, Biblio-Essais, 1994), 58.

4. *Ekklesia* literally means "summoned out of." The Greek word distinguishes the "called" group from everybody else.

5. For a history and analysis of this complex ceremony, see Crichton (1980).

6. 1 Corinthians 6:19

7. Ephesians 2:20–22; 1 Peter 2:4–5. See also 1 Corinthians 3:9, 16–17; Ephesians 4:12.

8. See, for example, Green (1983), 86–88.

9. Mark 3:20–21, 31–35. See also Luke 2:49–50, 11:27–28.

10. Olive oil symbolizes the Holy Spirit as saving, strengthening, nourishing, and health-giving. It signifies that the Christian is a disciple of the Anointed One, which is the meaning of the words "Christ" and "Messiah." Baptism also makes complex references to Noah and his ark, interpreting the Flood as the death of the old so that the new can begin afresh. The oil recalls the olive twig brought home by the dove to Noah in the ark, signifying that the Flood was receding and God was ready now to make peace with the world. Anointing with olive oil is the final act of initiation after baptism, assuring the initiate of support from the life-giving Spirit.

11. Psalm 51:7. Hyssop in the psalm is probably the plant known as the thorny caper (*Capparis spinosa*), and was used for sprinkling water in Jewish purification rites.

12. Colossians 3:13; 1 John 4:19–20. See also Romans 5:5. Christianity's most important prayer makes the next step, trusting God to "forgive us *as we forgive others*" (Matthew 6:12, 14–15; Luke 11:3–4; cf. Matthew 18:18).

13. Luke 6:29, 6:37; Matthew 5:23–24, 5:38–40, 18:21–22.

14. Luke 23:34.

15. Matthew 7:1–5; Luke 6:36–37.

16. John 1:4–5, 8:12.

17. Genesis 1:1–2:2. Genesis 6:13–8:14. Genesis 17:1–8. Genesis 22:1–19. Exodus 14:5–15:21. Isaiah 55:1–11.

18. Lent is a forty-day-long "low" period in the Church's liturgical year; it is a preparation for the week-long climactic remembrance of Christ's death and Resurrection. The forty days recall the Hebrew symbolism of forty as "a sufficiently long period of time": for example, Moses spent forty days with God, the Flood lasted forty days, Christ fasted for forty days. People pray especially intensely during Lent, and do whatever else they need to do to prepare themselves spiritually for Easter. They may fast, or not eat certain foods. The effect is to heighten and intensify the celebration of Easter, which includes feasting (on eggs, for example), and the return of ritual expressions of joy. Human restraint on eating during Lent

allows young animals to be born and grow, and the first new vegetables to mature. Cosmically speaking, Easter is Spring. The English word "Lent" is from the same root as "lengthen": the days are "Lentening."

19. Lent is often marked by "negatives," such as not ringing bells, not playing the organ, and not saying the prayer known as the Gloria or the word "Alleluia." "Alleluia" or "Halleluia" is from Hebrew *halelu-Jah*, meaning "praise God." It is used by the angels as a cry of jubilation in the Apocalypse (19:1–6). Joyfulness is its connotation; the forty preceding days without it serve greatly to increase its meaningfulness and power when Easter finally arrives.

20. The symbols derived from Scripture, in order of mention, are from Matthew 5:14–16; John 15:1–8; Isaiah 5:1–7; Ezekiel 19:10–14; Psalm 79(80):8–16.

21. Matthew 26:39; Mark 14:36; Luke 22:42; Matthew 6:10; Luke 1:38. In addition to these three instances, there are others: see, for example, Mark 3:35 and John 5:30.

22. Biblical scholars remind us that "the story" as we have it was written down, in four differing versions, after the Resurrection, and therefore from a post-Resurrection perspective. Mary's words, spoken within Luke's version of the "Infancy Narratives," which have been called "the Gospel in miniature," must in part be taken as a theological preparation for what follows. See R.E. Brown (1993).

23. John 2:1–12, especially 4–5.

24. John 19:25–27.

25. Matthew 16:18, 26:69–75; Mark 14:66–72; Luke 22:54–62; John 18:15–27.

26. Luke 1:46–55. "Yes, from this day forward all generations will call me blessed," she said, "for God has done great things for me. . . . He has pulled down the mighty from their thrones, and exalted the lowly. The hungry he has filled with good things, the rich he has sent empty away. He has come to the help of Israel his servant, mindful of his mercy, and according to the promises he made to our ancestors, to Abraham and to his descendants for ever."

27. Also venerated in early times were the Apostles (almost all of them martyrs), and the "confessors," which meant those who had not actually been killed, but who had suffered imprisonment, torture, or exile for their faith.

28. "Epiphany" means "showing" or "manifestation" in Greek. It can mean an individual mystical experience. In the Christian liturgical vocabulary it is the name of the feast on or near January 6, which celebrates the first four manifestations of Jesus to the world: at his birth, first to the Jewish shepherds (his own people) and then to the Magi (representing the rich, the intellectuals, the Gentiles, and people from countries far from the Holy Land); his baptism as an adult, when he was revealed as God's "beloved son"; and the first manifestation of his power, at the wedding at Cana when he turned water into wine.

29. Prudentius, "Hymn to Agnes," *Peristephanon* XIV.112–118. The *Passio of Perpetua and Felicity* includes the original diary which Perpetua kept in prison, before she was gored by a wild cow and then had her throat cut in the arena at Carthage on March 7, 203 A.D. Perpetua recorded a dream she had in which she, too, trod down a serpent as her soul prepared for her death: "Slowly, as though he were afraid of me, the dragon stuck his head out from underneath the ladder. Then, using it as my first step, I trod on his head and went up." Musurillo (1972), 112.

30. Genesis 3:15; Apocalypse 12:1–17.
31. This is the hagiographical background for Keats' poem "The Eve of Saint Agnes"; in England, however, January 21 is not spring but winter.
32. For a good recent account of the phenomenon of Lourdes, see Harris (1999).
33. A rosary is a string of beads used for counting prayers; it is arranged in a circle, with a short pendant ending in a cross. Its use began to be promoted, especially by members of the Dominican order, in the fifteenth century, although Christians were using strings of prayer beads before the ninth century. Because it is circular, the rosary is called after a garland of roses, known as a *rosarium*; compare the children's game, "Ring-a ring-a rosie" or "Ring Around a Rosie."
34. The underground watercourse was known to exist before Bernardette uncovered it.
35. By the mid seventh century, belief in the Immaculate Conception of Mary was common in the Eastern Church, where it arose first. A famous hymn by Andrew of Crete (died 740) calls Mary "alone wholly without stain." For a summary of the theology of the Immaculate Conception, see McBrien (1981), 885–889.
36. Luke 1:28.
37. For more on Catherine Labouré, see Laurentin (1980).
38. The vast theological system worked out by the Canadian theologian Bernard Lonergan (1904–1984) is based on five "transcendental precepts." The first of these, the indispensable beginning for all the rest, is "Be attentive." The others are: "Be intelligent," "Be reasonable," "Be responsible," "Be in love." Lonergan (1957) and (1971).
39. The original picture of the Madonna of Pompeii (of which this one is a copy) was given to the desperately poor town near this famous archaeological site by Bartolo Longo in 1876, and a church built for it. An orphanage and a home for children whose parents are in prison are among the many outreach programs associated with this church.
40. Luke 2:35.
41. For a reappraisal of the role of modern popular religious art, mainly in the lives of North American Protestants, see Morgan (1998).
42. Matthew 11:29.
43. (Deutero-)Isaiah 42:1–7, 49:1–7, 50:4–9, 52:13–53:12. Compare Matthew 12:17–21.
44. Luke 10:29–37.
45. This is a paraphrase of Matthew 25:35–46. See also Matthew 10:42, 18:5–6, 18:10; Mark 9:36–37; Luke 9:48.
46. John 19:33–37.
47. Matthew 25:1–13.

Seven: One Body: Chapels, Right Side

1. The spiral staircase was added after the seventeenth century, when the great staircase down to the church was reconstructed. See Krautheimer (1937), 22.
2. Saint Augustine (354–430 A.D.) was a Doctor of the Church and Bishop of Hippo

in Africa. "Doctor of the Church" is a title given to eminent ecclesiastical writers who are also saints. The first four Doctors of the Western Church were Ambrose, Jerome, Augustine, and Gregory the Great. The first four Eastern Doctors were Basil, Athanasius, Gregory of Nazianzus, and John Chrysostom. All these men are commonly depicted in churches, sometimes in groups of four.

3. Canons are priests attached to a cathedral or to a church. The word *kanon* means "rule" in Greek; a canon is called a *canonicus*, "one who lives by a Rule" in Latin. Canons Regular (as opposed to Canons Secular) are like monks in that they live in community; they do not, however, restrict their contacts with the outside world as monks do.

4. For the history of the mitre, see Noonan (1996), 364–371. The word "bishop" is from Greek *episkopos*, meaning literally "overseer" or "superintendent." A bishop has received the highest of the three "holy orders," which are those of deacon, priest, and bishop.

5. Acts 4:32. See also Augustine, Sermons 355 and 356, and Possidius, *Life of Augustine* (fifth century); P. Brown (1967).

6. Saint Dominic was an Augustinian canon before he founded his own order. The fourth Lateran Council (1215) forbade the introduction of new religious Rules, which is perhaps why Dominic adopted that of Saint Augustine. (Saint Francis had had his Rule approved before the council.)

7. Frutaz (1992), 175, note 110.

8. For the office of Commendatory Abbot, see G. and M. Duchet-Suchaux (1993), 111–112.

9. See Frutaz (1992), 103.

10. Stephen's story is related in Acts of the Apostles, chapters six and seven. Other figures revered as "first" Christian martyrs, but who died before Christ, are the Holy Innocents (the babies Herod killed in case Jesus was among them, according to the account in Matthew 2:16–18), and Saint John the Baptist (Matthew 14:10–12).

11. Acts 8:1–4; Tertullian *Apologeticus* 50.

12. *Peristephanon Liber* II; "The Passion of Lawrence" is one of the finest of the collection of fourteen poems.

13. Prudentius, "The Passion of Lawrence," lines 169–312, 401–408.

14. Hall (1974), 291.

15. The Rota is the supreme tribunal for the annulment of marriages. Its most famous case was the request (refused) of Henry VIII of England for the annulment of his marriage to Catherine of Aragon because she did not bear him an heir. The tribunal was called the Rota because the jurists used to sit at a round table.

16. The eight altars: one made for St. Peter's and now in the town of Boville Ernica; three at St. John Lateran; one at St. Paul's outside the Walls; one at the SS Apostoli; one at Santa Maria del Popolo (where des Perriers is buried); and the one now at Sant'Agnese's.

17. The vestment's name comes from Dalmatia (today, roughly Croatia) because it was once made of Dalmatian wool; the garment's design might also have been originally Dalmatian.

18. Becoming a deacon came later to mean reaching the penultimate of seven stages in the process of becoming a priest. (There are now only two stages.) The Second Vatican Council (1962–1965) encouraged men to become permanent deacons, and so returned to the earliest practice. Married men can become deacons. They can baptize and preach, but not consecrate the Eucharist. They are permitted to wear the priestly stole, but only over one shoulder and diagonally across the chest, to show that they are not priests. Priests wear the stole like an untied scarf around the neck (that is, over both shoulders), the two halves hanging straight down in front. Deacons now seldom wear the dalmatic, except on very solemn occasions; the distinctive stole normally takes its place.

19. Honorius of Autun *Gemma animae* I.212.

20. The liturgical colours are white or gold, red, violet or black, and green. On two days of the year the colour is pink, signifying subdued joy: Laetare Sunday during Lent and Gaudete Sunday during Advent. Both *laetare* and *gaudete* are words taken from the Masses for those days, and both mean "rejoice." See further Pastoureau (1988), a and b.

21. When Saint Benedict decided to withdraw from the world, he went to live in or near a village church, taking with him his devoted nurse. (Gregory the Great, *Life of Benedict*, Book II of the *Dialogues*, 593 or 594 A.D.) The passio of Nereus and Achilleus, brothers whose hypogeum survives in the Roman catacomb of Domitilla, tells us that the brothers each had a milk sister; their names were Euphrosyna and Theodora.

22. *superflui, miseri, caduci atque atrocissimi*

23. Bernard of Clairvaux, *De Consideratione* 5.11.24.

24. For details and dates for the sources of these Itineraries, see E.R. Barker (1913), 112–115.

25. Armellini (1876); Fasola (1954–1955).

26. Fasola (1954–1955), 8.

27. The Sancta Sanctorum, housed in the building called the Scala Santa, opens out of a private chapel built for the popes at the Lateran. In its present form it is the work of cosmatesque artists of the thirteenth century; the name "Sancta Sanctorum" was given it because it contained so many relics. On the walls are mosaics and frescoes, including a mosaic portrait of Agnes and a fresco of her martyrdom, because her skull was believed to be kept here. See Grisar (1907) and Pietrangeli (1995). Florian Jubaru found the skull, which was examined and its teeth found to be those of a twelve- or thirteen-year-old (Jubaru 1907, 8–9, 335–337). It was taken to the church of Sant'Agnese in Agone, where it is still revered and is displayed on the saint's feast day every year.

28. Frutaz (1992), 157, note 61.

29. Frutaz (1992), 156–157, note 59.

30. E. Stevenson (1896). These inscriptions are now in the passageway down, and are mentioned in Chapter One.

31. Réau (1955–1959), s.v. "Emerentiana." King Louis XI of France was hunting in the forest of Longué in Anjou in 1472 when he was struck down with violent stomach pains. He prayed to Saint Emerentiana, recovered, and later had a chapel

built for her. It is still there, at La Pouëze in Angers; in it is a statue of the saint.

32. The tradition is not merely an instance of picturesque realism; it refers to God's lament in Isaiah 1:3: "The ox knows its owner, and the ass knows the manger of its lord, but my people do not understand."

33. A Christmas crib embodies and conflates two Gospel accounts. There are no angel choirs and shepherds in the "infancy narrative" of Matthew, and neither magi nor star appear in Luke. See R.E. Brown (1993).

34. For the history of Roman cribs, see Escobar (1988). The Christmas cribs of Catalunya often include, among the people present in the scene, a little figure defecating. Modern tourists are shocked and fascinated; but the *cagoners* or "shitters," as they are robustly called in Catalan, are utterly traditional in showing human life in all its realism. The birth of Jesus is depicted as taking place in the midst of the most ordinary aspects of human life—not in some sanitized shop window.

35. The Te Deum is an early fifth-century hymn believed to be by Niceta of Remesiana (Bela Palanka in Serbia), who died in 414. Its opening words mean, "To you, O God, we offer praise; we acknowledge you as Lord."

36. The tiara, a beehive-shaped crown surmounted by an orb and a cross, is the pope's most formal headgear and is shown on top of his coat of arms. In 1963 Pope Paul VI was crowned according to custom, but later sold the papal tiara and gave the money to the poor. See Duffy (1997), 275. The symbolic crossed keys, one gold and one silver, are also part of the papal arms. They refer to the words of Jesus to Peter, giving him "the keys of the Kingdom" (Matthew 16:18–19): the gold key is for heaven, the silver key is for the earth. See Noonan (1996), 189–190.

37. For this account, I am indebted to Lequenne (1991).

38. The Franciscan habit is brown, grey, or black, with a hood. It is belted with a rope knotted three times, for the vows of poverty, chastity, and obedience. (The Capuchins, a branch of the Franciscans, are named for their *cappuccio*, or "hood" in Italian; they traditionally wore brown and were bearded, the old Cappuccini, of course, having white beards. *Cappuccino*, the frothy coffee, is named after the Cappuccini, because it is brown with a white "beard.")

39. The Cathari ("Pure Ones" in Greek), also known as Albigensians after the town of Albi in Languedoc, were neo-Manichaeans. They believed the world was controlled by a pair of powers: God (light) and Satan (darkness). According to the Cathari, if a person was not perfect, it mattered little what he or she did; among their anarchic beliefs they included total opposition to marriage. A small number of them were the real Cathari, who were believed to have reached perfection, and were called "Parfaits." The northern French used the existence of this heresy as a pretext for crushing Languedoc and annexing it to France.

40. Matthew 1:19. For a complex and eloquent meditation on the plight of Saint Joseph and his response to it, by a modern Catholic father of a family, see Baumann (1994).

41. Joseph was often a jokey figure in medieval drama; see Pastoureau (1991), 34–36. He is one of the models for Leopold Bloom in James Joyce's *Ulysses*: the indomitable ordinary man, loving, dependable, constant—and cuckolded by his wife Molly.

42. However, the *Protevangelium of James* 9:2 (fourth century) has Joseph say, "I already have sons and am old, but she [Mary] is a girl."

43. Early narratives concerning Joseph are the *Protevangelium of James*, *The Gospel of Pseudo-Matthew*, and the fifth-century Greek *History of Joseph the Carpenter*.

44. The history of devotion to Joseph is, of course, much more complicated than this suggests. See, for example, the article "St. Joseph" by Charles Souvay in *The Catholic Encyclopedia*, ed. Charles Hebermann et al. (New York: Universal Knowledge Foundation Inc., 1913), vol. VIII, 504–506.

45. The Canon of the Mass is the heart of the celebration, during which the consecration of the Eucharist takes place. Also during the Canon, prayers are said for Church members both living and dead, and the saints (men and women officially "canonized" as such) are remembered as being at one with the Church still in travail. The Canon ends with the solemn Great Amen.

46. For the saints in the Canon, see Kennedy (1963).

47. Pope John had already placed the Second Vatican Council under the protection of Saint Joseph, on March 19 (Joseph's feast day), 1961.

48. See Frutaz (1992), 93–96.

49. When Sant'Agnese's stood in open countryside, its parish boundaries were of vast extent. Now that the region has been built up, the same area comprises twenty-six parishes.

50. The community of Sant'Egidio, named after its mother church, Sant'Egidio (Saint Giles) near Santa Maria in Trastevere, Rome, began in 1968; its founder, Andrea Riccardi, was then eighteen years old. The community is international, admits men and women whether married or not, and today numbers about twenty thousand in Italy alone. The community is especially well known for having brokered the peace that ended the civil war in Mozambique (October 4, 1992), and for other peace projects in Africa and elsewhere. See Riccardi (1996).

51. For the custom of the Roman stations and its history, see Baldovin (1987).

Eight: Eternal Rest: Outside

1. There is no standard book on Santa Costanza's; I therefore append a list of articles, monographs, and extracts from books: Amadio (1986); Armellini (1982), 1068–1070; Bovini (1968), 270–300, and (1971), 33–63; Colvin (1991); De Angelis d'Ossat (1940); Deichmann (1982); Donati (1968); Frutaz (1992), 106–118 and notes; Jobst (1976); Lees-Milne (1988), 23–43; Lehmann (1955); MacDonald (1976), 104–108; Matthiae (1964), 116–117, 133–136; Monti (1992); Oakeshott (1967), 61–65; Polacco n.d.; Prandi (1942–1943); Sjöqvist (1946), 144–146; Stanley (1994); Stern (1958); van Berchem and Clouzot (1965), 1–8.

2. Krautheimer (1980), 66.

3. For the chi-rho sign, see Lactantius *The Deaths of the Persecutors* 44.5; Eusebius *Life of Constantine* 1.26–31. See further Bruun (1963); Marrou (1959); Sulzberger (1925).

4. See, for example, Homer *Iliad* I.482, XIV.16, XVI.391. (Ancient ideas about

colour, which seem very strange to us, often place surprisingly little emphasis on actual hue.)

5. On porphyry, see Klemm and Klemm (1993). On the discovery of the Porphyry Mountain, see G. Wilkinson, "Notes on a part of the Eastern Desert of Upper Egypt," *Journal of the Royal Geographic Society* 2 (1832), 53 f., cited by Klemm and Klemm. The explorations by Burton and Wilkinson were carried out in 1822–1823.

6. Frutaz (1992), 116.

7. Frutaz (1992), 206–207, note 18. Another porphyry sarcophagus was taken from the mausoleum to the Vatican in 1606; it may have been the tomb of Helena, Constantina's sister. Frutaz (1992), 207, note 22.

8. Most of the restoration was done in 1834–1840.

9. Winged genii or "cupids" are also found on the porphyry sarcophagus; they may well represent souls, *psychai*, in paradise. An ancient Roman genius was a representation of what today might be called the "self"; it was an embodiment of the traits that made up the individual's personality. A man had a genius, a woman a juno. (These winged figures, however, are all male, even though the sarcophagus contained a woman.) A genius was often portrayed as adult and bearded, but infant genii appear in the mosaics of Pompeii, for example. There are baby genii on the second-century Roman sarcophagus kept today in the Sala Giulio II in the canonry.

10. Visser (1991), 166.

11. A faded inscription over the sarcophagus niche records the removal, by Cardinal Fabrizio Veralli, of the remains of the mosaic.

12. Ezekiel 47:1–12.

13. Genesis 4:4–5; Exodus 17:5–6; I Kings 18:20–46; Daniel 13; Tobit 6:2–3.

14. The mausoleum of Constantine's son and Constantina's brother, the Emperor Constans (reigned 337–350), at Centcelles near the town called Constantí near Tarragona, Spain, is similar to Santa Costanza's. Its damaged mosaic cupola also depicts biblical scenes set in a wheel, but in three concentric rings. The porphyry sarcophagus, reused as part of the tomb of King Pere II in the nearby monastery of Santes Creus, is thought to have been taken from the mausoleum at Centcelles. See Camprubí (1952).

15. *Liber Pontificalis* II, 163; see Duffy (1997), 80–81.

16. Matthew 26:26–29; Mark 14:22–25, Luke 22:19–20; John 2:1–10; John 15:1–8. See further Jubaru (1904); Leonardi (1947).

17. Several of the disciples of Jesus were fishermen, until he promised them, "I shall make you fishers of men" (Luke 5:1–11). Fish were part of the miracles of multiplication, when Jesus fed the crowd with a few loaves and fish (Mark 6:35–44, 8:1–8). As well, he ate fish with his disciples after the Resurrection (Luke 24:41–43; John 21:1–14). A secret sign for early Christians was a fish. The acronym ΙΧΘΥΣ, "fish" in Greek, stood for *Iesous CHristos THeou Uios Soter*, "Jesus Christ Son of God Saviour." Tertullian (fl. 200) wrote, "We as little fishes, in accordance with our *ichthus*, Jesus Christ, are born in water" (*On Baptism* 1).

See further Daniélou (1961); Doelger (1910–1957), an exhaustive treatment; Morey (1910), (1911), and (1912); Thérel (1973).

18. See for example Fiocchi Nicolai et al. (1998). And for the subject generally, see Elsner (1995); C. Murray (1981); Rees (1992).

19. On the two apse mosaics, see Davis-Wyer (1961); de Francovich (1958); Grabar (1967); Oakeshott (1967), 64–65; Pietri (1976), vol. II, 1417–1421; Stanley (1987); Thérel (1973), 75–98; Tristan (1996); Vallin (1963).

20. It may have been depicted in the original apse mosaic of St. Peter's basilica in the fourth century. A mosaic of the scene, possibly in imitation of the earlier one, certainly occupied the apse there from the late twelfth to the sixteenth century; it was destroyed when the present basilica of St. Peter's was built. See Krautheimer (1980), 205.

21. Genesis 2:10–14.

22. John 10:1–16, 4:10–15, 7:37–38. See Underwood (1950).

23. See Galatians 2:7–8.

24. Matthew 16:18–19.

25. Ephesians 2:13–14. See Vallin (1963).

26. In the ancient world circles and spheres were thought to be "perfect" figures. From this point of view the mausoleum of Santa Costanza should be compared with its much larger architectural forerunner, Rome's Pantheon (which was not, however, built as a mausoleum). See further Hautecoeur (1954); MacDonald (1976); Poulet (1961). Schwarz (1958) discusses the possibilities of circular planning for the expression of meaning in Christian churches, in his First Plan, Second Plan, and Third Plan.

27. Olney (1972), 33, 49, 111 (where he points to the use of the image of life as a "road around" the self in the writings of Carl Jung).

28. Romans 8:9–11; I Corinthians 6:19.

29. Between the first and second niches on the left is an entry to a spiral staircase that leads up to a small tower on the roof; it was presumably made to give access to the roof for repairs. Steps also lead down, to a catacomb gallery. The niches received frescoed saints, painted between the fifteenth and the seventeenth centuries. Fragments of these remain.

30. In ancient Greek lists of the opposites, one is "the opposite" of two. One is singular, for example, while two begins plurality; one is whole, while breaking one makes two. Further down the list, one becomes male, and two female.

31. The church of Saint Bernard in Rome, San Bernardo alle Terme, is round, and was once part of the Baths of Diocletian.

32. Romans 6:3–4. For the importance of this symbolism for architecture, see Krautheimer (1942).

33. Krautheimer (1980), 49–50. He says the Lateran Baptistery "recalls nothing so much as late-antique buildings, such as S. Costanza on the Via Nomentana."

34. Genesis 1:2. The seventeenth-century inscription around the dove underlines this interpretation.

35. The inscription on the baptistery of the cathedral in Milan, attributed to Ambrose (ca. 337–397), describes in eight lines the importance of the number eight (symbolizing

salvation and regeneration) for the octagonal building and its octagonal baptismal pool. Baptism signifies "the death of the old Adam and the beginning of new life," "creation from the womb of water," and "rebirth into the spiritual octave."

36. The basilica was consecrated in 336; the Anastasis is known to have been in use by 350.

37. Santo Stefano Rotondo, built in the fifth century, has two concentric ambulatories inside, intersected by the shape of a Greek (equal-armed) cross.

38. *Liber Pontificalis* I, 180–181.

39. *Bonifatius vero, sicut consuetudo erat, celebravit baptismam Paschae in basilica beatae martyris Agnae. Liber Pontificalis* I, 227.

40. See, for example, Donati (1968).

41. Compare Romans 5:12–21, and I Corinthians 15:22 and 45. The word "Adam" is a modern scholarly conjecture; the two manuscripts have *adhuc* in one and *Adae* in the other, neither of which makes sense.

42. Compare the acronym ΙΧΘΥΣ, "Jesus Christ Son of God Saviour," creating the word for "fish" in Greek.

43. *Acta Sanctorum*, June Vol. V, 158–163. The *Acta Sanctorum* is a scholarly collection of documents relating to the lives of the saints. The work began in 1643 under the Jesuit John Bolland of Antwerp (1596–1665), and continues to this day. The Bollandists collect information in the pages of the organization's learned review, *Analecta Bollandiana*, published in Brussels since 1882. The many volumes of the *Acta Sanctorum* include the passios. The saints' lives are listed according to their feast days, and the months in which they fall. See further D. Knowles, in *Great Historical Enterprises*. Cambridge U.P. 1963.

44. Gallicanus was a fictional hero, created out of the figure of Constantina's second husband, Gallus. See Grégoire and Orgels (1954).

45. The basilica of SS Giovanni e Paolo, whose martyrdom occurred in 362, still stands on the Coelian Hill in Rome. It was built in 398. Underneath it are extensive excavations that can be visited; the church is built over an ancient titulus. There is also, underground, a pagan shrine to the Nymphs and the *confessio* of the two martyrs, with fourth-century frescoes. The church building now has, though with later decorations, a mostly twelfth-century appearance, and a magnificent campanile of the same century.

46. Julian the Apostate reigned from 361 to 363; he was born in 331. He attempted to restore the ancient Roman religion and to put down Christianity. Constantina's husband Gallus was a half-brother of Julian.

47. Ammianus Marcellinus *Rerum gestarum libri* XIV.1, 7, 9, 11.

48. Ammianus Marcellinus *Rerum gestarum libri* XXI.1.5.

49. An inscription dated 1256—found upside down and being used as a step in the passageway down to Sant'Agnese's church, and now affixed to the wall there—shows that the women were believed, in accordance with the passios, to be Constantina, Attica, and Artemia, and the men Saturninus and Sisinius.

50. Polacco (n.d.), 53.

51. Krautheimer (1937), 30. Some now wonder whether this "earlier basilica" might have been only the present basilica's foundations. See Frutaz (1992), 151, note 45.

52. Bacci (1902).
53. Ashby (1906).
54. Deichmann (1946).
55. The seventh century *De locis sanctis martyrum* also says: "*Beside* the basilica of Agnes, Constantia, daughter of Constantine, rests in a separate church" (emphasis mine).
56. It is admitted today that the great explorer of the catacombs, Antonio Bosio (1573–1629), had suggested the idea, but nobody took him seriously.
57. It was pointed out (Krautheimer [1960] refers to the objection) that the windows could conceivably have been there simply for the view; the walls of Roman circuses, open to the sky, were known to have been sometimes pierced by window-like openings.
58. See, for example, Lehmann (1955).
59. Exact measurements: the church was 98.3 metres long; the atrium was 59 metres long and 40.3 metres wide.
60. For an idea of what the building looked like, see Krautheimer's reconstruction of a similar basilica (1960), 20. For more on the funerary or cemetery basilica: Bovini (1968); Colvin (1991), 109–129; Deichmann (1946); Gatti (1960); Krautheimer (1960); Perrotti (1956) and (1961); Snyder (1985), 92–103; Tolotti (1982).
61. *Sancti Gregorii Papaci Opera Omnia*, vol. 2. Migne, *Patrologia latina 76, Homilia* XI and XII, columns 1114–1123.
62. The underground burial galleries at this site were the only ones of which extensive areas were known throughout the Middle Ages; from the fifth century the place was called *ad catacumbas* ("at the declivities") because of a natural depression between two hills at the site. In the sixteenth and seventeenth centuries, as the other underground cemeteries were rediscovered, they were all called by the same name, "catacombs."
63. Part of the ambulatory has been preserved and now houses the catacomb museum. See Tolotti (1982); Krautheimer (1980), 25. For the building's original appearance, see the reconstructions in Krautheimer (1960), 24, and (1980), 24.
64. Opposite San Sebastiano's today are the imposing ruins of a pagan circus, made in memory of Maxentius' son Romulus in 306–311. The plan of this complex, with its circular tomb, is very like that of a cemetery basilica with a mausoleum nearby; this is one reason why scholars sometimes explained the shell of the great apse at Sant'Agnese's as one end of the perimeter of a Roman circus.
65. *Liber Pontificalis* I, 180. Pope Damasus says in his inscription written for this place that he had actually met the martyrs' executioner when he was a child, and learned the details of their martyrdom from him: *percussor retulit Damaso mihi cum puer essem . . .*
66. Gatti (1960). It is not established beyond scholarly doubt that the "*basilica anonima sulla via Prenestina*" was a Christian basilica.
67. Krautheimer (1960), 28–29.
68. *Liber Pontificalis* I, 263: *Hic absidam beatae Agnae quae in ruinam inminebat et omnem basilicam renovavit.*
69. One of Deichmann's arguments in his 1946 article (p. 231) was that the *Liber*

Pontificalis finds it necessary to clarify that Honorius built *ubi requiescit*, "where [her body] rests."

70. Recent excavations have confirmed that the mausoleum and the basilica are two distinct buildings. Evidence was also found, under the narthex of the mausoleum, of the foundations of an earlier structure that was once an integral part of the basilica's foundations. What this might have been is still in question. Stanley (1994).

Nine: Finer Than Gold: Road, Crypt, and Tower

1. The popes had increasingly preferred to reside at the Quirinale Palace, and from the eighteenth century onward the Vatican's living quarters were almost deserted. See Girouard (1985), 123.
2. In 1947 the Quirinale Palace became the residence of the president of the Republic of Italy.
3. A truncated semi-circular tower still protrudes from the Aurelian Wall where the Porta Nomentana once stood, on viale del Policlinico. For a description of the via Nomentana at the beginning of the twentieth century, see Ashby (1906). The account gives an idea of how much beauty, and how much of historical interest, have been destroyed since then. See also Chandlery 1903.
4. Servius Tullius, a semi-legendary king of Rome, born a slave (*servus*), was once thought to have built these walls. He lived in the sixth century B.C. and did build walls, but not these.
5. Nomentum, founded by the Albans and conquered by Tarquinius Priscus in the fifth century B.C., was annexed by the Roman state in 338 B.C. Cicero's friend Atticus had his villa in the vicinity. The site was abandoned in the eighth century A.D., and the new town called Mentana grew up nearby. (The ancient site is in the area of Casali.) A Roman mile (the word "mile" means "a thousand" [paces]) is 1.480 modern miles.
6. The bridge is near the *Mons Sacer* or Sacred Mountain. It was said that the Roman plebeians withdrew to this mountain from the city along the via Nomentana in 494 B.C., returning only when the patricians granted them concessions (Livy 2.32 and 3.52). (Another tradition said that the Secession of the Plebs took place on the Aventine Hill, today in downtown Rome.) Not far from the Ponte Nomentano was the villa of the freedman Phaon, where Nero committed suicide in A.D. 68, having fled from Rome on horseback along the via Nomentana (Suetonius *Nero* 48–49).
7. The emblem of Shell Oil is a scallop shell (*coquille Saint Jacques* in French), which was and is the sign worn by pilgrims. The symbol began as a badge of pilgrims to the shrine of Saint James (*Saint Jacques*) at Compostela in Spain, and later came to distinguish Christian pilgrims in general.
8. Pope Innocent VIII endowed the Canons of the Saviour, newly arrived at Sant'Agnese's from Bologna in 1489, with the right to the toll paid by people passing through the gate. He also allowed the canons to live off the toll exacted for crossing the Nomentan Bridge.

9. *Liber Pontificalis* I, 127.

10. The discoveries did not prevent the placement of a statue of Pope Alexander I on the Porta Pia, in 1869, balancing a statue of Agnes. Both are by Francesco Amadori.

11. *Acta Sanctorum*, May Vol. 1. The *Hieronymianum* or "Martyrology of Jerome," a calendar dated 592–600, gives the earliest mention of the young martyr Alexander, on his feast day, May 3. Nothing is said of his being a pope, and the tutor Eventius is named first among the three martyrs.

12. For the following, see further Belvederi (1937) and (1938); Marucchi (1922); Styger (1935), 257–259; Testini (1969).

13. The passio preserves the fact that Alexander and Eventius were buried together in one place, and Theodulus apart.

14. The body of Saint Pancratius also lay obliquely with respect to his basilica. Not until the restoration of the church in the seventh century by Pope Honorius I (the builder of Sant'Agnese's) was the tomb moved into a straight position; Honorius explained what he had done in an inscription in the apse. See Delehaye (1933), 57.

15. The altar over the bones of Theodulus has completely disappeared. In the ninth century the bones of all three saints were brought within the walls of Rome and placed in the basilica of Santa Sabina, to protect them from the invading barbarian armies. The church on the via Nomentana subsequently fell into ruin and disappeared, until its rediscovery in the nineteenth century.

16. This altar frontal, dismissed in the seventeenth century as worth no more than material for making a step, had been prized in the Middle Ages: it had been carefully included in the left-hand (Gospel) *ambo* of the thirteenth-century altar complex. It was seen there by Pompeo Ugonio in the sixteenth century, and an engraving of it was published (posthumously) by Antonio Bosio in *Roma sotterranea* as late as 1632. Later, the frontal was believed to have been irrecoverably lost. It is .93 metres high by 1.35 metres wide; the two side pieces are .61 metres high and .83 metres wide.

17. The photograph published by Armellini in 1889 shows letters drawn on the marble on either side of the figure's head: SS AN and NEAS, "Sanctissima (SS) Anneas," "Most holy Agnes." These letters, together with a few other scattered initials, have since disappeared.

18. Exodus 17:11 (as long as Moses kept his arms raised, Joshua's army had the advantage over the Amalekites); Lamentations of Jeremiah 3:41; Psalm 140/141:2.

19. Homer *Odyssey* 13.355; Virgil *Aeneid* 2.687–688; Horace *Odes* III, 23, 1.

20. See, for example, Tertullian *On Prayer* 14.

21. In the passio of Marcellinus and Peter, "the executioner saw the souls of the [two] martyrs rising from their bodies in the form of young women, dressed in shining garments and adorned with gold and jewels; they were carried to heaven by angels." On *orantes* in general, see Grabar (1968), 72–74; Lowrie (1947), 645–69; Tristan (1996), s.v.

22. Luke 15:4–7; John 10:1–18.

23. The classic text on this subject is Paul's First Letter to the Corinthians, 15:35–58: "The trumpet shall sound, and the dead shall be raised, be raised incorruptible, and we shall be changed."

24. See Grabar (1968), 75.

25. There have been thirty-nine anti-popes, or rivals for the pope's chair, in the Church's history; Felix II was the third of these. The last was Felix V, 1439–1449.

26. *Liber Pontificalis* I, 208.

27. For Marangoni's dramatic account of the finding of the marble, and his foreman's saving it just in time from destruction, see the original Latin account, Frutaz (1992), 119–121, note 5. The top left-hand corner of the inscription was easily reconstructed.

28. For much of his pontificate, Damasus I was opposed by supporters of the anti-pope Ursinus. There were bloody struggles at the beginning of his reign, one of which took place inside the big cemetery basilica of Sant'Agnese.

29. During the years 1912–1939, ten small pieces of Damasus' inscription to the martyr Hippolytus were found cut up and used by medieval masons in the inlaid marble floor of the Lateran.

30. The poem says that she "suddenly left the embrace [literally "the lap"] of her nurse," when the trumpet mournfully sounded; the allusion is to the horn blast that customarily announced trials that could lead to capital punishment. The background of persecution against the Christians is supplied by the rest of the account. The Ambrosian hymn *Agnes beatae virginis* says that her parents tried in vain to keep her at home.

31. Clement of Alexandria (ca. 160–215) had already written opposing voluntary martyrdom: *Stromateis* 147, 173.

32. Teresa of Avila (1515–1582), *The Book of Her Life* in *Collected Works*, vol. 1, tr. Kieran Kavanaugh and Otilio Rodriguez (Washington: Institute of Carmelite Studies Publications, 1976), 55.

33. Damasus is quoting I Corinthians 3:16, and II Corinthians 6:16.

34. For the account that follows, see Krautheimer (1937).

35. Burial behind an altar placed over a saint's relics is called burial *retro sanctos*, "behind the saints." People often thought that burial near a certified saint would give them a better shot at heaven on "the last day."

36. Letter from the scribe Evarestus, "The Martyrdom of Polycarp." For the whole document, a letter written by Polycarp, and an introduction, see *Early Christian Writings: The Apostolic Fathers*, 113–135.

37. Athanasius *Life of Antony* 14; Jerome *Epistles* 107.1. See further P. Brown (1981), chapter 1, for this development.

38. Julian the Apostate, *Epistulae et leges*, ed. J. Bidez and F. Cumont (Paris: Les Belles Lettres, 1922). The translation is P. Brown's (1981), 7.

39. Gregory *Epistles* 4.30. See further McCulloh (1975–1976).

40. Gregory several times sent bishops and royalty filings from Peter's chains, enclosed in tiny key-shaped reliquaries (containers for relics). See Duffy (1997), 56. The very chains from which the filings were taken may be seen today in the basilica of San Pietro in Vincoli (Saint Peter in Chains), Rome. Two sets of chains are linked together. They claim to be (a) those that bound Peter in Jerusalem (Acts 12:6–9). They were sent to Rome by Eudoxia, wife of the Emperor Valentinian III, who replaced the fourth-century basilica, itself built on top of a third-century house, with the present church, consecrated in 439. They also claim to be (b) the chains that bound Peter in prison in Rome before his martyrdom.

41. Sozomen (fifth century) *Ecclesiastical History* 5.19.

42. Fiocchi Nicolai et al. (1998), 35–36; Carletti (1972), 22–25.

43. A poem for Hyacinthus and Protus, like the one for Agnes written by Damasus and inscribed on marble by Philocalus, is kept in the church of the Quattro Coronati in Rome. For a thousand years Seligenstadt in Germany claimed to have the bones of Saint Hyacinth; the Roman find showed that the German relics were false. See Hertling and Kirschenbaum (1960), 48. Hyacinth's grave had escaped rifling because the level of the pavement in the catacomb had been raised over that of his grave, and people had forgotten its existence.

44. Fiocchi Nicolai et al. (1998), 9, 65.

45. It was not uncommon for people to pre-empt the body of a living person who was likely to become a saint, by getting him or her to die in their town. We saw in Chapter Seven how Saint Antony of Padua, painfully dying, was dragged off in a cart by the Paduans, who wanted to ensure that he would be "theirs." Their enterprise has not gone unrewarded; Antony's cathedral still brings to Padua millions of pilgrims every year. One of the relics they may see—if they wish—is his tongue. Ancient Greeks also believed in the power of a hero's bones; Sophocles' *Oedipus at Colonus* shows how it came about that Oedipus died in Athens, and so deprived Thebes, his hometown, of his bones. See also Herodotus I.67–68 on the struggle for the bones of Orestes.

46. *Cappella* meant first a cloak, then a reliquary, then a chapel. (The Sainte Chapelle in Paris can be thought of as a large reliquary.)

47. See P. Brown (1981), 88–91.

48. On relics in general, see Geary (1978); Herrmann-Mascard (1975); Hertling and Kirschbaum (1960); Lefeuvre (1932); McCulloh (1975–1976); Niermann in K. Rahner et al. (1969), "Relics," vol. 5, 244–246; Pfister (1912); Rollason (1989); Rothkrug (1981); Smith and Cheetham (1875), vol. 2, 1768–1785; Snoek (1995); Sox (1985). On the importance of the Holy Places in the Christian sensibility and for the history of Christian art, see Loerke (1984).

49. Jean Calvin, *Traité des reliques* (Paris, 1629), 88, 92. Paulinus of Nola had written something similar in the late fourth or early fifth century: *Epistle 49, to Macarius*. However, the possibility of the survival of true relics of the Cross is strong enough to continue to inspire research. See most recently Matthew d'Ancona and Carsten Peter Thiede, *The Quest for the True Cross*. London: Weidenfeld & Nicolson, 2000.

50. For intelligent consideration of relics from the historian's point of view, see Geary (1978) and Herrmann-Mascard (1975).

51. *Life of Abbot Hidulfus, Acta Sanctorum* July 11; *Acts of the Benedictines*; *Acts of SS. Fructuosus, Augurius, and Eulogius*; Guibert, *On the Relics of the Saints*; Chaucer, *Prologue* to *The Canterbury Tales* lines 696–708; Lefeuvre (1932), 61; Sox (1985), chapters 2 and 3; Smith and Cheetham (1875), vol. 2, 1778.

52. For the concept of *communitas*, see V. Turner (1972) and (1973); V. Turner and E. Turner (1978).

53. Matthew 10:32–33.

54. A door from the new sacristy leads to the bridge-passage leading to the via Nomentana. Above this door there was once, outside, a bust of Agnes made from

two fragments of antique marble. One night in 1973 the statue's head was broken off and stolen.

55. Catacomb inscriptions show us that the people buried here were mostly very young: a large number of the adults died in their twenties. That might account for the fact that people seem to have been not only short in stature but also thin.

56. From very early times Paul has been depicted as balding and bearing his instrument of martyrdom, a sword; Peter is curly-headed and carries the keys of the kingdom (Matthew 16:19). The Sant'Agnese stone appears to be one of a minority of cases where the two men swapped hairstyles.

57. On the *fossores*, who were highly respected members of Christian congregations, with duties that were not only material but also spiritual (they came to count as members of the clergy), see Conde Guerri (1979).

58. For the archaeology of this area, see Fasola (1974). Other entries into the catacombs were once available. These led into the very restricted areas that had not been invaded by mud, and which appear to have been known in the Middle Ages. Earlier approaches to the present entry were first inside the Sacred Heart chapel, and then beside it; the door for the latter approach, facing into the church but now closed, is still marked *Coemeterium S. Agnetis.*

59. But Pope Paul V also named himself very visibly on the entablature of the ciborium over the altar.

60. Matthew 7:7–8; Apocalypse 3:20.

61. Genesis 3:9. For the *semantron* and its use, see Price (1983), chapter 4.

62. In Latin countries bells used to play the role of the Easter Bunny as the bringer of gifts. Children were told that the bells had flown away on Holy Thursday, like migrating birds, to Rome. They returned three days later, dropping Easter eggs in people's gardens as they made their way back to their church towers in time to ring out on Sunday. Probably because of their wide-open rims, bells were thought of as the very image of what was needed in giving birth without pain; it was sometimes a custom of pregnant women to pray in the church tower near the bells for an easy delivery. They would also pray that the baby would be "as sound as a bell."

63. The word *kumbalon* ("cymbal") comes from Greek *kumbos* ("a hollow") because of the two cupped shapes that are clashed together, as in the wooden version, castanets. *Kumb-* is the same syllable as we find in *katakumbas,* "in the hollows," the name of the first catacomb, now known as San Sebastiano's.

64. I Corinthians 13:1.

65. For the history and lore of bells, see Price (1983) and Rama (1993). An introduction to the history and art of "ringing the changes," where a series of bells is rung, with complex variations, by a team of ringers, will be found, for example, in Camp (1975).

66. Exodus 28:34.

67. The English word "bell" is onomatopoeic; it comes from the same root as "bellow" and French *bêler,* "to bleat." The word "belfry," now meaning a bell tower, originally had nothing to do with bells; it is from French *beffroi,* a wooden tower on wheels used in attacking city walls.

68. Isaiah 2:4 and Micah 4:3; the expression is reversed in Joel 4:10.
69. The science of bell making and bell tuning is far more complicated than this suggests, involving, for example, the contours of bells and the varying thicknesses of their sides. The alloy for a bronze bell in the Christian tradition is seventy-eight per cent copper and twenty-two per cent tin; it is the tin that is responsible for the ring. In addition, different religious and cultural traditions have different bases for a bell's tuning. For an introduction, see Rama (1993), 168–170. Some bells, for example the shrill warning bell or tocsin, were deliberately made non-consonant and therefore "non-musical" to the ear.
70. Acts 12:6–9.
71. For Roman campaniles, see Priester (1990).
72. On the *renovatio*, see the articles in R.I. Benson and G. Constable, eds., *Renaissance and Renewal in the Twelfth Century* (Cambridge, Mass.: Harvard U.P., 1982). Architectural reform appears to have begun at the great Abbey of Monte Cassino in southern Latium. Rome seems to have resisted building campaniles for a few decades after they began to sprout in other Italian towns. Priester (1990), 141–156.
73. The Divine Office is contained in the book called the breviary or Liturgy of the Hours, usually in four volumes covering the liturgical year. These are prayers, including the Psalms, spoken and chanted most especially in monasteries, at the Hours of Matins (four a.m.), Lauds (seven a.m.), Terce (nine a.m.), Sext (noon), Nones (three p.m.), Vespers (six p.m.), and Compline (nine p.m.). (Psalm 119:164 says, "Seven times daily I praise you.") In the fourteenth century the practice began of ringing, at non-monastic churches as well, the Angelus bell at six a.m., noon, and six p.m. to call to mind the annunciation of the angel to Mary that she would conceive God's son. The Angelus is still commonly rung.
74. Some said that Lucy tore her own eyes out and presented them to her suitor, who had been smitten by her beauty. Agatha figures in Lucy's story: Lucy's mother was healed of a hemorrhage at the grave of Agatha, and thereafter accepted Lucy's desire to imitate Agatha in remaining a virgin. A fourth-century inscription concerning Lucy survives.

Ten: Virgin Martyr: Tomb

1. Livy I. 58.
2. For Hestia/Vesta, see Vernant (1974). For Tyché/Fortuna, see Champeaux (1982) and (1987).
3. Porta Collina was not far from the old Porta Nomentana (now bricked up) and the Porta Pia, which replaced it. The *campus sceleratus*, for the burial alive of any vestal virgin who might sin, was near Porta Collina.
4. The Latin phrase *flexu in plateae* is obscure, but it could refer to a curved space, such as a Roman circus for races. The Loeb edition of Prudentius translates the phrase as "in the corner of the square."
5. For the church, designed by Rainaldi and Borromini, see Buchowiecki (1967), vol. I, 284–296; Ciofetta (1996); Parsi (n.d.), vol. II, 27–41; Sciubba and Sabatini

(1962); Sharp (1967), 29–32. Montagu (1985), vol. I, 150–156 and 216–217, describes and discusses the sculptures for the church by Alessandro Algardi and his pupil Ercole Ferratta.

6. "Agone" is from the Greek *agon*, "struggle," here meaning "sporting competition"; the word "Navona" is a corruption of *in Agone*, denoting the site of Domitian's *Circus Agonalis*.

7. See Marucchi (1909), 417.

8. A well-known example of a similar arrangement in the ancient world was that of the hero Oedipus at Athens. Shrines to Oedipus and to the Furies/Eumenides existed both at the Areopagus in central Athens and at Colonus outside the city walls.

9. For the process of canonization, see Woodward (1996). For the meaning of saints, see, for example, Cunningham (1980); Kieckhefer and Bond (1988); McGinley (1970); K. Rahner et al. (1969), vol. 5, "Saints"; Wilson (1983).

10. They were painted in the nineteenth century. In the sacristy of the church is a fine oil painting of Agnes surrounded by a crowd of female martyrs, each of whom carries her identifying attribute.

11. Animals in the stories of martyrs, even the animals in the arenas, often take the martyr's side. In real life, apparently, the wild animals would often refuse to attack victims in the arenas. See Salisbury (1997), 140.

12. For a good treatment of this complex and fascinating subject, see Heffernan (1988), especially his introduction.

13. David Barrett and Todd M. Johnson in *Our World and How to Reach It* estimated in 1990 that 26,625,000 Christians had been martyred since 1900. Cited in Bergman (1996), 17. See further Andrea Riccardi, *Il Secolo del martirio: i cristiani nel novecento*. Milan: Mondadori, 2000.

14. The Puritan poet Milton, in *Comus: A Mask* (1637), follows the last point in this schema to the letter. His virgin Lady is quite confident that "he, the Supreme good... Would send a glistring Guardian if need were / To keep my life and honour unassail'd" (lines 217–220). The Lady is not martyred, but she is rescued by supernatural means from her would-be seducer.

15. Vernant (1974). The god Hermes expressed "movement," while Hestia embodied "immobility."

16. Compare Matthew 22:15–22; Mark 12:13–17; Luke 20:20–26.

17. See, for example, Robert (1994) for Pionios, and Salisbury (1997) for Perpetua and Felicity.

18. A famous description of such a death is in Pericles' speech extolling soldiers who have died in war, according to Thucydides II.42–46.

19. Matthew 5:1–12; Luke 6:20–23; John 15:18–21. Mark 10:21, 13–14; Matthew 19:21, 23–26. Luke 10:21.

20. Both the Damasus inscription and, more clearly still, the Ambrosian hymn echo descriptions of sacrificed maidens in pagan mythology: the death of Polyxena in Euripides *Hecuba* 523–570 and Ovid *Metamorphoses* 13.456–480; and the death of Iphigenia in Lucretius *De rerum natura* 1.84–101.

21. Under the church of Sant'Agnese in Agone is a bas-relief by Giovanni Buratti, from an Alessandro Algardi design of the 1650s, that shows Agnes being led to the

fornix by Roman soldiers, trying (not entirely successfully) to cover her body with her hair. A bust derived from the bas-relief, the head and arms of Agnes, is in the Palazzo Doria Pamphili nearby. Inside the church, among scenes depicting the Agnes legend and related martyr stories, Algardi placed a flying putto in bas-relief, carrying Agnes' hair.

22. The young man has done nothing at all to merit the grace of God—yet he receives it. This scene was to be used as an illustration of the proclamation of the Council of Trent (1563): "We are justified by grace, because none of the things that precede justification, neither faith nor works, merit the grace that justifies." The intercession of Agnes and her complete forgiveness of her enemy save him: the scene was also to be used in support of the Catholic belief in the Communion of Saints. For an example of the use of the Agnes story in sixteenth-century theological debate, see Douglas-Scott (1997) on Tintoretto's altarpiece of Saint Agnes at the Madonna dell'Orto in Venice.

23. Matthew 27:11–26; Mark 15:2–15; Luke 23:2–7, 13–25; John 18:29–19:16.

24. This is an echo of the story of the three young men in the fiery furnace (The Book of Daniel, Chapter 3), a favourite subject in early Christian painting. The young men stand in the flames unharmed, with their arms raised in prayer; they are accompanied by an angel. They had been sentenced to be burned for refusing to sacrifice to idols. We may also recall the Liberian altar frontal, with Agnes as an "orant."

25. It was common practice for a victim being burned to be "finished off" with a sword; compare the death of Saint Polycarp.

26. In the medieval story of Lady Godiva, the lady rides through Coventry naked, covered only by her hair. "Peeping Tom" the tailor, the only man in town who dares to peer at her from his window, is struck blind for doing so.

27. Matthew 5:38–48; Luke 6:27–35, 23:34; Acts 7:60. See also Matthew 6:12; Mark 11:25; Romans 12:14–21, etc.

28. There is a pun in the text, on *leone* (condemned "to the lion") and *lenone* (condemned "to the owner of a brothel"). The quotation goes on: "The oftener we are mown down by you, the more in number we grow; the blood of Christians is seed." Tertullian *Apology* 50.

29. Robert (1994), *Pionios* VII.6.

30. For example, Aeschylus *Agamemnon* 198–254. The death of Iphigenia by stabbing at the hands of her father Agamemnon (a form of incestuous infanticide combined with human sacrifice) made the Trojan War possible; it also gave rise to crime upon crime in the House of Atreus, the family of Agamemnon and Iphigenia. See Aeschylus' trilogy, *The Oresteia*.

31. Tacitus *Annals* V.9. See also Dio Cassius *Roman History* 58.11; Suetonius *Tiberius* 61; Cyprian *De mortalitate* 15; Tertullian *De pudicitia* 1.221. In the *Acts of Paul and Thecla*, the girl begs the magistrate to allow her to remain a virgin until her execution by exposure to beasts in the arena.

32. See the excellent essay on a modern understanding of the virgin martyrs in Norris (1996), 186–205.

33. Augustine *Epistles* 121.9 and 228.7.

34. For the meanings of virginity for Christians in late antiquity, see P. Brown (1986)

and (1988); Chadwick (1960). Early Christian women have been the subject of enormous numbers of recent books and articles. For a good example, see Burrus (1987).

35. As we have seen, twelve centuries later, when as a child Saint Teresa of Avila discovered that her parents wouldn't let her run away to be martyred, she and her little brother knew exactly what to do next: they decided they should become hermits.

36. Ambrose wrote *De virginibus* for his sister Marcellina, who was a virgin dedicated to celibacy. The opening line of the Latin passio of Agnes addresses it to a community of celibate women.

37. Matthew 19:10–12. See also Isaiah 56:3–5.

38. The offence to the Roman state constituted by consecrated virgin women found expression in a command by Diocletian during the Great Persecution that professed (that is, formally dedicated) Christian virgins should be searched out and violated. (Codex Vat. Gr. 1669 fol. 401, cited in Jubaru [1907], 68.)

39. For the history and significance of this ceremony, see Metz (1954).

40. Mark 15:34; Matthew 27:47. His cry of affliction is the first line of Psalm 22—a prayer that ends in joy, with the coming of what Jesus called "the Kingdom of God." The crucified Jesus lived the beginning of this prayer in all its desolation; Christians believe that their response must be to ensure that the rest of the psalm is brought to fruition in the world's history.

41. Popular fairy tales and rhymes still include "Snow White" and "Mary had a Little Lamb."

42. Girard (1999) makes an excellent introduction to his work.

43. For examples in Greek mythology and literature, see Visser (1982).

44. See Liddell and Scott, *Greek-English Lexicon*, s.v.

45. Flavius Philostratus (third century A.D.), *The Life of Apollonius of Tyana*, Harvard U.P., Loeb Classical Library, Book 4, Chapter 10. See Girard (1999), 83–99.

46. John 11:49–50.

47. See further Barrett (1954–55); Gerke (1934); Kirschbaum and Braunfels (1971), vol. 3, columns 7–14; H. Leclercq, "Agneau," (1924); Tristan (1996), 123–141.

48. Isaiah 53:7; see the entire section, 52:13–53:12. The figure that Isaiah describes is taken by Christians to be the "type" of Christ.

49. John 1:29 and 36. Compare I Peter 1:18–20. Paul describes Christ as "our passover" (I Corinthians 5:7). For Christians Christ is also the "paschal lamb," the lamb killed for the Jewish passover, the blood of which the Israelites used to mark their doors so that the plague "passed over" them (Exodus 12:7). Jews did not interpret passover in terms of Isaiah 53, but Christians did. And Jesus as "paschal lamb" is consumed in the mystery of the Eucharist. In the Apocalypse, Christ as Lamb is mentioned thirty times. The Heavenly Jerusalem is "the bride of the Lamb," and the Lamb is the temple and the light of the city (Apocalypse 21:9–10, 21:22–24).

50. Matthew 18:12–14; Luke 15:4–7; John 21:15–17; Matthew 10:16.

51. John 12:24.

52. John 1:4–5.

SELECT BIBLIOGRAPHY

Adam, Adolf. *The Liturgical Year: Its history and Its Meaning After the Reform of the Liturgy.* Translated by M. J. O'Connell. New York: Pueblo, 1979.

Alexander, Suzanne S. "Studies in Constantinian Church Architecture." *Rivista di archeologia cristiana* 47 (1971): 281–330; 49 (1973): 33–44.

Alföldi, Andrew. *The Conversion of Constantine and Pagan Rome.* Oxford: Oxford U.P., 1948. Reprint 1998.

Amadio, Adele Anna. "I mosaici di S. Costanza." *Xenia, Quaderni* 7. Rome: De Luca, 1986.

Ambrose, Saint. "*De virginibus ad Marcellinam sororem,*" lib. I, cap. ii, iii, iv, v; "*De lapsu virginis consecratae,*" lib. I, cap. iii; "*De officiis ministrorum,*" cap. cciv; "*Epistolarum Classis I,*" cap. xxxvi. Fourth century.

(Pseudo) Ambrose. *Agnes beatae virginis.* See Jacques Fontaine et al., eds., 1992.

Pseudo-Ambrose. *Gesta sanctae Agnetis.* Fifth century. John Bolland, ed. *Acta Sanctorum, Januarii Tomus Secundus.* Paris: Victor Palmé, n.d. 715–718.

Ammianus Marcellinus (330–395). *Rerum gestarum libri qui supersunt* XIV, XXI. Loeb Classical Library. Translated by J.C. Rolfe. London: Heinemann; Cambridge, Mass.: Harvard University Press, 1972.

Andresen, Carl. *Einführung in die christliche Archäologie.* Göttingen: Vandenhoeck & Ruprecht, 1971.

Angenendt, Arnold. *Heilige und Reliquien. Die Geschichte ihres Kultes vom frühen Christentum bis zur Gegenwart.* Munich: C.H. Beck, 1997.

Armellini, Mariano. "La scoperta della cripta di S. Emerenziana." *Bullettino di archeologia cristiana* (1876): 150–153.

———. "Die neuentdeckte Frontseite des ursprunglichen Altars von S. Agnese." *Römische Quartalschrift für christliche Altertumskunde und Kirchengeschichte* (1889): 59–65.

———. *Le chiese di Roma dal secolo IV al XIX.* Reprint. Rome: Edizioni del Pasquino, 1982. (Originally published 1891.)

———. *Gli Antichi Cimiteri Cristiani di Roma e d'Italia.* Rome: Tipografia Poliglotta, 1893. New edition, Arnaldo Forni: 1978. 255–273.

Armstrong, Gregory T. "Imperial Church Buildings in the Fourth Century." *Biblical Archaeologist* 30 (1967): 90–102.

———. "Constantine's Churches: Symbol and Structure." *Journal of the Society of Architectural Historians* 33 (1974): 5–16.

Ashby, Thomas. "Classical Topography of the Roman Campagna." *Papers of the British School* 3 (1906): 38–46.

Astorri, Giuseppe. "Nuove Osservazioni sulla tecnica dei mosaici romani della basilica di S. Maria Maggiore." *Rivista de archeologia cristiana* 11 (1934): 51–72.

Averincev, Sergej. "L'or dans le système des symboles de la culture protobyzantine." *Studi medievale* 20 (1979): 47–67.

Bacci, Augusto. "Relazione degli scavi eseguiti in S. Agnese." *Römische Quartalschrift für christliche Altertumskunde und Kirchengeschichte* (1902): 51–58.

——. "Ulteriori osservazioni sulla basilica nomentana." *Nuovo Bullettino di archeologia cristiana* (1906): 77–87.

Baldovin, John F. *The Urban Character of Christian Worship: The Origins, Development, and Meaning of Stational Liturgy*. Rome: Pontificium Institutum Studiorum Orientalium, 1987.

Barker, Ethel Ross. *Rome of the Pilgrims and Martyrs: A Study in the Martyrologies, Itineraries, Syllogies and Other Contemporary Documents*. London: Methuen, 1913.

Barker, Margaret. *The Gate of Heaven: The History and Symbolism of the Temple in Jerusalem*. London: SPCK, 1991.

Barnes, Timothy D. "Legislation against the Christians." *Journal of Religious Studies* 58 (1968): 32–50.

——. *Constantine and Eusebius*. Cambridge: Harvard U.P., 1981.

Barral i Altet, Xavier. "Le cimetière en fête. Rites et pratiques funéraires dans la péninsule ibérique pendant l'antiquité tardive." In *Fiestas y Liturgia*, edited by A. Esteban and J-P Etienvre, 299–308. Madrid: Casa de Velazquez (Actas del coloquio, 1985), 1988.

Barrett, Charles Kingsley. "The Lamb of God." *New Testament Studies* 1 (1954–55): 210–18.

Bartolini, Domenico. *Gli Atti del martirio della nobilissima vergine romana S. Agnese, illustrati colla storia e coi monumenti*. Rome: S. Congregazione de propaganda fide, 1858.

Baumann, Paul. "Saint Joseph. A Family Man." In *A Tremor of Bliss: Contemporary Writers on the Saints*, edited by Paul Elie, 199–222. New York: Riverhead, 1995.

Belvederi, Giuseppe. "La basilica e il cimitero di S. Alessandro al VII Miglio sulla via Nomentana." *Rivista di archeologia cristiana* 14 (1937): 7–40, 199–224; 15 (1938): 19–34, 225–246.

Benedict of Nursia. *The Rule of Saint Benedict*. Ca. 535 A.D. Edited by D. Oswald Hunter Blair. Fort Augustus: Abbey Press, 1948.

Bergman, Susan, ed. *A Cloud of Witnesses: 20th Century Martyrs*. San Francisco: HarperSanFrancisco, 1996.

The Bible. *The Jerusalem Bible: Reader's Edition*. Garden City, New York: Doubleday, 1968. *The New English Bible: New Testament*. Oxford: Oxford U.P., 1961. *Novum Testamentum Graece*. Oxford: Clarendon Press, 1966.

Bibliotheca Sanctorum. Istituto Giovanni XXIII, Pontificia Università Lateranense. *Agnese di Roma* by Enrico Josi and Renato Aprile: Vol. I (1961), cols. 382–411. *Emerentiana* by Benedetto Cignitti and Francesco Negri Arnoldi: Vol. IV (1964), cols. 1161–1167.

Bishop, Edmund. *Liturgica Historica*. Oxford: Clarendon Press, 1918.

Boadt, Lawrence. *Reading the Old Testament: An Introduction*. New York: Paulist Press, 1984.

Bovini, Giuseppe. *Edifici cristiani di culto d'età costantiniana a Roma*. Bologna: Riccardo Pàtron, 1968. Chapters 5 and 6.

————. "Coemeteria-Basilicae d'età costantiniana a Roma." *Corsi Ravenna* 15 (1969): 91–97.

————. *Mosaici paleocristiani di Roma (Secoli III - VI)*. Bologna: Riccardo Pàtron, 1971.

Bowersock, Glen W. *Martyrdom and Rome*. Cambridge: Cambridge U.P., 1995.

Boyle, Leonard. *A Short Guide to St. Clement's, Rome*. Rome: Collegio San Clemente, 1989.

Bradshaw, Paul. *Early Christian Worship*. London: SPCK, 1996.

Braunfels, Walter, et al., eds. *Lexikon der christlichen Ikonographie*. Rome, Friburg, Basel, Vienna: Herder, 1973. "Agnes von Rom." Vol. V, cols. 57–63.

Brown, Peter. *Augustine of Hippo: A Biography*. London: Faber and Faber, 1967.

————. *The Cult of the Saints: Its Rise and Function in Latin Christianity*. Haskell Lectures on the History of Religions, n.s. 2. Chicago: U. of Chicago Press, 1981.

————. "The Notion of Virginity in the Early Church." In *World Spirituality. Christian Spirituality: Origins to the Twelfth Century*, Vol. I, edited by Bernard McGinn, John Meyendorff, and Jean Leclercq, 427–443. London: Routledge and Kegan Paul, 1986.

————. *The Body and Society: Men, Women, and Sexual Renunciation in Early Christianity*. New York: Columbia U.P., 1988.

Brown, Raymond E. *The Birth of the Messiah: A Commentary on the Infancy Narratives in the Gospels of Matthew and Luke*. Updated edition. New York: Doubleday, 1993.

Brown, Raymond E., Joseph A. Fitzmyer, Roland E. Murphy, eds. *The New Jerome Biblical Commentary*. London: Geoffrey Chapman, Cassell, 1990.

Bruun, Patrick. "Symboles, signes et monogrammes." *Acta Instituti Romani Finlandiae* I.2 (1963): 73–166.

Buchowiecki, Walther. *Handbuch der Kirchen Roms*. Vienna: Brüder Hollinek, 1967.

Burckhardt, Titus. *Sacred Art in East and West*. Translated by Lord Northbourne. London: Perennial Books, 1967.

Burrus, Virginia. *Chastity as Autonomy: Women in the Stories of the Apocryphal Acts*. Lewiston: Mellen, 1987.

Caiola, Antonio Federico. "Sant'Agnese nell'Almo Collegio Capranica." *Roma Sacra* 9 (1997): 1–11.

Cameron, Averil. *The Mediterranean World in Late Antiquity* A.D. *395–600*. London: Routledge, 1993.

Camp, John. *Discovering Bells and Bellringing*. Aylesbury: Shire, 1975.

Camprubí i Alemany, Francesc. *El monumento paleocristiano de Centcelles (Tarragona)*. Barcelona: Altés, 1952.

Carbonara, Andrea, and Gaetano Messineo. *Via Nomentana*. Rome: Istituto poligrafico e Zecca dello Stato, Libreria dello Stato, 1996.

Carletti, Sandro. *Le antiche chiese dei martiri romani.* Roma: Marietti, 1972.

Cecchelli, Carlo. *S. Agnese fuori le mura e S. Costanza (Le Chiese di Roma illustrate n. 1).* Rome: Casa Editrice, 1924.

Chadwick, Henry E. "Enkrateia." In *Reallexikon für Antike und Christentum* 5, 343–365. Stuttgart: Hiersemann, 1960.

—————. *History and Thought of the Early Church.* London: Variorum Reprint, 1982.

Champeaux, Jacqueline. *Fortuna: Recherches sur le culte de la Fortune à Rome et dans le monde romain des origines à la mort de César.* Rome: Collection de l'Ecole française de Rome. Vol. I (1982), Vol. 2 (1987).

Chandlery, P.J. *Pilgrim Walks in Rome.* London: Griffin, 1903.

Ciofetta, Simona. "Sant'Agnese in Agone." *Roma Sacra* 7 (1996): 45–50.

Coleman, Kathleen M. "Fatal Charades: Roman Executions Staged as Mythological Enactments." *Journal of Religious Studies* 80 (1990): 44–73.

Collinet-Guérin, Marthe. *Histoire du nimbe des origines aux temps modernes.* Paris: Editions Latines, 1961.

Colvin, Howard Montagu. *Architecture and the Afterlife.* New Haven: Yale U.P., 1991.

Conde Guerri, Elena. "Los 'fossatores' de Roma paleocristiana: Estudio iconografico, epigrafico y social." *Studi di antichità cristiana* 33 (1979): 1–212.

Consolino, Franca Ela. "Modelli di santità femminile nelle più antiche passioni romane." *Augustinianum* 24 (1984): 83–113.

Contessa, Fabrizio. *Sant'Agnese.* Milan: San Paolo, 1999.

Crichton, J.D. *The Dedication of a Church: A Commentary.* Dublin: Veritas, 1980.

Cunningham, Lawrence S. *The Meaning of Saints.* San Francisco: Harper and Row, 1980.

Daniélou, Jean. *Le Signe du temple.* Paris: Desclée, 1990. (Originally published 1945.)

—————. *Primitive Christian Symbols.* Translated by Donald Attwater. London: Burns and Oates, 1961.

Davies, John Gordon. *The Origin and Development of Early Christian Church Architecture.* London: SCM Press, 1952.

—————. *The Architectural Setting of Baptism.* London: Barrie and Rockliff, 1962.

—————. *Temples, Churches and Mosques.* Oxford: Basil Blackwell, 1982.

Davis, Charles. "The Christian Altar." In *The Modern Architectural Setting of the Liturgy,* edited by William Lockett, 13–31. London: SPCK, 1964.

Davis-Wyer, C. "Das Traditio-Legis-Bild und seine Nachfolge." *Münchner Jahrbuch der bildenden Kunst* 12 (1961): 7–45.

De Angelis d'Ossat, Guglielmo. "Chiesa di S. Costanza." *Palladio* 4 (1940): 44–45.

De Benedictis, Elaine. "The Senatorium and Matroneum in the Early Roman Church." *Rivista di archeologia cristiana* 57 (1981): 69–85.

de Blaauw, Sible. *Cultus et decor: Liturgia e Archittetura nella Roma tardoantica e medievale.* Vatican City, 1994.

de Bruyne, Lucien. "*Refrigerium interim.*" *Rivista di archeologia cristiana* 34 (1958): 87–118.

—————. "Les lois de l'art paléochrétien comme instrument d'herméneutique." *Rivista di archeologia cristiana* 35 (1959): 104–187.

de Francovich, Géza. "Studi sulla scultura Ravennate." *Felix Ravenna* 26–27 (1958): 124–136.

Deichmann, Friedrich Wilhelm. "S. Agnese f.l.m. und die byzantinische Frage in der frühchristlichen Architektur Roms." *Byzantinische Zeitschrift* (1941): 70–81.

————. "Die Lage der konstantinischen Basilika der heiligen Agnes an der Via Nomentana." *Rivista di archeologia cristiana* 22 (1946): 213–234.

————. *Rom, Ravenna, Konstantinopel, Näher Osten.* Wiesbaden: Franz Steiner, 1982.

————. *Einführung in die christliche Archäologie.* Darmstadt: Wissenschäftliche Buchgesellschaft, 1983.

Delehaye, Hippolyte. "Review of Pio Franchi de'Cavalieri, 'S. Agnese nella tradizione e nella leggenda.'" *Analecta Bollandiana* 27 (1908): 220–223.

————. *Les origines du culte des martyrs.* Brussels: La Société des Bollandistes, 1912. Reprinted in *Subsidia Hagiographica* 20, 1933.

————. "Martyr et confesseur." *Analecta Bollandiana* 39 (1921): 20–49.

————. "Loca sanctorum." *Analecta Bollandiana* 48 (1930): 5–64 .

Denomy, Alexander Joseph. *The Old French Lives of Saint Agnes.* Cambridge, Mass.: Harvard U.P., 1938.

Dictionnaire d'archéologie chrétienne et de liturgie. 15 vols. Edited by Fernand Cabrol and Henri Leclercq. Paris: Letouzey, 1924–1953.

Dodds, Eric R. *Pagan and Christian in an Age of Anxiety: Some Aspects of Religious Experience from Marcus Aurelius to Constantine.* Cambridge: Cambridge U.P., 1965

Doelger, Franz-Xavier Josef. "Die Symbolik des altchristlichen Taufhauses: Das Oktogon und die Symbolik der Achtzahl." *Antike und Christentum* 4 (1934): 153–87.

————. *Ichthus: Das Fischsymbol im frühchristlichen Zeit.* 5 vols. Münster: Aschendorff, 1910–1957.

Donati, Lamberto. *Polifilo a Roma: il Mausoleo di S. Costanza.* Florence: Leo S. Olschki, 1968.

Douglas-Scott, Michael. "Jacopo Tintoretto's Altarpiece of St. Agnes," *Journal of the Warburg and Courtauld Institutes* 60 (1997) 130–163.

Downey, Michael, ed. *The New Dictionary of Catholic Spirituality.* Collegeville, Minnesota: The Liturgical Press, 1993.

Duchet-Suchaux, Gaston, and Monique Duchet-Suchaux. *Les ordres religieux: Guide historique.* Paris: Flammarion, 1993.

Duchet-Suchaux, Gaston, and Michel Pastoureau. *The Bible and the Saints: Flammarion Iconographic Guides.* Translated by David Radzinowicz Howell. Paris and New York: Flammarion, 1994.

Duffy, Eamon. *Saints and Sinners. A History of the Popes.* New Haven: Yale U.P., 1997.

Dunbar, Agnes B.C. *A Dictionary of Saintly Women.* 2 vols. London: George Bell, 1904.

Duval, Noël. "Les origines de la basilique chrétienne: Etat de la question." *L'information d'histoire de l'art* 7 (1962): 1–19.

Early Christian Writings: The Apostolic Fathers. Translated by Maxwell Stamforth. Edited by Andrew Louth. London: Penguin Books, 1987.

Eliade, Mircea. *Images and Symbols: Studies in Religious Symbolism*. London: Harvill, 1952.

Elsner, Jas. *Art and the Roman Viewer: the Transformation of Art from the Pagan World to Christianity*. Cambridge: Cambridge U.P., 1995.

Emery, Pierre-Yves. *The Communion of Saints*. Translated by D.J. and M. Watson. London: Faith Fress; Les Presses de Taizé, 1966.

Enciclopedia Cattolica. 12 vols. Città del Vaticano, 1948.

Encyclopedia of Early Christianity. Edited by E. Everett Ferguson et al. New York and London: Garland Publishing, 1990.

Encyclopedia of the Early Church. Edited by Angelo di Berardino. Translated by Adrian Walford. 2 vols. Institutum Patristicum Augustinianum. Cambridge: James Clarke, 1992.

Engemann, Josef. "Bermerkungen zu spätrömischen Gläsern mit Goldfolien-Dekor." *Jahrbuch für Antike und Christentum* 11–12 (1968–1969): 7–25.

Escobar, Mario. "Il presepio romano." In *Le chiese sconosciute di Roma*, 290–309. Rome: Newton Compton 1988.

Eusebius of Caesarea (ca. 260–ca. 339). *The History of the Church from Christ to Constantine*. Translated by G.A. Williamson. Edited by Andrew Louth. London: Penguin Books, 1989.

Fanano, Eutizio. *Ugolino da Belluno: il Mosaico di S. Emerenziana*. Rome: Wanzer, 1968.

Fasola, Umberto M. "Le recenti scoperte agiografiche nel Coemeterium Majus." *Rendiconti della Pontificia Accademia Romana di Archeologia* 28 (1954–1955): 75–89.

—————. "La regio IV del cimiterio di S. Agnese sotto l'atrio della basilica costantiniana." *Rivista di archeologia cristiana* 50 (1974): 175–205.

Ferrua, Antonio. "Nuova luce sulle origini del culto di S. Agnese?" *La Civiltà Cattolica* 90 (1939, I): 114–129.

—————. "Sant'Agnese e l'agnello." *La Civiltà Cattolica* 1 (1959): 141–50. Reprinted in *Storia e Civiltà* (March–June 1997): 131–142.

Ferrua, Antonio, and Carlo Carletti. *Damaso e i martiri di Roma*. Vatican City: Pontificia Commissione di Archeologia Sacra, 1985.

Février, Paul-Albert. "A propos du repas funéraire: culte et sociabilité." *Cahiers archéologiques* 26 (1977): 29–45.

—————. "Baptistères, martyrs et reliques." *Rivista di archeologia cristiana* 62 (1986): 109–38.

Fiocchi Nicolai, Vincenzo, Fabrizio Bisconti, and Danilo Mazzoleni. *Le Catacombe cristiane di Roma*. Regensburg: Schnell & Steiner, 1998.

Fitzmyer, Joseph A. *The Acts of the Apostles: A New Translation with Introduction and Commentary*. The Anchor Bible. New York: Doubleday, 1998.

Fontaine, Jacques, ed. *Saecularia Damasiana: Atti del Convegno internazionale per il XVI centenario della morte di Papa Damaso I. 113–45. Studi di antichità cristiana* 39. Vatican City, 1986.

Fontaine, Jacques, et al., eds. *Ambroise de Milan: Hymnes*. Paris: Les Editions du Cerf, 1992. 363–403.

Franchi de'Cavalieri, Pio. *S. Agnese nella tradizione e nella leggenda. Römische Quartalschrift für christliche Altertumskunde und Kirchengeschichte*, Supplement 10, 1899.

Frend, William H.C. *The Archaeology of Early Christianity: A History*. London: Geoffrey Chapman, 1996.

Friar, Stephen. *A Companion to the English Parish Church*. London: Alan Sutton, 1996.

Frutaz, Amato Pietro. *Il Complesso monumentale di Sant'Agnese*. Rome: Nova Officina Poligrafica Laziale, 1992. (First published 1960.)

Frye, Northrop. *The Great Code: The Bible and Literature*. Toronto: Academic Press, 1981.

Garrucci, Raffaele. *Vetri ornati di figure in oro trovati nei cimiteri cristiani di Roma*. Rome: Salviucci, 1858. 128–137. Illustrations XXI–XXII.

Gatti, Guglielmo. "Una Basilica di età Costantiniana recentemente riconosciuta presso la Via Prenestina." *Capitolium* 35 (June 1960): 3–8.

Geary, Patrick J. Introduction to *Furta Sacra: Thefts of Relics in the Central Middle Ages*. Princeton: Princeton U.P., 1978.

Geertman, Herman. "The Builders of the Basilica Maior in Rome." In *Festoen opgedragen aan A.N. Zadoks-Josephus Jitta*, 277–95 Groningen: H.D. Tjeenk Willink, 1977.

Gerke, F. "Der Ursprung der Lämmerallegorien in der altchristlichen Plastik." *Zeitschrift für die neutestamentliche Wissenschaft* 33 (1934): 160–96.

Giannarelli, Elena. "Nota sui dodici anni — l'età della scelta — nella tradizione letteraria antica." *Maia* 29–30 (1977–1978): 127–133.

Girard, René. *Je vois Satan tomber comme l'éclair*. Paris: Grasset, 1999.

Girouard, Marc. *Cities and People*. New Haven and London: Yale U.P., 1985.

Glass, Dorothy F. *Studies on Cosmatesque Pavements*. British Academy at Rome International Series 82. 1980.

Goodenough, Erwin R. "The Crown of Victory in Judaism." *Art Bulletin* 28 (1946): 139–59.

Grabar, André. *The Beginnings of Christian Art, 200–395*. London: Thames and Hudson, 1967.

———. *Christian Iconography: A Study of Its Origins*. Princeton: Princeton U.P., 1968.

———. *Martyrium: Recherches sur le culte des reliques et l'art chrétien antique*. Paris: Boccard, 1946–1947. 2 vols. Reprint with new foreword, London: Variorum, 1972.

Green, Julien. *Frère François*. Paris: Seuil, 1983.

Grégoire, Henri, and Paul Orgels. "S. Gallicanus, consul et martyr dans la passion des SS. Jean et Paul, et sa vision 'constantinienne' du Crucifié," *Byzantion* 24 (1954): 579–601.

Gregory I, the Great (590–604). *Homilies* XI and XII. Jacques-Paul Migne, ed., *Patrologiae latinae* 76, cols. 1114–1123. *Epistle 4, Gregorii I Papae Registrum Epistolarum*. Eds. P. Ewald and L.M. Hartmann. Berlin, 1887–1899.

Grisar, Hartmann. "Di alcune statue pagane trasformate in figure di santi." *La Civiltà Cattolica* (1897): 210–215.

————. "Il tesoro della Sancta Sanctorum." *La Civiltà Cattolica* (1907).

Gunton, Lilian. *Rome's Historic Churches*. London: George Allen and Unwin, 1969.

Guyon, Jean. "L'Oeuvre de Damase dans le cimetière 'Aux deux Lauriers' sur la via Labicana." In *Saecularia Damasiana*, edited by Jacques Fontaine, 227–58. Vatican City, 1986.

————. "Damase et l'illustration des martyrs: Les accents de la dévotion et l'enjeu d'une pastorale." In *Martyrium in Multidisciplinary Perspective*, edited by Mathijs Lamberigts and Peter van Deun, 157–177. Leuven U.P., 1995.

Hall, James. *Dictionary of Subjects and Symbols in Art*. London: John Murray, 1974.

Hani, Jean. *Le Symbolisme du Temple Chrétien*. Paris: Guy Trédaniel, 1962.

Harris, Ruth. *Lourdes: Body and Spirit in the Secular Age*. London: Allen Lane, Penguin, 1999.

Hautecoeur, Louis. *Mystique et architecture: Symbolisme du cercle et de la coupole*. Paris: J. Picard, 1954.

Heffernan, Thomas J. *Sacred Biography: Saints and Their Biographers in the Middle Ages*. Oxford: Oxford U.P., 1988.

Herrmann-Mascard, Nicole. *Les reliques des saints, formation coutumière d'un droit*. Paris: Klincksieck, 1975.

Hertling, Ludwig, and Engelbert Kirschbaum. *The Roman Catacombs and Their Martyrs*. London: Darton, Longman, and Todd, 1960.

Herzog, Rudolf. "Zwei griechische Gedichte des 4 Jahrhunderts aus St. Maximin in Trier, II. Gedichte auf die hl. Agnes." *Trierer Zeitschrift* 13 (1938): 79–120.

Hopper, Vincent F. *Mediaeval Number Symbolism*. New York: Cooper Square, 1969. (First published 1938.)

Houston, Mary Galway. *Ancient Greek, Roman and Byzantine Costume and Decoration*. London: Black, 1931.

Hülsen, Christian. *Le Chiese di Roma nel medioevo*. Florence: Leo S. Olschki, 1927.

Janes, Dominic. *God and Gold in Late Antiquity*. Cambridge: Cambridge U.P., 1998.

Jeffers, James S. *Conflict in Rome*. Minneapolis: Fortress, 1991.

Jobst, Werner. "Die Büsten im Weingartenmosaik von Santa Costanza." *Mitteilungen des Deutschen Archaeologischen Instituts. Römische Abteilungen* 83 (1976): 431–437.

Josi, Enrico. "Coemeterium Maius, II: Il sepolcro di Santa Emerenziana." *Rivista de archeologia cristiana* 10 (1933): 13–16.

Jounel, Pierre. *Le culte des saints dans les basiliques du Latran et du Vatican au douzième siècle*. Ecole Française de Rome, 1977.

Jubaru, Florian. "La decorazione bacchica del mausoleo cristiano di S. Costanza." *L'Arte* 7 (1904): 457–468.

————. *Sainte Agnès: Vierge et martyre de la Voie Nomentane d'après de nouvelles recherches*. Paris: J. Dumoulin, 1907.

Kaftal, George. *Iconography of the Saints in Central and South Italian Painting*. Florence: Sansoni, 1965.

Kajanto, Iiro. "Onomastic studies in the early Christian inscriptions of Rome and Carthage." *Acta Instituti Romani Finlandiae* II, no. 1 (1963): 1–141.

Kelly, John N.D. *Early Christian Doctrines*. 5th ed. New York: Harper and Row, 1978.

Kennedy, Vincent Lorne. *The Saints of the Canon of the Mass.* Vatican City: Pontificio Istituto di Archeologia Cristiana, 1963.

Kieckhefer, Richard, and George Bond, eds. *Sainthood: Its Manifestations in World Religions.* Berkeley: U. of California Press, 1988.

Kirsch, Johann Peter. "Ausgrabungen in der Basilica der hl. Agnes in der Via Nomentana." *Römische Quartalschrift für christliche Altertumskunde und für Kirchengeschichte* (1902): 78–80.

Kirschbaum, Engelbert, and Wolfgang Braunfels, eds. *Lexicon der christlichen Ikonographie.* 8 vols. Freiburg: Herder, 1968–1976.

Kitzinger, Ernst. *Byzantine Art in the Making: Main Lines of Stylistic Development in Mediterranean Art, 3rd–7th Century.* London: Faber and Faber, 1977. Chapter 6.

—————. "Christian Imagery: Growth and Impact." In *Age of Spirituality: Late Antique and Early Christian Art, Third to Seventh Century,* edited by Kurt Weitzmann, 141–63. New York: Metropolitan Museum of Art, 1980.

Kleinbauer, W. Eugene. *Early Christian and Byzantine Architecture: An Annotated Bibliography.* Boston: G.K. Hall, 1992.

Klemm, Rosemarie, and Dietrich D. Klemm. *Steine und Stein-Brüche im Alten Ägypten.* Berlin: Springer, 1993.

Knipe, David M. "The Temple in Image and Reality." In *Temple in Society,* edited by Michael Fox, 105–133. Winona Lake: Eisenbrauns, 1988.

Koller, L. Peter. *Symbolism in Christian Architecture of the First Millennium.* (Self-published) Sydney, 1975.

Krautheimer, Richard. *Corpus Basilicarum Christianarum Romae: The Early Christian Basilicas of Rome (IV-IX Cent.).* Vol. I: *S. Agnese f.l.M.* (1937). Vol. II: *S. Lorenzo f.l.M.* (1962). Vol. III: *S. Pancrazio* (1967). Città del Vaticano, 1937–1977.

—————. "The Beginning of Early Christian Architecture." *The Review of Religion* 3 (1939): 127–148. Reprinted in *Studies in Early Christian, Medieval and Renaissance Art.* London: U. of London Press, 1971.

—————. "Introduction to an Iconography of Mediaeval Architecture." *Journal of the Warburg and Courtauld Institutes* 5 (1942): 1–33.

—————. "Mensa–Coemeterium–Martyrium." *Cahiers archéologiques* 11 (1960): 15–44.

—————. "The Constantinian Basilica." *Dumbarton Oaks Papers* 21 (1967): 117–140.

—————. *Rome: Profile of a City, 312–1308.* Princeton: Princeton U.P., 1980.

—————. *Early Christian and Byzantine Architecture.* 4th edition. Harmondsworth: Penguin, 1986.

Lamirande, Emilien. *What Is the Communion of Saints?* London: Burns and Oates, 1963.

Lanciani, Rodolfo A. *Pagan and Christian Rome.* London: MacMillan, 1892.

—————. *Wanderings Through Ancient Roman Churches.* Boston: Houghton Mifflin, 1924.

Laurentin, René. *Vie de Catherine Labouré, voyante de la rue du Bac et servante des pauvres 1806–1876.* Paris: Desclée de Brouwer, 1980.

Leclercq, Henri. "Agneau" and "Agnès (Cimetière de Sainte-)." In *Dictionnaire d'archéologie chrétienne et de liturgie.* Vol. I, cols. 877–905; 918–966. Paris: Letouzey, 1924.

Lees-Milne, James. *Saint Peter's. The Story of Saint Peter's Basilica in Rome.* Boston: Little, Brown, 1967.

——. *Roman Mornings.* London: Collins, 1988. 23–43.

Lefeuvre, Pierre. *Courte histoire des reliques.* Paris: Rieder, 1932.

Lehmann, Karl. "Sta Costanza." *The Art Bulletin* 37 (1955): 193–96, 291.

Leonardi, Corrado. *Ampelos: Il simbolo della vite nell'arte pagana e paleocristiana.* Rome: Edizioni Liturgiche, 1947.

Lequenne, Fernand. *Antoine de Padoue: Sa vie, son secret.* Paris: Chalet, 1991.

Liber Pontificalis. 2 vols. Edited with commentary by Louis Duchesne. Paris: Thorin, 1886, 1892. Reprint 1955–57.

——. *The Book of the Pontiffs (Liber Pontificalis) to* A.D. *715.* Translated with an introduction and commentary by Raymond Davis. Liverpool: Liverpool U.P., 1989.

——. *The Lives of the Eighth-Century Popes (Liber Pontificalis).* Translated with an introduction and commentary by Raymond Davis. Liverpool: Liverpool U.P., 1992.

——. *The Lives of the Ninth-Century Popes (Liber Pontificalis).* Translated with an introduction and commentary by Raymond Davis. Liverpool: Liverpool U.P., 1995.

Llewellyn, Peter A.B. *Rome in the Dark Ages.* London: Constable, 1993. (Originally published 1971.)

——. "The Roman Church in the Seventh Century: The Legacy of Gregory the Great." *Journal of Ecclesiastical History* 35 (1974): 363–380.

Loerke, William. "'Real Presence' in Early Christian Art." In *Monasticism and the Arts,* edited by T.G. Verdon and John Dally, 29–51. Syracuse: Syracuse U.P., 1984.

Lonergan, Bernard. *Insight: A Study of Human Understanding.* Toronto: U. of Toronto Press, 1957.

——. *Method in Theology.* Toronto: U. of Toronto Press, 1971.

Loomis, C. Grant. *White Magic: An Introduction to the Folklore of Christian Legend.* Cambridge, Mass.: Medieval Academy of America, 1948.

Lotz, Wolfgang. *Architecture in Italy, 1500–1600.* New Haven and London: Yale U.P., 1995.

Lowden, John. *Early Christian and Byzantine Art.* London: Phaidon, 1997.

Lowrie, Walter. *Art in the Early Church.* New York: Pantheon, 1947.

Luft, S.G.A. *The Christian's Guide to Rome.* Revised ed. London: Burns and Oates, 1990.

MacDonald, William L. *The Pantheon: Design, Meaning, and Progeny.* London: Allen Lane, 1976.

Mâle, Emile. *The Early Churches of Rome.* Translated by David Buxton. Chicago: Quadrangle, 1960.

Marrou, Henri Irénée. "Autour du monogramme constantinien." In *Mélanges Etienne Gilson,* 403–414. Toronto: Pontifical Institute of Mediaeval Studies; Paris: J. Vrin, 1959.

Martin, Thérèse. *Histoire d'une âme. Manuscrits autobiographiques.* Paris: Cerf, 1985. 153–154.

Marucchi, Orazio. *Eléments d'archéologie chrétienne.* Paris: Desclée de Brouwer, 1909. 416–419.

————. *Il Cimitero e la Basilica di S. Alessandro alla Via Nomentana.* Rome: Tipografia Editrice Romana, 1922.

————. *Le Catacombe Romane: Opera Postuma.* Roma: La Libreria dello Stato, 1933.

Marucchi, Orazio, and Augusto Bacci. "Scavi nella Basilica di S. Agnese sulla via Nomentana." *Nuovo Bullettino di archeologia cristiana* 7 (1901): 297–300; 8 (1902): 127–133.

Mathew, Gervase. *Byzantine Aesthetics.* London: John Murray, 1963.

Mathews, Thomas F. "An Early Roman Chancel Arrangement and its Liturgical Uses." *Rivista di archeologia cristiana* 38 (1962): 71–95.

————. *The Early Churches of Constantinople: Architecture and Liturgy.* University Park: Pennsylvania State U.P., 1971.

————. *The Clash of Gods: A Reinterpretation of Early Christian Art.* Princeton: Princeton U.P., 1993.

Mathieu-Rosay, Jean. *Chronologie des Papes, de St Pierre à Jean Paul II.* Brussels: Marabaut Aller, 1988.

Matthiae, Guglielmo. *Le Chiese di Roma dal IV al X secolo.* Roma: Cappelli, 1964.

————. *Mosaici medioevali delle chiese di Roma.* Roma: Istituto Poligrafico dello Stato, 1967. 169–79.

McBrien, Richard P. *Catholicism: Study Edition.* HarperSanFrancisco, 1981.

————. *Lives of the Popes.* San Francisco: HarperSanFrancisco, 1997.

McCulloh, John M. "The Cult of Relics in the Letters and 'Dialogues' of Pope Gregory the Great: A Lexicographical Study." *Traditio* 32 (1975–1976): 145–84.

McGinley, Phyllis. *Saint-Watching.* London: Collins, 1970.

McKelvey, Richard J. *The New Temple: The Church in the New Testament.* Oxford: Oxford U.P.,1969.

McVey, Kathleen E. "The Domed Church as Microcosm: Literary Roots of an Architectural Symbol." *Dumbarton Oaks Papers* 37 (1983): 91–121.

Metz, René. *La consécration des vierges dans l'église romaine: étude d'histoire de la liturgie.* Paris: Presses Universitaires de France, 1954.

Metzger, Bruce M., and Michael D. Coogan, eds. *Oxford Companion to the Bible.* Oxford: Oxford U.P., 1993.

Milburn, Robert. *Early Christian Art and Architecture.* Berkeley: U. of California Press, 1988.

Miquel, Pierre, and Paula Picard. *Dictionnaire des symboles liturgiques.* Paris: Le Léopard d'Or, 1995.

Montagu, Jennifer. *Alessandro Algardi.* 2 vols. New Haven: Yale U.P., 1985.

Monti, Paolo. "La poesia delle immagini nel Mausoleo di Costanza." *Bollettino della Unione Storia ed Arte* 85 (1992): 43–50.

Morey, Charles R. "The Origin of the Fish Symbol." *Princeton Theological Review* 8 (1910): 93–106, 231–246, 401–432; 9 (1911): 268–289; 10 (1912): 278–298.

————. *The Goldglass Collection of the Vatican Library, with an Additional Catalogue of the Other Goldglass Collections.* Vatican City, 1959.

Morgan, David. *Visual Piety: A History and Theory of Popular Religious Images.* Berkeley: U. of California Press, 1998.

Murray, Charles. *Rebirth and Afterlife: A Study of the Transmutation of Some Pagan Imagery in Early Christian Funerary Art.* British Archaeological Reports, International Series, 100. Oxford, 1981.

Murray, Robert. *Symbols of Church and Kingdom: A Study in Early Syrian Tradition.* Cambridge: Cambridge U.P., 1975.

Musurillo, Herbert, ed. and trans. *Acts of the Christian Martyrs.* Oxford: Oxford U.P., 1972.

Niermann, Ernst. "Relics." In *Sacramentum mundi* Vol. 5, edited by Karl Rahner et al., 244–246. 1969.

Noonan, Jr., James-Charles. *The Church Visible: The Ceremonial Life and Protocol of the Roman Catholic Church.* New York: Viking, 1996.

Norberg-Schulz, Christian. *Genius Loci: Towards a Phenomenology of Architecture.* New York: Rizzoli, 1980.

Norman, Edward. *The House of God: Church Architecture, Style and History.* London: Thames and Hudson, 1990.

Norris, Kathleen. *The Cloister Walk.* New York: Riverhead, 1996.

Oakeshott, Walter. *The Mosaics of Rome, from the Third to the Fourteenth Centuries.* Greenwich: New York Graphic Society, 1967.

Olney, James. *Metaphors of Self.* Princeton: Princeton U.P., 1972.

Onians, John. *Bearers of Meaning: The Classical Orders in Antiquity, the Middle Ages, and the Renaissance.* Princeton: Princeton U.P., 1990.

Onians, Richard Broxton. *The Origins of European Thought about the Body, the Mind, the Soul, the World, Time, and Fate.* Cambridge: Cambridge U.P., 1951.

Ousterhout, Robert G. "The Temple, the Sepulcre, and the *Martyrion* of the Savior." *Gesta* 29 (1990): 44–53.

Palmer, Anne-Marie. *Prudentius on the Martyrs.* Oxford: Oxford U.P., 1989.

Parsi, Publio. *Chiese Romane.* 2 vols. Rome: Liber, n.d.

Pastoureau, Marcel. *L'Eglise et la couleur, des origines à la réforme.* Bibliothèque de l'Ecole des Chartes 153, 1988.

————. "*Ordo colorum*, notes sur la naissance des couleurs liturgiques." *La Maison-Dieu* 176 (1988): 54–66.

————. *L'Etoffe du Diable: Une Histoire des rayures et des tissus rayés.* Paris: Seuil, 1991.

Payne-Carter, David. "Procession and the Aesthetics of Everyday Life in a Benedictine Monastery." *The Drama Review* 29 (1985): 42–47.

Perrotti, Raffaele. "Recenti ritrovamenti presso S. Costanza." *Palladio* 1956, fasc. I–II, 80–83.

————. "La basilica di S. Agnese fuori le mura. Considerazioni a proposito del restauro." *Palladio* 1961, fasc. III–IV, 157–164.

Pétrement, Simone. *La vie de Simone Weil.* 2 vols. Paris: Fayard, 1973.

Pfister, Friedrich. *Der Reliquienkult im Altertum.* 2 vols. Giessen: A. Töpelmann, 1909–1912. Reprint, Berlin and New York: de Gruyter, 1974.

Pietrangeli, Carlo, ed. *Sancta Sanctorum.* Milan: Electa, and Città del Vaticano: A.P.S.A., 1995.

Pietri, Charles. *Roma Christiana: Recherches sur l'Eglise de Rome, son organisation, sa politique, son idéologie, de Miltiade à Sixte III (331–440).* Bibliothèque des Ecoles françaises d'Athènes et de Rome. 2 vols. Rome, 1976.

—————. "Damase, évêque de Rome." In *Saecularia Damasiana,* edited by Jacques Fontaine, 31–58. Vatican City, 1986.

Polacco, Renato. *Il Mausoleo di S. Costanza.* Padua: Grafiche Messaggero di S. Antonio, s.d.

Potter, David. "Martyrdom and Spectacle. " In *Theater and Society in the Classical World,* edited by Ruth Scodel. Ann Arbor: U. of Michigan Press, 1993.

Poulet, Georges. Introduction to *The Metamorphoses of the Circle.* Trans. C. Dawson and E. Coleman. Baltimore: The Johns Hopkins Press, 1966.

Prandi, Adriano. "Osservazione su Santa Costanza." *Rendiconti della Pontificia Accademia romana di archeologia* 19 (1942–1943): 281–304 .

Pressouyre, Sylvia. *Nicolas Cordier: Recherches sur la sculpture à Rome autour de 1600.* 2 vols. Collection de l'Ecole française de Rome 73. 1984.

Price, Percival. *Bells and Man.* Oxford: Oxford U. P., 1983.

Priester, Ann Edith. "The Belltowers of Medieval Rome and the Architecture of Renovatio." Ph.D. diss., Princeton University, 1990.

Prudentius, ca. 400–405. *Peristephanon Liber.* In *Prudentius* vol. 2, edited by H.J. Thomson. Loeb Classics. Cambridge, Mass.: Harvard University Press; London: William Heinemann, 1979.

Quacquarelli, Antonio. "Il battesimo di sangue." In *Sapientia et Eloquentia.* Bari: Edipuglia, 1988. 289–302.

Rahner, Karl, et al. *Sacramentum Mundi.* 5 vols. London: Burns and Oates, 1969.

Rama, Jean-Pierre. *Cloches de France et d'ailleurs.* Paris: Le Temps Apprivoisé, 1993.

Réau, Louis. *Iconographie de l'art chrétien.* 3 vols. Paris: Presses Universitaires de France, 1955–1959.

Rees, Elizabeth. *Christian Symbols, Ancient Roots.* London and Philadelphia: Jessica Kingsley, 1992.

Riccardi, Andrea. *Sant'Egidio. Rome et le monde.* Entretiens avec Jean-Dominique Durand et Régis Ladous. Paris: Beauchesne, 1996.

Richards, Jeffrey. *The Popes and the Papacy in the Early Middle Ages, 476–752.* London: Routledge and Kegan Paul, 1979.

Robert, Louis. *Le martyre de Pionios prêtre de Smyrne.* Edited by Glen W. Bowersock and Christopher P. Jones. Washington, D.C.: Dumbarton Oaks, 1994.

Rollason, David. *Saints and Relics in Anglo-Saxon England.* Chapter 1. Oxford: Basil Blackwell, 1989.

Rordorf, Willy. *Sunday: The History of the Day of Rest and Worship in the Earliest Centuries of the Christian Church.* London: SCM, 1968.

Rothkrug, Lionel. "The 'Odour of Sanctity,' and the Hebrew Origins of Christian

Relic Veneration." *Historical Reflections / Réflexions historiques* 8 (1981): 95–142.

Rush, Alfred C. *Death and Burial in Christian Antiquity*. Washington: Catholic U. of America, 1941.

Salisbury, Joyce E. *Perpetua's Passion: The Death and Memory of a Young Roman Woman*. New York: Routledge, 1997.

Savio, Fedele. "Costantina figlia dell'Imperatore Costantino Magno e la basilica di S. Agnese in Roma." *Atti della R. Accademia delle scienze di Torino* 42 (1906–1907): 659–669 and 732–741.

Saxer, Victor. "Damase et le calendrier des fêtes de martyrs de l'église romaine." In *Saecularia Damasiana*, edited by Jacques Fontaine. Vatican City, 1986.

————. "Hagiographie et archéologie." In *Martyrium in Multidisciplinary Perspective*, edited by Mathijs Lamberigts and Peter Van Deun. Leuven U.P., 1995.

Schmitz, Philippe. "La première communauté de vierges à Rome." *Revue bénédictine* 38 (1926): 189–195.

Schumacher, Walter Nikolaus. "*Dominus legem dat.*" *Römische Quartalschrift für christliche Altertumskunde und Kirchengeschichte* 54 (1959): 1–39.

————. "Die Konstantinischen Exedra-Basiliken." In *La Catacomba dei Santi Marcellino e Pietro*, edited by Johannes Georg Deckers et al., 132–186. Città del Vaticano: Pontificio Istituto di archeologia cristiana, 1987.

Schwarz, Rudolf. *The Church Incarnate: The Sacred Function of Christian Architecture*. Trans. Cynthia Harris. Chicago: Henry Regnery, 1958. (First published 1938.)

Sciubba, Sante, and Laura Sabatini. *Sant'Agnese in Agone*. Roma: Marietti, 1962.

Sear, Frank B. *Roman Wall and Vault Mosaics*. Heidelberg: F.H. Kerle, 1977.

Seasoltz, R. Kevin. *The House of God: Sacred Art and Church Architecture*. New York: Herder and Herder, 1963.

Sharp, Mary. *A Traveller's Guide to the Churches of Rome*. London: Hugh Evelyn, 1967.

Sjöqvist, Erik. "Studi archeologici e topografici intorno alla piazza del Collegio Romano. L'origine del battistero costantiniano romano." *Skriften utgivna av Sveska Institutet in Roma* 1946. 144–146.

Smith, Molly Teasdale. "The Development of the Altar Canopy in Rome." *Rivista di archeologia cristiana* 3 (1974): 379–414.

Smith, William, and S. Cheetham. *A Dictionary of Christian Antiquities*. 2 vols. London: John Murray, 1875.

Snoek, Godefridus J.C. *Medieval Piety from Relics to the Eucharist*. Chapter 1. Leiden: Brill, 1995.

Snyder, Graydon F. *Ante Pacem: Archaeological Evidence of Church Life Before Constantine*. Macon, Ga.: Mercer, 1985.

Soave, Giuseppina. "Gli affreschi medioevali di S. Agnese fuori le Mura a Roma." *Rivista del R. Istituto d'Archeologia e Storia dell'Arte* 4 (1932–33): 202–210.

Sox, David. *Relics and Shrines*. London: George Allen and Unwin, 1985.

Stambaugh, John E. "The Functions of Roman Temples." In *Aufstieg und Niedergang der römischen Welt* 2:16:1. Berlin and New York: Walter de Gruyter, 1978. 554–608.

Stanley, David J. "The Apse Mosaics at Santa Costanza." *Mitteilungen des deutschen archäologischen Instituts. Römische Abteilung* 94 (1987): 29–42.

————. "New Discoveries at Santa Costanza." *Dumbarton Oaks Papers* 48 (1994): 257–261.

Stark, Rodney. *The Rise of Christianity: A Sociologist Reconsiders History*. Princeton: Princeton U.P., 1996.

Stern, Henri. "Les mosaïques de l'église de Sainte-Constance à Rome." *Dumbarton Oaks Papers* 12 (1958) 157–218.

Stevenson, Enrico. "Scoperte epigrafiche a S. Agnese f.l.M." *Nuovo Bullettino di archeologia cristiana* 2 (1896): 188–190.

Stevenson, James. *The Catacombs: Rediscovered Monuments of Early Christianity*. London: Thames and Hudson, 1978.

Stuhlfauth, G. "Das Schiff als Symbol der altchristlichen Kunst." *Rivista di archaeologia cristiana* 19 (1942): 111–141.

Styger, Paul. *Römische Märtyrergrüfte*. 2 vols. Berlin: Verlag für Kunstwissenschaft, 1935.

Sulzberger, Max. "Le symbole de la croix et les monogrammes de Jésus chez les premiers chrétiens." *Byzantion* 2 (1925): 337–448.

Swift, Emerson H. *Roman Sources of Christian Art*. New York: Columbia U. P., 1951.

Testini, Pasquale. *Archeologia cristiana. Nozioni generali dalle origini alla fine del secolo VI*. Rome: Desclée, 1958. (2nd ed. 1980.)

————. "Strutture murarie e fasi costruttive del santuario dei martiri nella catacomba di S. Alessandro a Roma." *Atti del VII Congresso Internazionale di Archeologia Cristiana 1965*. Città del Vaticano–Berlin, 1969. Vol. I, 711–738, ill. Vol. II, 359–371.

Thérel, Marie-Louise. *Les Symboles de l'"Ecclesia" dans la création iconographique de l'art chrétien du IIIe au VIe siècle*. Rome: Edizioni di Storia e Letteratura, 1973.

Thurston, Herbert J. *The Stations of the Cross: An Account of Their History and Devotional Purpose*. London: Burns and Oates, 1906.

————. *Familiar Prayers: Their Origin and History*. London: Burns and Oates, 1953.

Tolotti, Francesco. "Le basiliche cimiteriali con deambulatorio del suburbio romano: questione ancora aperta." *Mitteilungen des Deutschen Archäologischen Instituts, Römische Abteilung* 89 (1982): 153–211.

Toynbee, Arnold, ed. *The Crucible of Christianity*. London: Thames and Hudson, 1969.

Toynbee, Jocelyn, and John Ward Perkins. *The Shrine of St. Peter and the Vatican Excavations*. London: Longman, Green, 1956.

Tristan, Frédérick. *Les premières images chrétiennes*. Paris: Fayard, 1996.

Turner, Harold W. *From Temple to Meeting House: The Phenomenology and Theology of Places of Worship*. The Hague: Mouton, 1979.

Turner, Victor. "Passages, Margins and Poverty: Religious Symbols of *Communitas*." *Worship* 46 (1972): 390–412, 482–494.

————. "The Centre Out There: Pilgrim's Goal." *History of Religion* 12 (1973): 191–230.

Turner, Victor, and Edith Turner. *Image and Pilgrimage in Christian Culture: Anthropological Perspectives*. Oxford: Basil Blackwell, 1978.

Ullmann, Walter. *A Short History of the Papacy in the Middle Ages*. London: Methuen, 1972.

Underwood, Paul A. "The Fountain of Life in Manuscripts of the Gospels." *Dumbarton Oaks Papers* 5 (1950): 41–138.

Vallin, Pierre. "*Dominus Pacem dat*. A propos du mausolée de Constantina à Rome." *Recherches de science religieuse* 51 (1963): 579–587.

van Berchem, Marguerite, and Etienne Clouzot. *Mosaïques chrétiennes du IVème au Xème siècle*. Rome: "L'Erma" di Bretschneider, 1965.

van den Broek, R. *The Myth of the Phoenix According to Classical and Early Christian Traditions*. Leiden: Brill, 1972.

van der Meer, Frederik, and Christine Mohrmann. *Atlas of the Early Christian World*. London: Nelson, 1966.

Vernant, Jean-Pierre. "Hestia-Hermès. Sur l'expression religieuse de l'espace et du mouvement chez les Grecs." *Mythe et pensée chez les Grecs*. Paris: François Maspéro, 1974. Vol. I, 124–170.

Visser, Margaret. "Worship Your Enemy: Aspects of the Cult of Heroes in Ancient Greece." *Harvard Theological Review* 75 (1982): 403–428.

———. *The Rituals of Dinner*. Toronto: HarperCollins, 1991.

———. *The Way We Are*. Toronto: HarperCollins, 1994.

Ward Perkins, John Bryan. "Constantine and the Origin of the Christian Basilica" *Papers of the British School at Rome* 22 (1954): 69–90.

———. "Imperial Mausolea and Their Possible Influence on Early Christian Central-Plan buildings." *Journal of the Society of Architectural Historians* 25 (1966): 297–99.

Waugh, Evelyn. *Helena*. London: Penguin, 1988. (First published 1950.)

Weitzmann, Kurt, ed. *Age of Spirituality: Late Antique and Early Christian Art, Third to Seventh Century*. New York: Metropolitan Museum of Art, 1980.

White, L. Michael. *Building God's House in the Roman World: Architectural Adaptation Among Pagans, Jews, and Christians*. Baltimore: Johns Hopkins U.P., 1989.

Wilson, Stephen, ed. *Saints and Their Cults: Studies in Religious Sociology, Folklore, and History*. Cambridge: Cambridge U.P., 1983.

Woodward, Kenneth L. *Making Saints*. New York: Simon and Schuster, 1996.

Wyschogrod, Edith. *Saints and Postmodernism*. Chicago: U. of Chicago Press, 1990.

Zanchi Roppo, Franca. *Vetri paleocristiani a figure d'oro conservati in Italia*. Bologna: R. Pàtron, 1969.

Zettinger, Joseph. "Die ältesten Nachrichten über Baptisterien der Stadt Rom." *Römische Quartalschrift für christliche Altertumskunde und für Kirchengeschichte* 16 (1902): 326–49.

INDEX